BRITISH
MOTOR
COASTERS

Shell Mex & BP Ltd's tanker Ardrossan (1,529/68) arriving at St. Helier, Jersey on 1st April 1970. Note the discharging boom aft and the prominent rubbing bars fitted to the later series of their coastal tankers. DAVE HOCQUARD

BRITISH
MOTOR
COASTERS

CHARLES V. WAINE

Black Dwarf
Publications

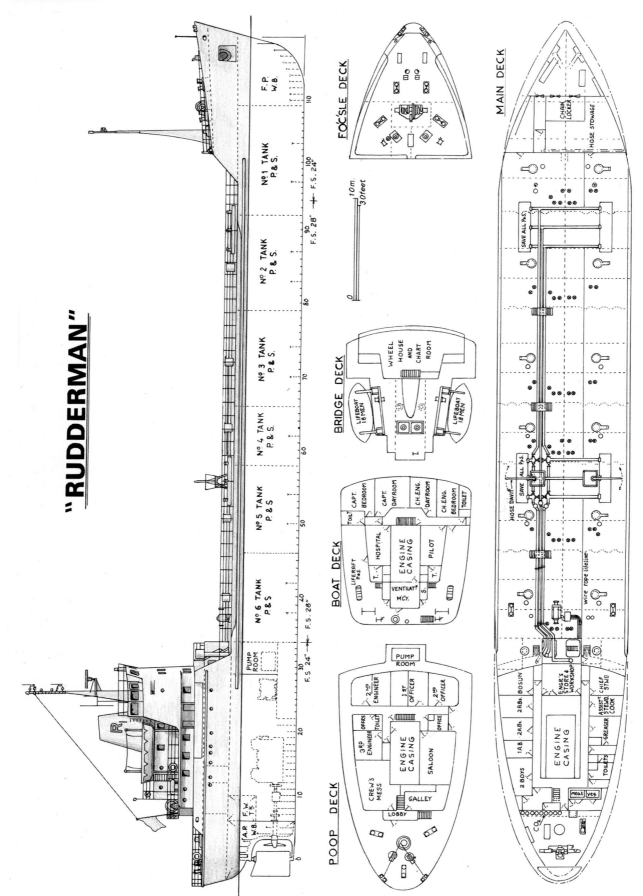

"RUDDERMAN"

FO'C'SLE DECK

10 m.
30 feet

BRIDGE DECK

WHEEL HOUSE AND CHART ROOM

LIFEBOAT 18 MEN

LIFEBOAT 18 MEN

BOAT DECK

TOILET
CAPT. BEDROOM
CAPT. DAYROOM
CH. ENG. DAYROOM
CH. ENG. BEDROOM
TOILET

T.
HOSPITAL
ENGINE CASING
PILOT
T.

LIFERAFT P&S
S.

VENTILAT. M'CY.

POOP DECK

PUMP ROOM

3RD ENGINEER
OFF'RS TOILET
2ND ENGINEER
1ST OFFICER
2ND OFFICER
OFFICE

ENGINE CASING
SALOON

CREW'S MESS
GALLEY
LOBBY

MAIN DECK

CHAIN LOCKER

HOSE STOWAGE

SAVE ALL P&S

SAVE ALL P&S

HOSE DAVIT

wire rope lifeline

ENG'R'S STORE & WORKSHOP

2 A.B.s BOSUN
1 A.B.
2 A.B.
2 BOYS

ENGINE CASING

ASSIST. STEW'D
CHIEF STEW'D
GREASER
COOK
TOILETS
meat
veg.
CO₂

F.P. W.B.

No 1 TANK P. & S.

No 2 TANK P. & S.

No 3 TANK P. & S.

No 4 TANK P. & S.

No 5 TANK P. & S.

No 6 TANK P. & S.

PUMP ROOM

F.W. TK.
A.P. W.B.

F.S. 24"
F.S. 28"
F.S. 28"
F.S. 24"

110
100
90
80
70
60
50
40
30
20
10

Rudderman (1,592/68) was one of the last vessels built with a conventional counter stern by Cochranes (see pages 184 and 201). From a drawing in Shipping World & Shipbuilder, December 1968.

CONTENTS

NOTE: Photographs are by the author unless otherwise stated. To avoid confusion where there are several vessels with the same name, the ship's name is followed by the gross tonnage and the last two digits of the year of build, thus: *Ability* (1409/79). Ship names in semi-bold italics in the text indicate that a plan is included for that vessel. Builders are often referred to as simply Goole or Everards, etc. Many of these companies were reconstructed during slumps or had owning/management splits but, as there are plenty of company books, it was felt inappropriate to go in to detail about their name changes in a book about ship design.

© Black Dwarf Publications & Charles V. Waine 2018

Designed by Neil Parkhouse

British Library Cataloguing-in-Publication Data. A catalogue record for this book is available from the British Library

ISBN: 9781903599 24 2

BLACK DWARF PUBLICATIONS LTD

Unit 144B, Harbour Road Trading Estate, Lydney, Gloucestershire GL15 4EJ
www.lightmoor.co.uk / info@lightmoor.co.uk / 01594 840641

Black Dwarf Publications is an imprint of Black Dwarf Lightmoor Publications Ltd

Printed in Poland
www.lfbookservices.co.uk

INTRODUCTION

My first interest as a youngster was primarily steam coasters in the 1940s and 1950s but I took an interest in motor coasters too. The interest was really the result of my grandfather having bought the disused Point of Ayr Lighthouse for a few hundred pounds in the 1930s and this is where I spent much of the school holidays, sketching the passing ships aided by Laurence Dunn's Ship *Recognition – Merchant Ships*. It was about a mile from the Point of Ayr Colliery, which had its own steam colliers and harbour. Also within sight was the Darwen & Mostyn Iron Works, which had its own harbour as well and handled a variety of cargoes for other local firms. Back then it was possible for youngsters to go on to quays as long as you kept out of the way of the work in progress and so I became familiar with the local ships and some of the crews. By coincidence, my aunt had worked with the daughter of Tom Coppack and so I got to know the Coppacks, who were the local coasting shipowners and they later helped me understand the business.

My grandfather used to have the *Journal of Commerce & Shipping Telegraph* and each week on Wednesday there would be descriptions of new ships. One week, **Marshlea**, built in Sweden for the Hindlea Shipping Co. Ltd of Cardiff, was featured with a photograph and I noticed the description of the decks was in error compared with the picture, so I wrote to the editor to point this out. He wrote to the owners who explained that I was right and sent a general arrangement drawing which the editor kindly sent on to me. It was the first general arrangement drawing I had seen and I was immediately hooked. This book is the result of sixty years of collecting ship plans and the generosity of shipowners, nearly all long gone, who found time to help me and trusted me to return plans promptly after I had traced them or gave me old plans no longer needed. Perhaps a special mention is due for the Robertson brothers, who opened their offices to me for a week when I was writing my first book *Steam Coasters & Short Sea Traders*. They lent me numerous plans and explained how they chose the type and size of ship for their fleet with regard to what they and their customers needed.

The Reverend William Jones, who sailed on several of their ships, added accounts of voyages plus photographs. Another important contributor was Everards, especially their marine superintendent Ken Garrett, who sent me a pile of old plans which he had saved and left me with no excuses not to write this book, and subsequently explained their ships and trades. To add to the picture, I asked around and received lots of help and contributions from in particular Tom Fish, Ken Davies, Ian Howe, Joe Keane, G.R. LeClercq, Douglas Lindsay, Dick Massey, Pat O'Driscoll and Chris Reynolds, along with many others over the years on the seagoing side of the business.

A word here for the photographers who caught the action and are acknowledged in the text. On the shipyard side, Eric Hammal who was Cochrane's naval architect, described the work that went into the design of a motor ship and Peter Coates, a marine engineer, helped regarding engines. Eric Hammal and Douglas Lindsay also kindly checked the final text. The illustrations are mostly the work of naval architects, draughtsmen and tracers many of whom are now anonymous and it is to their memory I would like to dedicate this book.

Charles Waine Ph.D, Albrighton 2018

BIBLIOGRAPHY AND REFERENCE SOURCES

Admiralty, *Naval Marine Engineering Practice*, Vols I & II, 1962
Atkinson, G., *J.&A. Gardner & Co. Ltd*, 2002
Atkinson, G., & Rix, J., *Rix Shipping*, 2014
Blackhurst, D., *Philip & Son Ltd, Shipbuilders & Engineers*, 2011
Bryans, P.J. (Ed.), *Channel Islands Merchant Shipping 1940-1945*
Burrell, D.C.E., *Scrap & Build*, 1983
Carter, C.J.M., *The Stephenson Clarke Fleet Story*, 1958
Chesterton, D.R., & Fenton, R.S., *Gas & Electricity Colliers*, 1984
Coppack, T., *A Lifetime With Ships*, 1973
Dakres, J.M., *A History of Shipbuilding at Lytham*, 1992
Dickson, J., & Pickard, G., *J. Crichton & Co., Shipbuilders*, 2002
Dunn, L., *Ship Recognition – Merchant Ships*, 1952
Fenton, R.S., *Cambrian Coasters*, 1989
Fenton, R.S., *Mersey Rovers*, 1997
Garrett, K.S., *Everard of Greenhithe*, 1991, 2nd Ed. 2017
Garrett, K.S., *Comben Longstaff & Co. Ltd*, 1996
Garrett, K.S., *R. Lapthorn & Company Limited*, 2001
Garrett, K.S., *Thomas Watson*, 2002
Garrett, K.S., *Union Transport 60 Years in Shipping*, 2006
Garrett, K.S., *Crescent Shipping*, 2010
Gray, E., & Fenton, R., *Ninety Years of the Ramsey Steamship Co. Ltd*, 2003
Harvey, W.J., *Arklow Shipping*, 2004
Huckett, Rev. A., *Rowbotham*, 2002
MacRae, J.A., & Waine, C.V., *The Steam Collier Fleets*, 1990
Mayes, G., *Short Sea Shipping 2001/2002*, 2001
Mitchell, W.H. & Sawyer, L.A., *Empire Ships of World War II*, 1965
Pollock, W., *Small Vessels*, 1946
Pollock, W., *Building Small Vessels*, 1948
Scott, R.J. *Irish Sea Schooner Twilight*, 2012
Somner, G., *DP&L. A History of the Dundee Perth & London Shipping Co Ltd and Associated Companies*, 1995
Staff of *The Motor Ship & Motor Boat, The Marine Oil Engine Handbook*, 5th Ed. 1919
Stuart, C., *Merchant Ships British Built 1952*, 1953
Tinsley, D., *Short-Sea Bulk Trades*, 1984
Waine, C.V., & Fenton, R.S., *Steam Coasters & Short Sea Traders*, 3rd Ed. 1994
Waine, C.V., *Coastal Vessels in Detail*, 2003
Winser, J. de S., *Coasters Go to War*, 2009
Winter, M.T., *The Portishead Coal Boats*, 2005

Periodicals and Annual Publications:
Coastal Shipping
Directory of Shipowners, Shipbuilders & Marine Engineers
Journal of Commerce & Shipping Telegraph
Marine News: Journal of the World Ship Society
Lloyd's Registers
Lloyd's Register List of Shipowners
Lloyd's Register Appendix
Reed's Nautical Almanac
Sea Breezes
Shipbuilding & Shipping Record
Shipping World & Shipbuilder
Ships in Focus Record
Ships Monthly
The Motor Ship

CHAPTER 1
THE POWER SOURCE

The early engines evolved from the stationary ones used in agriculture and other purposes, and are described as internal combustion engines, as the fuel is burnt inside the cylinder. They could be either 2-stroke or 4-stroke. In the 2-stroke engine, air was admitted, compressed by the rising piston, fuel injected and ignited at the top to drive the piston down by the resulting expansion of the hot gases. At the bottom of the stroke, the exhaust was partly pushed out by air as it was admitted, often in later years, from a pump on the engine or a turbocharger. They had the advantage of simplicity as they could be built without valves. This was an advantage because the valves were subject to high pressures and temperatures, and could distort and be burned away. This problem was much reduced as more heat resistant alloys were developed.

In 4-strokes at least two valves were necessary. A valve at the top of the cylinder opened and as the piston moved down it drew in air. The valve then closed and the piston compressed the air as it travelled upwards. Fuel was injected at the top, ignited and the piston driven down by the expansion of the hot gases. On reaching the bottom of the stroke, the exhaust valve at the top of the cylinder opened and as the piston travelled upwards the exhaust gases were expelled. One of the first marine engines was a 4-stroke paraffin motor produced by the Priestman brothers and fitted to a launch about 1888. This relied on spark ignition but the need for this was eliminated by Akroid Stewart's patents beginning in 1886. He relied on a hot bulb at the top of the cylinder to ignite the mixture which was injected into the bulb. His first engine had a compression of about 30 psi (pounds per square inch). Later engines achieved about 200psi but hot bulb ignition was still necessary and it was not eliminated until the arrival of Dr Rudolf Diesel's patent of 1892, where the compression was much higher at around 500psi and the energy of the compression and consequent heating of the mixture was sufficient to ignite it. He obtained patents in a number of countries and most of the early manufacturers bought the rights from him.

The first engines widely used were the semi-diesel hot bulb types, such as that from Bolinders of Stockholm* which worked at lower pressures and were used in some of the earliest British vessels. Other early makes were the 'Polar' from A/B Atlas Diesel, which could trace its origins back to an earlier company beginning in 1898, also Swedish, though they did not become popular in Britain until British Auxiliaries (later renamed British Polar) of Glasgow took out a licence in 1934. Crossley Brothers finally penetrated the marine market with a two-stroke in 1932. Mirrlees, the well known English firm, produced their first engine in 1897 but did not build popular marine engines for coasters and short sea traders until after the Second World War.

To start a Bolinder engine, the bulb on top of each cylinder had to be preheated with a blow lamp. This was because the energy of compression in these early engines was insufficient to heat the air enough to ignite the fuel when it was injected. Once running, the bulb would remain sufficiently hot to ignite the mixture. As the piston moved down it would uncover the exhaust port followed by the inlet port, using air compressed below the piston, which would flush out the remaining burnt gases before the air was compressed and more fuel injected at the top of the stroke. Injection was by air blast originally, which was supplied by a separate compressor, so changing to direct fuel injection later simplified matters but the pressures necessary to produce a good fine spray of fuel needed to be high – a few thousand pounds per square inch. Even in later years, starting from cold was assisted on some engines by the use of glow plugs or fuel heaters for example. Where these were not considered necessary in the post-war higher compression engines, a spray can of Easy Start could be resorted to and sprayed into the air intake or turbocharger when starting the bigger engines from cold! It reduced the ignition temperature of the fuel air mixture.

Tom Coppack has described what starting problems meant in practice. In 1928, they purchased the auxiliary ketch *Santa Rosa* (95/06) and soon replaced the Parsons engine with a more modern Kelvin but even so, it could not always be started. However, as she was just running on the very short trip from the Point of Ayr Colliery on the Dee round to Price's Patent Candle works at Bromborough on the Mersey she was never far from help. Coppacks' office would get a call from the lifeboat station at New Brighton for example, saying the *Santa Rosa* had signalled that she could

*A.J. & C.G. Bolinder's Mekaniska Verkstad Aktiebolag (MVAB) – Mechanical Workshop Stock (or Limited) Company in English – was founded in Stockholm in 1844 by the brothers Carl and Jean Bolinder. They produced their first crude oil marine engine in 1910 and by the 1920s reportedly had 80% of the world market. Although styling themselves in advertising as Bolinder's or Bolinders, they referred to their engines as a Bolinder. In 1932, the company merged with tractor manufacturer Munktell to become Bolinder-Munktell. In 1950, BM was bought by Volvo and, since 1995, has been a part of Volvo Construction Equipment.

not get started and was anchored off a certain point. Tom Coppack would then go to the chemists for a bottle of ether and armed with this highly inflammable liquid make his way to the ketch. A little of this always started the engine with quite a bang!

Parallel with the development of the semi-diesel, consideration was given to using gas engines, which were widely used in land based applications for industry. The problem was the supply of coal gas. Gas producers were compact and used about half the coal of a conventional steamer but they were temperamental and the gas had to be carefully scrubbed to remove dust. The other problem was that the engines could not be easily reversed. This was solved in the experimental coaster *Holzapaffel I* by using a hydraulic coupling consisting of two centrifugal pumps which delivered water to an ahead and an astern turbine. Losses in the coupling averaged about 15%. The Dutch coaster *Zeemeuw*, of about 560 deadweight tons, ran for a number of years with a similar arrangement. As oil products became more widely available, the simpler semi-diesel came to the fore and efforts to use coal gas were abandoned.

Meanwhile, the hot bulb engines were in use for small barges, fishing vessels and coasters in Europe and Russia, where Bolinders opened a second factory to produce their engines. So too did Nobel Marine, based in Petrograd, which was loosely associated with what was to become the 'Polar' brand. It was rather harder for the engines to make inroads into Britain as better winds and tides meant that traditional sailing craft were strongly established and cheap to run, compared with steamers. However, some owners saw the advantages of auxiliary power in sailing vessels, allowing them to sail in adverse winds. The 'Polar' name came about because of the success of the engine supplied in 1909 for *Fram*, the auxiliary sailing vessel used by Amundsen for his successful expedition to the South Pole.

These early engines were heavy with ones of 180bhp (brake horse power) weighing 10 tons, while a hundred years later, this power would be expected from an engine weighing at least ten times less. Because of the weight, the 2-stroke cycle was favoured as it gave good turning power for propellers at lower speeds and the best power to weight ratio. They were not particularly easy to start, requiring compressed air for this, so a small auxiliary engine which could be started by hand was needed to fill the compressed air tank before the main engine could be turned over. The other problem was heat and early engines easily overheated, which could be expected as, rather than burning fuel to heat water for steam to drive the pistons and ultimately the propeller, the fuel was being burnt directly in the cylinders of a reciprocating engine. Although this was more efficient, as it cut out the intermediate step and turned more of the fuel's energy into useful power, there were now carbon deposits to be regularly removed from the cylinders and exhaust ports. At least part of this was expensive lubricating oil, which was necessary to lubricate the piston and prevent damage to the cylinder walls. However, marine engines had the advantage of a plentiful supply of cooling water. Oil engines also had the further disadvantage that they could not be run particularly slowly for manoeuvring as steam machinery could. They took up less space though and could be started in a few minutes, as compared with steamers where it might take half a day at least to raise steam from cold, such that steamers continued to burn some fuel even at anchor.

During the First World War, there was much research and development of internal combustion engines generally, so that by the end of the conflict, there had been considerable advances. In addition, there were now many young engineers who had experience of virtually nothing else. Also, the Admiralty had ordered a considerable number of mostly Bolinder-powered barges and these were sold off at the end of the war, allowing several owners to enter the realm of motor shipping cheaply. Various new and second-hand engines were fitted to the numerous schooners which were still a significant part of the coasting trade to smaller ports, in order to extend their working lives.

The main development work on diesel engines had been on the continent and so it was logical that Plenty & Son of Newbury, well known for their steam engineering, should approach Kromhout to become licensees for the manufacture of their popular engines. These engines had cylinders of 335mm bore with a stroke 350mm. Their 4-cylinder (Kromhout 4M4) type developed 180bhp and weighed just under 10 tons with reversing gear. It was a 2-stroke, as many engines were at that time. In these engines each cylinder fires once per revolution and with the cranks set at 90 degrees there was a continuous turning movement on the crank shaft, this tending towards steady running and elimination of vibration. The air for scavenging was compressed in the crank case, it being drawn in on the up stroke of the piston through spring loaded, leather diaphragm valves, fitted with gauze strainers on the side of the crank case to prevent any solid matter entering with the air. On the down stroke, the exhaust port opened first, allowing the combustion products to pass out into the water-cooled silencer. Directly after this, the air inlet port opened and the air was deflected by a

specially shaped piston head to blow out remaining exhaust gases. The scavenging air in its upward flow from the crank case to the cylinder passed round the small end of the connecting rod, thus cooling the gudgeon pin and its bearing. There were four fuel feed pumps, one for each cylinder. The cylinder head or combustion chamber of each cylinder was entirely water jacketed, except for the top plate, but even under full load there was no red heat apparent. The water circulation in the jackets was provided by a plunger pump driven by an eccentric on the crank shaft. Water injection was entirely eliminated, which had been necessary on earlier engines.

The engine was started by means of the Kromhout rapid heater and this enabled starting from cold in five to six minutes. The heaters were lit like a gas jet without any pre-heating. When the top plate of each cylinder was sufficiently heated, compressed air was admitted to the forward cylinder and at the same time an injection of fuel was given by hand, this starting the engine running. The rapid heaters were then turned off and were not further needed, the engine retaining the necessary heat for both vaporisation and ignition under all conditions of load. The compressed air or in fact exhaust gases were bled off cylinder number two, to give about 180lbs pressure for future starts and also powered the ships' whistle. Reversing was done by the large hand wheel mounted on the after cylinder, which operated the reverse gear and the clutch and also controlled the engine's speed governor, so that the engine ran dead slow when the drive was re-engaged.

Beginning in 1920, the company began to manufacture their own design engine under the Plenty name. Everards became reliant on these engines and so when the builders collapsed in 1931, they purchased the diesel engine manufacturing side of the business and reconstituted it as the Newbury Diesel Co. Ltd, by which time the engines had become much more reliable. Under this new management, the engines were given some mild supercharging (3psi) and Bosch airless injection pumps on each cylinder.

Looking at their general economics in 1932, some interesting figures were produced by G.A. Brown in *Shipbuilding & Shipping Record*, which made a comparison between a small steamer and a motor vessel, and found that for the same power of about 128bhp, the machinery of the steamer weighed 35 tons against 24 tons for the motor ship and the motor ship burned 0.696 tons of oil a day compared with the steamers 4.35 tons of coal but coal was about £1 per ton compared with oil at £4 per ton. Even so, the running costs were £1 in favour of the motor vessel without taking into account the smaller crew but this was the peak of the slump and cheaply priced steamers were widely available. Also, steam engines did not require expensive spare parts and even if a boiler tube

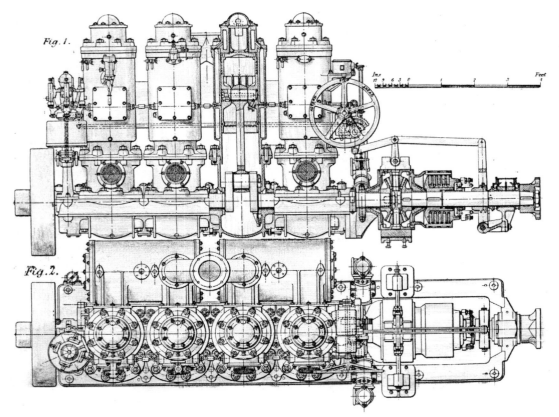

A 4-cylinder 2-stroke Kromhout (4M4 type) engine of 180bhp fitted to the coaster Neppo *(showing the side view and the top view), built at the Kromhout Works in Amsterdam. The cylinders were individually built up from machined castings assembled on to a cast bed plate and each had its own fuel feed pump. The combustion chambers were completely water jacketed, except for the hot bulb at the top of the cylinder. The large hand wheel on the aftermost cylinder operated a combined clutch and reverse gear, plus the engine governor, so the engine rpm was automatically brought to a suitable idling value. On the hand wheel being turned in either direction, the speed of the engine was slightly increased before the load came on and then ran at dead slow. The lubrication was fairly simple, with the main bearings and thrust block wick fed. FROM ENGINEERING, 27TH MAY 1921*

failed, it could be blanked off and the ship continue trading. However, very few smaller steam coasters had been built for more than a decade and as trade picked up, owners were tentatively looking to order motor ships as replacements for their ageing steamers. Owners were now being offered a greater choice of engines. Crossley Bros of Manchester, who had been manufacturing 2- and 4-stroke engines for many years and had originally been licensees of Nicklaus Otto engines manufactured by Deutz, introduced a 2-stroke marine engine fitted to a barge in 1933. The first engine, a 4-cylinder unit developing 100bhp at 450rpm (revolutions per minute), was fitted to F.W. Horlock's Thames barge *Resourceful* (100/30) and was still running over thirty years later. Deutz 4-stroke engines were also fitted to a number of new coasters in the 1930s. Most were direct drive, often via a clutch and a reverse gear, where the engine was not directly reversible. Propeller efficiency falls with increasing rpm but 4-strokes required higher rpm and so reduction gears were introduced. *Brockley Combe*, which had a Ruston engine giving 500bhp at 430rpm, was fitted with a reduction and reverse gear of 2.5 to 1 for a propeller speed of 172rpm. One of the problems encountered was vibration due to the various forces produced and it was found that 3-cylinder engines worked best with four bladed propellers and 4-cylinder engines with three bladed propellers. Best results in engines were where they had the ideal number of cylinders, so the engines were naturally self balancing, as for example an 8-cylinder 4-stroke and a 6-cylinder 2-stroke. For less balanced engines with other cylinder arrangements, various sprung engine mountings were developed. Another challenge was set by reduction gear boxes, as shipyard marine engineer Peter Coates explains:

'We always tried to arrange for 'bastard' reductions within the gear box, because what happened with gearboxes having equal perfect reduction ratios was that periodically a propeller blade would arrive at top dead centre at the same time as one of the cylinders arrived at top dead centre for its firing stroke; this created vibration in the whole of the propulsion system. This is also one of the many reasons for installing 6-, 8- or even 9-cylinder engines.'

Owners were not sure whether 2-stroke or 4-stroke engines were going to be the most satisfactory and both France, Fenwick & Co. Ltd and the Newcastle Coal & Shipping Co. Ltd built sisterships, with one of each type for comparison. France, Fenwick reported that both types had run satisfactorily for them but the Newcastle Coal & Shipping Co selected a Deutz 4-stroke for a later vessel in the 1930s, which may have also been influenced by cost. The numerous 'Chant' and 'Fabric' prefabricated coasters of the Second World War had clutch and reduction geared machinery and the engines fitted depended on what was available, although diesel engines of various makes became more freely available towards the end of the war.

Development of the 2-stroke continued although they had distinct limitations at higher rpm, as it became difficult to provide sufficient cooling. Crossley Bros continued to develop their loop scavenged engine which was valveless. In these engines, air was admitted on one side of the cylinder and exhaust released on the other through slots near the bottom, air under pressure being deflected up and around the cylinder in a loop to force out remnants of the exhaust gases. Some makes had a poppet valve. These spring loaded valves in the cylinder heads were operated by a cam and these could get up to 25% more compressed air into the cylinder but this was offset in the valveless engine by using exhaust stroke pressure charging. By careful arrangement of the exhausts, the exhaust pulse from an adjacent cylinder could be used to produce a back pressure pulse to compress the air in another cylinder before the exhaust port closed. This effect increased with the engine under load with no loss of power and was used in the Crossley 2-stroke engines popular for small coasters in the 1950s.

The need to provide quick reversing began to be addressed with the fitting of controllable pitch propellers and the up-river collier *Mitcham*, delivered in 1946, was designed and built with the fitting of one in mind but it was not ready before the ship entered service and the first vessel delivered with one was thus *Wandsworth* in 1950. A few of the largest coastal and short sea vessels were fitted with the smallest engines from the Sulzer or Doxford ranges, whose main market was much larger ocean going vessels. The popular choice post-war was British Polar, who reported in 1949 that there were thirty-four vessels at sea with their 2-stroke engines and twenty with more than five years service. Most had electric slip couplings, while nine of them had hydraulic couplings. However, by the later 1950s, Deutz 4-strokes were making inroads and, from 1956, all Robertsons' new vessels had these engines, as did the last two delivered to John Stewart & Co. (Shipping) Ltd. Ken Garrett, marine superintendent of Everards, noted that their British Polars tended to regularly need parts, while the Deutz did better but if something did fail it could be expensive to fix.

Brons also made inroads and superseded Crossley as the preferred 2-stroke engine in the Rowbotham fleet in the 1960s but perhaps the most novel installation was that for J. & A. Gardner,

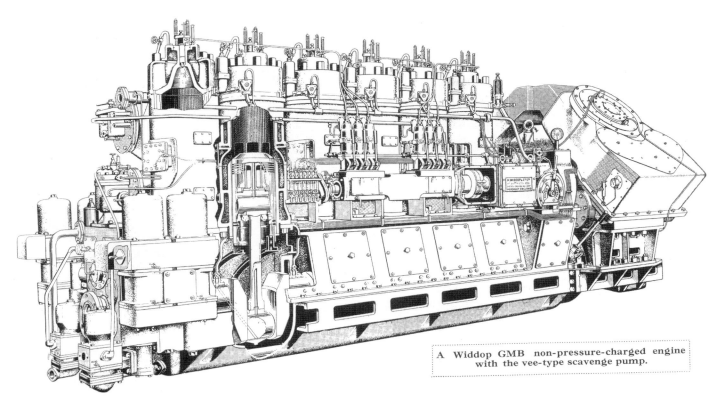

A Widdop GMB non-pressure-charged engine with the vee-type scavenge pump.

who chose a vee 12 Dorman 4-stroke of 495 horsepower at 1500rpm with a 6 to1 reduction gear. The total weight was less than 6 tons, giving a high power to weight ratio – a policy they continued in later vessels although not with quite such high rpm. The most popular choices for these smaller vessels were Lister-Blackstone and Kelvin. Geoff LeClercq notes in the days of uncertificated engineers:

'It was a case of learn quick or no job. Engineers we weren't, engine drivers more like, look often at the oil, water and fuel. All the companies had good trouble shooting teams, mostly ex-engineers and would get to you wherever you were. Most was routine maintenance and problems were sorted out and very rarely was a shipyard called in. If at sea, the final resort was a tow-in, if possible by another company ship, when beyond the efforts of the engineers, as with lost propellers.'

Ken Garratt also observed:

'when I moved from steam to motor I was appalled at the vibration and frequency of breakdowns. In my early years at Everards, when they still had many Newburys, tow-ins were unfortunately not a rarity. A chief engineer would come on the radio with a tale of woe. It was then up to me to negotiate a tow to somewhere for repair. Sometimes one of our own ships could do the job for a modest bonus to the crew. Meanwhile, the engineer superintendent would be organising spares or even a replacement engine.'

The later 1960s saw Newbury cease engine manufacturing, as by then Everards were their only customer and lighter, faster running, geared 4-stroke engines rather than heavier 2-strokes were becoming the order of the day. This was exemplified by Everards, who replaced all the Newbury engines in their Exelship 2600 vessels with 4-stroke Mirrlees-Blackstone or 'Polar' engines, both types with reduction/reverse gear boxes. Ruston engines, more commonly found in tugs, were also fitted to some vessels.

It is interesting to note that a 4-cylinder Sulzer engine of 1924 gave 80bhp at 400rpm but, by the 1970s, an engine of the same 240mm bore could well develop eight to ten times the power. The very low power of this 2-stroke trunk piston design of 1924 was in part due to crank case compression, which severely limited the amount of scavenge air available. Diesels designed as heavy duty and usually low rotational speed were primarily produced for propulsion of smaller vessels like coasters. Power to weight ratio was fairly low, prioritising low maintenance and good reliability even with less skilled engineers. Engines of medium to high rating, running at 700-1000rpm, were designed as geared propulsion units. They were mostly 4-stroke, with a single stage turbocharger and aftercooling, straight or vee with a maximum of twenty cylinders, and usually with two inlet and two exhaust valves in each of the separate cylinder heads. Pistons were usually cooled by splash or directed oil and the cylinders by coolant. The valves were operated by a side mounted cam shaft,

The Widdop 6-cylinder 2-stroke medium speed (about 300rpm) GMB6 engine. It was loop scavenged by a v-type scavange pump (the angled box on the far end of the drawing). The bore was 12.5 inches and the stroke 18.5 inches. Though more popular for tugs and trawlers, an 8-cylinder version was selected for Constantine's collier Thameswood in 1957. This engine was rated at 1135bhp and drove the propeller via a flexible coupling and single reduction gear to give a service speed of 11 knots. FROM THE MOTOR SHIP, OCTOBER 1958

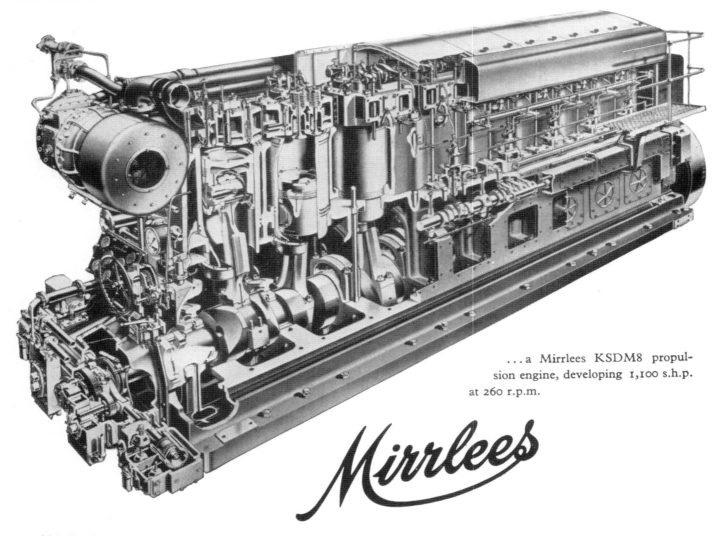

...a Mirrlees KSDM8 propulsion engine, developing 1,100 s.h.p. at 260 r.p.m.

Mirrlees

with roller followers and push rods. The increase in unmanned engine rooms favoured the use of shielded fuel pipes and pumps, in view of the fire risk from fractured high pressure fuel lines spraying fuel into the engine room. Engines generally had built on coolant and oil circulating pumps, together with a seawater circulating pump and fuel surcharge pumps. Starting was generally by compressed air directly to the cylinders.

In the 1970s and '80s, the move was very much towards turbocharged and intercooled 4-strokes, with smaller British engines displaced by Caterpillar and Cummins from the USA, and Alpha packages which came with gearbox and controllable pitch propeller from Denmark, while Everards chose some MaK engines from Germany. Allen, probably best known for generating sets in larger ships, supplied a few main engines from the 1930s onwards and was selected by Rowbotham for some ships, whilst Danish Callesen engines superseded Alpha in the last vessels built for London & Rochester (Crescent Shipping).

Geoff LeClercq comments:

'The slow running non-turbocharged engines were over engineered and had many back-up/get you home systems which the newer high speed engines, Cummins, Rolls-Royce etc, never had. The knowledge of the older MWM, Deutz, Brons, Stork etc were at their peak for reliability and someone somewhere would know the problem, how to fix it and where to get spares if needed. Most of the running repairs were easily done and would get you home for the fit-team to arrive! A tribute to British engineering was an ancient 5-cylinder 2-stroke Crossley salvaged from a sunken Harker oil barge somewhere on the Severn and refitted in the Island Commodore, which had been sold to the West Indies. It started to smoke and splutter after a week into the Atlantic crossing but continued to run without stopping from Guernsey to Marigot (St. Martens). It was still running to the very end when a hurricane parted her anchor at Guadaloupe and drove her ashore.'

CHAPTER 2
THE PIONEERS

There are various rules for the measurement of hull dimensions. Within these pages, as far as possible, the moulded dimensions, as used by naval architects and builders, are given unless otherwise stated. In moulded dimensions, the length between perpendiculars used was originally defined as the horizontal length from the after side of the stern post to the fore side of the stem bar where it intersected the upper deck (also sometimes referred to as the main deck), projected forwards if necessary (see plan of *Cromarty Firth*, page 47). There was a slow change to defining the fore perpendicular as the intersection between the fore side of the stem and the load water line, and the aft perpendicular where the stern post intersects the load water line or, if no stern post, the centre of the rudder stock, as for example in a vessel with a spade rudder. This definition was common from the 1940s onwards. Breadth moulded was defined as the maximum breadth between the external sides of the frames amidships but excluding the thickness of the plating. Depth moulded is the vertical distance at midships from the top of the keel or keel plate to the top of the deck beam (or underside of deck) at the side of the ship (that is excluding the deck camber which was usually about one fiftieth of the breadth). Draught moulded was taken as the distance up to the load water line. Sheer is the longitudinal curvature of the deck. Rise of floor is the rise of the bottom shell plating either side of the keel measured at right angles to the centre line of the ship and can be seen on body plans and midship sections. Flare is the outward curvature of the forward sections above the water line at the bow. When moulded dimensions are not available, especially for older vessels, the official registered dimensions are quoted. The registered length was measured from the foreside of the tip of the stem bar to the after side of the stern post or rudder stock if there was no rudder post. Registered breadth was also the extreme breadth measured over the plating (but excluding any belting or rubbing bars). Registered depth (depth of hold) was measured from the top of the ceiling in vessels with ordinary floors and double bottomed ships or from the tank top if no ceiling was laid, to the top of the deck beams amidships. Neither of the above length measurements take into account the overhang of the stern beyond the rudder post or rudder, so that the overall length of the ship could be several feet greater.

Ship's names are followed by gross tonnage/last two digits of year of build, to avoid confusion where there are several vessels of the same name.

Unlike steam, internal combustion engines crept into the coasting trades as auxiliary engines in sailing vessels and motor lighters. Around the Mersey area, steam barges towing a dumb barge were widely used. The only area almost completely reliant on small steamers was the Forth & Clyde Canal and adjacent waters. As the advantage of motors steadily declined as the size of vessel increased, these particularly small vessels would show the greatest gain in cargo capacity. The canal locks limited vessels using it to 66 feet and so weight and space saving was particularly valuable.

The first man to venture into motor vessels in a big way was John M. Paton, who left Paton & Hendry to form the Coasting Motor Shipping Company of Glasgow, set up in January 1912. A well known figure in his fifties, he probably had little trouble attracting shareholders, investing £8,000 of the £50,000 nominal capital himself. The initial order was for eight vessels, four of which were suitable for the Forth & Clyde Canal, with the registered dimensions 65.6ft x 18.4ft x 8.6ft. First to be delivered was *Innisagra* (94/12) in May 1912, with the remainder following by the end of the year, three with Bolinder engines and the forth with a Beardmore. This was in line with the company's decision to try different engines and compare the results. In appearance, they were closely similar to the small steamers in use, though *Innisagra* could carry rather more at 140 tons at a speed of about 8 knots. However, she could only carry this maximum through the Crinan Canal, as the Forth & Clyde was too shallow for a full cargo.

The order for the four larger vessels, each to carry about 230 tons with 120bhp engines, was divided between John Cran & Co. and Jeffrey & Co., both of Leith. First to be delivered was *Inniskea*, with the registered dimensions 93ft x 18.7ft x 9.5ft. There was then a pause, perhaps while further consideration was given to the draught of the vessels, which was reduced by about a foot in the remaining three, which were slightly longer to compensate. Cran's vessel, at 99.0ft x 18.8ft x 8.4ft

and with a shorter poop, was smaller than Jeffrey's, which were 100.1ft x 18.9ft x 8.6ft and had a quarter deck. At the time, owners often only specified deadweight, speed, draught and possibly any other restrictions, other details being left to the yards. Initial results must have been encouraging, as two further canal sized vessels were ordered together with four larger vessels, the latter divided between MacGregor and Jeffrey. However, at about 74 feet, these four were unable to use the Forth & Clyde Canal but could use the Crinan Canal and again there were slight differences in design.

Originally an outline design for a vessel able to carry 460 tons very similar to contemporary steamers was considered but finally an order was placed with Chalmers, Rutherglen for four vessels able to carry about 350 tons on a draught of 9ft 8ins. However, the design of this last group does not seem to have been well thought out. The early engines were noisy and produced a fair amount of vibration, and possibly for this reason all the crew were moved to the forecastle, as can be seen in the *Innisshannon* (238/13), 115.7ft x 21.6ft x 9.6ft registered. By the time the second vessel was built, some of the shortcomings in the design were probably becoming apparent, with bulwarks seemingly added aft to protect the lifeboats and bars to protect the wheelhouse windows. Even so, it must have been quite an experience to be at the wheel, fully laden and hove to in a gale, with seas crashing over the bow or trying to hang on to the wheel light ship! There was then a pause of about a year, during which time the wheelhouse position was reconsidered and it was moved aft, with accommodation for the chief engineer and captain beneath what was now an open bridge, as seen in *Innisvera* (238/14). The arrangement was changed for the crew too, who now had some berths below the main deck, allowing the forecastle to be shorter and the hatch slightly longer. It was probably found that the space previously under the forecastle and separated from the hold by a wooden bulkhead was difficult to stow, and would in many cases set the vessel down by the head if used for cargo.

Although large deep bilge keels were fitted to minimise rolling when passages had to be made in light condition, as would be the case in the Isles trade, the provision of water ballast was minimal and so the vessels would have been difficult to handle in bad weather. Clearly insufficient thought had been given to this and the aft peak would only hold 8 tons and the forepeak not much more. One of the problems met with when motor vessels ventured into open water was that when the screw came out of the water, the engine would speed up and the fuel would be reduced by a governor but on plunging back the engine could stall. Compressed air for restarts could soon run out, leaving the vessel helpless. The horizontal exhaust under the stern may have also caused problems, with following seas producing back pressure in the system, although it may have been fitted with some form of flap non-return valve and seems to have been retained in later reconstructions.

Profile of Innisshannon *(238/13), based on a general arrangement drawing and photographs published in* Shipbuilding & Shipping Record, *29th January 1914. The layout was revised for later vessels in the series, as shown in the general arrangement of the* Innisvera *(238/14), page right.*

Possibly following service as an Admiralty water boat, the *Innisshannon* herself was rebuilt to correct some of the shortcomings of the design, with her bridge and accommodation moved aft, although no wheelhouse was fitted. The lack of ballast was addressed by fitting a cellular double bottom forward able to hold 40 tons.

Although the vessels could carry considerably more than steamers of the same size, there was no infrastructure to support the venture. Expansion was so rapid there was no time for the engineers

M.S. "INNISSHANNON"

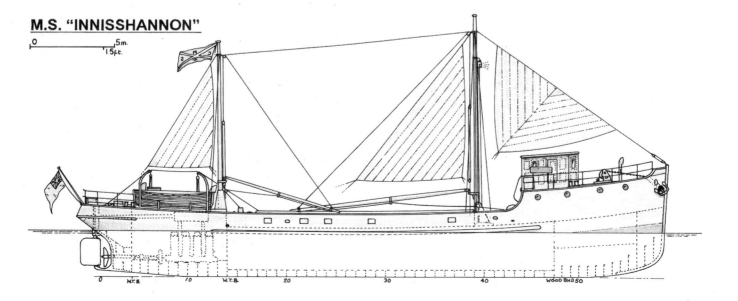

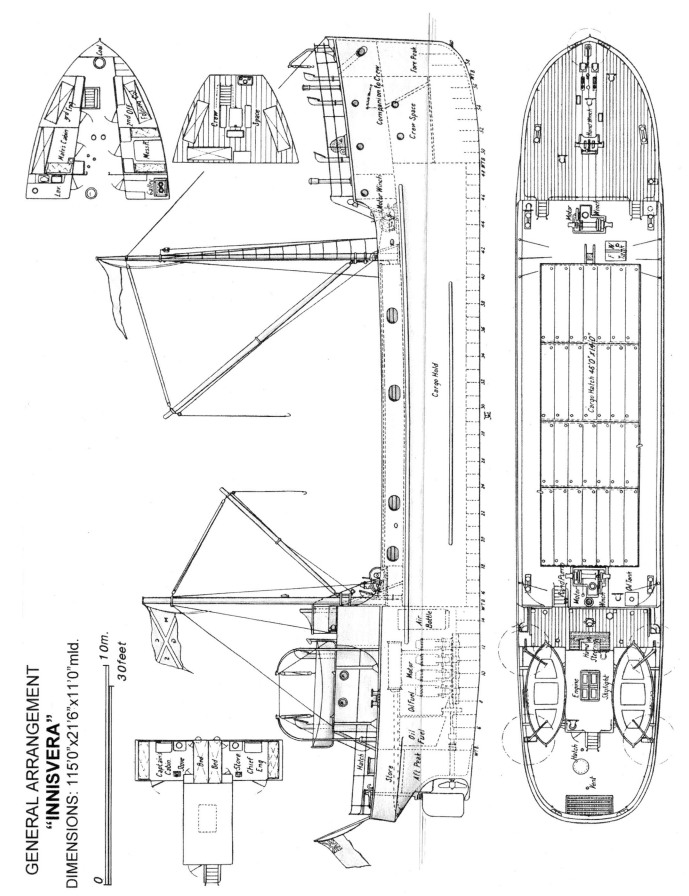

GENERAL ARRANGEMENT
"INNISVERA"
DIMENSIONS: 115'0"x21'6"x11'0"mld.

30feet

10m.

Innisvera built in 1914 for the Coasting Motor Shipping Co. Ltd by William Chalmers & Co. Ltd. From Shipbuilding & Shipping Record for 21st January 1915.

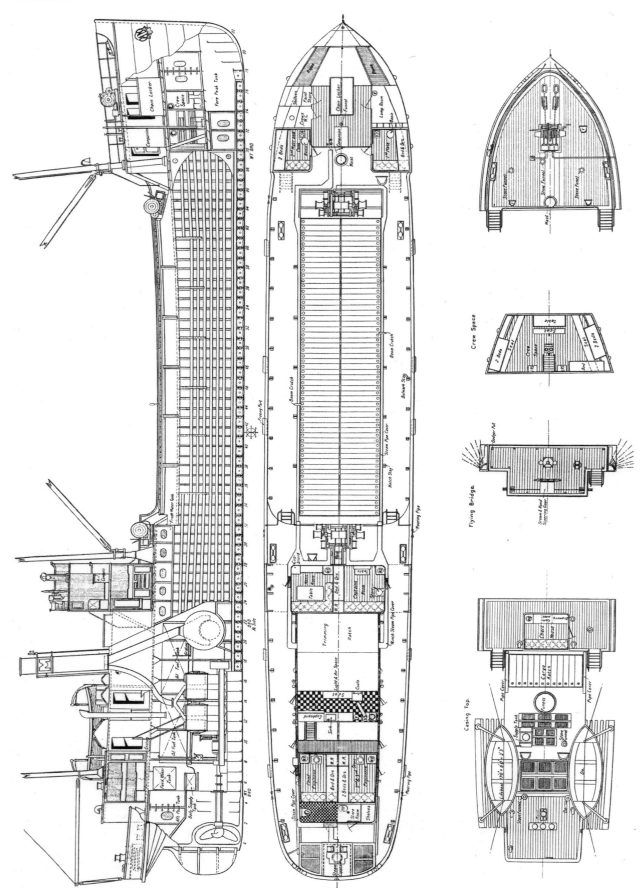

Isleford (4/4/13) was begun as a steamer but changed to a motor ship during building. The 50 foot long hatch was suitable for long steel and similar cargoes, and was probably attractive to the Admiralty, who immediately purchased her following delivery. Cargo battens running horizontally along the frames in the hold are shown on this very detailed drawing from Shipbuilding & Shipping Record, 22nd May 1913.

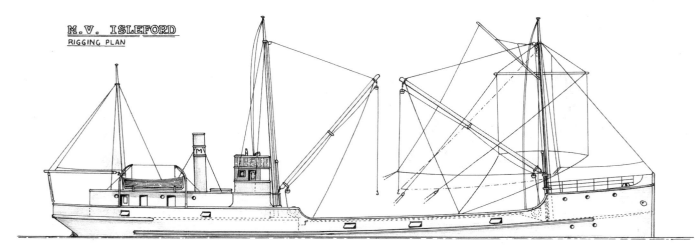

M.V. ISLEFORD
RIGGING PLAN

to be given sufficient training or the designs given sufficient trials. With the outbreak of war in the summer of 1914, the younger and more able men were taken by the armed services, leaving older men set in the ways of steam. Even as late as the 1950s, there were men choosing to return to steamers from motor vessels as they preferred working on the former. However, the war also brought salvation for the fleet when six of the larger vessels were sold to the Admiralty as water boats and four to the Russian Government. Two had been lost following engine breakdowns. This left the company with canal-size vessels for canal and sheltered water work, which were described in a contemporary report as very successful. The final verdict is perhaps illustrated by the fact that, at the time of his death in November 1917, Paton was the owner of a steam coaster and the Coasting Motor Shipping Co. was continuing to sell ships, with the last sold in 1919.

Almost unnoticed in February 1913 was the delivery of the *Isleford* (414/13), to another Glasgow owner, Mann, McNeal, with the registered dimensions 149.8ft x 25.6ft x 10.0ft. Ordered from the Ardrossan Shipbuilding & Dry Dock Co. and designed as a steamer, at a late stage it was decided to fit a 4-cylinder Bolinder 2-stroke engine of about 350bhp at 250rpm. An oil-fired donkey boiler had to be fitted, as all the deck machinery remained steam. This was as recommended by Mr Milton, chief engineering surveyor of Lloyd's. The crew quarters was given special attention, as one of the reasons given for the difficulty of attracting good crews for motor vessels was said to be the lack of good accommodation. The arrangement of the fuel tanks at the sides of the engine room allowed what would have been bunker space to be used for cargo. The original sail plan for the steamer was apparently just fore and aft sails but a square sail was added to the foremast so the vessel could switch to sail in the event of a breakdown. The trial runs loaded were quite impressive, with a speed of almost 9 knots at 228rpm and the engines could be reversed in 5 seconds. However, the slowest possible engine

Rigging Plan of the Isleford *(414/13). The sail plan was increased apparently as a precaution when the decision was taken to change from steam to motor at a late stage during construction. From* Shipbuilding & Shipping Record, *22nd May 1913.*

Innisowen *after lengthening and fitted with a Bolinder engine to bring her into line with the rest of the fleet of John Summers & Sons, Shotton, Chester. Sketched from an old photograph, she apparently still retained the original derrick length. Her bluff lines contrast strongly with the vessels designed by the engine importers, Pollocks, which were much more successful in service both for John Summers and other owners.*

Coppack Bros' Fleurita, 171 gross, of 1913 is seen on 1st September 1958 being overhauled in Port Dinorwic on the Menai Straits. She had just come out of dry dock (off picture to the left), where the hull had been repainted and work on the topsides and deck was continuing afloat. Sold to Civil & Marine Ltd, for work on the Thames, she foundered there in 1965.

speed was found to be 120rpm ahead and 180rpm astern. Fuel consumption proved to be about 19 gallons per hour. Following ten days of trials, she was bought by the Admiralty and remained in their service for a number of years after the 1914-18 war.

It was perhaps appropriate that the last of the Coasting Motor Shipping Co's vessels should be bought by John Summers & Sons, another pioneer owner of motor coasters, who had a large steel works on the banks of the River Dee at Shotton, near Chester. They soon sold *Innisdhu*, probably because of the poor deadweight/ draught ratio, but opted to send *Innisowen* to Crichton's yard nearby for lengthening and fitting a Bolinder engine, to bring it in to line with the rest of the fleet. The company had initially owned some small steamers in earlier times but with rising freight rates and probably fewer small steamers available, they returned to shipowning. Their wharf had tidal restrictions and so the motor vessel *Ogarita* (95/11), 88ft × 19.1ft × 7.1ft registered, which had a particularly shallow draught, was purchased. She was immediately followed by *Carita* (141/13), 96ft × 21.5ft × 7.7ft registered, and *Fleurita* (171/13), 103.2ft × 22.1ft × 8.3ft registered, delivered from the local shipyard of Abdela & Mitchell. Unlike the Coastal Motor Shipping Co. vessels built the same year, their design proved excellent and would have been based on drawings supplied by Bolinders' agents James Pollock, Sons & Co Ltd. Pollocks were primarily still consultant engineers and naval architects based in London and did not open their own shipyard until 1916. Clearly happy with the vessels designed by Pollocks they purchased the *Sir William* (170/14) from Liverpool owners. Although the Bolinder engines could be temperamental at times, the advantage for the company of being able to move more shipments when tides were poor outweighed the costs. The early runs were mostly short, often to Liverpool or Birkenhead, so that if a problem arose it was easy for a company with their engineering facilities to make or repair parts and quickly dispatch a fitter if needed. Tom Coppack discussed them with Summers' manager at the time and he was adamant that for the ordinary tramp owner carrying cargoes to out of the way places, they were not a practical proposition, with stops for adjustments being all too frequent. The manager's notebook reveals that even after lengthening in 1925 to 88.7 feet, *Innisowen* (142/13), drew 1ft 6ins forward and 5ft 2ins aft light ship. It can be compared with *Carita*, of a similar size but which drew a more favourable 2ft forward and 5ft aft, and could load 175 tons on 7ft 3ins, while *Innisowen* could manage 195 tons but needed 8ft 6ins. In later years, following the Second World War, Coppacks took on the *Fleurita* and Tom Fish of Connah's Quay recalls her:

'*Fleurita* of Coppacks never went south of the Lleyn Peninsula and was really a bit too small for voyages as far as Belfast but we had to do them and could really suffer weather delays. We left Connah's Quay the last week in September with parcels of goods stowed for discharge at Douglas, Ramsey, Belfast, and Drogheda. The weather was really bad and we were caught in Belfast, we would often get as far as The Mew and have to turn back and it was five weeks before we finally made it to Drogheda and back to Connah's Quay. She had been built as a flush decker with shorter voyages in mind but Coppacks increased the height of the bulwarks at the bow to shoulder height. This helped as long as the seas were not coming over the top of it. As she was flush deck, this water would tend to run right down the deck and off the stern. On one occasion she started to run a bottom end bearing and we had to make for shelter in Skerries Roads between Drogheda and Dublin with two of the crew pumping oil over it to keep it cool. The captain considered it pure luck that we managed to get in. Occasionally there was a Belfast to Barrow cargo and a 'one-off,' was a full cargo – 45 tons of telegraph poles for Douglas from Connah's Quay. Bricks, tiles and general building materials were usually loaded at Connah's Quay and one of the destinations was Dublin. Electrical goods for Ward & Goldstone were also taken there from Connah's Quay. The worst cargo out of Dublin we ever had was some canned fish which had been condemned and had been crushed into square bales and it was covered in flies. It was loaded for Barrow in the hold and as deck cargo. When we arrived we were ordered to anchor off. It was eventually discharged by dockers on treble time. Meanwhile some of the crew jumped overboard for a wash to try and get rid of the smell. The next cargo was to be stone from the Rivals but as the ship was still covered in flies a call was made*

JAMES POLLOCK, SONS & Co. Ltd.

Naval Architects, Shipbuilders and Engineers.

3, LLOYDS AVENUE, LONDON, E.C.
AND
SHIPYARD, FAVERSHAM, KENT.

Sir William (170/14). Although built by Abdela & Mitchell Ltd at Queensferry on the Dee for J.H. Vernon of Liverpool, the original design was clearly the work of Pollocks, as this contemporary postcard, probably showing the vessel on its trials, indicates. She was a small vessel with the registered dimensions 98.1ft x 21.1ft x 9.6ft. Purchased by John Summers & Sons from Vernons in 1915, she was renamed Felita, retaining the somewhat precarious work/lifeboat position, which could just be reached by the long cargo derrick for launching. She was probably needed by them to keep pace with the increased demand for steel products as a result of the First World War. Following the war, exports of corrugated steel sheets, which were taken to Liverpool and Birkenhead, was important initially but as the company began to supply the car industry with sheet steel, a lorry fleet was built up and the smaller vessels sold. WAINE COLLECTION

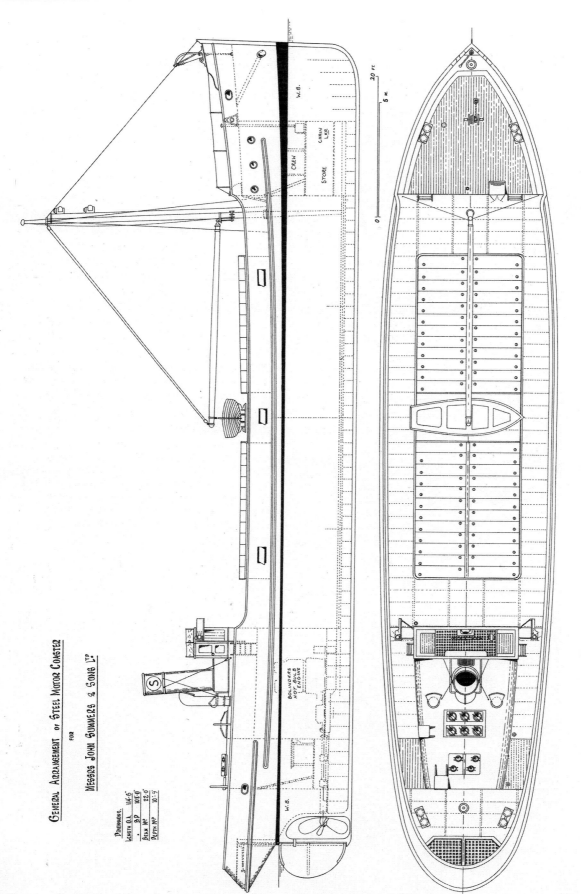

GENERAL ARRANGEMENT OF STEEL MOTOR COASTER

FOR

MESSRS JOHN SUMMERS & SONS LD

DIMENSIONS.

LENGTH O.A.	114'-6"
" B.P	108'-0"
BEAM MD	22'-0"
DEPTH MD	10'-3"

The original plan of the Indorita submitted to Lloyd's for approval about 1914. The transverse dotted lines indicate the positions of the deck beams, though unusually the frames were not numbered. Comparison with the vessel as built shows some changes such as the straight casing aft. This would have simplified construction as the original design involved unnecessarily complex plate bending.

at Holyhead to get some 'Flit' flyspray and the flies were literally shovelled up from the cabin floors!

Although the hatches were supposed to be on before casting off (the quarry jetties), the foreman would often start throwing the lines off to avoid paying overtime before the crew had battened down. The River Loyne was lost off Penmaenmawr when she took a heavy sea on board before the hatches were secured (but the practice continued in subsequent years). It was also necessary to leave the ballast in, so that the rudder and screw were in as deep as possible to aid manoeuvring when going alongside and might not be out before leaving. The ship might sail with the decks awash while some of the ballast was still being pumped out. However, if one could get on three hours before high water and get loaded quickly, the tide could be caught up the coast to the Stack and then stay in close under Carmel Head and inside the West Mouse, etc to avoid the weather. When loading stone dust in a wind, it was necessary to ask for an extra 10 tons or so, as this much could be blown away during loading.'

The success of the small ships resulted in John Summers ordering two larger vessels from Abdela & Mitchell. One of the original drawings for *Indorita* has survived, which was submitted to Lloyd's for approval about 1914. The plan shows a rather sparse vessel, with a small open bridge very similar to the slightly smaller *Fleurita* but with the addition of a raised quarter deck and half height forecastle. Early photographs show a more substantial higher open bridge and it is probable that she was modified during construction. For example, the final approved plan for the rudder was practically rectangular, with a sloping top edge and a horizontal lower edge. The light ship weight was about 130 tons. The design avoids all the shortcomings of the Scottish vessels, with good provision for water ballast, the aft peak holding 25 tons and fore peak 30 tons. Another improvement was the placing of the fuel tank amidships between the hatches, well away from any fire risk and forming an integral part of the hatch structure, so reducing weight but still easily inspected for leaks, whilst the fuel would easily flow to the engine fuel pumps. However, there was the risk of grab damage and possible penetration during discharge of bulk cargoes. The original Bolinder engine developed 160bhp at 220rpm. With the registered dimensions 108.6ft x 22.1ft x 9.4ft, the manager's notebook records she could carry about 260 tons on a draught of about 9ft 8ins and the light ship trim was 3ft forward and 5ft 11ins aft. Steamers able to carry a similar cargo were about 20 feet longer and would draw about an extra foot of water.

They were clearly very successful, as virtually no changes were made to the design and similar vessels were being built a decade or so later. However, *Indorita* herself and her sister had a difficult start in life. Laid down in 1915, the Admiralty considered modifying them for Naval service but this was not proceeded with and they were left while the yard concentrated on war work. Labour difficulties following the war delayed her launch until 7th February 1920 and even then the yard had forgotten to fit the side keelsons, the Lloyd's surveyor handing the yard a list of rectifications needed. She was finally completed in August 1920, followed by her sister *Eldorita* in September 1920. They were soon

This photograph of **Indorita** (201/20) taken in the 1930s shows the plan submitted to Lloyd's was generally followed, with an open bridge. A wheelhouse was added in the 1940s. It seems that although designed with hawse pipes for the stockless anchors, they were never fitted and the anchors were handled by a davit and hoisted on deck. Although the original plan shows only three wash ports, the photograph shows five. This could be the result of a later revision of the plans, experience in service or after new regulations issued in the 1930s, following inquiries into the loss of several colliers on the east coast. JIMMY HARTERY

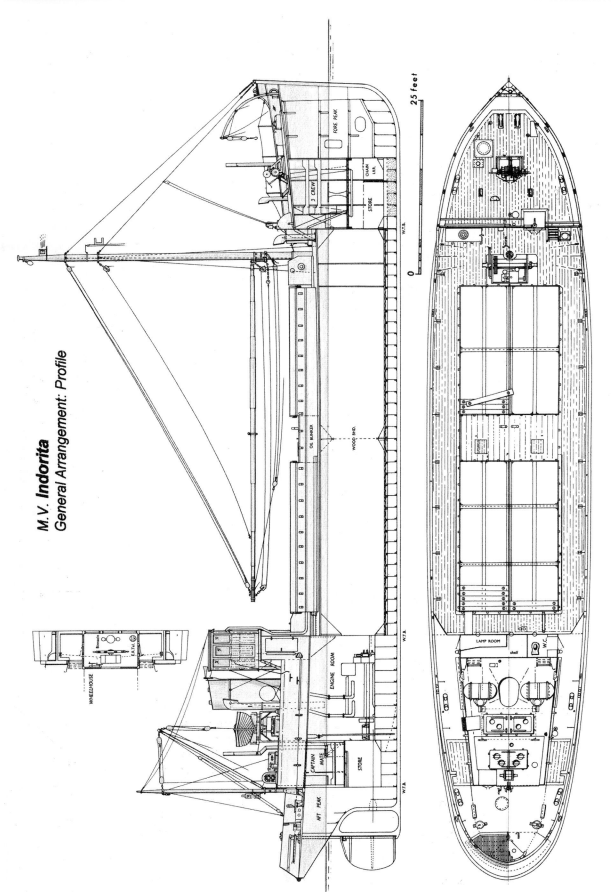

M.V. *Indorita*
General Arrangement: Profile

25 feet

0

FORE PEAK

CHAIN LKR.

3 CREW

STORE

W.T.B.

OIL BUNKER

WOOD BHD.

ENGINE ROOM

CAPTAIN

MATE

STORE

AFT PEAK

WHEELHOUSE

W.T.B.

W.T.B.

W.T.B.

LAMP ROOM

shelf

W.C.

ABOVE: Indorita (203/20) in her final form when fifty years old, from a detailed survey made during the early 1970s by the author.

employed carrying pig iron from Barrow, Millom and Workington, cargoes for which they had been specially strengthened so they could safely rest aground alongside when fully laden.

Basic slag, a by-product of the steel making process, often provided a northwards cargo for the British Basic Slag Company, as it was widely used as a fertilizer and frequently taken to the small harbours along the banks of the Solway Firth. They were not confined to company work especially during the 1930s and a variety of cargoes were found for them by J.S. Jones of Liverpool, who specialised in the coasting trade. During the Second World War, they were taken up as water boats on the Clyde and at the end of the conflict were offered for sale, as the company had had two larger vessels delivered just after the outbreak of hostilities.

Purchased in 1946 by Coppack Bros, the local owners, who had close ties with the Summers, *Indorita* then worked widely on the Irish Sea. Although there were now engineers with considerable experience of Bolinder engines, even they sometimes found them difficult to start. After several attempts, a really explosive mixture could build up in the funnel and there could be quite a bang when the engine eventually fired. Finally, on one occasion it was too much for the old silencer and a hole was blown in the front of the funnel, the blast being sufficient to also blow out the bridge windows, doors and lift the roof!

This problem was ended in 1958 with the fitting of a new 6-cylinder 2-stroke Crossley engine, producing 240bhp at 300rpm. The manufacturers recommended fitting twin silencers and although they could have been fitted horizontally within the engine room this was not advised, as experience had shown soot was enclined to accumulate, so the consultant engineers suggested a new oval funnel to contain the two silencers. The final cost of the engine and fitting was estimated at about £2,500. The old propeller was retained but was probably overloaded, as examination at the end of her life showed some blade-tip erosion due to cavitation. It is a tribute to the original design and engine that this was the first major change in thirty-eight years of service, although there had been improvements to the accommodation and a wheelhouse fitted to keep her up to date in that respect, with a WC and lamp room added below it.

Captain Joe Keane, as a young man of twenty-four and master of *Indorita* from January 1959 to July 1960, recalls:

'She was always loaded by the stern 3ins so she would steer well, say forward 9ft 9ins – aft 10ft. Stone cargoes, steel and wheat, etc, partly filled hatches and wheat, oats, etc, had to have some bagged to stop shifting during passage! Indorita was a very strong ship, specially built for Summers Steel Mills. During heavy weather I could hoist a sail between the forward mast and wheelhouse, this would increase speed by 1 to 1.5 knots and stop her rolling 50%. I would make a passage whilst coasters twice her size would be sheltering! No radar then on Coppack coasters, everything was done by local knowledge of tides and recognition of landfall, etc! In fog we would stop ship and listen for fog signals when a couple of miles off. Indorita had a new Crossley main engine fitted in '58. In 1959 this engine exploded whilst approaching Drogheda! We had RNLI assistance and were towed to Dublin.

I have sailed through the Menai Straits on occasions when the weather was too bad to round the South Stack and Skerries on passage from Quarries to Liverpool. But usually we sailed close to the shore when rounding the South Stack to dodge the tide and

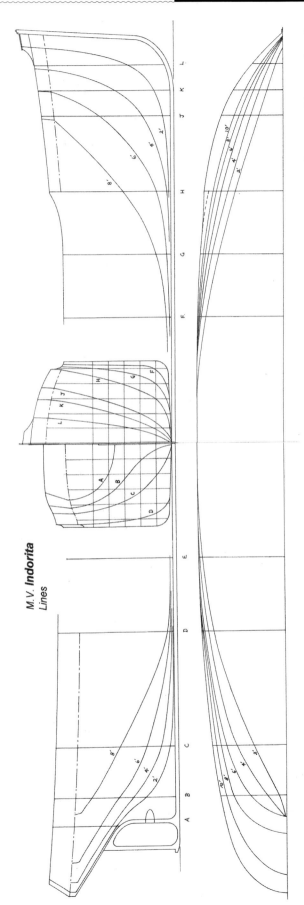

M.V. *Indorita*
Lines

Lines of the Indorita from original sections and a survey made by the author and the owner, J. Antony Hind, in the early 1970s. Her finer lines forward are in contrast to those seen in Neppo and small steamers of the period.

Indorita looking aft on the port side, just below the bridge, in 1972. Prominent in the foreground is a drum of lubricating oil and opposite, running along the side of the engine room casing, are the rod and chains of the steering gear from the bridge to the rudder quadrant aft, commonly fitted to coasters of this period. Rods were used where the motion was simply backwards and forwards, and chains elsewhere. The chain in the foreground runs round a pulley, the cover for which is just visible, in order to pass upwards to the bridge. The bottle screw between the chain and rod was for taking out the slack as the chain wore over the years. Also visible are the cast iron steps and hand rail for access to the bridge. The liferaft container partially obscures the engine room entrance and beyond is the curved hood of the entrance to the officers' cabin. Also just visible at the top of the picture is the keel of the work/lifeboat. Apart from the fairlead on the rail aft, there is the mounting for attaching the log for determining the distance run.

then went up inside the Skerries, very close to West Mouse, Middle Mouse and East Mouse avoiding all the traffic and tide. Approaching Bar Light Vessel in fog we would watch for a big vessel at anchor and stay close to or anchor and await clearance. We knew the channel and time between all buoys as good as the Pilots!'
Tom Fish adds:
'Indorita *made similar runs to* Fleurita *but went a little further to the much more exposed Creesloch (Sheephaven Bay), round by Tory Island, for silver sand for Pilkingtons glass which was taken to Garston. She was uncomfortable loaded; used to roll quite a lot and would put both bow and stern in. It would be quite a challenge to turn and run for shelter at night. After calls at Douglas, Ramsey and Belfast, there would be 40-50 tons left for Drogheda cement works; gear wheels, etc and frequently sacks of grinding*

Eldorita (201/20) on 3rd March 1948, shortly after her sale to Captain Shaw, apparently having her wartime grey hull repainted white. Note the small steadying sail stowed lashed to the derrick. She subsequently reverted to a traditional black hull and eventually foundered in the North Sea about 35 miles north-west of the Hook of Holland in December 1966, by which time she was owned by the Colchester Shipping Co. Ltd. ROBERT SHORTALL

pellets. This was often followed by an inward cargo of stone from one of the North Wales quarries.'

Following a dry docking it was found that the bottom was set up, the result of a grounding, and not worth repairing and so she was sold to the scrap merchants Oldham Bros. However, whilst laid up awaiting disposal she caught the eye of J. Antony Hind in 1971, a naval architect, who thought she could be returned to service. He formed the Golden Cross Shipping Co. Ltd and following some work, she left in these colours under her own power for Manchester dry docks, where it was decided not to proceed with further repairs. She made her last voyage as a motor coaster back to lay up at Birkenhead docks, where she was sold back to local scrap merchants. She was subsequently sold on to Spanish breakers and left under tow for Spain in 1974.

Eldorita was also sold in 1946 and passed to Captain Hugh Shaw of Arlingham, near Gloucester. By this time the ship's boat had been moved aft and was stowed fore and aft, rather than athwartships as in *Indorita*, with a derrick for launching. In 1949, she was fitted with a reconditioned Ruston engine made in 1935. Captain Shaw used *Eldorita* mostly in the Bristol Channel trade, until he sold her to the Colchester Shipping Co. (R.S. Banyard, manager) of Tiptree, Essex in 1963.

Pat O'Driscoll recalls going to collect her:

'Our first trip was from Barry to Bridgwater with coal. Then we brought her round to Wivenhoe shipyard to be converted for carrying sand and gravel between Colne, London or the Medway. The sides of the hold were boxed-in with timber, in line with the hatches, so it was easier for grab discharge. The mast and derrick were taken out and replaced with a light signal mast, which could be lowered. Ballast (a mixture) came by tipper lorry from Haybridge Hall pit and was shot into the hold at Maldon and supposed to be trimmed but that could be omitted. Once we loaded at Felixstowe and took the cargo to Fulham above bridges but the cargoes were mainly for Ham River. We also went to Dover once or twice. When we were unable to discharge at Margate, as the weather was too bad for us to get in there (no shelter apart from a breakwater) we had to take the cargo to Rochester instead.

Living conditions in the Eldorita were quite good. The foc'sle had four built-in bunks in pairs, although only two were occupied, with two drawers beneath each pair and narrow seat lockers. It had originally been lined out with varnished wood, but now had Formica on top. High on the port side was a brass clock and an electric fan and there was also a coal-fired Rayburn stove. The after cabin was palatial with very nice panelling. There was an oil-fired stove and the bunk openings were roughly oval and there were drawers beneath the seat lockers, a rack for glasses, a clock and a barometer.'

Other small coasters of a similar design were built under Pollocks supervision, including *Christo* (140/16) built for Wilfred Christopherson of Ipswich. She traded for a number of owners and by 1963 had become *Limelight* of Ross & Marshall's Light Shipping Co., the well known Clyde puffer owners who were making the change to motor coasters.

At the end of the First World War, there were considerable numbers of 'X' lighters surplus to Admiralty requirements and these were purchased by a number of owners, mostly for sheltered water work within river limits, although a few were classed to work a little further afield. The Etna Stone & Shingle Co. (Snettisham) Ltd, had their motor 'X' lighter *Beatrice Hope* (142/16) classed for coasting service with the limits of Harwich, Dover, Dunkirk and Bologne. Owners such as Everards and Metcalfs gained experience of oil engines as a result of operating them. One of the largest owners eventually was J.J. Prior (Transport) Ltd, based on the Thames, who used them to transport sand and gravel from Prior's Quarry at Fingeringhoe to London, where they had a base at Orchard Wharf.

A group of narrower barges were apparently ordered by the war department with dimensions to suit continental canals. The Lytham Shipbuilding & Engineering Co. completed four, with registered dimensions 99.3ft x 16.4ft x 7.3ft, for John Summers, which were then used locally running between the Dee and Mersey until 1939, when all were sold to Risdon Beazley Ltd, Southampton. J. Crichton & Co. on the River Dee built a longer, 126 foot version, four of which were also purchased by John Summers for local work and then sold off in 1947. A fifth, slightly longer version, the *Fer* (151/21), 129.5ft x 16.4ft x 7.3ft, was completed at Saltney for the Darwen & Mostyn Iron Co. Ltd, Mostyn, registered at Chester and powered by a 125nhp Bolinder semi-diesel. She was sold to Captain James Screech of Appledore in 1948, who sold her on to Captain Richard H. Clark and she then traded locally until 1954.

Very few new motor vessels were built but it is misleading to think vessels with motors were not in use, as the auxiliary steel motor schooner *Eilian* had been built at Amlwch as early as 1908. Further new auxiliaries were built and by the time *Neppo* (240/21), 115.6ft x 20.0ft x 9.3ft registered, was delivered to London based Van Oppen & Co., the sail plan was much reduced. The type was widely built for Dutch owners subsequently. Though built in Holland, *Neppo* was constructed under the supervision of Flannery & Gregson, who had offices in Rotterdam, London and Liverpool. Ballast

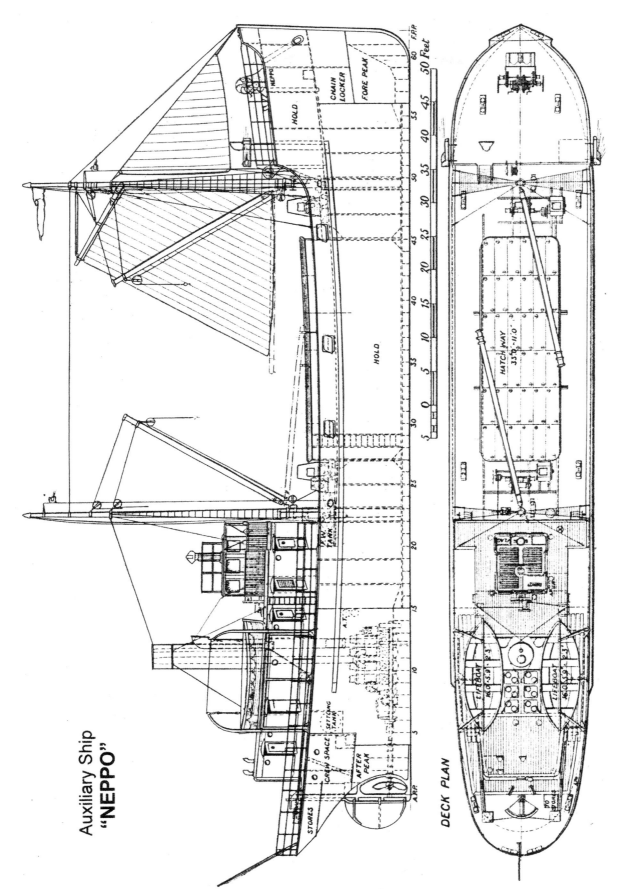

Auxiliary Ship
"NEPPO"

50 Feet

F.P.P.

NEPPO

CHAIN LOCKER

FORE PEAK

HOLD

HOLD

F.W. TANK

STORES

CREW SPACE

SETTLING TANK

AFTER PEAK

A.P.P.

DECK PLAN

HATCH WAY
33'0×11'0

LIFE BOAT
16'0×5'9×2'3

LIFE BOAT
16'0×5'9×2'3

Neppo (240/21) from a drawing in Engineering, 27th of May 1921. Though designed by a British firm of naval architects with an office in Holland, the style of the design is Dutch. The Kromhout engine is illustrated in Chapter I.

Wooden Motor Coaster

DIM: 100'-6" O.A. 95'-0" B.P. x 23'-0" x 9'-0"

General arrangement drawing of a 250 ton wooden motor coaster with Vickers-Petters engines, published in Shipbuilding & Shipping Record, 20th January 1921. Utilising the fact that the vessel shown is twin screw and by a process of elimination using Lloyd's Registers, photographs and plans of vessels in the series, the one illustrated here is almost certainly Heather Pet (164/21).

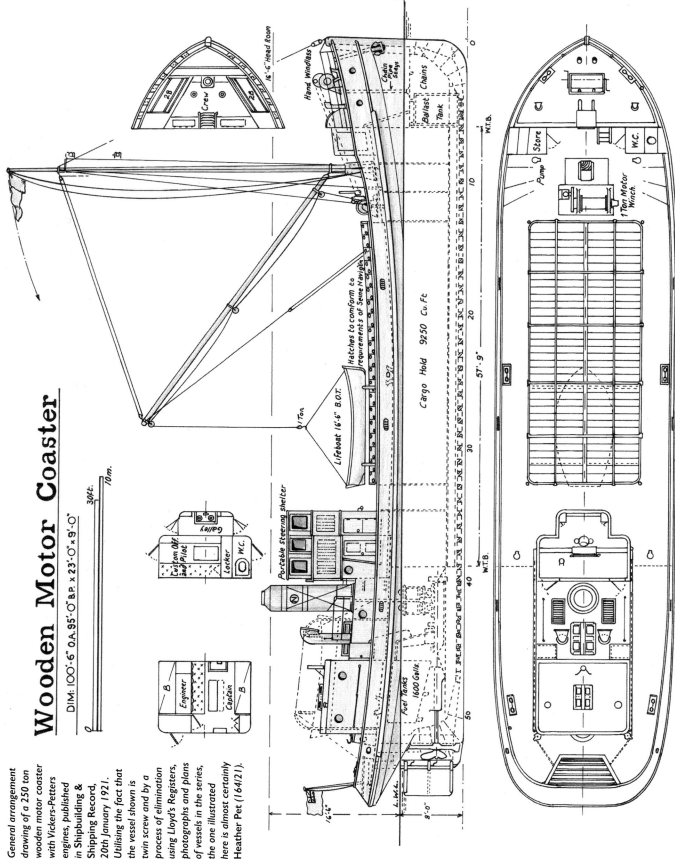

capacity was low at 17 tons but she was expected to run loaded in both directions. The engine was the Dutch-built Kromhout 4M4 type, developing 180bhp at about 300rpm.

There were still hundreds of schooners and other sailing craft serving the smaller ports and these were progressively fitted with auxiliary engines. By the later 1930s, more and more were becoming motor ships with auxiliary sail and were able to trade successfully into the 1950s. Replacement coasters ordered following the First World War were practically all steam, as owners were expecting the size of cargoes to be larger in the 1920s. There was no real experience with oil engines for this size of vessel and there was a plentiful supply of local coal and labour. Lorries had increased in size and many soldiers had learned to drive during the war, so it was possible, often using war surplus lorries, to easily distribute larger cargoes from the deeper water harbours. However, the war had completely changed the coasting trade, with coasters diverted to war work and Government control of railways effectively moved traffic from sea to rail, so it was not until 1937 that the volume of the coasting trade recovered to that of 1913. Conversions of steam vessels to motor were rare except for the smallest craft, where the relative cargo capacity increase was greatest. One company which did have a conversion was the Brito-Franco Shipping Co. Ltd, managed by A. Tate. Their old iron steamer *Helenic*, 135ft x 21.2ft x 11.4ft registered, though built in 1874 was still in such good condition it was decided to fit a Vickers-Petters engine of 152bhp, which gave a loaded speed of 8.25 knots carrying 360 tons of coal on 11 feet draught. As with most steam coasters of the time, she was schooner rigged with fore and aft lower sails only.

It seems that Vickers-Petters, the engine makers, were also associated with the ordering of four wooden motor coasters around 100 feet in length, from local builders on the Thames, which had been designed by their consultant naval architect R.C.W. Courtney. Two were to be twin screw and two single screw. A staysail was to be carried in case of breakdown. Though primarily of wood, steel was to be used for bulkheads, casings, hatch coamings and some other items. The frames were of English oak, with bottom planking of 3.5 inch thick elm and sides of 2 inch Oregon pine, and with an outer skin of 1.5 inch English oak with a sealing layer of tarred felt between them. The yards involved were Wills & Packham of Sittingbourne, Kentish Shipbuilding & Engineering Co. Ltd of Whitstable and Short Bros of Rochester. Construction seems to have started in 1920 but with the rapid slump in trade following the First World War, probably the original prospective owners pulled out. Short Bros launched their vessel *Rochester Castle* and then suspended work until 1923, when she was completed for their own account and eventually ran speed trials on 5th June 1925, achieving 8.54 knots from her twin 96bhp Gardner 4-cylinder 2-stroke engines. As completed, her galley was placed forwards in place of the store on the port side, whilst the casing above the engine room was the same height as the accommodation below the bridge and was continuous with the aft accommodation, which was attractively fitted out and apparently of wood. A towing hook was fitted. She was able to carry a deadweight of about 250 tons on a draught of 8ft 6ins according to *Motor Boat* magazine. The vessel was eventually sold about two years later to the United States Trading Co. of New York and renamed *Duvalla*.

Two were built by Wills & Packham and registered in 1921; certainly one had been completed earlier and was eventually sold to a partnership of captain, engineer and a merchant based in Newquay, and was named *Harparees* (161/21), while the other was the twin screw version and was registered to Vickers-Petters Ltd, London as **Heather Pet**. Sold on, she was eventually bought by Everards in 1927. She was later re-engined with a Newbury oil engine and renamed *Assurity*. She then traded for the company until 1956 and was finally broken up in 1959. Photographs show that she was closely similar to the plan with the galley aft as shown but neither vessel had the wheelhouse extended over the galley and the aft accommodation was lower, the same height as the central casing.

Similar vessels were built in steel, mostly from the 1930s onwards. Typical of these was *The Miller* (117/32) and the slightly smaller **Golden Grain** (101/34), with the registered dimensions 82ft x 17.4ft x 7.6ft, completed by H. Robb Ltd, Leith for E. Marriage & Son Ltd, East Anglia Mills, Felixstowe, to carry grain cargoes in bulk for their mill. It was also welded where welding was best for the builders and owners. As early as 1920, Cammell Laird had built the entirely welded motor coaster *Fullagar* as an experiment but it was to be more than twenty years before welding was widely used as the answer to the urgent need for coasters in World War Two. **Golden Grain** carried 125 tons on a draught of 7 feet. The engine was a British Kromhout of 100bhp at 320rpm, with clutch and reverse gear, and with most lubrication by a pressure system. A dynamo was fitted to provide electric light. The pitch pine mast lowered but only a hand winch and windlass were fitted, as the vessel would be loading and discharging using shore cranes and elevators. Many similar vessels with local variations were built to serve around the Humber, Severn and the Mersey areas.

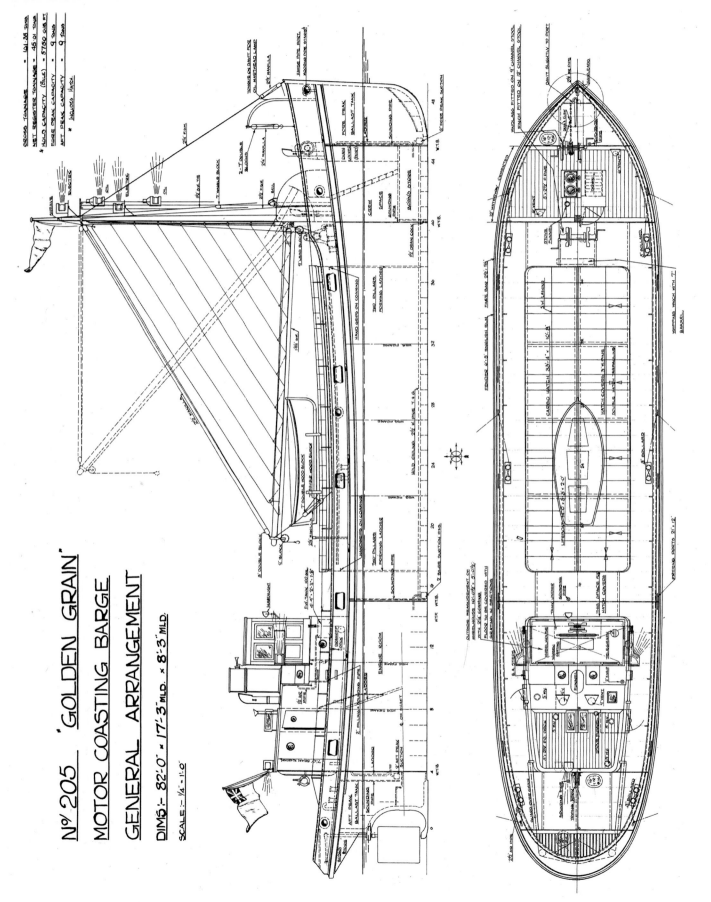

Nº 205 "GOLDEN GRAIN"

MOTOR COASTING BARGE

GENERAL ARRANGEMENT

DIMS:- 82'-0" × 17'-3" MLD. × 8'-3" MLD.

SCALE :- ¼" = 1'-0"

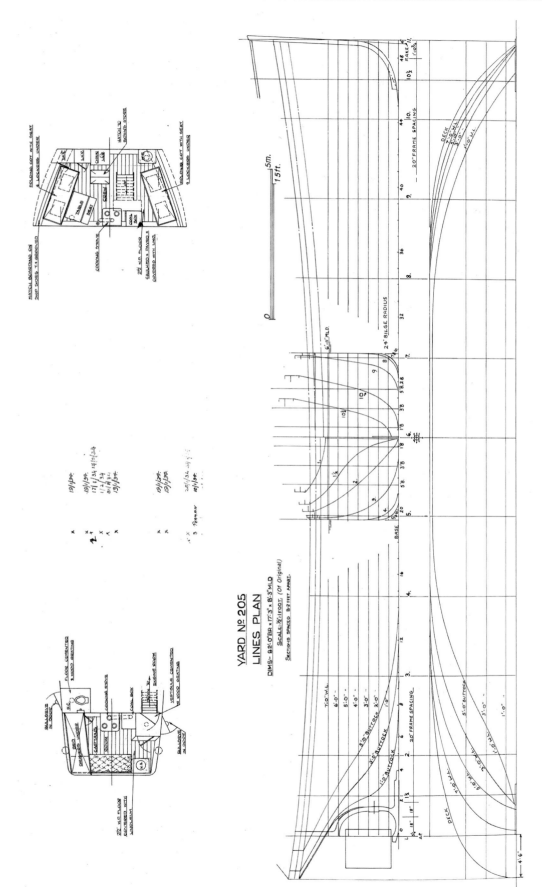

YARD Nº 205
LINES PLAN

DIMS:- 82'-0"BP × 17'3" × 8·3"MLD
SCALE ½"=1 FOOT (Of Original)
Sections spaced 8·2 feet apart.

Golden Grain general arrangement and lines plan.

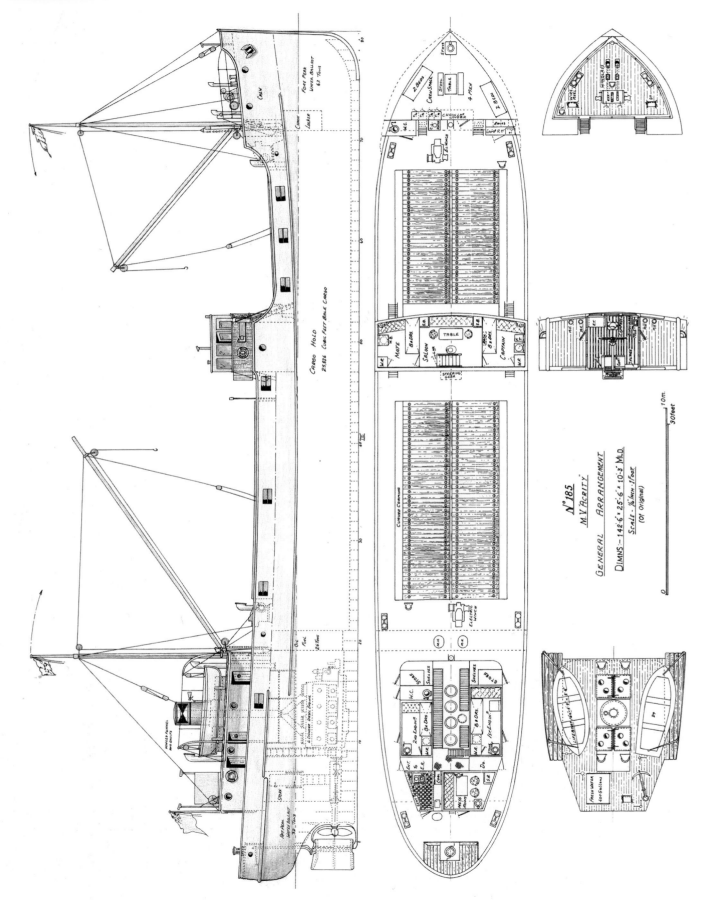

Nº 185
M.V. "ACRITY"
GENERAL ARRANGEMENT
DIMNS:- 142'·6" × 25'·6" × 10'·3" MLD.
SCALE - ¼ INCH : 1 FOOT
(Of Original)

CHAPTER 3
THE 1930S: DECADE OF DEVELOPMENT

Note: The dimensions used in this chapter are molded dimensions unless otherwise stated.

Everards were one of the early adopters of auxiliary power and built the sailing barge *Grit* in 1913, with an engine supplied by Plenty & Son of Newbury, who were originally Kromhout licensees. Alfred M. Everard had served his apprentiship as a motor engineer and later gained further experience in the Royal Naval Air Service during the 1914-18 war. The barge was lost in 1916 but a Dutch-built steel schooner was acquired in 1920. This had a Kromhout engine which was replaced with another Plenty engine. She was rebuilt in 1925 to become their first motor coaster, appropriately named *Capable*, and further motor barges were added to the fleet. Everards had become tanker owners and these were steamships, as the edible oils carried generally needed steam heating coils, but a milestone was reached in 1926 with the small tanker *Prowess* (207/26), which was a motor vessel. Steam was retained for the larger tanker *Authority* completed in 1928 but she was the last steamer built for the company, although they were to purchase many second hand and war surplus steamers.

Also in 1928, the first true motor coaster, *Ability* (262/28), registered dimensions 115.1ft x 23.2ft x 9.5ft, was delivered by Fellows & Co. Ltd, Great Yarmouth. Designed for the east coast, south coast and continental trades, she was intended to be able to compete with Dutch vessels, carrying about 250 tons on 9ft 6ins and was followed by a sister, *Amenity*. They had Plenty P50 semi-diesel, hot bulb engines with five cylinders of 335mm diameter by 390mm stroke, delivering 250bhp at 300rpm. The starting was still with rapid heating burners, which needed to be on for three minutes or so before the engine could be started. The 5-cylinder arrangement and well designed engine bed

Ability (262/28) was essentially Everards' first true motor coaster and was fully equipped to discharge herself, with two derricks and associated winches. ALEX DUNCAN, J. &M. CLARKSON COLLECTION

reduced vibration. The water jacketed exhausts were paired for the end two cylinders, with the centre cylinder separate, and all three exhausts led into a secondary silencer in the funnel. Silencing was also helped by a long intake pipe for the air to the crank case valves. The *Motor Boat* observer at the trials reported that the engine was practically inaudible on deck and the exhaust almost smokeless, although the haze of burnt lubricating oil was obvious. The engine was non-reversing and fitted with a bevel gear and large plate clutch. A single cylinder 10hp Plenty engine drove a pump and compressor to provide compressed air for starting the main engine and electric light for the engine room was provided by a dynamo on the main engine. The fuel tanks were placed at the sides of the engine room. Two engineers were carried and trials were done with 35 tons of water in the forepeak. The hatches were designed with a view to protecting cement cargoes and heavily constructed. Two 9hp Brons' engined winches were fitted. No lamp or electric pre-heating was needed for starting these. A half-compression device was used and two men were needed to swing the engine, so as soon as the flywheel rotated at the desired speed, the engine was turned over to full compression and started immediately.

Trade picked up in the 1930s and the company built larger coasters, with *Ability* herself being lengthened in 1938 to 136.8 feet, increasing her capacity to 300 tons. The engines were all from Plenty & Son, Newbury. This company collapsed at the bottom of the slump and Everards found themselves forced to take over in 1931 to ensure a supply of spares. A new company, The Newbury Engine Co. Ltd, was formed to take on the oil engine manufacturing part of the original business and Everards' engineers all went to the factory for training prior to working on the ships. The fleet expanded rapidly, the smaller vessels built by Fellows, Great Yarmouth, which the company had also acquired. George Brown & Co., Greenock built the larger ones and *Acrity*, 142ft 6ins x 25ft 6ins x 10ft 3ins, shows the arrangement used for most of those over 130 feet in length, although all the following vessels had the bridge raised by placing its superstructure on the raised quarter deck. The transverse fuel bunker incorporated as part of the engine room forward bulkhead was to become standard practice. The size was slowly increased so that, by the beginning of the war, the final group were some 20 feet longer and in total, represented twenty-two vessels.

In the later vessels, such as *Sincerity* of 1936, the crew and engineers were aft, with cabins arranged around the engine casing, most of which opened on to the deck. The deck hands had a six-berth cabin at the after end and at the forward end was a small saloon for the engineers. The larger crew's mess room was adjacent to the galley but it was to be another decade before individual cabins were provided for all hands. Most were built by George Brown but the final group was split with Goole Shipbuilding & Repairing Co. Efforts were also made to improve the efficiency of the smaller propellers turning faster in motor vessels, which was eventually resolved by fitting a reduction gear, often incorporating reverse. Everards found that a polished bronze propeller and a streamlining piece added to the stern frame and rudder of *Activity* made her 0.4 of a knot faster than her sister *Assiduity*, with an ordinary stern frame and a cast iron propeller.

Acrity (403/34), reverted to a 4-cylinder engine, with a much revised specification termed the Newbury Sirron – a brand name created by spelling the designers name, Norris, backwards. This engine incorporated rotary valves controlling exhaust opening, with scavenging and supercharging of about 3lbs per square inch by rotary chain driven blowers and all forced lubrication. These changes gave a better power to weight ratio, allowing one cylinder to be eliminated. Fuel consumption was about 15 gallons per hour for a service speed of 9.5 knots. There was a clutch allowing the engine to be warmed up but this engine was directly reversible by moving the cam shaft. Each cylinder had a Bosch fuel injection pump working at 3,500psi. The engine produced about 400bhp to give a service speed of 9.5kts, assisted by a streamlined balanced rudder. The cargo gear was powered by electric winches. *Acrity* could carry about 520 tons on a 10 foot draught.

Meanwhile, prompted by David Williamson Ltd of London, the National Physical Laboratory's model testing tank was used to determine the best lines for their small motor coaster *Affaric* (239/34), being constructed by the Goole Shipbuilding & Repairing Co. Ltd, the first time this had been done. The idea was to produce a motor coaster which would be equal to or better than the small Dutch coasters so active in British trades. Earlier work had shown that a well shaped cruiser stern, with a smaller, faster turning propeller necessary with direct drive oil engines, showed a gain in propulsive efficiency of about 2.5%. The new study produced such a marked improvement that rather than simply add 15 feet to the parallel mid body for the larger sister *Arrivain* (273/34), it was decided to carry out further tank tests on a second model. The first model decided upon had a block coefficient of 0.71. The stern frame was of cast steel, with a fin integral with the stern post which was to be bossed out in line with the propeller and this was paired with a streamlined rudder of

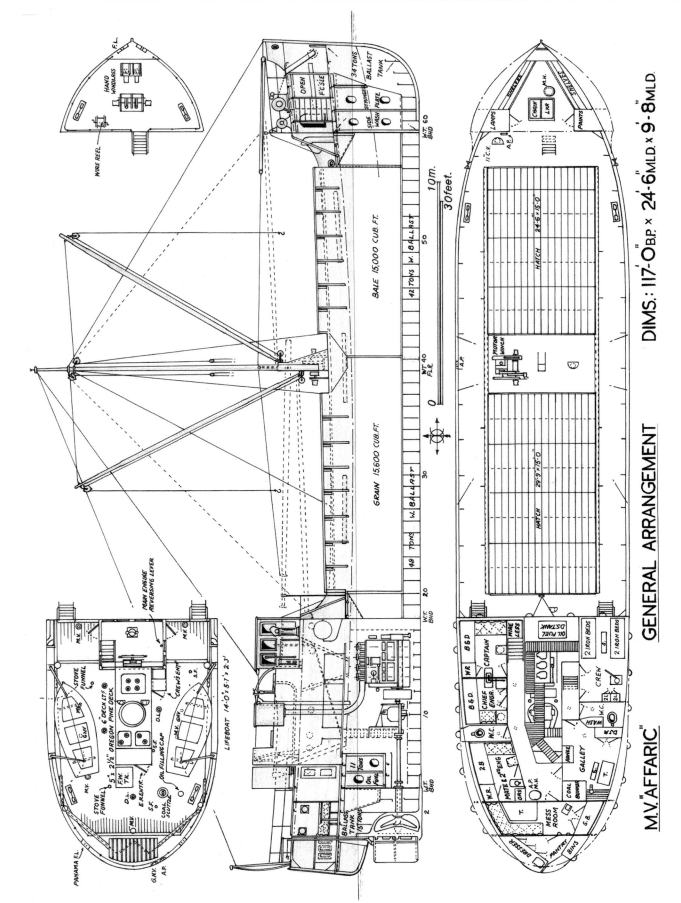

M.V. "AFFARIC" GENERAL ARRANGEMENT

DIMS.: 117'-0 B.P. × 24'-6 MLD. × 9'-8 MLD.

Clichy, 310 gross tons, was built for T.E. Evans & Co. Ltd, London as Andoni *in 1935, who sold her in 1936 and transferred the name to a larger ship. The buyers were the Dundee, Perth and London Shipping Co. Ltd, Dundee, who renamed her* Clova *and later sold her on to the Lockett, Wilson Line, London. Although a single deck rather than a 'tween deck ship more commonly associated with liner trade companies, their good cubic capacity and ability to offer a 'little and often' service made them attractive. She was photographed arriving at Jersey and renamed* Clichy *shortly after her sale to the Channel Shipping Co. Ltd, Jersey. By this time the derricks had been dispensed with, as loading and discharge at ports became more mechanised. Subsequently, the mast and winches were removed and two light and signal masts were placed fore and aft. In 1967, she was in good enough condition to warrant the fitting of a new Rolls-Royce engine and went on to serve several more owners before she reached the end of her days in the West Indies in the 1990s.*

DAVE HOQUARD

double plate construction, so that the stiffeners would not interfere with smooth water flow. A four-bladed propeller was found to give the best performance and tests indicated that a 200bhp engine, running at 300rpm, would give about 9 knots, a high speed for such a small cargo vessel. The engine chosen was a direct reversing, airless injection, 4-cylinder, 4-stroke Deutz of 250bhp, which was arranged for bridge control, whilst for the larger vessel a 6-cylinder Deutz of 350bhp was selected. A full cellular double bottom was used and, with the fore and aft peaks, gave a ballast capacity of 120 tons, which could be discharged in about three hours. This addressed the problem experienced with earlier motor coasters, which frequently had to run for shelter in even average heavy weather. To compensate for the loss of capacity, the hatch coamings were raised giving a good stowage rate of a little over 50 cubic feet per ton. The deadweight of the smaller vessel was 333 tons on 8ft 10.5ins and the larger sister 370 tons on 8ft 10ins. A low profile and folding masts were incorporated to make the vessels even more versatile. The Dundee, Perth & London Shipping Co. purchased *Affaric* and *Arrivain* in 1939, renamed them *Crombie* and *Cortachy*, and replaced the Deutz engines with 2-stroke Crossleys. Both had long lives with various owners.

Goole soon built on the experience and attracted orders from other London owners, developing their 'Proficient' type motor coaster. It incorporated a sharply raked stem, which was found to reduce overloading on the engine in rough head seas. They built several variations in the mid and later 1930s, with a raised quarter deck in the larger vessels and obtained an order from Everards for a vessel already under construction, who had hitherto been loyal to Browns, resulting in the *Sequacity* (870/37).

Shipbuilding had been given a boost in 1935 by the British Shipping (Assistance) Act, which offered loans to owners building new ships. T.E. Evans of London took advantage of the scheme to buy three sisters, delivered in 1936, for their trade to shallow water Spanish ports and the earlier *Andoni* (310/35) was sold to the Dundee, Perth & London Shipping Co. Ltd. Each of the new vessels had cost a little over £16,000. They were later to prove just as useful in home waters as, after the war, *Andoni* (678/37) and two of her smaller sisters, *Benguela* and *Loanda*, were bought by Metcalf, the latter becoming *Monica M* (534/36) in 1946 when name changes were again allowed, having been bought by Metcalf in 1943.

Dick Massey recalls:

'In June 1956 I signed on the motor vessel Monica M, *owned by Metcalf Motor Coasters Ltd of London.* Monica M *had been built in 1936 with a Mirrlees engine. She was a typical design of that period*

with a forecastle head, raised quarter deck and a poop containing all the crew accommodation. There was one long hold with a temporary separation bulkhead, accessed by two hatches covered by steel MacGregor roller hatch covers. The Monica M was on the Gravesend slipway at the time I joined her, still being refurbished after being raised from the bottom of the River Thames, having been sunk by a collision with the Edward Cruse, a London County Council sludge vessel. Known as the 'Bovril boats' locally, these vessels were on a tight schedule to keep London's sewage on the move to the dumping ground in Black Deeps. Unfortunately, a collision happened in dense fog, sinking the Monica M in Erith Reach on 12th November 1955, with no loss of life but taking her new 600bhp Lister Blackstone engine, fitted that June, to the bottom. Raised on 22nd, she was beached at Belvedere, Kent where temporary repairs were carried out. She was then refloated on 18th December and taken to Gravesend for reconditioning. Now the repairs were almost completed. Being an insurance job, the refurbishing was only up to the standards that were in place when she was first built, the only modernisation appeared to be the installation of radar. The last coats of paint were soon applied, the wife of one of the Company's directors gave a blessing at the re-launching and we were soon on our way to Falmouth with orders that, weather permitting, we were to carry on to Porthoustock and load granite chippings. After a few teething problems in the engine room we arrived at Falmouth. The winds were fresh from the south and this closed Porthoustock, so we anchored in Carrick Roads, Falmouth.

The ship being light dragged her anchors, though owing to the weather, we had two anchors down. When the weather improved we were ordered to retrieve the port anchor. As the anchor came to the surface – what a sight! – threaded in around the flukes was a very thick cable. After many hours of struggling to clear the cable, it was dropped where we laid, but now we had missed the tide for Porthoustock, so we stayed as we laid to the starboard anchor, and hoping that with the shift in the wind, that anchor would come up clear the next day. The plan then was to haul this anchor early, giving us time to clear it if need be. As the chain came aboard it was obvious that all was not well and as the anchor broke the surface, there was a repeat of the previous day, however with the experience gained then, we were able to clear it by the time the pilot came aboard. The loading port was only just along the coast and with the sea calm enough; the hatches were opened ready to receive the cargo, as we understood the loading would be very quick. Porthoustock is a very small Cornish cove with a stony beach. The ship was secured aft on a rocky outcrop and run forward to get the bow on to the steep beach. This was necessary to get the loading chute into No. 2 hold and with a few mooring lines ashore the ship was secured several feet off the small wharf. This was no more than a natural sheer rock face with the stone silo built on top looking like a medieval fort. Long steel trough-like chutes were lowered down; two to each hatchway, then loading began with the pilot standing on the wheelhouse top, half invisible in dust, controlling the loading with signals to the unseen operators in the silo with blasts on a pea whistle. Very soon we had the forward deck awash – the engineers were having trouble getting the water ballast out of the forward double bottom tanks, as the pumps had to pull the water uphill. There was a temporary stop to the loading as the ballast was slowly pumped out. By now the pilot was getting worried as the tide was falling, so the decision was made to get the rest of the cargo loaded and get out of there. As the silo held just the right amount of cargo for the ship, loading was easily completed, but the ballast was still not out which meant that the ship was well over her legal loaded draft and huge fines apply for doing this. We returned to Falmouth and berthed at the local shipyard for them to sort out the problem which proved to be some fault in the mono ballast pump. The pump had two rubber impellers that had been damaged by being left dry while the ship was under repairs. New parts were soon on their way to Falmouth from the factory, and a few days later with the ballast removed, the local Board of Trade surveyor passed the ship as seaworthy for passage to the River Thames.

On arrival at the River Thames, the orders were to proceed to Deptford Creek to discharge our cargo and then return to Falmouth (Porthoustock) to load granite chippings for the Thames again. It was mid summer and the return round trip was completed in good weather with no hold-ups; this time the discharging berth was Bow Creek. The next orders were to load cement at Northfleet for delivery to Inverness, and the loading and long passage north were without any memorable incidents. On arrival at Inverness I received advice there was a job coming up shortly on the steamship Holdernook and on the strength of that I paid off the Monica M.

A particular feature of the Monica M was the early type of steel hatch covers designed by Robert and Joseph MacGregor. All the sections except one were successfully salvaged when the ship had sunk. There was no training programme for ship's crews on the safe working of these potentially dangerous hatch covers. The earliest covers I sailed and worked with were classed as single lift hatch covers as on Monica M. The forward hatch had, I think five sections, the aft seven sections. The procedure for opening the hatches was; the derricks were topped up, (lifted). The cargo runner (or cargo whip) was removed

from the cargo winches, then the wire rope for heaving and lifting the lids was run to the cargo winch. This wire was attached to the first lid either by shackle or on some there was a 'T' lug for the eye of the wire to be placed over. When this was done, all the securing wedges, which were located in individual sockets on top of the lids, were knocked free with a sledge hammer. Next the securing clamps holding the lids together were knocked free, then the 'T' bolts that hold the lid down on the hatch coaming and make a watertight seal, there being a thick rubber seal set in a channel on the underside of each lid. This same sealing system was used across each contact surface between the lids. Each lid would have at least two or three 'T' bolts each side. When all these bolts had been removed, the two screw jacks that forced (compressed) the hatch lids together were slacked off. The next job was to lower the wheels, two on each side of a lid with special shaped round bars around three feet long. First a locking pin was removed, the handle inserted in a slot outside the wheel and with a hefty pull on the handle, the wheel carrier was rotated through 180 degrees, the wheel brought into contact with the track on the hatch coaming and so lifting the lid. I think the Monica M still had the earlier type, so to put the wheels down, hydraulic jacks like car jacks had to be used between the hatch coaming ledge and a lug on the side of the lid. With the weight on the jacks, the wheels could be rotated 180 degrees – in the case of Monica M's No. 2 hatch, starting from the forward lid. The sequence was necessary as when the wheels were raised to lower the lids, each lid was locked into its neighbour. So starting from forward, with one man each side of the hatch each wheel was lowered and pinned in position. When all the wheels were down, the wire rigged to the winch, hove all the lids forward lightly against the screw jacks. A wooden wedge was then placed to jam the wheels of the second lid from aft. This was to allow the aftermost lid to be winched aft. On the side of each lid was a pivot pin that matched up with a cup in the extended hatch coaming. As the first lid was heaved aft it reached its point of balance and with the lid wire heaving, the lid was tipped up vertical and secured by two heavy hooks. Then someone had to scramble across the top of that lid to release the wire rope. If the hold was empty, it was a long drop to the bottom of the hold. The wire was then fixed to the next lid and the wooden wedges moved along to the third lid. If the ship was empty and there was a considerable slope, an extra wire was rigged as a check to stop the lids running uncontrolled.

For closing, the process was reversed, but using two winch wires, one to heave the lid down and one to check it's descent on to the track on the coaming. When the wheels were sitting in the correct position in the coaming track, the second wire was used to pull the lid forward. The forward most wheels would then be carefully wedged and the wires removed and attached to the next lid to be lowered. This was easy and safe when the ship was loaded, but empty with the bow high, great caution was required – many a hatch lid has ended up down the hold when the crew returned late from the pub and caution went with the last pint. There was no sort of safety gear except perhaps a rot prone net made from sisal rope. The next improvement was when all the lids were connected together with wires or chains (concertina lids) followed by the two lids hinged together and operated by hydraulic rams. They were far safer at sea in bad weather with seas breaking over the vessel compared with canvas tarpaulins and wooden hatch boards.

The Monica M system required much maintenance to keep all those bolts greased and easy to use. The wheel ball-races required two types of grease, one for the race itself and another very thick yellow waterproofing grease to try and keep the seawater out. The wires were stowed away, though some ships left them rigged as lifelines for crossing the hatch when at sea as the paint was slippery when wet. They also needed painting regularly. There was no reduction in crew with them as it was already the minimum for safe manning. In 1960 she was transferred to the Wimaisia Shipping Co. Ltd also managed by T.J. Metcalf and in 1971 she was sold to a Greek owner.'

In the 1930s, industrial activity in the Thames area was increasing with Ford car plant, Firestone tyres, Reeds paper mills and many others. This increase in trade tended to favour local owners. T.J. Metcalf, who was originally the manager of Crawley's water boats, became a barge owner and eventually set up on his own account but the connection was not severed as he had married Crawley's daughter. His first motor barges were two 'X' craft purchased in the mid 1920s and a small new coastal tanker followed in 1929. It was Dutch-built, as were several more coasters, until 1935 when Burntisland built the Charles M, followed by the slightly larger Daniel M (448/36), 150ft 0ins x 26ft 3ins x 11ft 6ins, able to carry about 651 tons on a draught of just under 12 feet.

Dick Massey recalls:

'I joined the Daniel M in August 1955 at Norwich. Metcalf's trade was NE ports like Blyth to Norwich power station. The newer larger ships; coal from NE to English Channel ports but very rarely beyond Hayle in Cornwall. Stone was loaded at Newlyn and Porthoustock for the Thames for example, Bow and Deptford Creeks. The quarries at Dean and Berry Head were almost reserved for Everards. Lots

of coal to many small fishing ports around Moray Firth, also Perth and Dundee. Coal was also loaded at Keadby. Metcalf masters were a mix of southern Irish and eastern Scottish and crews a very mixed bunch. The Master of the Daniel M and later Monica M was John Findlay from Cullen near Buckie. She had two hatches with wooden hatch boards and two masts each fitted with a steel cargo derrick. There was a crew of seven: Captain, mate, two engineers, two deck hands and a cook steward. The Deutz main engine, the engine room and accommodation was all aft. The galley cooker and heating used coal.

The ship was employed on a regular run with various side trips carrying coal from Blyth. It was a fine grade suitable for the automatic feed system at Norwich power station. At Blyth the loading of the cargo took about one hour. The coal arrived at the staiths in 5-ton wagons from the mines close by, pushed by a small steam engine so that when over the chute a handle was pulled, the bottom of the wagon opened and the coal fell out. Blyth was a very busy coal port with many different types of coal being loaded on to a variety of ships which sailed to all the ports from the Shetland Islands to Land's End, small ports in Northern Island and the Baltic. The coal trade was in its heyday, many ships on arrival at the pilot boarding station would receive loading orders for the loading staiths which ran for a long distance each side of the river. The staiths at the west end were more suitable for loading the larger ships; if your orders were that your cargo was ready and waiting you would be ordered to the appropriate chute number and with a loading rate of 500-1,000 tons per hour the small ships took longer to batten down the hatches than to load coal! On the other hand, the orders might be to proceed to South Dock and await instructions, which might mean a wait of a day or a week. The Daniel M when at Norwich power station could expect to stay for three or four days depending on the stockpile there. The unloading system was a simple overhead single track girder crane that had a small grab which lifted about a ton each time – with over 500 tons to unload that is a lot of movements to and from the ship with working restricted to the 8 hour working day.

Norwich is up the River Yare, part of the Norfolk Broads with many hire boats and navigation restricted to daylight hours only. This all added up to a very easy working system for the crew. Half the crew lived round Norwich and the other half near Blyth so half the crew got time at home. In the winter time, with the short days, it was not uncommon for the ship to have to stop and moor up for the night depending on the captain's favorite riverside pub, which was where we could spend the evening – no wild parties, just a beer or two, a game of darts and back on board. There was no TV, though someone might have a portable radio. Great Yarmouth was the other favorite place to wait for a suitable tide for the crossing of Braydon Water, this being a large mere with a shallow channel passing through it. With the cargo being mainly coal, the cargo holds required very little cleaning which was unfortunate for us as we were paid a bonus if we had to clean the holds! We had a deduction of about a pound a week from our pay and

Daniel M outward bound from Mast Parrel Wharf, Woolwich on 31st March 1968. By this time various additions and modifications had been made. In order to comply with the revised regulations for preventing collisions at sea, ships over 150 feet in length were required to carry two white lights on their centreline, with the aft light at least 15 feet higher than the forward light. The vertical light height in total was to be less than the horizontal distance between the lights. As can be seen from the plan (overleaf), the original foremast light has been lowered somewhat, the main mast extended and a signal yard added. Other additions include a short radar mast on the wheelhouse and a very tall funnel for the coal fired galley range aft. Her design, with a railed quarter deck edge continuous with the bulwarks of the well deck forward, can easily be confused with a single decked ship such as Brockley Combe at a distance but the line of freeing ports for the well deck can just be picked out below the bulwark forward, which indicate that there is a well deck. DAVE HOCQUARD

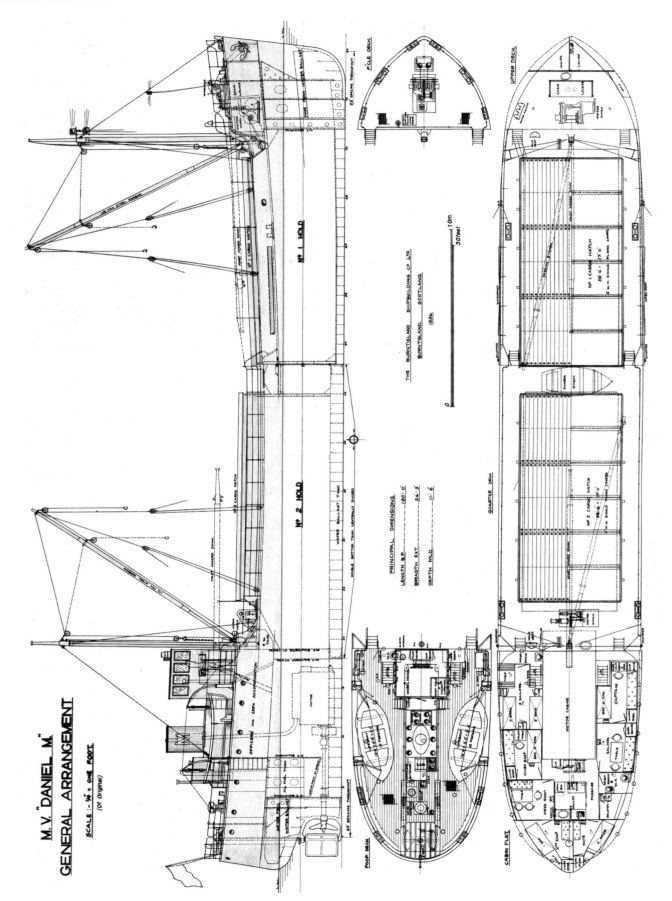

this was given to the cook to provide the whole crew with three meals a day, which rather depended on his capabilities. On the Daniel M we fed very well as we spent a long time in port and with somebody away visiting family, or on a Sunday we might have all been ashore for a meal or two, so the cook was able to manage very well … the 'extras' we bought ourselves.

The river part of each voyage to and from Norwich normally took 5 hours each way. At Great Yarmouth there were two opening bridges to navigate, the first one coming in from the sea was the main road, this carried the principal traffic through town and ships were normally only allowed to pass through with the tide against them or at slack tide. The next bridge was the railway's main passenger line and here a ship might have a long wait, depending on the trains. On this river the captain consulted not only the tide tables but the railway timetable as well, and as there was a second railway bridge at Reedham, to be considered with a third railway bridge if bound for the upper part of the city of Norwich, the waiting time for these bridges could add on several hours, which could extend the river trip to eight or more, so one cargo of coal was all that could be done in a week. As winter approached a second ship, the Rose Julie M, would be diverted to also bring coal to the power station, not only to keep the stock pile full, but as the river had been known to freeze over and the ice stop ships, it was hoped the extra shipping would keep the river navigable. On occasions there might be a cargo of scrap metal to load at Norwich. This would normally go to Middlesborough and add almost another week before getting back to Blyth to start the round again. The Daniel M also occasionally carried coal to the Thames and Medway, usually with a return cargo of scrap metal for Middlesborough.'

Daniel M had been transferred to the Mac Shipping Co. Ltd, a Glasgow subsidiary, in 1952. On 5th June 1961, she was severely damaged in a collision with the Marsund (498/51) in the North Sea Canal, while on passage from Amsterdam to London. She was beached and later towed in for repair and continued in service until 1971, when she was broken up at Broom by Van Den Bossche.

Ships like **Daniel M**, fitted with rod and chain steering gear, often required relieving tackles. Dick Massey explains:

'On ships with bridge amidships, it was impossible to have good tension on the chains. Buffer springs were fitted, but with all the grease and oil that was required for ease of use, coal dust and debris would get into the links of the chains in port, then as the steering gear was in use, the debris would be squeezed out allowing the chains to resume their earlier tension. However, with the rudder quadrant jiggling about, there was always the danger of a chain dropping off the grooves in the quadrant, so the use of the relieving tackles was very important, as this stopped the rudder from slopping about. Steering gear required regular maintenance but was often missed, though with relieving tackle requiring to be tensioned, defects were often spotted before a problem occurred. With the advent of nylon rope, some ships used heavy nylon rope instead of iron rods. These could be set up bar-tight. Because the nylon had a lot of stretch, this took up a lot of the shock loads. With the rudder held steady, many ships steered far better and with no kick-back at the wheel. Then came hydraulic and electric steering gears – now there was almost no feeling on the wheel, so the old saying at the change of the helmsman that she was carrying so much wheel to port or starboard; without a rudder indicator, there was no feel as to the load on the rudder.

As steering gear improved, loads on the rudder stock were reduced. With rod and chain, there was either a single tiller bar or the quadrant system; there was a great deal of stress. Mainly the pull caused wear in two basic positions, either in the eight o'clock and four o'clock position with a quadrant or, with the tiller bar system, in the ten o'clock and two o'clock positions in the upper bearing of hardwood (lignum-vitae or later oak), with twelve o'clock taken as dead aft. This upper bearing was hidden under a grating that the mooring ropes would be stowed on. The ropes shed all sorts of debris, including sand, coal dust and fibres; mixed with the heavy grease, it turned into a good grinding paste! Annual surveys often missed this wear problem, so by the time the four-yearly survey came round there could be a considerable amount of wear and the top of the rudder stock could be slopping around. The use of the relieving gear took up most of the movement and in doing so, hid the signs of wear. We used the tackle on the Daniel M and Monica M.

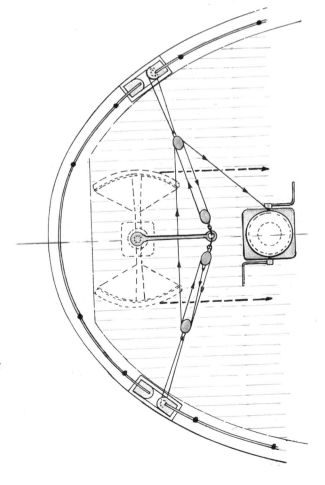

Relieving Tackle: This clever arrangement of blocks uses the friction in the tackles to prevent rudder 'kicks' reaching the helmsman to a large extent in bad weather. It was arranged so that as the rudder was turned, the tackle on one side pays out rope exactly matching the shortening occuring on the other side and the rope is kept tight by the hand capstan adjusted as necessary.
FROM A DRAWING BY DICK MASSEY OF ITS USE ON DANIEL M

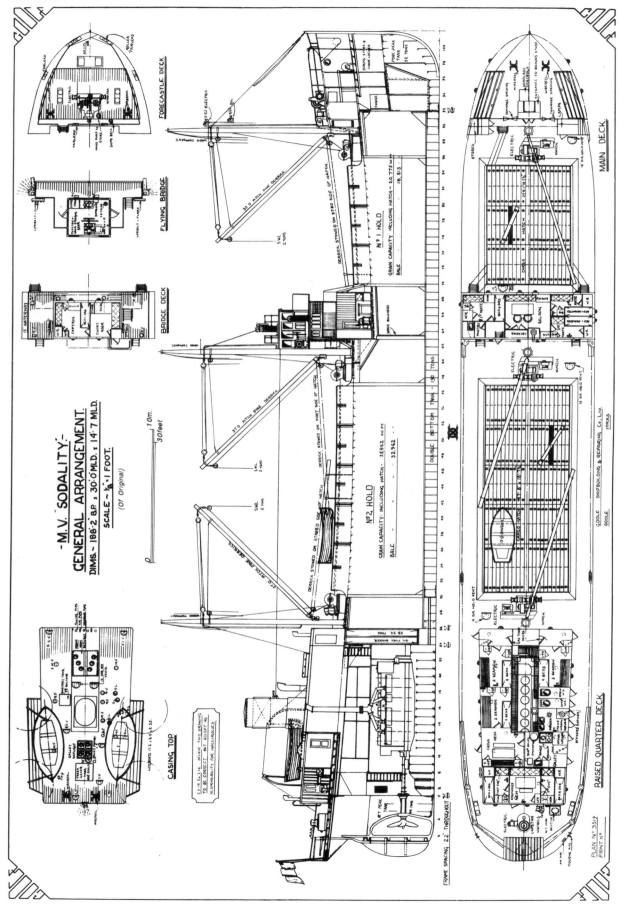

This general arrangement drawing of Sodality (829/38) shows her conversion by Goole Shipbuilding & Repairing to a motor vessel from a steam coaster hull begun by Williamson at Workington. Note the characteristic and attractive decorative border that Goole applied to their drawings.

Hydraulic steering varied; some had a multi-piston slave motor mounted on to the stock, so again there was true rotation. There were many variations on the push-pull double acting rams; mainly double with one each side of the tiller arm. This again caused some wear points, but as the rams needed to be protected from the weather, they were often in a compartment known as the steering flat or a large box right aft as seen in Lady Sylvia. *Many ships had emergency steering tackles, as was required by regulations, stowed close by the steering gear. Hydraulics took up the shock loads to the rudder and steering system and eliminated the need for relieving tackles.'*

John Stuart had built six steamers at rock bottom prices to use up First World War surplus tug engines and R. Williamson & Son also built some steamers at Workington. This yard built large coasters and the last hull of their series, Yard No. 244, was laid down in 1932 for their own account. However, construction ceased with the death of Mr Williamson and eventually the almost completed hull, yard and machinery were offered for sale. The build quality of Williamson ships was well regarded and attracted the attention of Everards, who bought the hull in April 1938 and after some further work and clearing the weeds which had grown around the slipway, it was eventually launched as *Sodality* (829/38). It was towed round to Goole Shipbuilding, who installed a 7-cylinder Newbury 'L' type engine (700hp/300rpm) and prepared the final general arrangement drawing with their characteristic boarder of the period. The engine gave her a speed of about 10 knots. The motor ship, compared with the steamer *Corinia* (870/28) built earlier to the same dimensions, had a deadweight of 1,218 tons against the steamers 1,200 tons and a slightly better cubic capacity at 56,727 compared with about 55,000, when she was finally completed in September 1938. The characteristic feature of a Williamson ship, the curved hatch coamings, are visible on the plan. The steamer origins are clearly revealed by the small propeller in the large aperture intended for the larger, slower turning propeller associated with steam machinery. With the more compact machinery, it was possible for all the crew to be accommodated in the forward end of the deck house, where the boiler and bunker would have been. Deck machinery was electric and this avoided having individual oil engines exposed on deck, relying on a generator in the engine room, where it was protected from the elements. As late as 1960, Coppacks considered converting their steamer *Hove* and using the boiler as the oil fuel bunker, extending the after hold into the bunker space and fitting a Crossley engine. Lloyds were not happy with the proposal and as their vessels had always been classed with them, the idea was scrapped, as was the ship.

Up to the mid 1930s, the only experienced motorship yards were Fellows, which was owned by Everards and Browns, but, from the mid 1930s, other yards began getting orders. Lewis built for Horlocks, whilst Scotts of Bowling built two for Gardners of Glasgow. Pollocks built the twin screw *Lanada*, with a deadweight of about 250 tons on a draught of 8ft 3ins as a speculation and sold it to Watsons as *Lady Sheila* (213/35), who soon ordered another, *Lady Stella* (213/35) to complement their motorised sailing barges with the china clay trade to Reed's paper mill at Aylesford in mind. A slightly larger vessel was delivered in 1938. Meanwhile, in Bristol, Hills began building for the Ald Shipping Co. This company had been formed in 1923 by A.L. Duggan, using his initials for the title, together with his partner, W.J. Bardwell, and was managed by A.L. Duggan & Co. The registered address was at Charles Hill's office in Bristol. Both were employees of Hill's and they continued to handle Hill's (Bristol City Line) business for many years. Their first motor vessel, *Castle Combe* (454/36), 155ft 0ins x 27ft 6ins x 10ft 9ins, was paid for by a 100% government loan of £16,045 via The British Shipping (Assistance) Act, 1935. She was followed in 1938 by the larger **Brockley Combe** (662/38). Funnels were originally black with a white 'A' but by the time the motor coasters arrived, it was yellow with a red 'A' corresponding with the houseflag, and hulls had changed from black to grey. Initially, some steam coasters were owned and although they traded widely there were regular shipments of Newlyn roadstone to Bristol and a weekly cargo of cement from Rochester. The first motor coaster – and first new ship – was very much an 'in house' affair, as she was built by Charles Hill's yard in Bristol as a raised quarter deck coaster. Welding was extensively used and a 'simplex' streamlined rudder was fitted. A 7-cylinder Ruston engine of 500shp at 430rpm was attached to a 2.5 to 1 reverse/reduction gear box, giving a favourable propeller speed of 172rpm. Fitting this higher rpm engine allowed a more compact engine room.

Captain Ernest Greenway was in the *Castle Combe* at Rouen on 9th June 1940 having discharged a cargo of Welsh coal and was loading wheat for Manchester. There was some air activity overhead and the German army was reported nearing Paris. Confusion reigned but Captain Greenway managed to get clearance to sail and took the *Castle Combe*, without a pilot, down to the Seine anchorages. In the estuary he sighted the **Brockley Combe** waiting with a coal cargo and went alongside to warn the master of the situation, who took his ship first to St. Malo and then across to Weymouth, still with

TOP: **Castle Combe** *(454/36) on 12th August 1939, showing her original, conventional raised quarter deck layout.*

ABOVE: *This second photograph shows her as* **Alfred Plym** *and after a post-war rebuild. She was lengthened by inserting a third hatch, mast and derrick in front of the bridge, and extending the raised quarter deck to the forecastle. The height of the mast was governed by the new requirement that vessels over 150 feet in length were required to have a second mast, with a white light 15 feet above that of the foremast.*
BOTH WAINE COLLECTION

the coal cargo. *Castle Combe* was sold in 1953 and renamed *Alfred Plym*. Though British vessels sold to Greek owners were often rebuilt in various ways it was quite unusual for a British owned vessel to be extensively rebuilt. She was lengthened in 1955 by inserting an additional hatch, mast and derrick adjacent to the bridge and the well deck eliminated by extending the raised quarter deck, probably because a larger ship was needed. With yards having full order books and freight rates favourable, a rebuild was probably the best option, however by 1958 and a time of falling freight rates, she had been sold to Italian owners.

Brockley Combe (662/38), 171ft 3ins x 29ft 0ins x 15ft 6ins, was also a product of Hill's yard and was most likely proceeded with as freight rates were improving. Some of the steamers were sold, probably to help finance the new ship, as a government loan was not available. Apart from the increase in deadweight, she differed from *Castle Combe* in having no raised quarter deck and so was somewhat easier to construct, with welding again being widely used. The same machinery combination was fitted despite the larger hull but even so, a speed of 10 knots was recorded on loaded trials with 900 tons of coal. With her flush deck, she was more in the style of contemporary Dutch coasters though larger. She survived the war but was subsequently wrecked on Les Minquiers reef off Jersey in December 1953. The coastal trades were declining as oil replaced coal and the last of the company's ships were sold in 1960, with the Ald Shipping Company being wound up in 1964, although A.L. Duggan & Co. continued as agents for other coasters like *Eldorita*, which brought cargoes of stone from Newlyn to Bristol.

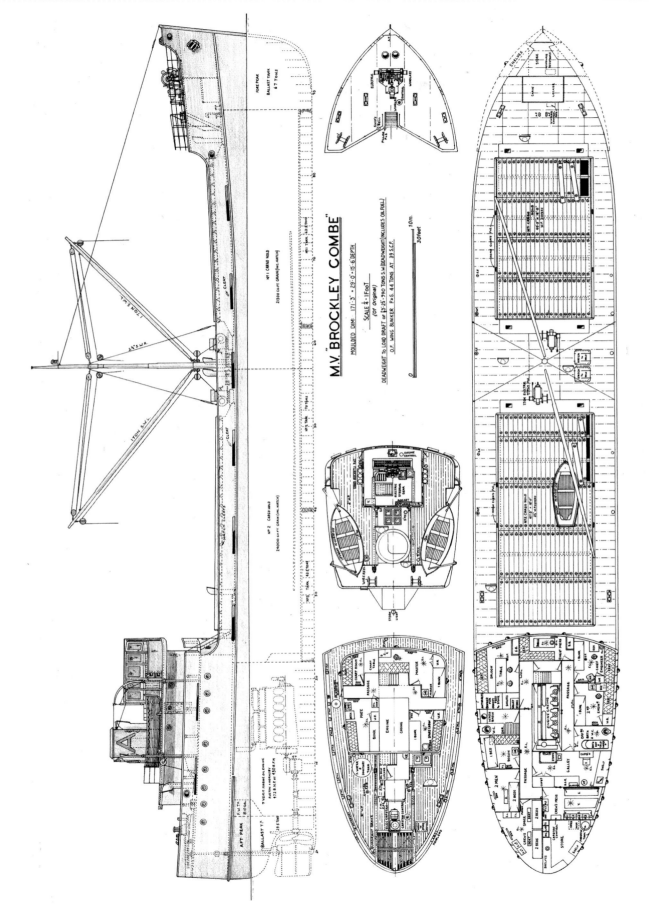

The grey hull of Brockley Combe (662/38) was more typical of Dutch coasters but her plain and rather chunky superstructure aft was otherwise characteristic of British-built or designed motor vessels of the 1930s and 1940s.
WAINE COLLECTION

Hotwells (499/50) was a small collier ordered in 1949 by Osborn & Wallis Ltd to supply Portishead power station from the South Wales coalfields and was closely similar to the owners' St. Vincent, built some years earlier. The main engine was a turbocharged Ruston & Hornsby with a reverse/reduction gear box. Unusually she had a MacGregor steel forward hatch cover in the well deck and an old style wooden hatch cover for the raised quarter deck hatch. However, as the voyage was short, in favourable weather this wooden cover was left off. She later became W.N. Lindsay's Rosewell. Douglas Lindsay recalls that she was rather scruffy but had a remarkable capacity for getting around the Scottish coast and made regular voyages to the Shetland Isles without difficulty. However, the gearbox was her weakness and it broke down quite a few times, usually resulting in her being laid up for a month or so. In order to conform to the new rules for a second mast carrying a navigation light, which came into force shortly after her completion, another mast was added behind the bridge.
M.T. WINTER COLLECTION

Osborn & Wallis of Bristol, who were heavily involved in supplying coal to Portishead power station, had their fleet maintained by Hills and probably on seeing the success of these vessels, ordered their first motorship. Hills completed *St. Vincent* in 1940, which had similar hull dimensions to the *Castle Combe* of 1936 and the same gross tonnage of 454. The main engine was also a Ruston, driving the screw via a reverse/reduction gear box, although in this case a 6-cylinder 4-stroke. A novel feature for the time was MacGregor rolling steel hatch covers for the forward hatch, although the main hatch retained wood covers. The design proved very successful during the war years and a sister incorporating a few slight changes was completed as *Hotwells* (499/50), 155ft 0ins x 27ft 0ins x 11ft 9ins. The voyages were short, usually loading at Newport or Ely harbour, Penarth. Plans were discussed with the builders for two similar but slightly larger vessels in 1950 and were proceeded with when it became clear that they would be needed for the new power station at Portishead, resulting in *Colston* (586/55) and *Brandon* (586/57). Though built in the 1950s, the design was very conservative so they looked like 1930s vessels and even reverted to all-wooden hatch covers. In the 1960s, the power station changed to larger vessels and eventually part was closed and the remainder changed to oil firing, so the ships then carried coal to East Yelland and Hayle power stations for which their size was well suited. The company ceased trading in 1970, by which time the latter pair had been sold to W.E. Dowds of Newport and were to have several more owners over the years, clearly demonstrating how well designed and built they were.

Cromarty Firth, 160ft 0ins x 28ft 0ins x 12ft 3ins, was built to a more traditional design with a raised quarter deck and bridge amidships. However, the lower headroom needed for an oil engine by this time led to the added complication of two steps in the strength deck. It is interesting to

M.V. "HOTWELLS."

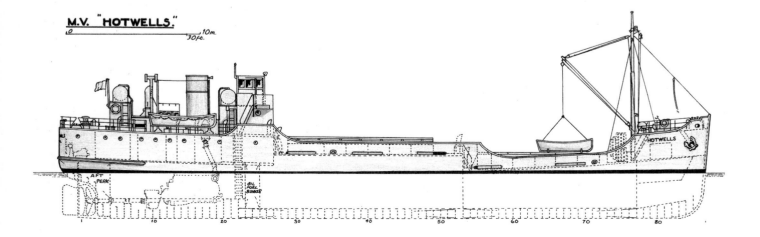

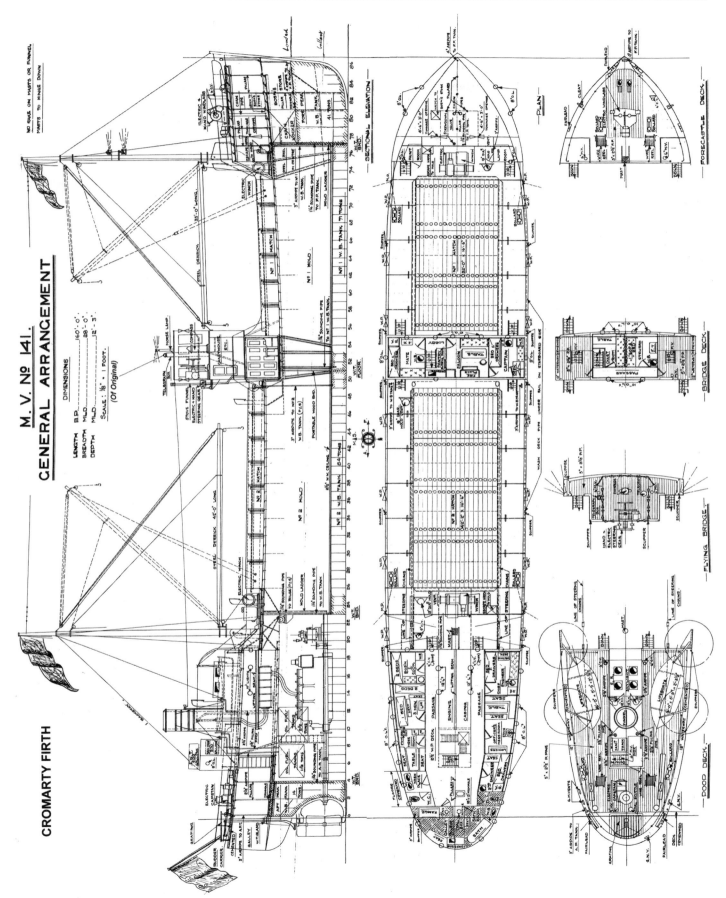

M. V. No. 141.
GENERAL ARRANGEMENT

CROMARTY FIRTH

DIMENSIONS

LENGTH   B.P.   160'-0"
BREADTH MLD.   28'-0"
DEPTH   MLD.   12'-3"

SCALE : 1/8" = 1 FOOT.
(Of Original)

— SECTIONAL ELEVATION —

— PLAN —

— FORECASTLE DECK. —

— BRIDGE DECK. —

— FLYING BRIDGE —

— POOP DECK. —

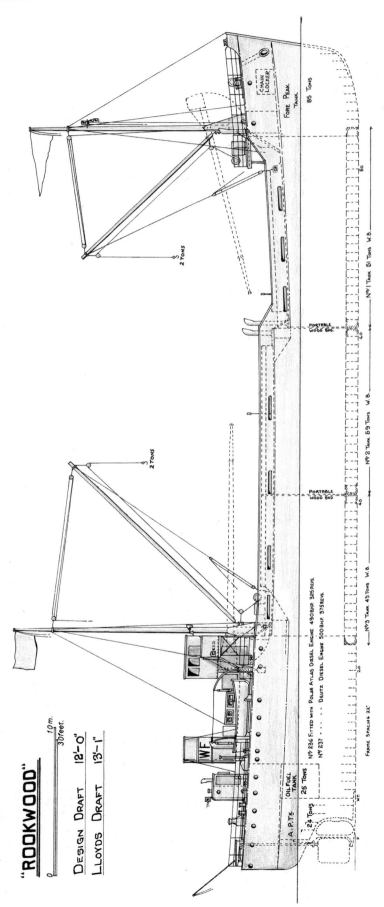

Rookwood (633/36) and her sister Lockwood (633/36) were the first motor vessels built for France, Fenwick & Co. Ltd of London and were fitted with a Deutz 4-stroke and a 'Polar' 2-stroke main engine respectively, to see how the types compared. Both achieved 10 knots on trials, so exceeding the contract speed of 9.5 knots. The lesser design draft was probably in respect of some restriction imposed by their intended trade or cargo.

"ROOKWOOD"

DESIGN DRAFT 12'-0"
LLOYDS DRAFT 13'-1"

note that when Hill's built their second vessel, *Brockley Combe*, they decided on a continuous main deck, as was common in smaller motor coasters. Lewis' had built a similar style vessel, as well as a smaller pair for F.W. Horlock's Ocean Transport, taking advantage of the Government scrap and build programme. *Cromarty Firth*, built for G.T. Gillie & Blair, also received a full loan of £17,880. She had a deeper double bottom than required by Lloyd's rules, for increased ballast and strength. Heavier plating was used at the fore end which had extra stiffening. The bridge accommodation was panelled in oak, with chrome fittings surmounted by a teak wheelhouse. Power came from a 'Polar' of 500bhp at 375rpm, giving about 10 knots in service. Fuel was carried in free standing tanks. Trials were difficult due to gales, so in the afternoon she sailed for Granton, averaging 8 knots in strong head seas and winds on the voyage. She then loaded 730 tons of coal for Aberdeen and averaged 9.5 knots despite head winds. The vessel had a long life, becoming *Herriesdale* in 1957 and from 1962 was under Greek owners, who moved the bridge aft and modernised her appearance.

There was also a significant order from collier owner William France, Fenwick & Co. of London for two small (for them), low air draft (folding masts) motor coasters for Henry Robb's yard, Leith. The moulded dimensions were 175ft 0ins x 28ft 6ins x 12ft 6ins, giving 800 tons deadweight on 12 feet and a maximum of 965 tons on 13ft 1ins. A streamlined rudder was fitted and nine crew were provided for in the sunken poop. *Rookwood* had a 4-stroke 8-cylinder Deutz (500hp/375rpm), while Lockwood had a 2-stroke 7-cylinder 'Polar' (490bhp/325rpm) supplied by British Auxiliaries, Glasgow. The auxiliary engines were all Deutz in *Rookwood* but Paxman and other British makes in *Lockwood*. Both were built for £18,500 for long term charter on a tonnage rate basis to a regular customer. The charter did not work out well and so after three years the arrangement was terminated by mutual agreement. Both makes of main engine had proved reasonably satisfactory for the company, however with no work for them they were offered for sale by auction but were withdrawn. Shortly afterwards, *Rookwood* was sold for £19,000 to F.W. Bowles & Sons for conversion to a sand dredger, while *Lockwood* was sold to the Channel Islands Steam Ship Co. for £28,750,

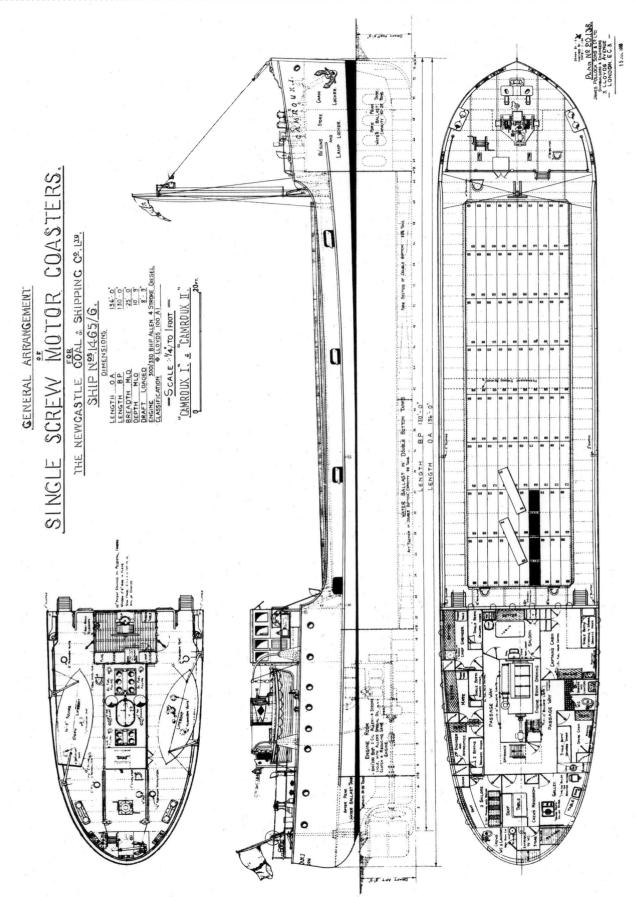

Most general arrangement drawings in this book have had to be slightly rearranged to fit the format, but this general arrangement of Camroux I (324/34) and Camroux II (323/35) is reproduced exactly as it was drawn. Drawings (as tracings) were printed as blue-prints (white on blue) and later dye-line prints (black on white) on rolls of chemically treated paper, usually from 24 to 36 inches wide so any reasonable length could be printed. This illustration was taken directly from an original dye-line print.

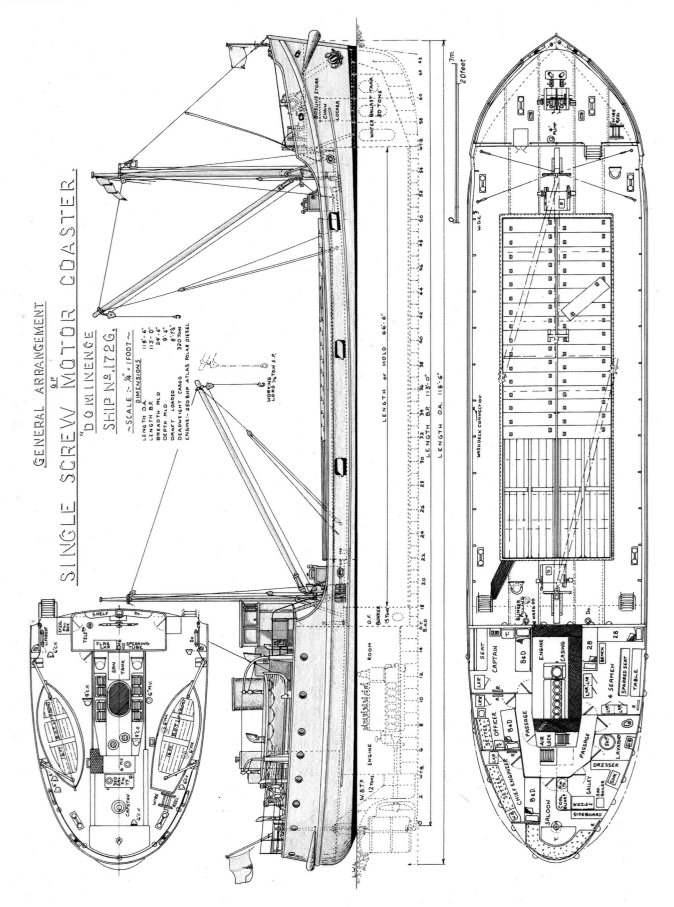

GENERAL ARRANGEMENT
OF
SINGLE SCREW MOTOR COASTER.

"DOMINENGE"

SHIP No. 1726.

~SCALE :- ¼" = 1 FOOT ~

DIMENSIONS

LENGTH O.A.   118'-6"
LENGTH B.P.   113'-0"
BREADTH MLD   24'-6"
DEPTH MLD   9'-6"
DRAFT LOADED   8'-7¾"
DEADWEIGHT CARGO   320 Tons
ENGINE:- 260 BHP ATLAS POLAR DIESEL

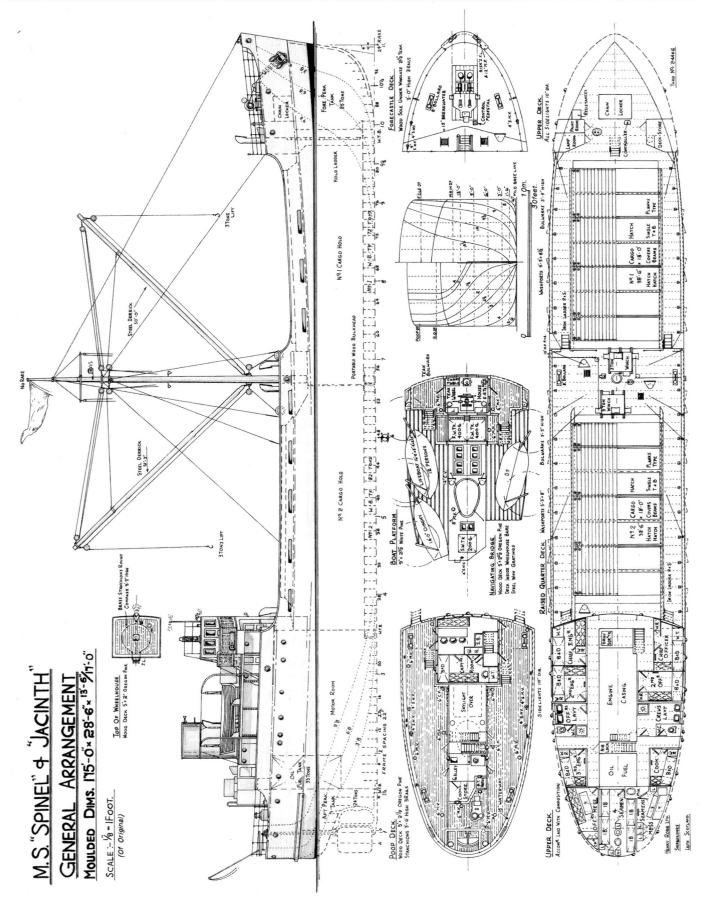

M.S. "SPINEL" & "JACINTH"
GENERAL ARRANGEMENT
MOULDED DIMS. 115'-0" x 28'-6" x 13'-6"/11'-0"
SCALE :- 1/8" = 1 FOOT.
(Of Original)

as by then war had broken out and prices had risen in the expectation of good freight rates. Renamed *Alderney Queen*, she was sunk off the Pembroke coast on 9th October 1940.

France, Fenwicks order may have been triggered by the Newcastle Coal & Shipping Co. Ltd, who had acquired an up-river wharf on the Thames at Fulham which required the navigation of nineteen bridges, some with very little headroom. To serve the wharf, they ordered a pair of low air draft, 420 ton deadweight coasters, *Camroux I* (324/34) and *Camroux II* (324/35), 130ft 0ins x 25ft 0ins x 10ft 9ins, from Pollocks at Faversham, which were named after their 'Camroux' brand of coal. They were followed by the slightly larger *Camroux III* (409/35). They were quite a feature on the Thames, with their beautifully kept white hulls. With the introduction of smokeless zones in the 1950s and the general move to oil and gas, the first two ships were sold in 1960 to J. Hay & Co., Glasgow and became *The Marquis* and *The Marchioness* respectively, until 1966 when they were sold on and left the coasting trade.

Apparently, the London & Rochester Trading Co. Ltd were not very impressed with their Goole 'Proficient' type coaster *Crescence* and ordered a similar sized vessel from Pollocks, which they named *Dominence* (261/40), 118ft 6ins x 24ft 6ins x 9ft 6ins. The company were primarily a barge and lighterage operator on the Thames and *Dominence* was only their second coaster, although they had experience with motor barges which ventured round the coast adjacent to the Thames. She was designed to carry 320 tons on a draught of 10ft 3ins at about 8 knots. She was delivered in the early part of the war and taken up immediately for Government work, being used to evacuate troops and later as a water boat. It seems she was damaged whilst engaged on exploding magnetic mines and was laid up until 1945, when a new Crossley 4-cylinder 2-stroke engine could be obtained for her; at 240bhp, it was 10bhp less than the original 7-cylinder 2-stroke 'Polar' engine. She traded for the company until 1969, when she was broken up at Rochester.

By 1936, Everards had seventeen motor ships under six years old. Their rapid expansion from cement and other local trades into the coal trade, to small southern and western harbours with stone and china clay as a return cargo, probably contributed to the collapse of Robinson, Brown of Newcastle and their fleet of small steamers in 1935.

In 1936, Robertsons were the largest owners by tonnage in the coasting trade, with thirty-eight vessels but just one was a motor ship. Experience with oil engines in larger coasters was, as the Robertson brothers explained in 1974, limited and had resulted in them ordering a steamer, completed in 1936, but also investing in motor ships, the first of which was *Sapphire* (933/35), delivered the previous year. She was the first big motor coaster Ailsa had built. They had reason to be cautious. Kincaids, the local builders of Burmeister & Wain engines for larger ships, went into partnership with MacCallum & Sons Ltd forming the Kindiesel Shipping Co. to own *Kindiesel* (339/36). It was fitted with a new type of small marine engine designed by Kincaids and in the first year was out of service for over six weeks, whilst the following year this was only reduced to a month. It was then completely overhauled and so was out of action for six months with further losses, now, at least in part, due to trading conditions for the size of ship. It was finally sold in January 1942 to Lovering & Sons, Cardiff and in 1951 to Norwegian owners.

Robertsons fared better and further motor coasters were ordered. Henry Robb used the lines and experience of building the same size *Rookwood* and *Lockwood* for France, Fenwick & Co., to build *Spinel* (650/37) and *Jacinth* (650/37) for them. As Robertsons required cabins for a third engineer and second mate for their more distant voyages, the accommodation was rearranged and the captain now had a cabin behind the officers saloon, which was moved up to the poop deck. The single mast amidships reduced weight and the raised quarter deck was slightly shorter, so the deadweight was reduced to 880 tons on a draught of 13ft 0.5ins. They chose locally made 7-cylinder 2-stroke 'Polar' engines manufactured under licence in Glasgow by British Auxiliaries Ltd. Both were requisitioned by the British Government in 1939 and *Spinel* had to be abandoned at Dunkirk with a cargo of cased petrol in May 1940, as she was trapped in the inner basin. Salvaged by the German Navy, she was used to carry supplies to the Channel Islands during the occupation, where, as the Allied Forces advanced, she had to be laid up due to fuel shortages. With the arrival of British forces she was recovered and became *Empire Spinel* of the Ministry of War Transport. Her management was placed with Robertsons and she was repurchased by them in 1946. She then traded for the company until 1970, when she arrived at Dalmuir to be broken up.

Jacinth fared rather better when taken over by the British Government on the same day and like her sister was used to carry cased petrol. She spent much of the war on requisition until August 1944. She then traded for the company until 1966, when she passed to Greek owners for £10,500 and was renamed *Thessaloniki*. She had been built at a cost of £24,100. Both had been fitted with

Jacinth (650/37) arriving at Preston with a cargo of Scandinavian packaged timber, an important trade for Robertsons' ships. The steel banded packages were secured with wires and chains, and look distinctly loose at the end of this voyage. The cargo in the forward well deck was protected somewhat by the breakwater at the after end of the forecastle. DAVE HOCQUARD

new 'Polar' engines in 1957 of the same size as originally fitted. At some time after the war, the front and side of the poop deck was plated in below the bridge wings to give more shelter to the saloon on both vessels.

Robertsons, had a near sister to *Sapphire* built by Inglis which they named **Cameo** (946/37) but, like several other British owners, turned to Dutch yards for their small and medium sized coasters. Dutch yards had much experience building small motor-sailers and motor vessels, assisted by the good mortgage facilities attractive to Dutch captain owners. Generally in the size range 200 to 500 tons deadweight, they were often on charter to British operators. Koster was successful at attracting orders from Metcalf and Rix, aided by his son who had served his apprenticeship in a British yard. However, *Prase* (374/38) and *Cairngorm* (394/38) were built by A. Vuijk en Zonen. Reverend William Jones recalls them among the regulars in the later 1940s, loading limestone at the company's quarry at Llandulas, along with the British-built *Spinel* and her sister *Jacinth*. The two Dutch vessels were only near sisters; they were both the same registered length but the slightly broader and deeper *Cairngorm* was able to carry about 40 tons more than *Prase*. The pair were legendary for the way they battled through stormy seas which often delayed larger vessels. Vuijk also built for H. Harrison (Shipping) Ltd, London and *Saint Kentigern* for J. & A. Gardner, Glasgow.

Cameo (946/37) from A. & J. Inglis was the second motor vessel built for Robertsons and was closely similar to the first, Sapphire (933/35), from Ailsa, which had cost £24,350. The latter had a 2-stroke 'Polar' main engine, while this vessel had a Burmeister & Wain 2-stroke made by Harland & Wolff.

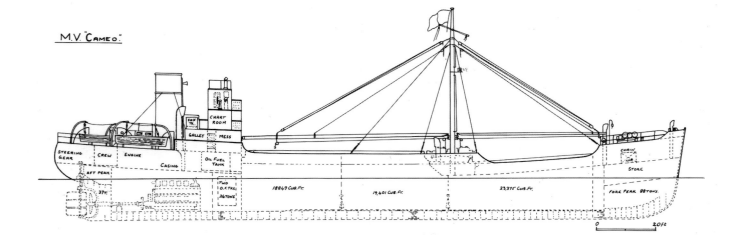

M.V. "CAMEO."

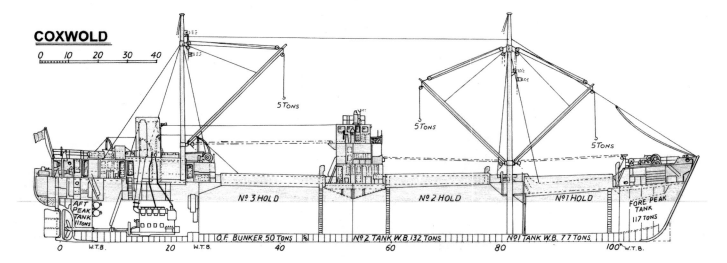

COXWOLD

0   10   20   30   40

5 TONS

5 TONS

5 TONS

NO 3 HOLD   NO 2 HOLD   NO 1 HOLD

AFT
PEAK
TANK
11 TONS

FORE PEAK
TANK
117 TONS

O.F. BUNKER 50 TONS   NO 2 TANK W.B. 132 TONS   NO 1 TANK W.B. 77 TONS

0   W.T.B.   20   W.T.B.   40   60   80   100   W.T.B.

Coxwold (1,124/38) was unusual in having the bridge placed between the hatches on the raised quarter deck, rather than at the forward end of the raised quarter deck, where it could be incorporated in the steelwork needed to compensate for the step in the strength deck. The deck gear was electric for the 5-ton capacity derricks, while the main engine was a 'Polar' M44M (725 bhp/300rpm). From a plan in Shipbuilding & Shipping Record, *14th April 1938*

James Fisher of Barrow went to nearby Vickers-Armstrongs for their first motorship *Shoal Fisher* (698/37), with the registered dimensions 185ft x 30.3ft x 11.3ft, which was designed for special cargoes of exceptional dimensions and built with increased scantlings, with much of the vessel electrically welded. Fishers had close ties with Vickers and often carried major items for them. Deadweight tonnage was 1,055 with provision for 323 tons of ballast. The fuel oil bunker, lubricating oil, etc, was arranged in the more modern form of a cross bunker and double bottom tanks to give a range of 7,000 miles or about four weeks at sea. Deck and steering gear was electric and the steering gear incorporated a rudder brake, which avoided the need for relieving tackles. The accommodation was of an exceptionally high standard. The plan was probably passed round other builders for tender as De Haan & Oerlemans, Heusden built the almost identical, though slightly smaller, *Kyle Fisher* (604/39) which had a Sulzer (500bhp/300rpm) diesel giving a speed of 11 knots, while the earlier vessel had a 'Polar' engine.

Occasionally an order was split and *Coxwold* (1,124/38), 210ft 0ins x 32ft 9ins x 15ft 3ins, was built for E.E. Atkinson & Prickett of Hull, while near sister *Thixendale* (1,092/38) was built by Vuijk. It was closely similar to the Goole-built vessel, with the bridge between hatches two and three rather than at the forward end of the raised quarter deck.

Unlike owners who were venturing into motor ships for the first time, John Summers at Shotton were by then ordering a second generation of motorships for work on the Irish Sea, as some of their fleet were more than twenty years old. An order was placed with Scotts of Bowling for two coasters of the maximum size which could reach their jetty on the higher tides, roughly every two weeks, and the smaller ships sold. In a break with tradition they were named *Hawarden Bridge* (297/40) and *Staley Bridge*. The drawing shows *Staley Bridge* (297/40), 130ft 0ins x 24ft 6ins x 10ft 0ins, as refurbished after the war and with higher bulwarks at the bow, as can be seen compared with the trials picture of *Hawarden Bridge*, which was similarly modified.

Ken Davies recalls:

'I joined the Hawarden Bridge *as a deck boy in October 1956. She carried 7 crew and a boy. The master was Joseph Peers who had been master of her sister* Staley Bridge *when both ships had supported the Normandy Landings. Both ships had a brass plaque in the saloon acknowledging this service. He had started in schooners and his first command had been* Innishowen *and he told many hair-raising stories about bad weather in that little craft. The mate was James Hopwood who had been master in* Eldorita *and* Warita. *The chief engineer was Ken Griffiths who had risen quickly with Everards and Coppacks. The second engineer was Bill Dowell who had sailed in the Point of Ayr colliers, two very experienced able seamen and a young ordinary seaman completed the crew.*

The main engine was a 4-cylinder Newbury Sirron and electric lights came from a dynamo on the main engine, which charged batteries to keep us in lights when in port, which occasionally needed topping up from a small generator. The deck gear of two winches and a windlass were hydraulically powered and very efficient but noisy. The capstan aft was hand powered via two handles. Fortunately the skipper was a competent handler of his ship and the capstan was seldom used.

The main work was to bring pig-iron from Workington, Millom and Barrow-in-Furness to Summers' jetty adjacent to the steelworks. This meant a cargo roughly every fortnight when the tides were big

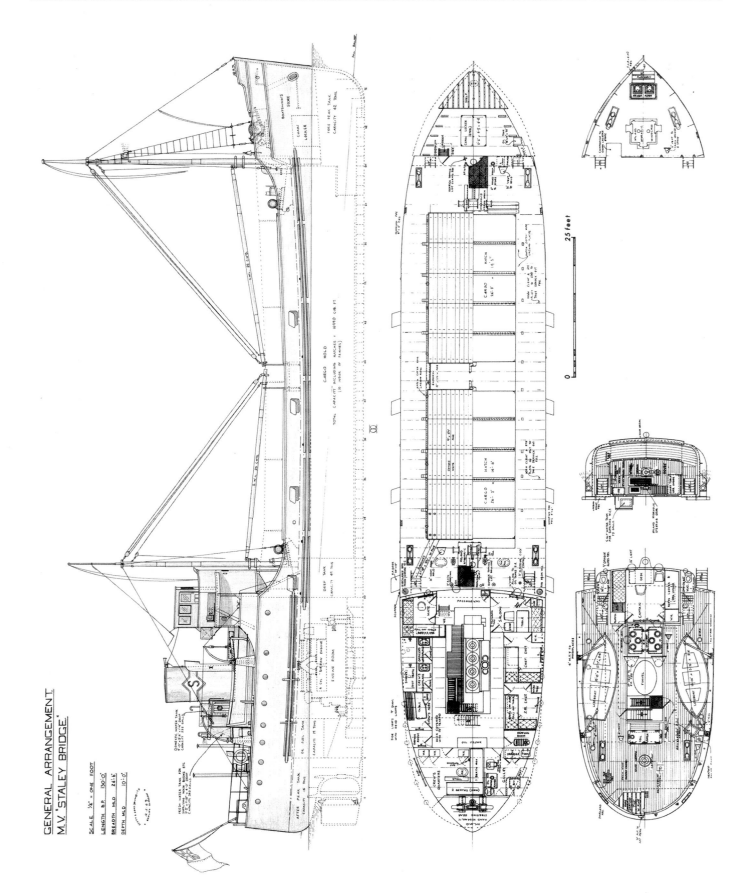

GENERAL ARRANGEMENT
M.V. "STALEY BRIDGE"

SCALE ⅛" = ONE FOOT

LENGTH B.P.   130'-0"
BREADTH MLD   24'-6"
DEPTH MLD   10'-0"

enough to accommodate the fully laden vessels which carried around 320 tons on their summer marks. Berthing at the jetty was an interesting experience. The ordinary seaman and I would have an early start as Summers were proud of the high standards of ship's maintenance they set. We would ensure any bits of rust breaking through the paintwork were scoured away and the grease would be cleaned off the brasswork around all the ports and scuttles and especially the bell on the forecastle head. All brasswork would then be cleaned with vinegar and polished to a high shine. Up would go the houseflag and a clean red 'duster' hung at the stern ready for our approach to the home port. On the way up the river we would strip the hatches and get ready to berth. We would be riding the flood tide up river and somewhere abeam The Rock at the north end of Connah's Quay, the anchor would be dropped, we would swing stem to tide and would be dropped gently on to the jetty. She would be secured with additional large coir ropes which the ordinary seaman and I had to secure round the jetty beams with large shackles. This entailed climbing down to sit facing the jetty on the longitudinal timbers. To leave our hands free to secure the shackles, we would hold on to the next longitudinal by tucking our toecaps under it.

We would then top the derricks and lift out the crossbeams, hurried along by the shore gang who discharged the cargo on a 'job-and-finish' basis. They were hefty individuals whose preference was for Barrow, Millom and Workington in that order. Every pig had to be lifted and thrown into a skip almost chest high. The Workington pigs were huge and the Millom pigs small so the men had to bend almost twice as often. The medium sized Barrow pigs were considered 'just right'. As the channel could only be navigated in daylight, a night in was almost guaranteed.

When leaving the jetty the ordinary seaman and I would be sent ashore to release the bigger ropes and single up to a couple of lines shortly before the flood tide was due. The ship would be lying on the ground and the flood tide would come up river in a bore several feet high. It could be seen rolling up from just above Flint, sometimes with fishing boats riding on its crest. It would sweep round the ship which would rise rapidly, hence the need for secure moorings. The order to let go and heave away would be given and the windlass would heave her out into the stream by the anchor.

In between pig iron cargoes, with the exception of the very occasional load of bricks from Connah's Quay to Drogheda, we sailed light. On a few occasions we went to Ellesmere Port and loaded wood pulp which had just arrived aboard Scandinavian vessels and take it to Mostyn, from whence it was carried by rail to Courtaulds at Greenfield. As we left the same Scandinavian vessel would be docking, as these steamers of around 2,000 tons could only dock with a half cargo. Occasionally there was a cargo of baled 'fibro' (rayon staples) at Mostyn for York Dock, Belfast and a return cargo of potatoes might be loaded for Liverpool in season. This varied work was supplied by J.S. Jones, Rumford Street, Liverpool. Sometimes there would be grain to be loaded overside by elevator from an Empress liner in Liverpool for Barrow or else flax seed for Greenock. These cargoes were detested for dust. An interesting experience was the occasional load of sand/gravel aggregate from Piel Island, Barrow, a lonely place owned by aggregate suppliers Summerfields. A frequent cargo was flour and cattle-feed from Birkenhead to Belfast, Derry or Glasgow. The flour was loaded at Spillers Creek. We would then cross the dock to the UVECO mill for the cattle feed. There was usually a night in one side or the other. Coal was a very occasional cargo. As shipping was not their main business, Summers could afford to decline punishing quarry work but one interesting diversion was a cargo of limestone dust from Maryport the short distance to Garliestone. It encroached everywhere and seemed to consume the paintwork, we only did one cargo! More pleasant was the occasional run up the River Weaver to Winnington, where caustic soda in drums was loaded for Carrickfergus. The annual survey was on Scott's slipway at Bowling on the Clyde which took about a month and there was a very friendly atmosphere for us there and in the village.

The 'bridge' boats were noted for their lack of comfort at sea. The bridge was high, perched above the captain's flat so that they rolled terribly, particularly when crossing Morecambe Bay with a load of pig iron. They had a low forecastle head about three feet high surrounded by bulwarks and I remember being told that that this was because a higher forecastle head might get under Summers' jetty when the tide rose. However, in any head wind stronger than force 4 they would scoop up water and the foredeck was almost permanently awash. They also slammed badly when light. Being somewhat underpowered, they frequently failed to make headway in anything above a force 6 and in winter we quite often anchored in Moelfre Bay or Ramsey Bay waiting for the wind to abate. One difference between the sisters was that Staley Bridge had an oil fired galley stove while Hawarden Bridge had an anthracite fired range. No cook was carried and as cooking at sea in winter is difficult and sometimes dangerous, the ordinary seaman and I would prepare a large pan of scouse, or else lentil soup with a lump of boiled ham boiled in it. This could be lashed on to the range and brought on to heat as required. In port we would do ourselves proud with a full roast dinner followed by apple duff and custard.'

LEFT: By the time Hawarden Bridge *(297/40) was completed and this photograph taken of her on delivery, the Second World War had started and ships' names were confined to name boards hung on the bridge when required. COURTESY BSC ARCHIVES*

BELOW: Hawarden Bridge, *seen here loading drums of chemicals and following post-war refurbishment, during which the raised spurketting plates (white) were added and the bridge and accommodation modified by Scotts, the original builders. These modifications are shown on their revised general arrangement drawing of her sister* Staley Bridge. *The short signal mast aft was probably a wartime addition so that the appropriate signal flags could be flown and was retained subsequently. COURTESY BSC ARCHIVES.*

Both ships were sold in 1967 and *Staley Bridge* retained her name with a number of owners. Initially owned by Captain Wharton, Liverpool, she was sold following damage in the English Channel and was used for salvage work for a time. Sold by Salvage & Cable (Folkestone) Ltd to J.P. Rowland in 1976, she was soon after broken up at Bow Creek. *Hawarden Bridge* was sold to I.W. Marshall of St. Thomas, Barbados and had an unusual fate. On 14th March 1978, she was found drifting and abandoned 15 miles north-north-west of Great Issac Light with the engine room flooded. The life rafts were missing, as was the compass and radio equipment, so she was towed into Miami by a US coastguard cutter. No trace of the crew or the owner was ever found, so on 3rd November 1978, she was towed out of Miami and scuttled to form an artificial fish reef.

The first of the larger motor colliers for the east coast coal trade was built in the 1930s, beginning with *Eildon* (1,447/36), 240ft 4ins x 37ft x 20ft 6ins, delivered by Grangemouth to George Gibson & Co. They had requested the 'Maierform' hull which had been achieving very good results. However, as there was no time for model tests, a predicted form to give 11 knots with 950 bhp at 255 rpm was used as a basis. A 'Polar' M46M giving 870bhp at 250rpm was selected and on trials at maximum power of 925bhp, a speed of 11.725 knots was reached, at a displacement of 2,890 tons on a mean draught of 14ft 11ins and a block coefficient of 0.76. Summer deadweight was 2,180 tons on 15ft 5ins. After delivery she went into the coal trade from Scottish ports to the Thames and

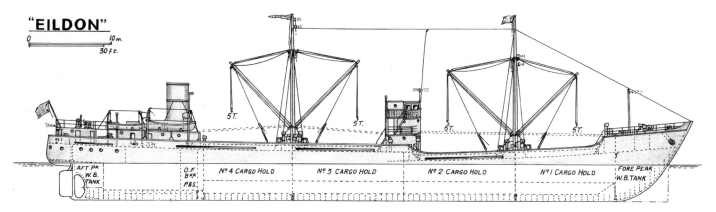

"EILDON"

0   10 m.

30 ft.

AFT PK. | O.F. | Nº 4 CARGO HOLD | Nº 3 CARGO HOLD | Nº 2 CARGO HOLD | Nº 1 CARGO HOLD | FORE PEAK
W.B. | BKR. | | | | | W.B.TANK
TANK | P.B.S. | | | | |

Eildon of 1936 was the first collier built with 'Maierform' lines, which particularly affected the form of the bow, as shown in this profile from Shipbuilding & Shipping Record *of 29th October 1936.*

on these runs fuel consumption was about two tons per day. She was not confined to the Thames and took gas coal to Jersey for example. She served the company well and was finally sold out of the fleet in 1967 to Greek owners, M. Gigilinis & D. Kalkasinas, who renamed her *Paskalis*.

Early Motor Tankers

The rise in petrol consumption led to the construction of fuel depots and the building of small tankers to serve them. Most were steam but the small estuarial tankers were motor. For example, the little *Bargate*, with an overall length of 84 feet, was built by J. Crichton, Saltney, near Chester in 1916 for the Anglo-American Oil Co. She was able to carry 90 tons on a draught of 5ft 3ins and was powered by a 75 bhp Gardner engine. A requirement of the contract was that she should load a cargo at Barrow and deliver it in good condition to their depot at Caernarvon. This was completed successfully and she then proceeded to Southampton depot, where she was to be based. Crichtons also converted the larger motor barge *Silver Queen* (165/12), 95ft 0ins x 18ft 0ins x 11ft 0ins, to a tanker for the company under the direction of their marine superintendent Mr J.F. Wakeham. She had been built by H.&C. Grayson as a self discharging grain barge. She was designed using the Isherwood system of construction, to allow the conveyor along the centre line to be as low as possible. The longitudinal stringers were placed on the outside of the hull in the form of rubbing strakes, leaving the hold sides clear of internal obstructions. Following conversion, she was classed with Lloyd's 'A1 Motor Barge' for limited coasting service between Barrow and Caernarvon in the four summer months, carrying about 220 tons of petroleum in bulk on a draught of 9ft 11ins. As the drawing shows, the accommodation was minimal, although similar to the small sailing vessels of the period. The company later took delivery of *Southgate* (143/25) and *Caldergate* (138/26) from the Amble Shipbuilding Co., which were classed for coasting except the west coast, Cork to Pentland Firth. Similar barges were built for other owners to work on the Severn Estuary up to Stourport and elsewhere.

The Anglo-Persian Oil Company, later to become British Petroleum, had barge style vessels for bunkering larger ships and in the early 1930s came under Shell-Mex & BP, the combined distribution arm of the respective companies. They had several motor tankers for coastal work, including *Shellbrit 2* (695/28), *Shellbrit 3* (460/34) and *Shellbrit 4* (349/28). A company whose fleet was later to be merged into Shell Mex & BP was that of the National Benzole Co., unique in that the mixture was produced as a by-product from the distillation of coal tar, much of which was carried out in the northern coal, iron and steel manufacturing areas. The company initially used a steam tanker and the Dutch built barge *Ben Johnson* (ex-*Ioline* – 183/13) to collect and distribute the benzene mixtures, which were blended with imported petrol to produce their 'National Benzole Mixture' that was widely sold by garages. Demand increased in the 1930s and the Rowhedge Ironworks Co. built a series of vessels for the company. The barge *Ben Sadler* (289/31) was specially built to run to London from Thameshaven with four tanks holding 300 tons in a double hull, to reduce the risk of spillage and fire in the event of a collision. The barge incorporated extensive welding using the Quasi-Arc system. It was followed by the *Ben Henshaw* (377/33), 135ft 0ins x 25ft 0ins x 12ft 0ins, which was built to carry a similar amount but with a forecastle and poop for coasting service on a draught of 10ft 6ins. She was fitted with twin engines exhausting to a funnel fitted with a spark quenching device and an oil trap. She was able to maintain 9 knots in bad weather and could then maintain steerage way in the event of the breakdown of one engine. The design incorporated the latest thinking on rudders, with a streamlined semi-balanced one of Oertz type.

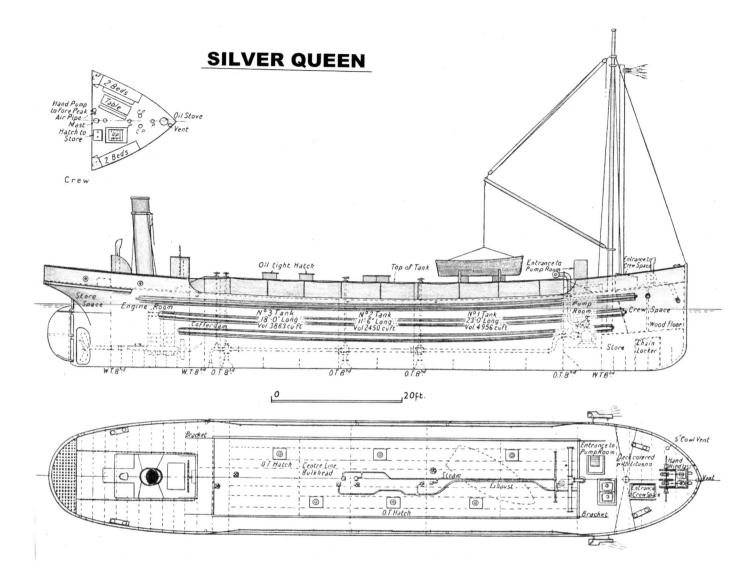

Silver Queen (165/12) after conversion to a tanker, from a drawing published in Shipbuilding & Shipping Record of 5th May 1921

The hull was built on the transverse system, with scantlings and general construction particularly heavy, as the vessel was expected to load and discharge aground, and withstand the corrosion associated with petrol and salt water. Salt water (as ballast) was put in the empty cargo tanks and was also used to wash them. Cargo discharge was unusual in that one pump was driven by steam from a shore supply, although the other was diesel driven from the engine room. The design was clearly very successful as the *Ben Hebden* (410/47) was built to the same design fourteen years later, although experience had shown that there was no need for twin engines and a single, more powerful, 6-cylinder 2-stroke 'Polar' (560bhp/375rpm) was fitted. Other minor changes were the incorporation of a raked stem and the fore peak ballast tank increased from 22 to 45 tons, by moving the chain locker up on to the main deck. The same pump room arrangements were retained.

In the company's fleet these were large tankers and the smaller tanker *Ben Johnson* (228/38), with the registered dimensions 112.2ft x 22.7ft x 9.4ft, was built for the company. She was able to carry 220 tons on about 9ft 3ins. The pump room was conventional, with a Worthington-Simpson duplex pump of 100 tons per hour installed, driven by a 30bhp Paxman diesel via a shaft through the bunker housed inside a gas tight tube. The main engine was a 7-cylinder 2-stroke 'Polar' of 280bhp.

By this time electric light was almost universal, with a main engine driven dynamo supplying enough power at sea so that a separate generator need not be run until needed, if electric deck gear was fitted. Above about 500 tons deadweight, combined hand/electric steering gear was desirable, so that with power assistance in congested waters hard over to hard over could be carried out in about twelve seconds.

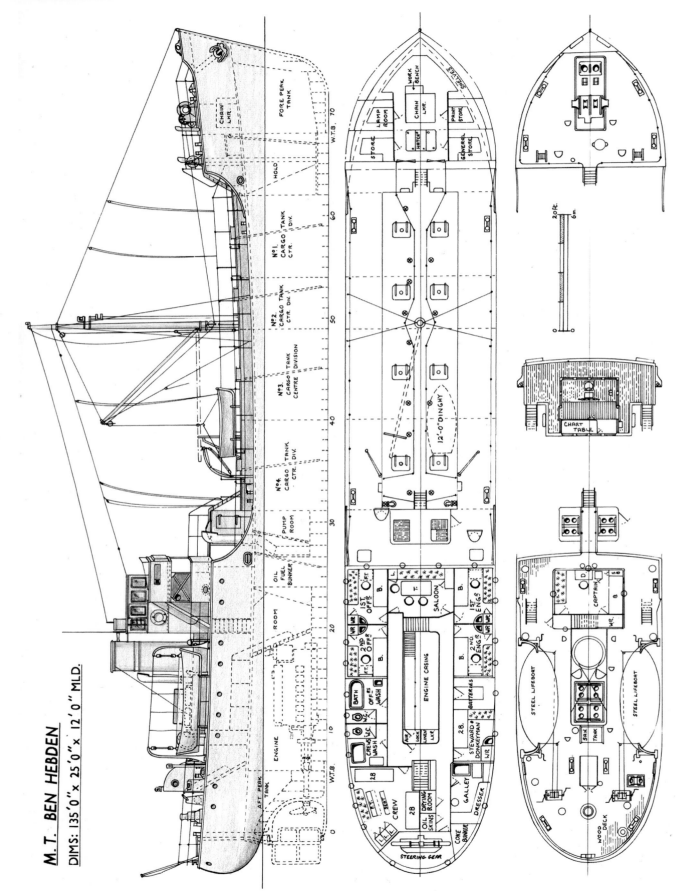

M.T. BEN HEBDEN
DIMS: 135'0" x 25'0" x 12'0" MLD.

CHAPTER 4
WAR TIME AND PREFABS

Note: The dimensions used in this chapter are molded dimensions unless otherwise stated.

With the outbreak of war, shipyards were often given orders for vessels similar to those they had recently built. For example, *Shoal Fisher* (697/37) had been built by Vickers-Armstrongs Ltd, Barrow, in 1937 and they were building a similar vessel for Fishers which was launched as *River Fisher* but was then taken over and completed for the Ministry of War Transport as *Empire Jack* (734/41), with the registered dimensions 185.0ft x 30.3ft x 11.5ft. The vessel was designed with a particularly large after hatch, measuring 53ft 2ins x 22ft 8ins, to carry gun mountings when required and so was critical to the war effort. *Empire Jill* and *Empire Judy* were then built to the same plan by Austins, though with increased fore and aft peak ballast, and completed in 1942 and 1943 respectively. All were managed by Fishers and were bought by them and renamed *River Fisher*, *Race Fisher* and *Stream Fisher* respectively in 1946. During the war, some ships were requisitioned but for the most part owners retained their ships, although were subject to a system of control for voyages and freights for which a scale of official freight rates was set up, to give a reasonable return to owners.

Pollocks built the smaller *Empire Creek* (332/41), 130ft x 25ft x 10ft 9ins, and *Empire Crag* (332/41), able to carry 430 tons on 9ft 10ins. They were powered by 330bhp, 6-cylinder, 2-stroke Crossley engines, which gave a speed of 9 knots. Following the war, they traded for a number of London and south coast owners: *Empire Creek* as *Springcreek*, *Goldcreek* and *Milborne* respectively, and *Empire Crag* as *Springcrag*, *Walcrag* and then *Colne Trader*, latterly as a sand carrier on the Thames for J.J. Prior. A similar type, though of shallower draught at about 9 feet, was built by Pimblott (e.g. *Empire Kyle*), Watson and also Richards, totalling twelve vessels. A slightly longer and narrower version – the 'Severn Collier Type' – was built to carry south Wales coal to the new Castlemeads Power Station at Gloucester. All six were built in 1943 and perhaps the most striking feature was the lack of bulwarks, which were replaced by rails, though they were still classed 'coasting service Great Britain & Ireland'. Four were built by Dunstons and two by Harkers. Dunstons' version had the moulded dimensions 140ft x 21ft 6ins x 10ft 0ins, while Harkers were deeper at 10ft 6ins. The former were able to carry about 356 tons on about 10ft, while the Harker vessels carried 430 tons on 10ft 6ins. There were also differences in the lengths of the forecastle, poop and its accommodation, although all were fitted with Crossley 5-cylinder, 2-stroke engines of 275bhp to give a speed of about 9 knots.

Following the end of the war, they were all sold off in 1947. Although Osborn & Wallis and the Ald Shipping Co. had managed them locally, only the *Empire Laird* was bought by Ald and renamed *Monkton Combe*, with the classification extended to 'Continent between River Elbe and Brest'. Sold in 1950 to become *Halronell* of James Tyrrell, she was lost after striking Black Rock off Carnsore. They proved popular with sand and aggregate companies, and four eventually became sand dredgers. Harkers

Race Fisher (ex-Empire Jill – 739/42), together with a sister ship was built by S.P. Austin & Son Ltd, probably because Vickers, who had built the first of the class, were fully occupied with warship construction. The registered dimensions were 185.0ft x 30.3ft x 11.5ft and both were powered by 'Polar' 2-stroke engines.

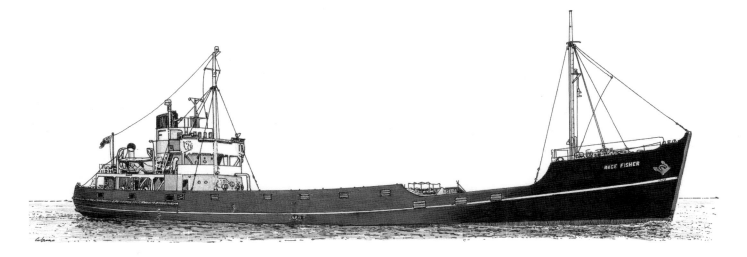

"EMPIRE CREEK"

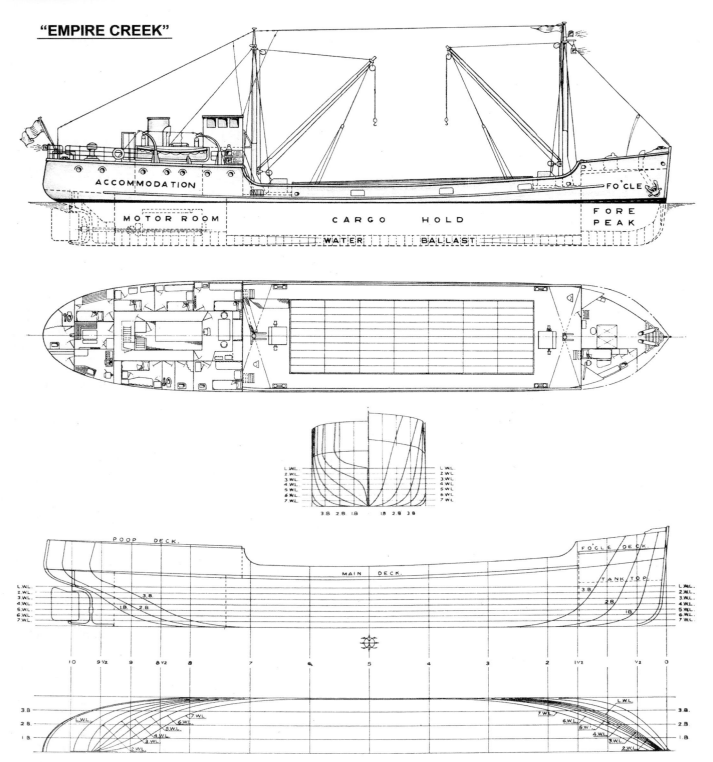

*Empire Creek (332/41) and
Empire Crag (332/41) were
built by J. Pollock, Sons & Co.
Ltd, Faversham for the war effort
based on their own designs.
Walter Pollock, a qualified naval
architect and engineer, wrote
several books on building and
operating small ships.* FROM
BUILDING SMALL SHIPS, 1948

were allocated the management of the two they built for the Ministry of War Transport, *Empire
Reaper* (332/43) and *Empire Rancher* (332/43). They were not the most graceful of vessels, with a
block coefficient of 0.79 loaded corresponding to a displacement of 597 tons on 9ft 0ins draught.
Light displacement was 315 tons, drawing 7ft 3ins aft and 3ft 3ins forward. The two Harker-built
vessels were purchased by the Anglo-Danubian Transport Co. Ltd and placed under the management
of Anglo-Continental Waterways Ltd as *Browning* and *Shelley* in 1947. The following year, *Shelley* was
sold to Coppack Bros & Co., Connah's Quay and renamed *Normanby Hall*, by which time the hatch
had been divided by fitting a mast amidships flanked by two derricks and motor winches. The original

Ordinence (321/41) was built as Empire Kyle by I. Pimblott & Sons Ltd and had a deadweight of 350 tons and the registered dimensions 131.7ft x 24.7ft x 8.6ft. She was one of a number of small coasters built for the war effort to pre-war designs. Sold off in 1946 to the Erskine Shipping Co Ltd, she was renamed Turgail and managed by Freight Express, who had offices in London and Greenock. She passed to Dutch owners for a short time, before being purchased by the London & Rochester Trading Co. Ltd in 1956 and renamed Ordinence. She is seen here off Ronez Quarry Jetty on 21st June 1959, as the crew complete battening down the fore hatch following loading. The cluttered nature of the poop decks of these small coasters is well illustrated here with water tanks, skylights, ventilators, stove funnels and, for the unwary, the steering chains running along the deck from the wheelhouse to the rudder quadrant. DAVE HOCQUARD

Halronell (313/43) was built as the small collier Empire Laird to serve Gloucester Power Station. At the end of the Second World War, the fleet was sold and this vessel was bought by the managers, the Ald Shipping Co. Ltd, Bristol, renamed Monkton Combe and sold after a few years to James Tyrrell of Arklow. She was part of the change from schooners to motorships and the beginnings of the large motor coasting fleet that was built up at Arklow. The exposed nature of the hatch sides and adjacent deck are well illustrated in this Dick Scott photograph of her with a full cargo. As reference to the plan shows, there was no sheer on the deck, so she has clearly been loaded to trim some inches by the stern for easy steering on passage. Seas frequently broke over the hatch, as the photograph taken from the wheelhouse of sister ship Normanby Hall by Tom Fish illustrates (page 66). RICHARD J. SCOTT

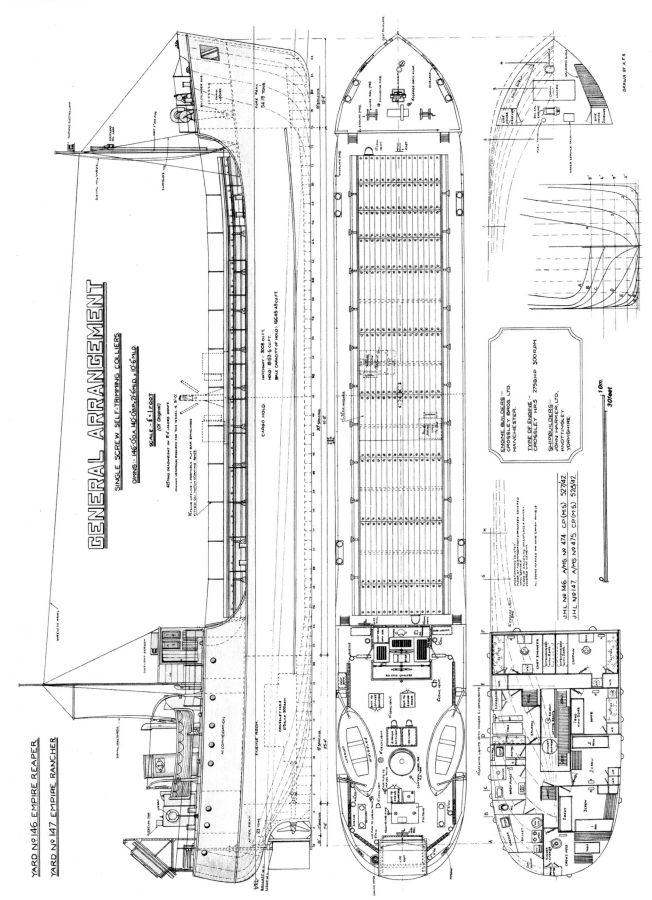

General Arrangement has been combined with the lines plan in the illustration and also shows the proposed position for mast and winches, as well as the funnel mark of the Anglo-Danubian Transport Co. Ltd obtained from other drawings.

Tom Fish recalls:

'There was a variety of loading overside from ocean ships in Liverpool, Birkenhead and sometimes Belfast, such as Belfast-Liverpool oranges on one occasion. More usual was the flour run from Birkenhead to Glasgow and cattle feed, etc from the Mersey for Spillers, Buchannon and UVICO to Belfast and Londonderry. Pig iron was carried from Millom to Newport and very occasionally to Summers Wharf (on the River Dee opposite Connah's Quay) if their two boats could not cope. Most of the cargoes were arranged by J.S. Jones, the brokers in Liverpool, with the cargoes from Connah's Quay handled by Coppacks. Much of this trade went when the railway closed the dock (at Connah's Quay). In 1954 she was regularly on road stone: Trevor and Rivals [quarry jetties] to Carriers Dock and also Manchester. Occasionally there were cargoes from Penmaenmawr [quarry] to Collingwood Dock or Preston. A good sea boat loaded and comfortable, but with no bulwarks, seas on the quarter would sweep right over the hatches. An extra third tarpaulin was put on followed by wire strops to make sure all was secure. Like most coasters she used to 'thump' light. On one occasion we had loaded 150 tons of slates at Dinorwic and completed in Bangor. We then sailed past Puffin Island and on for the Skerries – weather was fine and calm, but we met a heavy swell against the tide that shook the lifeboats in the chocks. The captain was soon on the bridge asking why I was not further out from the Skerries. We would go through the Menai Straits in bad weather but if you did so, you would lose a tide to anchor off Caernarvon or Dinorwic and wait for slack water to proceed through the narrow Swellies, but then start to meet the tide coming the other way and so would be stemming it for the remainder of the voyage to Liverpool. We would go round the Skerries in ballast but in bad weather use the Straits. As discharging ballast could take three hours we might come off the quarry still with some ballast.'

Ken Davies adds:

'It was the attraction of having a cook in addition to master, mate, two engineers and two ABs, that led to me moving across the river to Coppacks Normanby Hall which was loading basic slag at Connah's Quay for the Isle of Man, a by-product of Summers steel making. The cargoes were similar to Hawarden Bridge, although we never carried pig-iron while I was aboard and had far fewer grain cargoes. Coal cargoes to Dublin, Waterford and New Ross were quite common, invariably coming back via the roadstone quarries of Carreg-y-Llam, Port Rivals, or once or twice to Port Trevor before the jetty closed. The master was Gwenlyn Jones with a fine sense of fairness, but he was not noted for 'going wind-bound'. Having discharged the basic slag in October 1957 we made our way to Carreg-y-Llam. The wind freshened from the west and we were lucky to get a load. The jetty extended from the rocky coastline which had claimed many ships. We went alongside and had a thoroughly uncomfortable time. As Normanby Hall had no bulwarks, by the time she was down to her marks the foredeck was already awash. It was then a frantic rush to batten down and drop off the jetty. We were all soaked to the skin being waist deep in water as we drove home the last wedges – carried out with great diligence as the lack of bulwarks combined with a freeboard of a few inches impressed us all with a strong sense of safety. "Well Kenny my lad" the shipper said to me, "you have had a grand christening at the quarries; you will never load in weather worse than that – we wouldn't hold her on the quay." Indeed the wreck of the Amy Summerfield, by then a boiler and a scattering of scrap metal on the beach a few yards from the jetty, bore grim testimony to the dangers of treating the quarries lightly. We would frequently get two cargoes of roadstone between flour and coal cargoes, our only respite was a return cargo of potatoes. This trading pattern of short runs working 'watch-and-watch' meant a hard life with little sleep. From the Mersey it was usually 18 hours to Belfast, 24 to Derry or Waterford and 14 to Drogheda, Dublin or Dundalk. It was not unusual to make an overnight passage to Ireland in time for an eight o'clock start and finish to sail in the evening. This meant working watch-and-watch all night on the passage out, doing a full day's work then work watch-and-watch through the following night. One watch would loose a watch below to load at the quarries, and arrival at Carriers might be in the small hours. She would be discharged by mid-day, often to sail for another load at a quarry jetty that evening and repeat the pattern if no other cargo was available.

She was not a handsome ship, but was popular with her crews and remarkably comfortable at sea, having an easy motion. Partly because the bridge consisted of no more than a wheelhouse on the poop and partly because, having no bulwarks, she carried little water [on deck] in bad weather. Only when taking a gale on the beam did she roll. The crew was very mixed. There were two Lister driven winches on deck and a small motor under the forecastle head which drove the windlass. Motor deck gear was seldom popular with crews as they had to be started with a crank handle. The man performing

*A typical view, from the wheelhouse of **Normanby Hall**, of seas breaking over the hatch, which was unprotected by bulwarks. Though these made deck work easier, Lloyd's made no distinction for loading and insurance purposes and it is therefore likely that because of this and the shortage of steel during the war, they were built without bulwarks. TOM FISH*

this action would get a good motion going, then a companion would pull down a small lever to activate the compression. If successful first time, the handle would be quickly removed and the compression lever secured with a wedge. Frequently they failed to fire. They allowed for much less variation in operating speed than either hydraulics, electrics or steam.

I returned to her in 1963 having been deep sea. Some interesting changes had taken place aboard and the ordinary seaman's post had disappeared as times had become tough for small shipowners. She had also become a slower ship due to having lost a screw which had been replaced by one that was too large and heavy for her. Life was less hectic as she struggled to do Belfast in 20 hours so as a consequence we rarely arrived in time for an eight o'clock start and always got a night in Belfast. The round of cargoes were still similar but now we only managed two cargoes a week instead of three. An interesting deviation was a cargo of bricks from Connah's Quay in October 1964, which Coppack's were anxious to get to Limerick before the winter set in. The bricks were on pallets and not the lengthy loading of stacking the bricks by hand in the hold. Unusually we sailed at night, the pilot being persuaded to make an exception as it was brightly moonlit and the buoys could be picked out by torchlight. It took us about four and a half days to reach Limerick after taking the full force of an Atlantic westerly. We had one night in Limerick and then went down the Shannon to Kilmore to load ground kelp for Bridgewater, punctuated by a spell at anchor in Brandon Bay. The Atlantic rollers looked truly formidable and, breaking with custom, she rolled like a pendulum as we sailed across them.

The Normanby Hall's survey fell due and we went to one of the floating dry-docks in Ellesmere Port. We left a week or so later to load. Some years previously most of her bottom plating on the port side had been replaced. This had given her a list to port which had been mostly compensated for by putting some concrete blocks in the bilges on the starboard side. Shortly after Eastham Locks we noticed the list had become far more pronounced and I was sent to investigate. Removing a hatch board I could see the starboard side of the hold was filling with water. I called the mate, grabbed a couple of crowbars and a hammer and went down the hatch. When we lifted a ceiling board we could see water was coming in quite rapidly from the port side. When we lifted a couple of boards on the port side, water gushed from an open rivet hole. A length of broomstick hammered into the hole soon swelled and made a tight seal. In the meantime the old man had radioed ashore and as we approached Alfred Locks we were refused entry as they did not want us sinking there. Then, furnished with a two tug escort, we returned to dry-dock.

On 6th of October 1965 she ran aground in fog, while on passage Birkenhead to Belfast with flour, near Tara Point at the entrance to Strangford Lough. A meeting point for the tides, it made it difficult to judge your position and although refloated, she sank in Belfast Lough two days later while being towed towards Carrickfergus.'

During the war, some larger vessels were built in ones and twos. For example, Goole built *Empire Cliff* (873/40) and *Empire Foreland* (873/41), 190ft x 30ft x 13ft 6ins, carrying about 1,125 tons on 13ft 2¹/₂ins. They later built *Ability* (881/43) and *Amenity* (881/44) to a similar plan, as the pressures of war work eased and owners were granted building licences. Both the 'Empire' ships were managed by Everards and it is interesting to note that the pair later built for that company did not have the strongly raked stems of the 'Empire' version. The largest group were six built in 1941. They were conventional, long-raised quarter deckers, based on the design of the *Yewmount* (859/39), 198ft 6ins x 33ft x 13ft 10ins, which had just been completed before the war by Scotts of Bowling for John Stewart & Co. (Shipping) Ltd. Scotts, Inglis and Harland & Wolff's Glasgow yard each built a pair and they were mostly placed with liner companies except for *Empire Shoal*, which was managed by Everards. They proved attractive to their respective managers and at the end of the war were purchased by them, Everards renaming theirs *Angularity*.

The need for coasters to support the D-day landings was met by mass producing a standard design, following experience gained with prefabricated tugs. A coaster with a hull of proven performance was selected, with the moulded dimensions 140ft BP-27ft-11ft as the prototype. From this a hard chine design which could be built from flat plate with little bending, was prepared. Tank tests showed that a slightly swim shaped (barge style bow) was unsatisfactory. This was discarded and finally replaced by two easy chines, rather than a single abrupt one which had been initially tried in place of the partial swim shape. The stern was also modified and completed with a square transom. The skeg was altered to an aerofoil shape and this improved performance, saving 5.5% on horse power at the propeller. Except for the twisted plate needed for the skeg, every plate was flat or curved in one direction only and so easily rolled. In order to cut down work, the sheer was omitted and intermediate curves were replaced by known radii, so dimensions of all plates could be easily calculated. The original design requirement was a tanker carrying fuel in bulk or in cans, hence the hatches, but as 'Pluto', the cross channel fuel pipeline, progressed, the need for tankers was reduced and during construction some were changed into dry cargo carriers. The vessels had to be able to ground on the beaches, possibly under air attack, so to minimise the chance of petrol leaking on to the surface of the water and causing a major fire hazard, a double hull design was used and closely subdivided.

The hull was split up into units, transverse for the bow and stern, and longitudinal units for the mid-body, which had longitudinal frames. The bow and stern transverse frame arrangement allowed a simple ring weld when the sections were mated. This was aided by leaving a degree of flexibility in the ends by not welding the last few inches, until the units were lined up in the shipyard doing the final assembly. The sections were made by firms such as bridge builders and structural steel workshops with no shipbuilding experience. As no unit weighed more than 13 tons, they could

The tanker **Chant 58**, *401 tons gross, not long after completion in 1944 and in wartime rig, with guns amidships, a float ready for immediate launch aft and hand rails running along the sides of the trunk. Stops were fitted on the guns so a gunner intent on shooting down an enemy aircraft could not hit any part of the ship. In civilian use, with the gun mounting and float removed, rails were generally fitted along the side deck. JOHN CLARKSON*

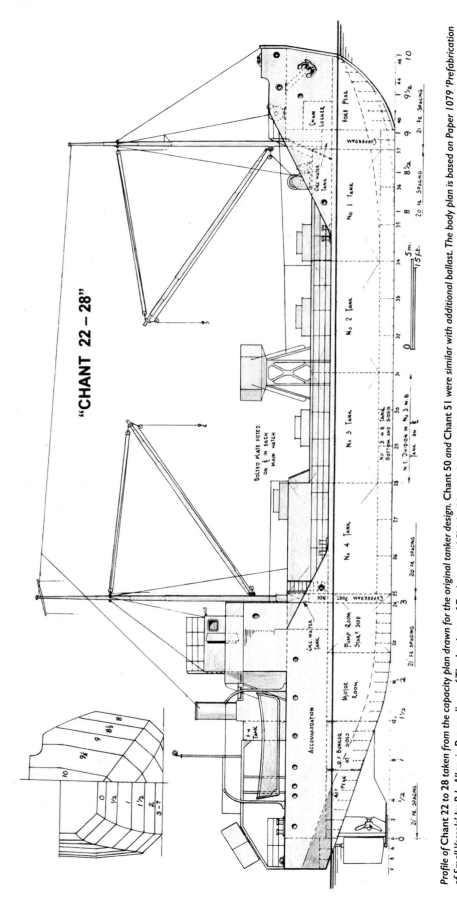

Profile of Chant 22 to 28 taken from the capacity plan drawn for the original tanker design. Chant 50 and Chant 51 were similar with additional ballast. The body plan is based on Paper 1079 'Prefabrication of Small Vessels' by R.L. Allan, in Proceedings of The Institute of Engineers and Shipbuilders in Scotland, Volume 90 (1946/7).

easily be moved by road to the shipyards, where the units could be assembled into a coaster in three to four weeks. A variety of engines were fitted and the vessels were rather underpowered at 8 knots, due to the lack of availability of more powerful engines.

In all, forty-three of the tankers were produced in 1944 and assembled by Burntisland (four), Furness (sixteen), Goole (nine), Readhead (two) and Scarr (twelve). The registered dimensions were expected to be 142.25ft x 27.0ft x 8.5ft and the gross tonnage 402.4. Built under British Corporation survey, each seems to have been officially measured and the gross tonnages recorded varied from 401 to 403. All were given numbers from *Chant 1* to *Chant 69* but gaps in the sequence appear to correspond with the twenty-five completed as the 'Empire Fabric' Class dry cargo coasters. Deadweight on summer draught for the tanker was given as 480 tons, including fuel stores, etc. Cargo was 350 tons at 50 cubic feet per ton at 98.5% full, allowing 1.5% for expansion.

Though the management of the tankers was placed with coastal tanker owners such as the Bulk Oil SS Co., T.J. Metcalf, Everards and a relative newcomer, Coastal Tankers Ltd (*Chant 58*), at the end of the war none were sold to British owners. It was rumoured that as no less than five had capsized and sunk within a year of completion, they were not offered to British owners for this reason and all were sold overseas. However, in the 1950s, Rowbothams bought *Pinard* (ex-*Chant 11*) and a little later Everards bought *Theodora* (ex-*Chant 53*) and *Frans* (ex-*Chant 27*), which were renamed *Averity* and *Auspicity* respectively. A generic capacity plan for *Chant 22-28* and *Chant 50-51*, prepared by Goole Shipbuilding & Repairing in March 1944 and sent to Everards in respect of *Auspicity* in 1961, has a note that 'on Chant 51, *50 tons ballast added to the bottom*'. This would have increased the double bottom water ballast from 66 tons to 126 tons so perhaps the capsizing risk had been identified. Strangely this double bottom ballast is not listed in Lloyd's Register, although the fore and aft peak ballast is. No more were lost to capsizing. *Auspicity* was classed by the British Corporation for '*Baltic, Mediterranean and European Coasting including Great Britain and Ireland but not north of 65 degrees north*. Tanker for

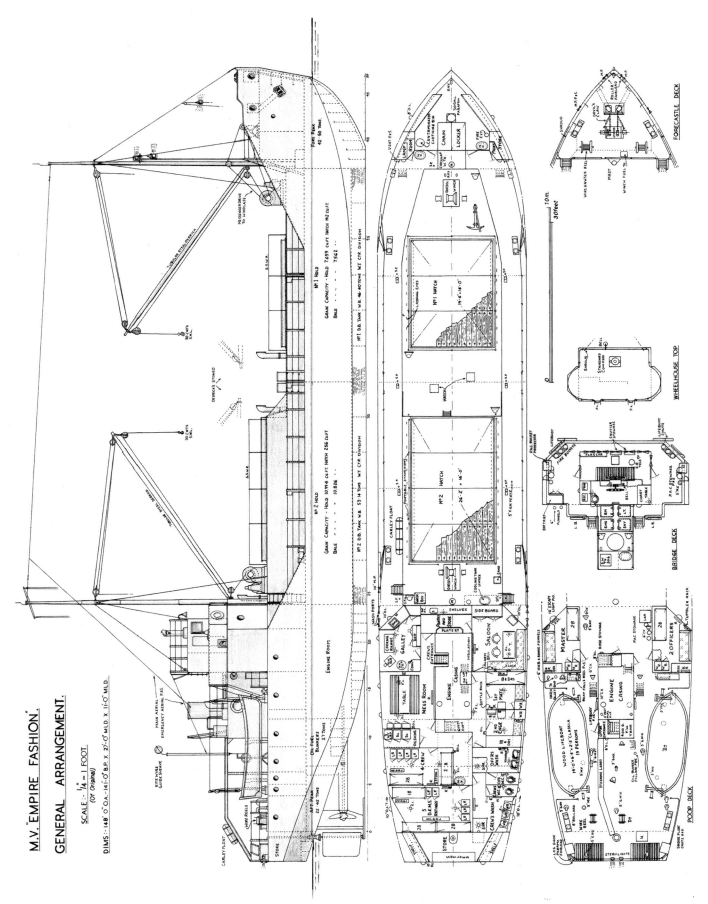

M.V. EMPIRE FASHION.

GENERAL ARRANGEMENT.

SCALE :- 1/4" = 1 FOOT.
(Of Original)

DIMS :- 148'-0" O.A.-141'-0" B.P. X 27'-0" MLD. X 11'-0" MLD.

Frivolity (410/44), here in Everard colours, was one of the 'Fabric' coasters, a dry cargo version of the 'Chant' tankers. She is almost fully laden but the slope in the side deck shows how the raised after hatch on the trunk made it possible to load with slightly more cargo aft and hence a few more inches of draught aft to aid steering.
WAINE COLLECTION

oils flash point above 150 degrees Fahrenheit.' She was equipped with heating coils and a donkey boiler fitted in 1955, which had a prominent funnel just in front of the bridge. In 1969 her old Crossley engine was replaced by a Newbury. Latterly, she was carrying lard from the Continent to the Thames until sold to Greek owners in 1972 and was broken up in 1974.

The situation with the 'Empire Fabric' series of dry cargo coasters was rather different. They were sold widely to British owners and Everards had nine, with Hull Gates, Metcalf, Captain Griffen and others one each. The details recorded seem to have depended on how individual surveyors or societies applied their rules to what was a very odd ship. The British Corporation recorded the forecastle as 14 feet, Lloyd's recorded it as 17 feet. Aft, the poop deck was recorded as 38 feet by the British Corporation which is the distance from the rudder post to the front of the poop at the side of the ship, while Lloyd's recorded it as 48 feet, the distance from the stern to the fore end of the poop on the centre line. The nett tonnage was sometimes recorded as 178, although most were given 190 and gross 410. The only obvious difference from the tankers was the extension of the raised part of the trunk. Ballast in the double bottom was recorded as 99 tons, with fore peak 43 tons and aft peak 24 tons. As completed, they were double hulled like the tankers and this is the case in respect of *Empire Fashion*, 141ft x 27ft x 11ft, which became Everards' *Frivolity*. She had a deadweight of 450 tons on a draught of 9ft 7ins. Grain capacity was 19,001 cubic feet in the double hull form, which gave a not very generous stowage rate of 42 cubic feet per ton, so some owners took out the inner hull and this was done with *Hullgate* and Metcalf's *Jim M*, increasing the latter's capacity to 23,601 cubic feet.

Dick Massey recalls the 'Chants':

'I joined the Jim M at the end of June 1957 in Drypool's yard in the Old Harbour at Hull. I was to spend nine months aboard this ship the first time, then later I signed on again as mate for a further three months. Jim M was one of the wartime 'Chants' – this stood for channel tankers, though twenty-five of them were completed as dry cargo ships which carried just over 400 tons of cargo. My first contact with these ships was at the age of seven when we lived at Howden and I used to have rides on low loader lorries delivering parts of a ship for assembly by Henry Scarr's yard at Hessle on the River Humber. This was part of England's entry into prefabricated shipbuilding. The design was for speed of building. Normal building was a very complex system from designing to lofting with individual wooden templates to be made for plates, the frames individually bent and the plates bent to match using bending rolls. A riveted ship then had to have many tens of thousands of rivet holes punched followed by the actual riveting together of the components.

The main design feature of the 'Chants' was that there was little rolling of any plating; the builder cut every part from flat plate as each part of the ship was built, and one set of templates would be used for marking out multiple pieces; they were then welded together, often using jigs, which allowed the components to be rotated so welding was as easy as possible, to produce pieces up to a maximum of about 13 tons or as large as road transport allowed. The parts would then be transported to various small shipyards for assembly. With quite small engines and a flat bottom to allow for beaching, they

were intended to be follow-up ships for the invasion of France. Built like a box with a point at the bow, they were not good sea ships. There were stories of 'Chants' capsizing on river trials with no ballast in the double bottom tanks – from then on these tanks were kept full if there was no cargo in the holds.

With the end of the war, these ships were decommissioned and sold or transferred to various owners. Many of them lived to give good service, several of them to cross the North Atlantic to Canada while others went to the Ionian Sea and further afield and reported to be still in service in the late 1990s. This one, Jim M was bought by Metcalf Motor Coasters. She was most suitable for the East Coast trading to small, shallow, drying harbours. They were easy to work on having two masts, two derricks, two cargo holds and two hatches covered with wooden hatch boards over steel beams. There were two cargo winches, the forward one connected to the windlass for heaving up the anchor. This connection amounted to an endless chain being driven by the forward winch, kept on tension by a block and tackle on the foremast. Of all things this was the most dangerous and most likely to break down at the worst time so a spare chain joining link was always kept on hand.

The crew's accommodation was quite spacious, as in their original guise these ships would have had a larger crew than the seven men carried in peace time. The standard crew on small coasters at that time was captain, mate, two engineers, cook steward and two deck hands. These should all be qualified men but more often than not from the captain down, promotion came from the ability to do the job in a seamanlike manner. Many times if a small coaster was in trouble through some navigational error or poor ship handling, inevitably this was attributed to ex-deepwater ship men without local 'hands on' experience. On this ship we were all coaster men with a thorough knowledge gained from visiting the same ports many times, and this made for an easier working routine throughout the ship. In the later part of this year (1957) road and railway was making a great challenge by carrying freight in bulk often more quickly and efficiently, so that often after discharging cargo there would be no new loading orders for a week or more, but this was not a holiday for the crew – for the mate, with orders from the marine superintendent, would have the crew doing maintenance that was usually done at dry docking time, and this may have helped balance the profit and loss for the ship.

For the first few months the ship was employed in carrying coal from Blyth to places like Norwich, up the River Yare above Great Yarmouth. Going to Norwich was always a time of concern for the captain as the Jim M never steered very well in shallow rivers, being dead flat bottomed. If she touched the mud, she just slid sideways, sometimes not stopping until she touched bottom on the other side of the river – not that the Yare was a very wide river. In the narrower parts it was about 100 feet wide with very few straight sections. Meeting another ship was always an interesting manoeuvre as both ships had to edge over as far as they could to the bank, and this might end up with both ships touching the bottom and sliding into the channel. With practice if we knew we were to meet another ship, the captain had favourite trees that we could get close enough to, to get a mooring wire round and hang on and let the other ship go past without any dramas.

At that time the Norfolk Broads were a Mecca for hire boats both sail and motor; they had instructions to pass port to port and to be confronted by a coaster must have terrified some of the crews, especially on a bend that turned to starboard as the deepest water was on the outside of the bend, with no room for anything on the port side as our stern would be almost touching the river bank. One of the crew would always be on the forecastle head to wave directions as to which way we needed the hire boats to go. I only remember having one bad collision with a cruiser and that was because it was tied up right by a big sign that said 'No Mooring Here'.

Depending on the tides at Great Yarmouth bridges, we might have been late getting away, so just before dark, a suitable place to moor for the night would be found, normally within rowing distance of one of the many waterside pubs along the river. Next morning at first light we would continue towards our destination, whether up or down stream depending where we were bound. As the unloading at Norwich was always slow whatever the cargo, the crew knew to expect a few days there and if loading away with malting barley after discharging our coal cargo, we could expect to be there a full week, with all the pleasure boats going by all day, mostly with friendly waves from the people aboard them. Whilst the ships were moored they posed no threat or even looked intimidating. With this holiday atmosphere all around, Norwich was a popular port with ships' crews. We did in fact load malting barley at Norwich for discharge at Boston, Lincolnshire, where the receiver of the barley was a local brewery far up a very narrow creek. With a local pilot on board, we made our way to the little quay, about one third the length of the ship. This creek was very deep for its width, from memory not more than 50 feet wide, and there being nowhere to turn we were all puzzled as to how we would escape from there.

As soon as we arrived, the pilot was gone with a wave of the hand, calling out "See you when you are ready to leave". From the Brewery staff we learned a little about the place; their grain was normally

brought by sailing barge, the Thyra *from their parent company's grain mill and silo at Old Harbour, Hull. The brewery silo could only hold a little over 100 tons and we had over 400 tons, so we were another week or more in port, the ship's owners being paid demurrage, that is compensation for every day over the agreed time when the ship should be empty of cargo. As freights were becoming hard to come by, they were happy for their ship to be used as a floating warehouse, and with the mill workers happy to open and close the ships hatches as required, most of the crew disappeared for a few days. My parents at that time were based and working in the town of Louth close by. They also had my Vespa motor scooter with them so I came back to the ship each day to check how things were going. The creek dried out completely at low tide and we still had no idea how were going to get the ship stern first back down the creek for a mile or so. We assumed the pilot would have a launch to act as a tug and tow us stern first to where we could turn round. We spent about ten days in that creek. When we had a date when all the cargo would be out, the local ship's agent sent telegrams to the absent crew members. The captain and cook at Woodbridge came back by car – the chief engineer lived in Gravesend and the second in Dartmouth, the rest of us were local. Sailing day came and the pilot arrived just after high tide, but no launch. The pilot asked if we were ready to depart, yes, "Ok take in all your stern lines" – we had men from the brewery letting our ropes go and the pilot told the foreman, "Ok, phone Joe and tell him we are ready". He then had us let go all the headropes and with the engine going slow ahead, drop the port anchor. With the tide ebbing the ship was stationary in the middle of the creek, engine stopped. The next thing the water was flowing past the ship at six knots, the anchor chain was shortened until the anchor started to drag and the ship was being pushed stern first down Witham Creek. The water that was used came from a sluice gate (operated by Joe) on the main River Trent to Boston canal, with access to the River Witham and the Wash. Later we met up with the mate of the* Thyra, *David Nash who told us that the method used to get the* Jim M *out of Witham Creek had been used for over sixty years. By the time we got the ship out of the creek and turned around, the tide had fallen too low for the passage over the shallows into Boston Deeps, so a safe anchorage was found to await the next tide. Orders were then to proceed to Blyth to load house coal for Whitstable in Kent. This was to set the pattern for the next few months, Blyth to Drakes Wharf at Strood near Rochester, and the occasional trip to Whitstable, with the ship returning each time with the holds empty. Winter gales were well set in, so the return passage north often took many days. Every anchorage that could provide shelter along the coast was used.*

In anything but calm weather, the main deck with no sheer and about 9ins of freeboard, Jim M *was awash, holding many tons of water once a big sea had filled it. This gave the ship a list making the weather deck almost submerged. With shorter seas, like crossing the Wash, the wave frequency was so quick, they just thumped aboard and bounced off. Like many small ships, 'Chants' had more buoyancy aft. If the ship was loaded just a few tons less than her marks, they were a far better sea ship. Empty and head to wind and sea they were prone to pounding and with their small engine power, were difficult vessels to work to windward. Fortunately, the* Jim M *had a worm steering box similar but much larger than that used in cars. This system gave a true rotation to the rudder stock and so side loads were negligible. Each time there was a lull or break in the weather a few miles might be gained, or we could even be blown further back. Crossing the Wash into a north west gale was never possible, even though this wind would be blowing off the land, the coastal land being low and flat gave no shelter. Once past the Wash it was often possible to stay very close inshore and get some shelter off the high cliffs along the Yorkshire coast. Harbours were to be avoided as there would be harbour dues to pay, so we had lots of anchoring drill. The captain and engineers carefully studied fuel consumption and bunkers remaining each time the ship had to run back for shelter, as the owners considered this a waste of fuel, so to stay or go was a big decision. Also that most important person, the cook only had enough money to buy one week's food at a time – what a situation, use fuel or have the crew on short rations. Somehow these small ships' cooks managed and we never starved.*

Then one day while on a voyage north the coastguard at Gorleston signalled 'call your owners by r/t' [radio telephone] and we were instructed to enter the nearest port and prepare the ship for laying up. The nearest port was Great Yarmouth on the River Yare. While awaiting the tide to enter the river, speculation was of whether we had a job tomorrow – soon enough we would know our future. On entering the river the harbourmaster hailed the ship with new orders to proceed to the lower quay at Southdown on the Gorleston side of the river, to moor there and await further orders. The owners' agent was soon aboard to tell us what plans were for the ship – until further information became available we were to resume our normal duties! This uncertainty went on for a few weeks, then we had another visit from the agent – we were all to remain working on board until further notice, and get paid. This was happening all along the coast, then in mid-December it was if a dark cloud had been lifted, there was freight to be moved everywhere.

Drakes at Strood had no coal left in stock, with the cold weather well established, coal was in short supply. For the next two months we moved coal from the nearest coal ports on the Humber to Strood, then with all coal stocks replenished, another slack period was forecast in the coal trade. Our next orders were 'proceed to Greenwich to load scrap for Middlesbrough'. On arrival at Greenwich we found that our loading berth was next door to a local riverside pub with the name of Cutty Sark *– the* Cutty Sark *was in drydock nearby. Robinsons wharf was a very small wharf jammed in between a narrow lane and the River Thames. There was no crane here, just a couple of steel chutes hinged off the quayside, the outer end being supported by the ship's derricks. It was obvious it was going to take many days to load 400 tons, with the average loads arriving being two or three tons. Our ship's second engineer spent each evening searching through the scrap looking for brass and other non-ferrous metals that had been missed by the scrap dealers. This was then sold back to the yard and the money then passed on to the cook to buy extras for the galley. Eventually we arrived at Middlesbrough to have the scrap discharged in under two hours using electro-magnetic grabs, then we moved upstream to load bagged fertiliser for Whitstable. On arrival, there was talk of the ship being laid up, and consequently I left the* Jim M *on the 24th of February to join the seagoing barge* Gazelle *the next day.*

I rejoined the Jim M *in July 1958 at Drake's Wharf, Strood, as mate. From there we departed for Immingham on the River Humber to load fertilizer for Ipswich and this was the routine for the next two and a half months. My personal wish was to move on and upwards with Metcalfs, and I had made a request to the company's marine superintendent for the opportunity to move on to one of their larger motor ships. Unfortunately for me the situation at that time was that there was a difficulty in finding suitable masters and mates for their smaller ships. The larger ships had larger crews with far better accommodation, modern navigation bridges – all the extras that made life easier on board – the downside was very little time in port, as the larger ships traded to the more modern ports where turnaround time instead of days was reduced to hours. My request was met with a firm "No, you are far more important to the company in the smaller ships where a hands-on approach is very important and to have a friendly relationship and rapport with the dockers and ship workers in the smaller ports". The freight rates paid to deliver cargoes to these smaller ports was far higher, as door-to-door delivery made economic sense to the cargoes' owners. However road transport was soon to start making inroads to this small ship trade.*

About this time some businessmen with agricultural interests in the Wash area formed a group often referred to as the Fosdyke Trading Company, although the ships were registered to the B.W. Steamship, Tug & Lighter Co. Ltd, Hull, in which G.F. Birch, a local Spalding mill owner, was one of the partners. They purchased three ships, one a 'Chant' they named Fosdyke Trader, Yarvic, *a puffer which they had lengthened by 20 feet and completely rebuilt as a motor ship, and the old and well known* Lizzie and Annie *which was also completely overhauled to suit their requirements. For the next few years these ships were kept very busy carrying the agricultural produce and requirements locally and to the near Continent, mainly Holland and Belgium. The area round the Wash is often referred to as New Holland as the area and crops are very similar to western Holland. Very soon small coasters from Holland were trading to all the ports round the Wash, then in the 1960s Dutch farmers started to buy up local farms and produce the same crops nearer the British market and soon the* Fosdyke Trader *was sold, becoming the* Fort Carillon *in 1961,* Janoline *in 1972 and the* Fermont *in 1975. She was beached on the south side of Seal Island, Nova Scotia in a sinking condition in November 1991 and abandoned. The smaller ships continued to trade, mainly carrying grains and animal feeds from Hull to the Wash ports. With the building of the Humber Bridge, lorries could now deliver easily and this was the end of the shipping side of their business. The* Yarvic *moved south to Kent, owned by Tony Lapthorne of Hoo on the Medway, while the ancient* Lizzie and Annie *went to Whitby to become a sand barge.'*

A shelter deck version of the 'Chants' was produced for the Far East and some of the 'Fabrics' were later modified. Captain J.H.K Griffin of Bideford bought the *Empire Farringay* in 1946 and, renamed *Farringay*, she carried coal throughout the 1950s to the local gas works at Bideford. As gas coal is bulky, various modifications were made and the trunk was widened and raised to form a quarter deck. This changed the gross tonnage to 461, grain capacity to 25,500 cubic feet and her deadweight to about 533 tons on a draught of a little over 11 feet. By the 1960s, she was carrying china clay to Preston. She started out with a 6-cylinder Petter engine which gave a speed of about 7.5 knots but she eventually finished up with triple screws driven by an 8-cylinder Kelvin and two 4-cylinder units on wing shafts, varying in age from 1965 to 1972. She was still in fine condition when Captain Griffin sold her to Greek owners for £15,000 in the latter part of the 1970s and she traded for a few more years as *Clare*.

This photograph, taken on board the 'Fabric' coaster Jim M *in July 1958, graphically demonstrates that using the side deck for access forward even in favourable summer weather was not advisable!* Dick Massey

At the end of the war, Captain J.H.K. Griffen bought the 'Fabric' coaster Empire Farringay *(410/44) and, renamed simply* Farringay, *ran her as a captain/owner for many years. He carried out extensive modifications, extending the trunk forward to include the forward hatch to increase cargo capacity, a similar arrangement to those produced for Far East service, though they were shelter deckers. He also fitted bulwarks in place of rails. He maintained her in good condition and so she lasted some thirty years in the coasting trade. DAVE HOCQUARD*

Apart from the 'Chants', a small number of conventional tankers were built. Three were built by Browns, joining the Everard fleet in 1946 and a few smaller ones by Rowhedge, Harkers and Pimblott. Most of the larger tankers were steam but towards the end of the war, a series of tankers were produced for service in the Far East. Some were steam but the majority were diesel, fitted with British 'Polar' 2-stroke engines. Sheer was also eliminated in this design but compensated for by increasing the erections at bow and stern. The most obvious feature was the large bridge amidships, as the poop was wholly used to accommodate the much larger Asian crew, as seen in the general arrangement of *Empire Tedilla* (947/46),190ft x 34ft x14ft 9ins. The pipework, valves and stripping valves were all inside the tanks with the hand wheels only on the deck. Theoretically, three compatible grades could be carried but in practice they probably only carried one grade as leaking valves could not be seen. In later tankers, the pipework was arranged on deck and it was possible to uncouple sections of pipe so that any possibility of contamination could be completely avoided. Japan surrendered before some of the vessels were commissioned and *Empire Tedson* was completed as *Arduity* for Everards. Having her from new had the advantage of clean tanks and so she was used for vegetable oils, lubricating oils and other clean products. Her sister *Amity* (ex-*Fossarina*, ex-*Empire Tedassa*) carried the first cargo of bulk lard from Brussels to Liverpool successfully and it became an important trade. The bridge layout and officers accommodation was retained but the much smaller European crew of eleven were able to have large single cabins, while on the boat deck, there was a single crew's mess with a single enlarged galley and the stewards' mess was converted into the crew's recreation room. The after galley, etc was converted to stores. Also, with the smaller crew, the lifeboats on the navigating bridge deck were no longer needed. *Arduity* was lengthened in 1956 and sold to Portuguese owners in 1969.

All were fitted with twin boilers which provided steam to run the pump room, deck gear and heating coils as required. On delivery, they were mostly split between the Anglo-Saxon Petroleum Co., who managed and later bought some of those in the Far East, and Everards, who took many of the remainder or later bought them in the 1950s. Everards used them in a variety of trades, particularly where heating of the cargo was required to keep it fluid enough for easy pumping, such as the basic oil used in the manufacture of lubricating oils and palm oil. Grease and printing ink, the latter which was loaded in Hamburg, required considerable heating. Often they worked on time charter or contracts of affreightment.

With the ending of the war, the emphasis tended to be on exports as the cost of the war had almost bankrupted the country. There were also shortages of a variety of materials while companies made the change to peacetime working and delivery dates stretched into years. One of the early post war deliveries was *Thorium* (604/47) for ICI Alkali Division, which was unusual in having a 'box' hold — that is a double hull similar to the 'Empire Fabric' type. It was part of the original design, as the vessel was intended to carry limestone from the company quarry and easy grab discharge was wanted with no difficult to reach parts. Although built by Grangemouth Dockyard, she was actually a repeat of *Cerium* (532/43), built by Goole Shipbuilding & Repairing, which had introduced the box hold design. The new vessel could carry about 653 tons, 100 tons more than the earlier vessel. *Thorium* had the moulded dimensions 185ft x 28ft 3ins x 11ft 10ins but the yard's own drawing gives 189 as the length BP and she was powered by a 7-cylinder, 2-stroke British 'Polar' engine of 520bhp. She was sold in 1964 to W.N. Lindsay Ltd, Leith, who renamed her *Roseburn* and in 1967 transferred her to W.N. Lindsay (Shipowners) Ltd. Douglas Lindsay, who was mate when the vessel was first acquired by his father, W.N. Lindsay, recalls:

'The Thorium *was built for ICI to hump limestone from their quarry at Llandulas on the North Wales*

M.V. "Empire Tedilla"

Diesel Coastal Tanker
General Arrangement.
Scale:- ⅛" = 1 Foot.

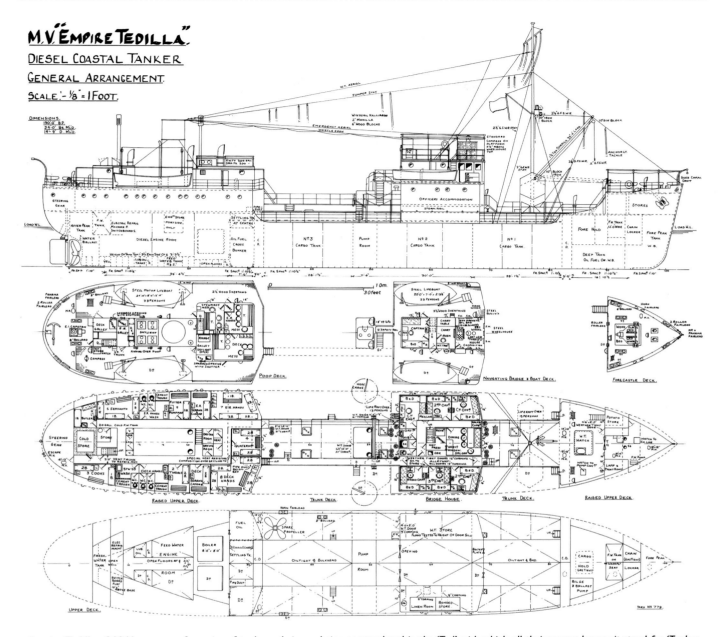

Empire Tedilla of 1946 was one of a series of tankers, their use being encapsulated in the 'Ted' with which all their names began; it stood for 'Tanker Eastern Diesel'. Production capacity for the more demanding requirements of larger diesel engines was becoming available in the latter part of the Second World War, although the series also included the 'Tes' tankers which were steam ('Tanker Eastern Steam'). Earlier in the war, a series of steam tankers were built modelled on the Pass of Melfort design, which had been developed by the Bulk Oil SS Co. during the 1930s. However, by this time, with progressive modifications such as the elimination of sheer, the bridge amidships and the increase in breadth, they were essentially a new design. Empire Tedilla herself was bought by her eastern managers, the Anglo-Saxon Petroleum Co. Ltd and renamed Forskalia but returned from the Far East after being bought by Harker (Coasters) Ltd and renamed Danesdale H in 1949. She was soon sold on to Shell-Mex & BP Ltd and renamed Shell Driller in 1952, for their UK-based operations. With the pipework incorporated within the tanks, any leaks could be difficult to spot and as charterers pressed for less risk of contamination and owners wished to avoid claims, pipework was progressively moved on deck in post war vessels. She was scrapped in 1966.

coast to their chemical works at Fleetwood and occasionally other cargoes. In many ways she was a precursor of modern coaster design, with one long hatch and hopper sides. These hopper sides extended the full length of the hold to make discharge quicker and easier with no side overhangs to trim out from. This was fine for ICI's stone cargoes but once sold into the general tramping trade they reduced the hold's cubic capacity a good deal. This meant she could not take her deadweight of lighter cargoes, and several times W.N. Lindsay considered cutting the hopper sides out, but they were an integral strength member of the ship's construction and if cut out would have needed to be replaced by other longitudinal stiffening and the cost always outweighed the earnings benefit. Another not too obvious feature on the plan is the long overhang at the fore end of the hold. If this could be filled the ship trimmed about six inches by the

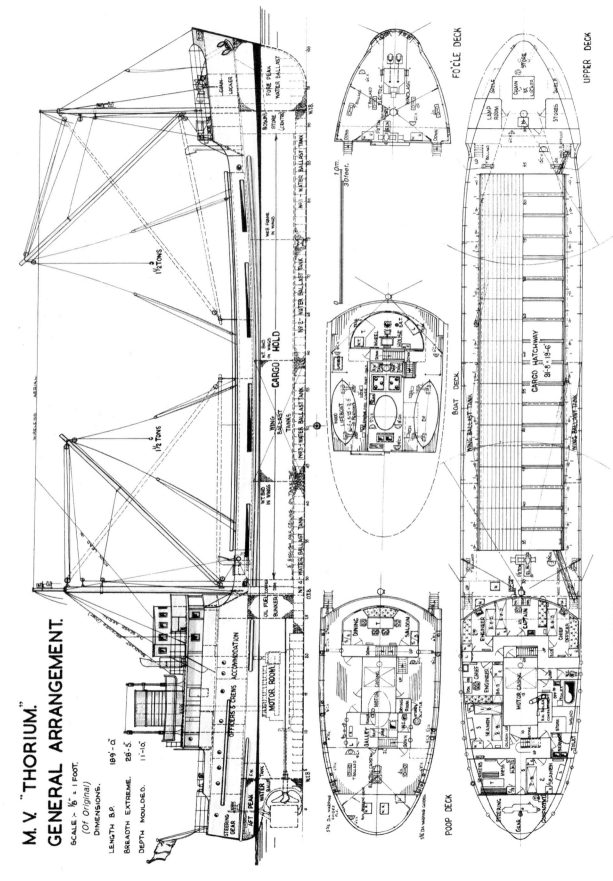

M.V. "THORIUM."
GENERAL ARRANGEMENT.

SCALE :- 1/8" = 1 FOOT.
(Of Original)
DIMENSIONS.

LENGTH B.P.   189'-0"
BREADTH EXTREME.   28'-5".
DEPTH MOULDED.   11'-10".

THE BURNTISLAND SHIPBUILDING COMPANY, LIMITED, BURNTISLAND, SCOTLAND.

FO'C'LE DECK

UPPER DECK

BOAT DECK

POOP DECK

stern, but it was long enough that getting cargo in there was always difficult. There was a booby (access) hatch at the fore end and a grain loading pipe could be put through that, but for other bulk cargoes, especially lighter ones, the long fore end was always a nuisance. However she was a good sea boat and a tough thing capable of punching through fairly rough conditions, although her beltings were at sea level in loaded trim and caused a lot of spray to fly up from them when slapped underneath by a sea.

The booby hatch was almost the end of the ship while I was on her. We were punching our way north with a coal cargo off Rattray Head in dirty weather when she slowly stopped rising to the seas. She got a dead feeling and old Sandy Richie, her skipper said "She's leaking. We're going to have to get her in.". The weather was bad enough for it to be a bit dodgy turning her through the seas that were running, so old Sandy took the wheel himself, watched for a bit of a lull, and put her hard to starboard. With one enormous roll to starboard we got round and ran before the weather into Peterhead, doing its job as a refuge port. By the time we got in, the foredeck was awash, but the leak didn't seem to be getting any worse. Investigation showed that the booby hatch, at the fore end had some fractured welds that attached it to the deck and each sea coming aboard was pushing some water into the hold. The deck plating and the butts of the shell plating had been electrically welded though the remainder was riveted. It all got sorted out, the hatch re-welded to the deck, and the cargo was eventually delivered to Kirkwall, but I have to say a ship not rising to the seas is a horrible feeling.

The ship was in trouble twice in its ICI days, going aground/ashore on Morecambe sands. The first time was early in her career and she was extensively rebuilt. The second time was less dramatic. Other than that she was a good sound vessel, her 'Polar' engine never missed a beat and she went about her business with the minimum of fuss for the time W.N. Lindsay had her. Running in the general tramping trades with some emphasis on the north of Scotland meant that she carried a wide variety of bulk cargoes and her life was very different from her first incarnation carrying limestone. Another feature which anticipated modern coaster design was that she had very high coamings and low side decks, almost like a [trunk deck] tanker. In a ship with wooden hatch boards and tarpaulins, this made hatching up hard work. The boards had to be thrown up over head high from the side decks and by the time you had done a side you knew you'd been working hard. I believe the ship may still be trading round Turkey with her original 'Polar' engine [she was acquired by Turkish owners in 1985]. If so, she is a remarkable survivor and shows how sound and practical her design was.

When W.N. Lindsay came to sell the Roseburn in 1973 I happened to be on leave and my father invited me along to the handover in London. She was sold to Aegean Island Greeks who put her under the Honduras flag (as Stavros Emmanuel). The agreed purchase price was £15,000. We assembled in the office of our sale and purchase broker, T.W. Tamplin, based in the old Baltic Exchange Chambers in St. Mary Axe. The senior broker, Cyril Warby, conducted proceedings.

The ship was lying at Bow Creek and the buyer's superintendent was dispatched to check her over and make sure everything was the same as when they made their main inspection some weeks before. He also sounded the fuel tanks, as this fuel would be a separate purchase. The buyer's party consisted of two rather sharp young men who had fairly fluent English and a grizzled older man who sat at the back and said very little. He had very much the air of an old sea captain.

Late in the morning word came through from the superintendent that the ship was fine and they could go ahead with the purchase. There then followed a bit of discussion about how payment was to be made. Banker's draft? Certified cheque? The older buyer looked puzzled and said something, pointed in Greek to the young men in front of him. One of them smiled and said "No problem", then produced a suitcase. Inside it was £15,000 in cash. Warby's people had to set to and count it, in mainly £20 notes. This took half an hour before it was agreed there was indeed £15,000 in the case. My father, escorted by one of Warby's assistants and one of the sharp young men, took the suitcase down to the bank next door to the Baltic, and there the bank staff had to go through it all again before accepting the deposit.

In the meantime the Bills of Sale had been drawn up, and were ceremonially signed as soon as the bank party returned. The superintendent was phoned to say the ship was now theirs and his crew, who had been sitting in the ship's messroom waiting, immediately spread out to look at their new purchase. Our captain shook hands with the superintendent, wished him all the best, and left. With the ship sold in nice time for lunch, the buyers were invited to join us in the better restaurant in the Baltic's basement but they declined, being keen to get the new registration completed and to go aboard their purchase. Through this, the now empty suitcase had sat on the broker's office floor and my father picked it up to return it to the buyers. The older man finally cracked a smile, patted father on the shoulder and said, "You have it. Special present from me" and father had it for the rest of his life.'

At the end of hostilities, yards which had been exclusively employed on naval work began to look for peacetime work and Vosper Ltd, Portsmouth, began offering a smart little coaster able to

carry about 350 tons on a draught of 9ft 6ins at about 9.5 knots, powered by a 'Polar' 4-cylinder, 2-stroke of 360 bhp at 350 rpm. Displacement was expected to be 550 tons. They eventually found a customer in T.G. Irvine of Sunderland and as *Ferndene* (313/49) joined his fleet of small coasters. The large square windows of the saloon, captain's day room and the general layout is reminiscent of the Dutch coasters being built just before the war. Ballast was low at a total of 73 tons including the double bottom, for a vessel with the moulded dimensions 125ft x 23ft 6ins x 10ft 4ins but she was quite fine lined with a block coefficient of 0.71. She was the last of his fleet by 1974, when *Ferndene* was scrapped.

Leading owners slowly began to get new vessels delivered and *Sapphire* (1,000/49), 199ft 10ins x 34ft 0ins x 14ft 9ins, joined William Robertson. James Robertson explained that they would have preferred an all-aft design but were eventually persuaded by the builders, Grangemouth Dockyard,

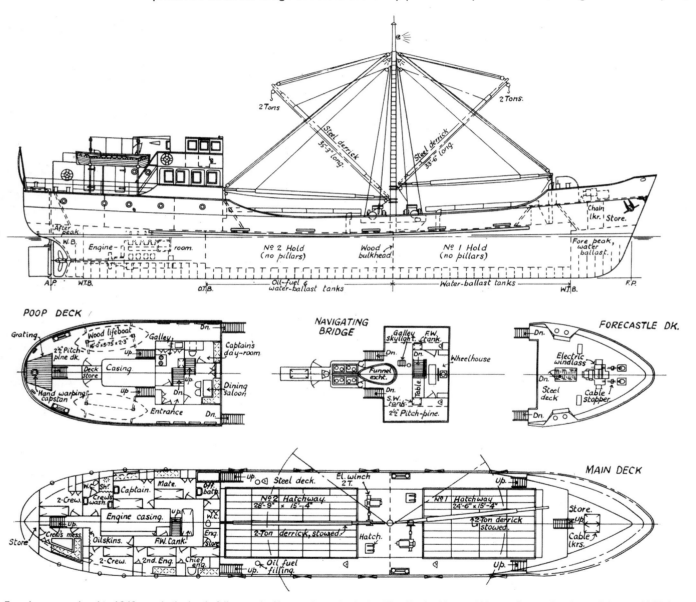

Ferndene, completed in 1949, was built closely following this Vosper plan published in The Shipbuilder and Marine Engine-Builder *in February 1947. It was intended to be a standard design with slight variations to suit owners, the company looking to find civilian work at the end of the Second World War. However, it seems that only this one example was built and the company in fact found plenty of naval work to occupy their Portsmouth yard. The design was very Dutch in style and may well have been based on a Dutch design, as for example the prominent combined bulwark and mooring bollards. The stem was well raked, as was the latest practice at the time, with the upper part of rounded plate construction merging with a convex stem bar lower down. A streamlined rudder was fitted beneath the cruiser stern. Coasters of this size did not necessarily have double bottoms but one was included in this design as were cargo battens. The proportion used for ballast or fuel oil could be varied to suit the owner and as completed she could carry up to 37 tons, enough for up to 7,000 miles. Only the winches were electric, with a hand windlass and capstan. There were two 3-cylinder Russell Newbury engines of different sizes driving generators, and one also included a clutch driven pump and compressor for starting air, although the 'Polar' 2-stroke main engine also incorporated a compressor as well as a scavenge air pump. The vessel achieved 9.75 knots light, with a fully loaded speed of 9.57 knots, easily exceeding contract speed.*

that they could give them a better ship with 3 tons extra deadweight for example. In service she proved inferior to the all-aft ships and so they decided to sell her when only nine years old. Her raised quarter deck design made her attractive as a collier and she was purchased by A.S. Davidson, the Belfast coal merchants, for £67,500. Robertson's vessels were strongly built to load limestone at their North Wales quarries and both the bridge and the poop were inset, and the stern protected by heavy belting. Davidson's office was called 'Mayfair' and so they renamed her *Mayfair Sapphire*. Davidson's was taken over by Cawoods and in 1971 her owners became Cawoods Fuels (Northern Ireland) Ltd, Belfast. They sold her to Cypriot owners for about £26,000, to become *Ioulia K* and she was eventually broken up as *Babi* in 1983.

Everards continued with their low profile raised quarter deckers, begun in the 1930s and suitable for the West Country coal trade, as for example *Austerity* (592/47). *Sonority* and *Severity* were the largest that Fellows' yard could launch into the River Yare but the style of vessel was continued with deliveries from other yards and ended with *Century* (780/56) and *Clarity* (764/57) from Goole. The characteristic low profile of bridge forward of amidships and masts at each end with the derricks facing each other, was augmented at the after hatch by a kingpost and derrick directly behind the bridge, as this last pair were over 200 feet in length. The smaller *Sonority* (589/52), 174ft x 27ft 6ins x 11ft 7ins, with a deadweight of 750 tons, had a 5-cylinder, 2-stroke Newbury engine of 500 bhp to give 11 knots and was designed by Reg Stanley, Fellows' naval architect. As Fellows' yard was owned by Everards, Mr Stanley may well have had a hand in the design of the similar size vessels delivered from other yards. Ethel Everard recalled that she was launched by Mrs Tracey Fowler of the Cantley sugar factory at Great Yarmouth at the second attempt, as the bottle failed to break the first time! Sugar beet was often to be a cargo until the trade fell away in the 1960s. Cement to northern destinations such as Lossiemouth ended in the 1960s also, as cement factories or at least bulk-rail bagging-plants were built in Scotland by the cement manufacturers. Return cargoes could be coal to Hythe Quay, Colchester, both household and gas coal for the gas works there. It was not uncommon to be brushing along the bottom of the channel to reach the quay! Coal was also taken to Ilfracombe, Truro, Hale, Padstow, Looe and Teignmouth, often loaded at Blyth. It was then a short voyage to Dean Quarry. In order to secure return cargoes, Everards purchased Dean Quarry at St. Keven, Cornwall in 1956 and a quarry in Guernsey in 1960, so that if the weather was bad for one, they could always load at the other. This convenient arrangement collapsed literally, when part of a graveyard fell into the Guernsey quarry. Further quarrying was banned there and it was decided

Austerity of 1947 loading china clay at Par on 28th June 1964. She has the typical low profile of Everard coasters built from the mid-1930s to the 1950s. Return cargoes of china clay were important, as were stone cargoes from Cornwall. However, as the cargo to Cornwall was often coal, the hold had to be very carefully cleaned out before china clay was loaded, as it was often destined for paper mills. Clean cargoes ensured regular work for owner and crew.
DAVE HOCQUARD

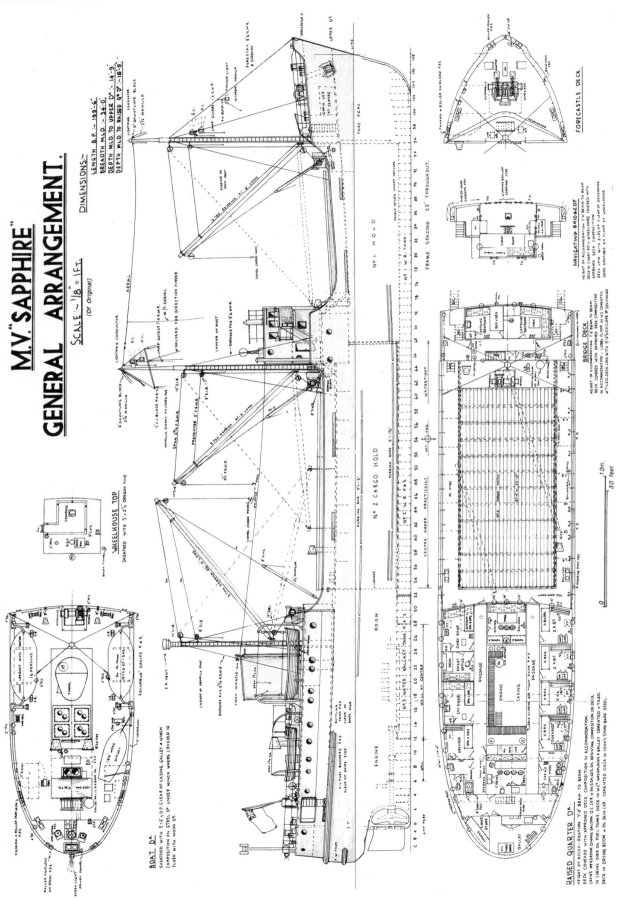

M.V. "SAPPHIRE"
GENERAL ARRANGEMENT.

SCALE ~ 1/8" = 1 FT.
(of original)

DIMENSIONS:-

LENGTH B.P. :- 199'-6"
BREADTH MLD :- 34'-0.
DEPTH MLD. TO UPPER D :- 14'-9
DEPTH MLD. TO RAISED Q'R D. :- 18'-9

WHEELHOUSE TOP
SHEATHED WITH 5' x 2¼" OREGON PINE

BOAT DK.
SHEATHED WITH 5' x 2' D.P CLEAR OF CASING GALLEY & WINCH
COMPOSITION ON STEEL D' UNDER WINCH WHERE CROSSED IN
FLUSH WITH WOOD D'S

FORECASTLE DECK.

NAVIGATING BRIDGE?

HEIGHT OF ACCOMMODATION 7'6 BEAM TO BEAM.
DECK IN CHART RM. & WHEELHOUSE COVERED WITH
APPROVED DECK COMPOSITION
IN ACCOMMODATION - LOBBY FLOOR IN W/C CEMENTED
& TILED. DECK LAND WITH 5' x 2' D.P. CLEAR OF DECKHOUSE.
WOOD GRATINGS ON FLOOR BY. WHEELHOUSE

BRIDGE DECK.

HEIGHT OF ACCOMMODATION 7'6 BEAM TO BEAM.
DECK COVERED WITH APPROVED DECK COMPOSITION ON DECK.

RAISED QUARTER D.

HEIGHT OF ACCOMMODATION 7'-0 BEAM TO BEAM.
DECK COVERED WITH APPROVED DECK COMPOSITION IN ACCOMMODATION.
IN CASING OVER OIL FUEL TANKS DECK IN W/C WASHPLACES & GALLEY COMPOSITION & TILED.
DECK IN DRYING ROOM & OIL SKIN LKR CEMENTED. DECK IN COOK'S STORE BARE STEEL.

No 1. HOLD

No 2 CARGO HOLD

ENGINE ROOM

FRAME SPACING 22" THROUGHOUT.

CENTRAL GIRDER PRACTICALLY

ABOVE: General Arrangement of Sapphire completed in 1949, showing profile and higher decks (above), with the upper (or main deck) on the following page. The vessel proved to be a retrograde step for Robertsons and was not as efficient in service as the 'all-aft' designs introduced before the war and developed subsequently.

NEXT PAGE BELOW: General Arrangement of the upper (or main deck) of Sapphire.

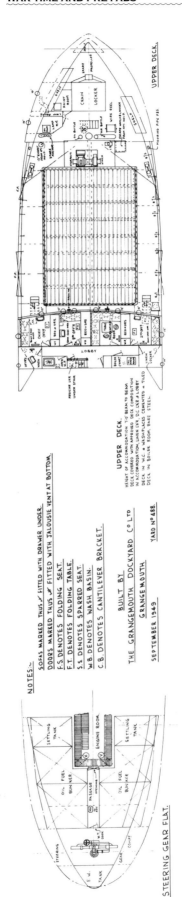

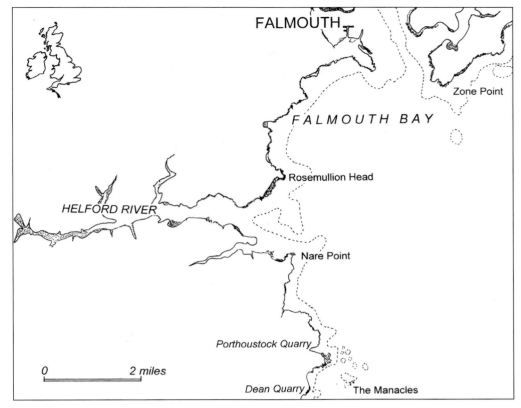

to sell Dean in 1970 as the single quarry was not really viable. Less common were cargoes of china clay from Par or Fowey to Antwerp and Ghent, and, in December, cargoes of sugar beet for the British Sugar Corporation at Selby from Cowes. Though comfortable sea boats, as time went on the two-berth cabins and the large number of hatch boards to be manhandled made keeping crews increasingly difficult, though the last of the vessels, *Clarity*, had steel hatch covers, while *Continuity* and *Centricity* were about the largest for the mills at Selby.

During the war, Everards moved into larger four hatch ships, beginning with the delivery of *Supremity* (2074/44) and the deeper draughted *Superiority* (2,145/47). It is probable that they were built to 'Icemaid' collier dimensions, as there was a pressing need for colliers and so approval for their building would have been straightforward to obtain. *Icemaid* (1,964/36) was a collier built for the Gas, Light & Coke Co. by S.P. Austin & Son Ltd, Sunderland in 1936, with the registered dimensions 270ft x 40ft x 17.2ft ,and her lines and details were used for a standard series of steam colliers built during the war mostly by the Grangemouth Dockyard Co. The maiden voyage of *Superiority* was from Goole to the Thames via King's Lynn, where 1,995 tons of sugar beet were loaded, bound for the sugar refineries. She was unable to load her full deadweight of 2,550 tons because of the tides. Perhaps with this in mind, they ordered the slightly smaller sisters *Stability* (1,490/49) and *Security* from Goole, which were more versatile, three-hatch, raised quarter deckers. With the moulded dimensions 225ft 6ins x 36ft 0ins x 16ft 0ins, they could carry 1,740 tons. They were powered by Newbury P type 4-cylinder, 2-strokes of 800 bhp at 250 rpm, to give a speed of 11 knots. Though fitted for timber and able to carry 1,600 tons of wood pulp, they were initially running coal from Blyth and beet from King's Lynn. They soon proved their worth and the

Map showing the location of Dean and Porthoustock quarries south of Falmouth. In the 19th and 20th centuries, quarries were often developed on the coast where good hard rock could be got for roadstone, which could then be easily distributed by sea from very basic jetties. These were two of the well known quarries frequented by coasters. Dean Quarry had a particularly dangerous approach, past the Manacles which had claimed many a passing ship. Efforts were made to reduce the danger by blasting but this did not lower the rocks sufficiently to remove them as a hazard. The quarry was purchased by Everards in 1956 and supplied their ships with a return cargo for a number of years after delivering coal to nearby ports.

Another important source of stone was the Channel Isles and this photograph shows *Marshlea*, with her hatches off, carefully approaching Ronez Quarry, to load on a misty day. The hatch beams have been left in place, as the stone cargo would flow either side of them and was just brushed off before the hatch boards were replaced. She was built in 1957, especially for a ten year time charter to the quarry company but in later years return cargoes of cement became more important and she was converted into a dedicated cement carrier after she was sold to Ronez Ltd.
DAVE HOCQUARD

opportunity was taken to improve the design by increasing the breadth by about two feet and their carrying capacity but staying under 1,600 tons gross. This was a significant figure, as a full time radio operator with a fully equipped radio room was required if they were any larger. First of the improved deadweight class was *Speciality* (1,570/51), 225ft 4ins x 37ft 10ins x 16ft 0ins, from Grangemouth, able to carry 1,850 tons. Goole also participated in the building programme and a total of ten vessels of the improved class had been reached when the last was delivered in 1958. *Singularity* was specially prepared for the Coronation Review in 1953 and had a mizzen mast added to her outfit.

Although having the same dimensions, there were design differences between the two yards and the Grangemouth vessels had a few inches less sheer aft, resulting in a slightly lower stern which curved inwards to give a vertical bulwark. This was not a feature of the Goole vessels, which had a straight raked stern similar to the bow and no stanchions to the boat deck. These were fitted from new in the Grangemouth vessels, as they were needed to prevent the lifeboats swinging in

Yorkshire Coast (750/59), with her MacGregor hatches rolled back, is seen going alongside Ronez Quarry, Jersey. The nice clean hold and the frames and strong hatch coaming show up prominently. The size and design of the hold was probably chosen with long steel cargoes in mind. She belonged to the Tyne-Tees Steam Shipping Co. Ltd, part of the Coast Lines group who were mostly in the liner trades but as she was a single deck ship, she was able to carry bulk cargoes when liner work was short.
DAVE HOCQUARD

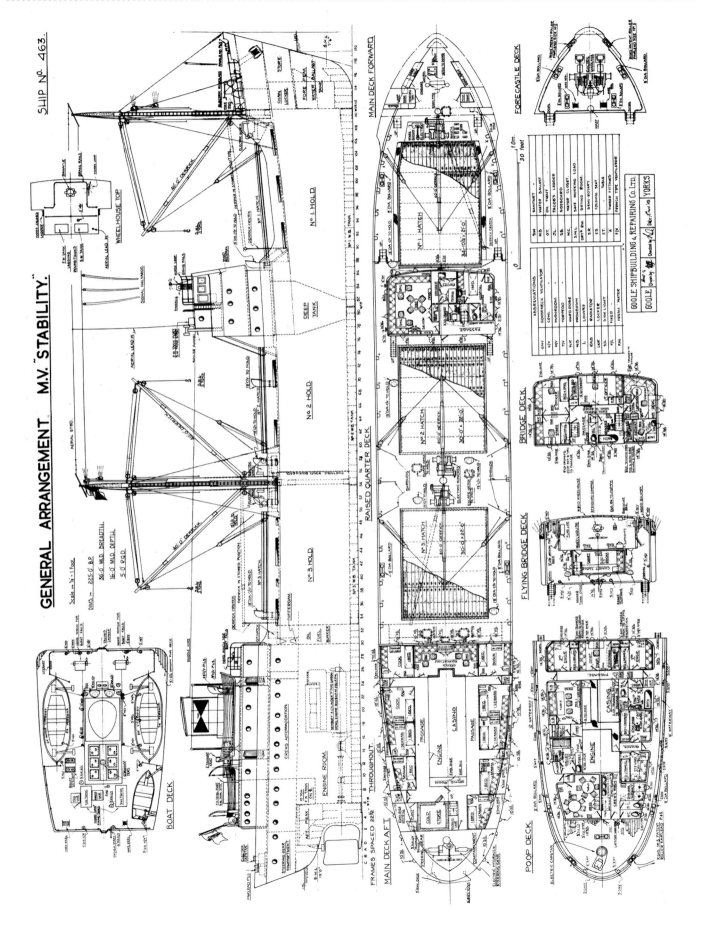

GENERAL ARRANGEMENT M.V. "STABILITY."

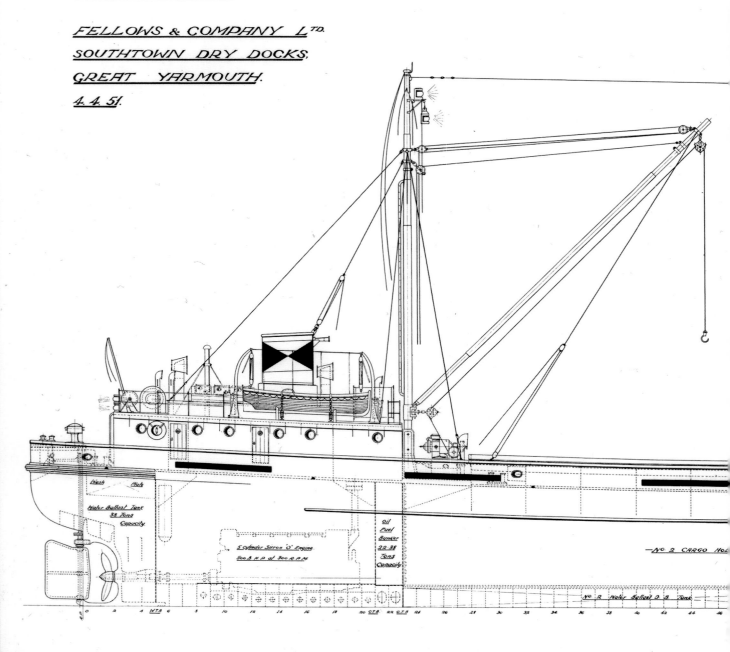

Nºˢ 356 & 357.

GENERAL ARRANGEMENT – PROFILE.

SCALE :- ¼" = ONE FOOT.

FELLOWS & COMPANY Lᵀᴰ.
SOUTHTOWN DRY DOCKS,
GREAT YARMOUTH.
4. 4. 51.

ABOVE AND TWO PAGE SPREAD FOLLOWING: This particularly stylish general arrangement drawing was produced by Reg Stanley, who was the resident naval architect at Fellows & Co. Ltd, Great Yarmouth. It depicts Sonority of 1952, which was built for F.T. Everard & Sons Ltd (and owners of the yard) along with a sistership. It was produced on two sheets, probably because the drawing office only had a 24 inch width printer and so this limited the height of the prints that could be produced. It is reproduced here exactly as drawn in all its intricate detail. The original drawing had a very simple border but some yards still used the more intricate borders which were popular in the steam era. An attractive and ingeneous border was that used by Goole, as shown on the drawing of Sodality (page 42), where the stylised name of the yard was used to embellish the corners. The original drawings were traced onto special waxed, fine tracing linen,

32

<u>DIMENSIONS.</u>
<u>LENGTH. B.P.   174'-0"</u>
<u>BREADTH. MLD.   27'-6"</u>
<u>DEPTH. MLD.   11'-7"</u>

Chain
Locker

Wash Plate

—No.1 CARGO HOLD—

Head Bulkhead

Fore peak Water Ballast Tank.
89 Tons Capacity.

No.1 Water Ballast D.B. Tank.

the waxing process making it reasonably transparent but often with a bluish tint. It was glossy on the back and matt on the working side. Even so it did not take ink well and was usually prepared further by gently rubbing it all over with French chalk powder, which was then removed to make it a more ink receptive matt surface. In the 1960s, plastic tracing film became generally available and this could be used either with ink or special pencils; it was considerably more transparent although some types were prone to tearing easily. In the larger yards, the naval architect would hand over to the draughtsman who usually did the tracing, adding details as they became available from equipment suppliers, although some yards used tracers also. The drawing was continually updated and in the case of Sonority here, all the work was done by Reg Stanley himself. This pair of drawings are numbered 32 and 33 but there is also a

Nᵒˢ 356 & 357.

GENERAL ARRANGEMENT – DECKS.

SCALE:- ¼" = ONE FOOT.

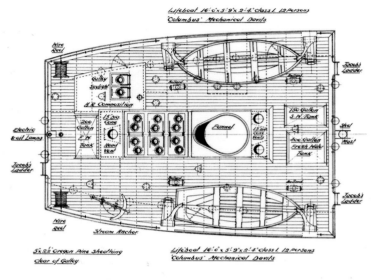

— CASING TOP —

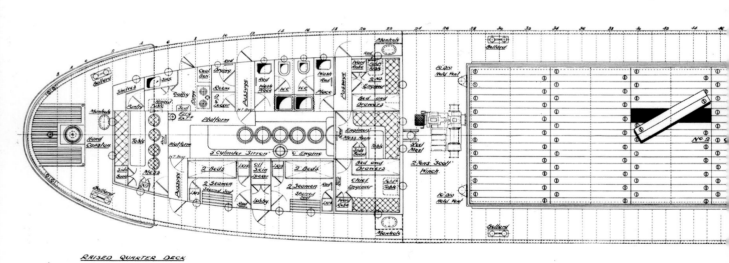

RAISED QUARTER DECK

surviving 'as fitted' deck plan, which is numbered 60, the main changes being the addition and positioning of wire reels. In general, unless there was time or the owner requested it, no final 'as fitted' drawing was made. As can be seen here, they were often beautiful examples of industrial art and although it was possible to make corrections to them, care had to be taken that it did not leave vague outlines when printed. Everard vessels were built with both the bridge and boat decks cantilevered out and so free of supports to foul the jetty, which also made moving a mooring rope forward or aft particularly simple. However, it was realised that if the ship was listing and attempts were made to lower the lifeboat on the high side, it would be able to swing in under the boat deck and become trapped. To prevent this, the vessels with this type of boat deck were fitted with two vertical bars, running from the edge of the boat deck to the bulwarks below, which prevented this happening.

33

ELLOWS & COMPANY Lᵀᴰ.
OUTHTOWN DRY DOCKS,
REAT YARMOUTH.
4. 51.

DIMENSIONS.
LENGTH B.P.	174'-0"	
BREADTH MLD.	27'-6"	
DEPTH MLD.	11'-7"	

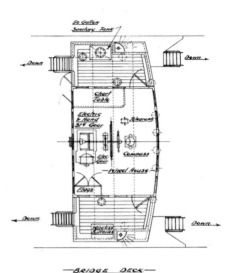

—BRIDGE DECK—

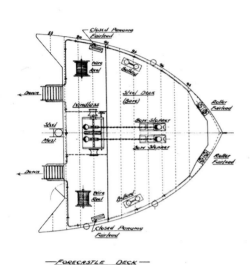

—FORECASTLE DECK—

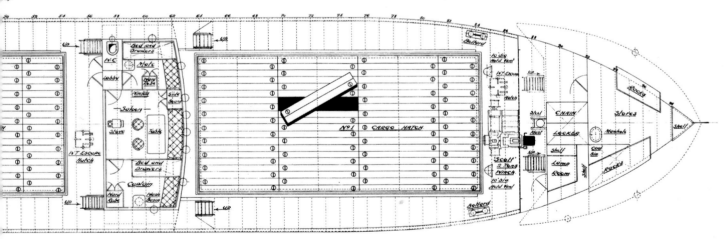

—MAIN DECK—

under the cantilevered out boat deck. The freeing ports also differed, with Grangemouth-built ships having the three for the well deck placed further aft. Their vessels also had slightly rearranged accommodation in the bridge superstructure, which meant there were only two portholes on the starboard side at raised quarter deck level, rather than the three of the Goole ships which had 12ins portholes rather than 10ins. Not surprisingly, deadweights also varied, so that the last of the class, *Fred Everard* (1,542/58), had a deadweight of 1,883 tons. Deliveries were initially rapid, with four from Grangemouth between August 1951 and June 1952, and two from Goole. They were painted corn yellow and were soon known as the 'yellow perils'. They proved comfortable for the crew and good sea keeping boats. Initially fitted with wooden hatches, later ones had MacGregor steel hatches.

They also proved ideal for expanding Everards trading area, as they were suitable for the Baltic (coal out – timber/pulp home). G.R. LeClercq recalls how these cargoes were discharged in Belfast and Dublin using the single derrick rig: '*The dockers got a list on as soon as possible, then they rigged a rope guy through blocks to hang from the mast with enough weight of old iron hooks, chain, etc to bring the derrick back aboard with an occasional pull of a rope on the head of the derrick by the hatch man/guy man. This proved very quick and efficient and all general, timber, telegraph poles, pulp and paper were handled in this way.*'. Rates were initially favourable and it was worth going out in ballast to Norway and Sweden for pulp in the 1950s, the rules permitting generous amounts of cargo on deck. Mediterranean trades were also entered, for example, phosphate rock was loaded in Casablanca. In the latter case it was important that they had a prompt voyage, as they could run out of fresh water. *Stability* was the largest for Camber Quay, Portsmouth with coal for the gas works, while *Similarity* carried coal for many years to Kingsbridge, Devon. Sometimes coal was carried for Stephenson Clarke if they were short of ships and *vice versa*. Return cargoes of stone for the Thames could be loaded at their quarries. Another regular cargo was cement clinker from Tunnel Cement at West Thurrock to Glasgow, where it was ground and bagged for sale. It was not popular with the crews because of the dust and made the decks slippery when wet. The company's long association with Unilever and its predecessors lead to several of the ships carrying grain and soya beans from the Continent to their plant on the Thames. Most served the company for over twenty years, though two were lost and one scrapped following a collision.

CHAPTER 5
POST WAR PRIORITIES AND THE NEW LOOK

In this chapter moulded dimensions are given unless otherwise stated.

With the gas and electricity undertakings Nationalised there was a priority given to building collier ships but even prior to this, major coal suppliers had placed orders for new colliers. Most were large vessels and not strictly coasters, although some smaller vessels were needed for destinations with draught or other restrictions.

Many of the colliers built after the war continued to be steam but the smaller vessels were mostly motor ships. Stephenson Clarke had a number of customers on the Thames and south coast where smaller ships were needed and had four built between 1947 and 1950 from different yards. *Henfield* (1,098/49), 212ft 5ins x 34ft 3ins x 15ft 4ins, was one of a pair from Grangemouth able to carry 1,530 tons on a draught of 14ft 7¼ins. After twenty years with the company, she was sold to Greek owners, renamed *Danae III*, then *Tsimentefs* and was finally broken up as *Thanassis*. These were followed by several three and four hatch vessels, such as *Amberley* (1,934/53), 249ft 5ins x 38ft 6ins x 18ft 6ins, able to carry 2,405 tons on a draught of 17ft 3½ins. The special features to suit the vessel for the coal trade were hopper sides, extensive ballast capacity and wire compressors, commonly used for mooring colliers. They were also designed to be self-trimmers, that is they could be loaded with coal to their summer load line and be on the lowest trimming charges, and this had to be officially demonstrated and a certificate issued by a British Transport Docks Port. The owners did have a slight advantage as they could choose the type of coal and the port likely to be most favourable to the ship. The accommodation was of a high standard with single berth cabins but the bridge accommodation was unusual in having the officers' cabins on the raised quarter deck and the captain, saloon and pantry above on the bridge deck. *Amberley* was delivered with radar, which was expensive at the time but attracted a reduced insurance premium. It was very useful in the crowded waters of the Thames and south coast, where they would frequently be sailing. She foundered off the Wash on 2nd April 1973, after developing a list during storm force north westerly winds while on her regular passage from Goole to Shoreham with coal. The crew were rescued by helicopter and she sank near the East Dudgeon Buoy. Stephenson Clarke's biggest motor vessels, such as *Minster* (3,194/46), were largely confined to supplying the gas and electricity companies.

Henfield, 1,098 gross tons, was one of the smallest colliers built for Stephenson Clarke following the Second World War. She was completed in 1949. The solid foremast and stumpy kingpost aft were purely to support the tackle used to open the steel hatch covers, which stowed concertina fashion vertically at the ends of the hatches rather than beyond them. The accommodation was in a sunken poop at main deck level, so the line of the raised quarter deck bulwarks continued right aft, merging with the poop deck on which the boats were stowed. WAINE COLLECTION

AMBERLEY

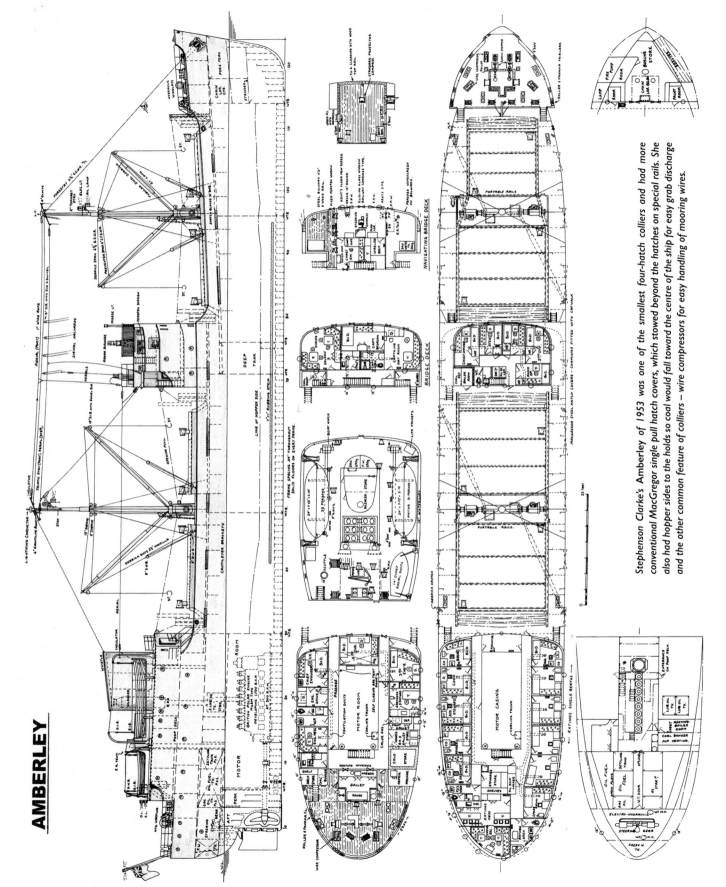

Stephenson Clarke's Amberley of 1953 was one of the smallest four-hatch colliers and had more conventional MacGregor single pull hatch covers, which stowed beyond the hatches on special rails. She also had hopper sides to the holds so coal would fall toward the centre of the ship for easy grab discharge and the other common feature of colliers – wire compressors for easy handling of mooring wires.

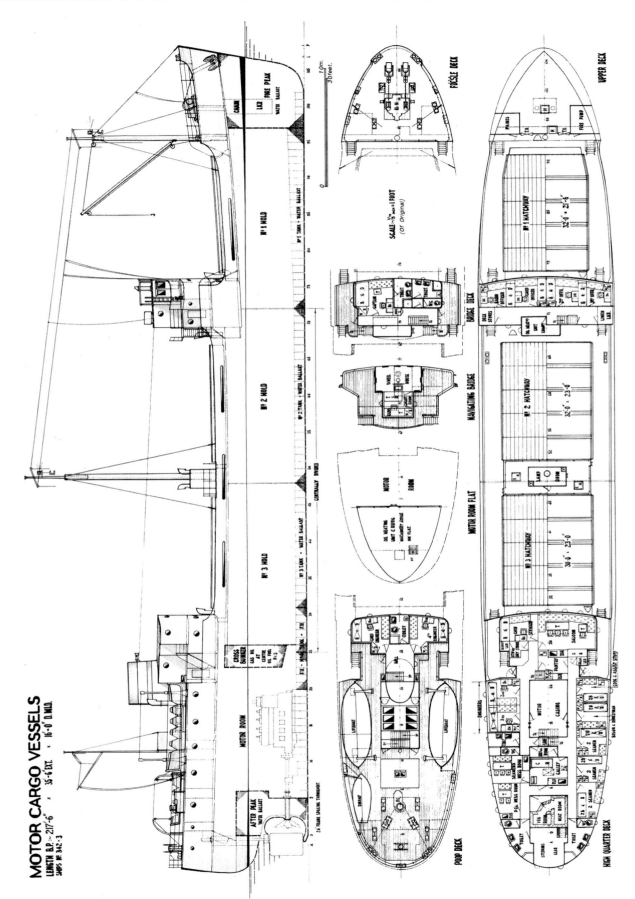

In many cases the shipyard knew the proposed name for a ship by the time the updated General Arrangement drawing was being prepared and construction was imminent but apparently not here. The plan shows the sisters Eskwood (1,273/51) and Copsewood (1,272/51), which were built for the Constantine Shipping Co. Ltd by the Burntisland Shipbuilding Co. Ltd.

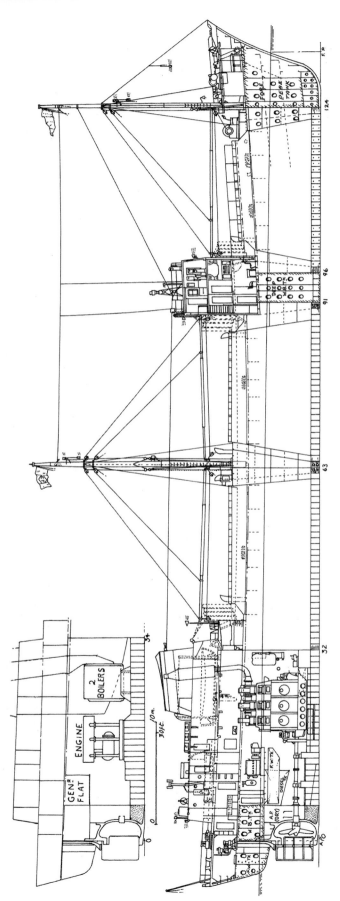

Profile of Cardiffbrook which was built in 1952 with a Doxford engine, while her sister Cardiganbrook was fitted with steam machinery. The layout of the latter's steam machinery is shown (top) for comparison. As can be seen, in vessels of this size there was little difference in the space required (or weight) for either type of machinery so it was a matter of reliability, fuel consumption and fewer crew needed in the motor ship. They were both built for the Williamstown Shipping Co. Ltd (Comben Longstaff & Co. Ltd – managers).

Constantines of Middlesbrough were active in the east coast coal trade to smaller London wharves and often carried coal to the cement works at Swanscombe with a return cargo of cement, although they also regularly carried grain cargoes for smaller ports. As alluded to above, coal trade vessels tended to have wire compressors for mooring, which assisted temporarily holding the ship as it was moved to and fro beneath coal shoots, and more bulkheads in the holds so that two or more grades could be carried by the same ship. These features are seen in *Copsewood* (1,272/51), 217ft 6ins x 35ft 4ins x 16ft 1in, and sister ship *Eskwood* (1,273/51). Both were completed in November 1951 by the Burntisland Shipbuilding Co. Ltd and were powered by a direct reversing British 'Polar' 4-cylinder, 2-stroke of 640bhp at 250rpm. Deadweight was 1,675 tons on a draught of 15ft 8½ins. Crew accommodation was fairly generous in the poop, which was stepped up from the main deck and, unusually, the officers' saloon was aft; usually it was below the bridge, so it was the steward who had to brave the elements to bring meals from the galley. Deck gear was all electric, with electro-hydraulic steering gear, and no cargo handling was expected to be done but one derrick was fitted to the foremast. She served the company well and was not sold until 1967, when she went to the Knossos Shipping Co. Ltd, Cyprus, for about £25,000 and was renamed *Dora*.

Although the war had ended seven years previously, there were still shortages of steel for the shipbuilding industry but a surplus of aluminium production, which was now needed in reduced quantities. Its use in shipbuilding offered the possibility of reduced weight and easy availability, so it was utilised for some funnel casings and lifeboats. Popular engines also had long delivery times and were more expensive than steam plant, which was more readily available.

It is interesting to note that Comben Longstaff, having managed motor coasters for a number of years, placed orders for steamers with Lewis of Aberdeen. Steam machinery runs slowly at 70 to 100rpm, whereas diesel engines run two or three times faster with a higher rate of wear. They are also made up of more complicated parts which require replacing more often. In the coal trade the voyages were short and fuel consumption less important but reliable deliveries, especially in winter, were essential if the shipping company was to retain the contract. The relationship between owner and builder was close, and became even closer when Andrew Lewis became a director of the Williamstown Shipping Company. It is interesting to speculate that this closer tie was a precursor to the ordering of *Cardiffbrook* (1,812/52) to be powered by the first Lewis-built Doxford 3-cylinder opposed piston engine, while her sister was to be the steam *Cardiganbrook* (1,780/52). Both engines developed 1,100bhp to give a service

speed of 11.5 knots. The moulded dimensions were identical at 250ft 6ins x 38ft x 17ft 9ins, but the motor ship was able to carry four more tons at 2,272 tons. Hold volume was 119,948 cubic feet (grain), 2,620 cubic feet more cargo space, as the engine room was slightly longer in the steamer. The steamer would require about two extra crew (firemen) but they were offset against engine room spares, etc, at £5 to £10 less a day and boiler oil was considerably cheaper as was the machinery, so in these larger vessels the motor advantage was still small. Obviously Mr Longstaff continued to favour steam, as Lewis went on to build the closely similar steamer *Devonbrook* (1,414/54).

In the 1930s, experiments with the streamlining of railway locomotives in particular had been carried out to improve their aerodynamics. Although the gains were marginal, from a public relations point of view it was very successful and showed the railways were keeping up with the times, although few could actually afford air travel. The general styling began to spread to motor vessels in the 1950s, firstly on the continent and then little by little to British ships. In the 1930s and 1940s, funnels had been utilitarian cylinders to house silencers; now they became a focal point of designs, as is well illustrated by **Cardiffbrook**, where the funnel is considerably larger than needed, although the extra space was often used to conceal water tanks which had cluttered decks in earlier vessels. Some of the most streamlined superstructures were created by Hills of Bristol for the Bristol Steam Navigation Co. in the 1950s.

Corbrae (2,002/52), 258ft x 39ft 3ins x 18ft 11ins, was the first motor collier for William Cory & Son, who had been in the London coal trade from about 1785. Typical east coast collier features are the lack of cargo handling gear, permanent bulkheads between holds, small bunker capacity because voyages would be short and the superstructure as compact as possible for unobstructed loading and discharge. She was the typical size of the smaller four-hatch Thames colliers. The crew accommodation was good on these larger vessels and she was powered by an 8-cylinder, 2-stroke 'Polar' engine, and could carry 2,760 tons on a draught of 17ft 6ins. Corys considered a service speed of about 10 knots the most economical, as at higher speeds the finer lines of the hull and more powerful heavier machinery meant that less coal would be delivered with the same dimensions. Corys slowly withdrew from the coal trade in the 1970s and eventually sold *Corbrae* to Stephenson Clarke who ran her as *Brightling* but they soon resold her to overseas owners.

Most of the gas and electricity colliers were steam but one special group, the 'flatirons', were particularly suited to motor. These large, low air draft vessels were built to serve gas and electricity plants on the Thames beyond the fixed bridges, of which there were eighteen between Tower Bridge and Wandsworth gas works. *Wandsworth* (1,875/50) was the first coaster to be fitted with a variable pitch propeller to improve manoeuvrability and it was also expected to reduce engine wear, as the engine could be warmed up with the propeller in neutral. The British 'Polar' 8-cylinder, 2-stroke of 1,180bhp at 225rpm gave a speed of 11 knots and was still reversible, so some manoeuvring was done with the propeller stopped because of the risk of fouling mooring wires. Once the vessel was clear, full use of the variable pitch propeller was made via a direct combined pitch/rpm lever in the wheelhouse. Between 1950 and 1958, a series of nine vessels were delivered, with the slightly smaller *Mitcham* (1,787/46) acting as a pathfinder. With an overall length of around 275 feet they were the longest vessels which could safely turn in the river at Wandsworth. The first five, including *Kingston* (1,873/56), 261ft 6ins x 39ft 4ins x 18ft 6ins, which could carry 2,875 tons on 17ft 1in, were followed by the remainder from Hall, Russell, plus Alexander Hall who built one. In order to ballast down sufficiently to pass under the bridges, water ballast was 1,058 tons. Considering the amount of traffic, collisions with the bridges were rare, although *Dulwich* hit Vauxhall Bridge on the way up and suffered extensive damage amidships. Found to be seaworthy, she proceeded to discharge, only to hit another pier of the same bridge on the way down river!

Piloting colliers up the Thames was an exacting business, as recalled by Bob Holland and Dick Waterhouse and told to Captain MacRae:

'Fulham IX and Fulham X had a single screw driven by Mirrlees engines, they were nicely fitted out below and even had a cafeteria for the crew. To go from ahead to astern the engines had to be stopped and re-started in reverse using compressed air. Most motor ships were direct drive like this but not all of them. Fulham VIII was a pilot's nightmare and gave much trouble with her two engines coupled to one shaft. If you were in trouble on her and wanted a double ring astern you'd get it alright, but when you wanted to go ahead it took too long for the engineers to uncouple it. It took several seconds and it was vital that when the pilot wanted the ship to stop it did stop. The usual procedure was to go up against the tide and come down on the ebb. Bob Holland obtained his experience by steering for other pilots as they did not like the idea of helmsmen off the ships. Sometimes the ship's bosun would be at the wheel, but few seamen liked steering up through the bridges, even though the vessels had longer

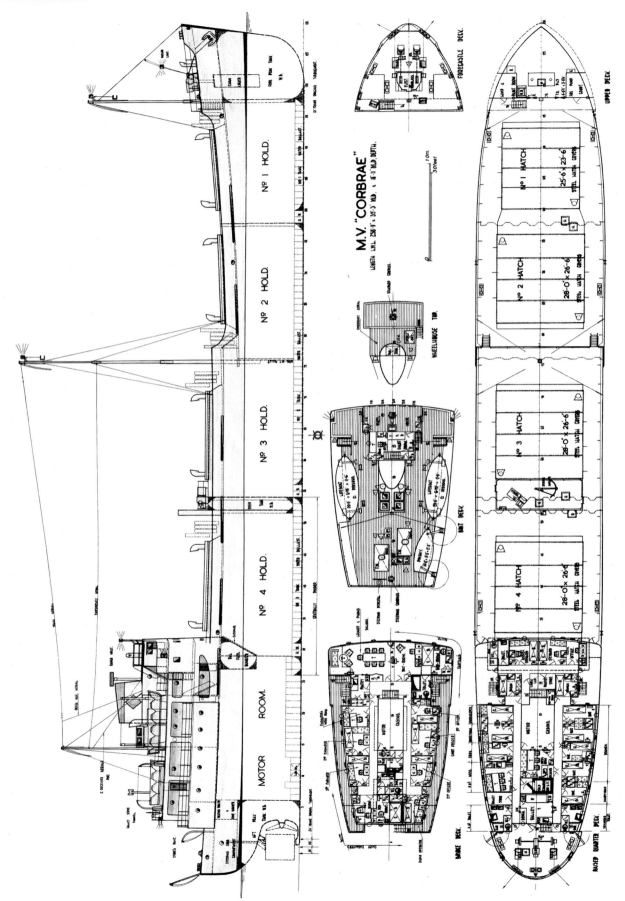

rudders than normally fitted, to improve the response. In the mid-1950s there would be an average of about five ships going up on each tide and making their way through tugs with barges and other traffic. There was a difference in handling steam and motor colliers. With a steamer, say, nine times out of ten when you rang 'full astern' you would get a kick ahead first to break the vacuum in the engine, which you did not want. With motors you got the movement you wanted as soon as you rang for it. Sometimes you got the wrong movement though, if the engineer misread the telegraph indicator. On one occasion the pilot on Harry Richardson (1,198/50) got 'full ahead' and finished up under a jetty at Rotherhithe!

The pilot usually arrived five hours before high water to take the ship down and would let-go about four and a half hours before high water. If, having left Fulham and on arrival at Battersea Bridge, he could see five and a half courses of stones on the pier, and next Victoria Rail bridge showed four courses of stones, the pilot had a comfortable margin. Then on reaching Westminster Bridge there was five and a half or six courses of stone showing he could get down to London Bridge safely and transfer to a loaded collier and bring her back up. On the other hand if it was five courses of stones at Battersea, three and a half at Victoria Rail Bridge and five at Westminster it would be essential to hurry back and keep the loaded collier head-up ready to go. The tide might be late, but that could not be counted on. A tide's work would be, say, one down, one up and another down.'

London & Rochester Trading Co. continued expanding their coasting from their Thames barge operations as the war ended, beginning a smart series of two hatch coasters with *Eminence* (555/45), followed by *Faience* (552/48), which delivered their first cargo of coal to East Yelland power station, on the River Taw in north Devon, from South Wales. For this trade cargo gear was not needed and so *Luminence* (558/54), *Militence* (561/56) and *Nascence* (563/56), 175ft x 27ft 6ins x 11ft 9ins, were built without cargo gear but retained wooden hatches, which meant plenty of work for the crews. They were able to carry around 750 tons on about 11ft 3ins. With the exception of *Eminence*, all were built by Clelands and the last two with Newbury engines, as Everards had become major shareholders in the company. *Luminence* was lost on this run on 1st March 1967, when she struck a rock while on passage from East Yelland to Ayr, where coal was loaded for the power station in later years. They also served the power station at Hayle from Barry in earlier times and took coke from Portsmouth to the Channel Islands. The crew was employed on a share basis, in the same way as crews were traditionally paid on Thames barges and fishing vessels, with wages determined as a fraction of the freight earnings. The vessels were well maintained and manned with a rota for washing up, cooking and serving duties for the deck hands. Mates were expected to work alongside the crew on all tasks, such as cleaning out the holds, washing down decks and the accommodation.

They proved adaptable and *Faience* was modified in 1964 as a temporary oil rig supply vessel, while purpose built vessels were constructed for London & Rochester subsidiary Offshore Marine Ltd. Earlier, *Luminence* had been selected to open what became known as the Crescent Line between Whitstable and Esbjerg in 1959. It was begun to offer shippers the possibility of avoiding congestion and labour delays in London docks. The most obvious change to *Luminence* was the addition of a mast and two derricks amidships to serve the two hatches. She was also fitted with refrigerated chambers for butter and cheese. The box shaped dotted line and the note about hold lining may relate to this on the plan of *Nascence*, as the plan of *Luminence* had been lost around this time. The Crescent Line was successful

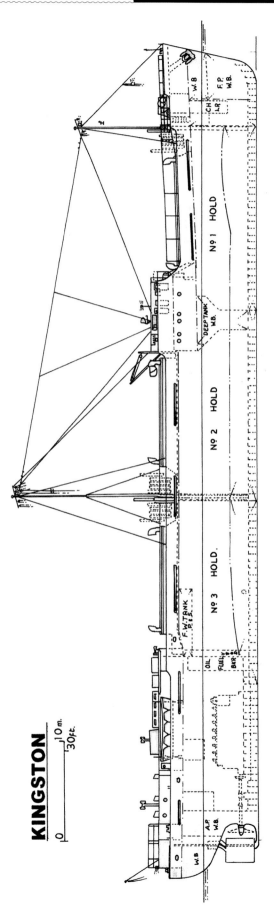

KINGSTON

Kingston was built in 1956 for the South Eastern Gas Board to carry coal to their plant beyond the low fixed bridges of the Thames, hence the very low profile and lowering masts.

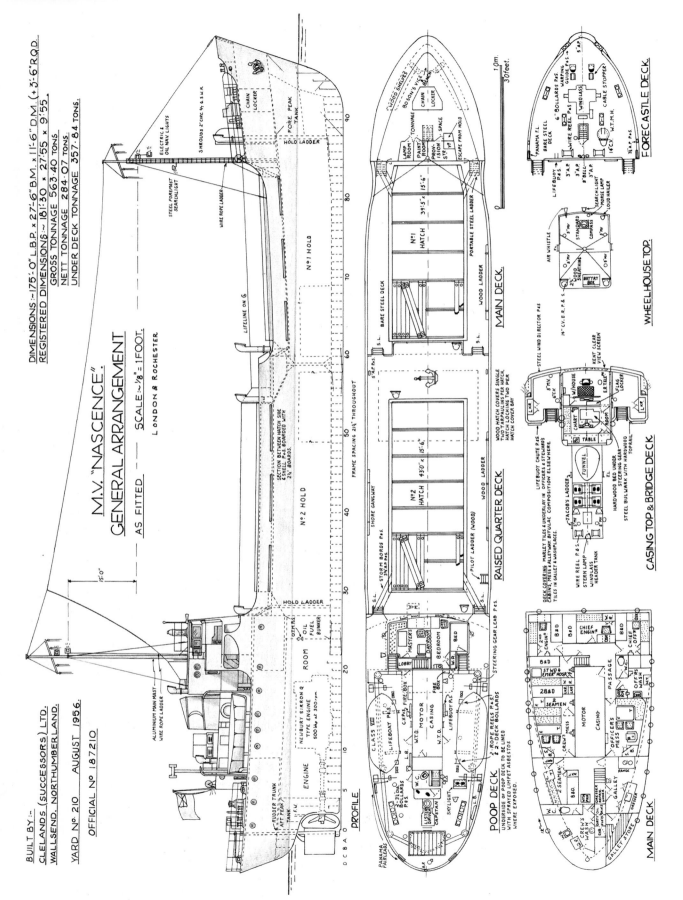

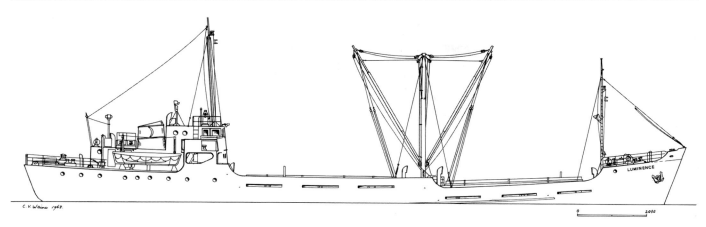

and *Luminence* was replaced by a shelterdecker more suited to liner trading, which was renamed *Resurgence*. *Luminence* returned to the coal trade where she was lost in 1967. Clelands built a similar vessel, *Heathergate*, for their associated Hull Gates Shipping Co. Ltd, Hull. The London & Rochester Trading Co. found employment for two larger versions of their two-hatch type: *Pertinence* (868/58) was geared, with two 2-ton capacity derricks as the older geared ships were coming to the end of their lives in the fleet, but sistership *Quiescence* (868/59) was gearless. Their long sequence of two-hatch, raised quarter deckers, often with a mast between the hatches, was completed by the largest and gearless *Crescence* (999/65), from an unusual source, J. Samuel White in Cowes. She was built with the coal trade in mind and had two Lister Blackstone engines giving 660bhp at 750rpm reverse/reduction, geared to a single screw at 250rpm.

Thomas Watson continued to expand into coasters, although by this time it was owned by the Bradley family, who also had a stevedoring and agency business based on the Medway at Rochester. They had begun the move into coasters from sailing barges in 1935 and, by 1938, had purchased three small coasters from Pollocks. They had been sending their sailing barges coastwise to load china clay and then make their way up the Medway to Aylesford and Reeds paper mill. Clay was usually loaded at Par or Charlestown and the return cargo westwards was often cement. The first post-war new-build order went to Philip & Son, Dartmouth, who mainly built tugs, lightships and other specialist vessels, often for export. *Lady Sylvia* (371/52), 136ft 2ins x 25ft x 10ft 9ins, could carry 425 tons on a draught of 9ft 9½ins and had a light displacement of 270 tons. The main engine was a 6-cylinder, 2-stroke Crossley of 570 bhp at 400 rpm, giving about 10.5 knots. The price including extras was £52,425 and she was registered in the names of D.J. Bradley and D.J. Bradley junior for a short time, before Thomas Watson (Shipping) Ltd was formed in 1953.

Dick Massey recalls:

'Frank Mumery was master. Frank and his father were each master of the Lady Sheila *and the first* Lady Stella, *the father retired and Frank became master of the* Sylvia *from new. The dinghy lashed in the rigging was in her early days – later a special davit was installed right aft sitting on the box that housed the steering gear. It was a typical Dutch barge's steel work boat. Her hull design was a copy of a trinity house light ship adapted to become a coaster. She had two hatches and one long hold.* Lady Sylvia *was fine in the bow and full in the stern, the long poop giving great buoyancy. A bulk cargo like clay, coal, grain, durite, etc had to be loaded aft, filling No. 2 hatch to the coamings and the after end of the forward hatch, leaving any space right forward. There were no side bilges outboard of the double bottom tanks, only here was she constructed differently to a normal ship. From the tank top to the ship's side there was a false bilge running all the way fore and aft, port and starboard. This sloping ceiling reached about 3ft in and 3ft up the ships side.*

We often loaded newsprint in large rolls for Aberdeen and this made stowage difficult as the paper must be stowed thwartships; we nearly lost the ship because of this stowage. The Lady Sylvia *had no cargo battens, that is timber lining along the ship's side covering the sharp frames and it was essential to avoid damage to the delicate rolls which had to be stowed away from the ship's side. The false bilge was the next problem as the first layer of rolls were stowed in the bottom of the hold, the lower edge of the outboard rolls would be touching the inner edge of the false bilge. Each roll of paper was about 3ft wide and this gave a space from the top of the first roll to the real ship's side of about 3ft so as the hold was filled there was a gap to the ship's side. The stabilising of the stack came from the rolls of paper held within the hatch coaming, this weight of paper on top had always stopped the lower rolls from moving.*

This sketch shows how Luminence of 1954 was fitted with cargo gear for liner trading. Having established the trade, she was replaced by a more suitable ship. She returned to tramping and the coal trade but retained her cargo gear.

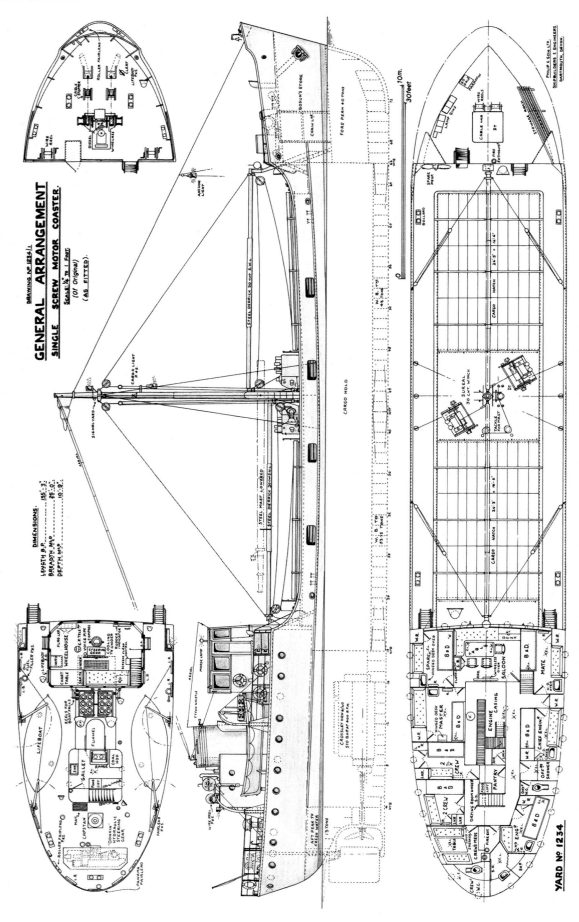

DRAWING Nº 1234/1

GENERAL ARRANGEMENT

SINGLE SCREW MOTOR COASTER.

SCALE ¼" TO 1 FOOT.

(Of Original)

(AS FITTED).

DIMENSIONS:-

LENGTH B.P. .... 155'-3"
BREADTH M.D. .... 29'-0"
DEPTH M.D. .... 10'-9"

PHILIP & SON LTD.
SHIPBUILDERS & ENGINEERS
DARTMOUTH, DEVON.

YARD Nº 1234

Lady Sylvia, completed in 1952, came from the yard of Philip & Son, Dartmouth, a yard more usually associated with the building of tugs and similar craft. The mast and winch platform formed part of the hatch-side girder to maintain longitudinal strength amidships. It also made it easier for those working winches to see into the holds.

But this time it was raining all the time when the paper was being loaded. Spring tides had passed and there was a chance that the Lady Sylvia *could be neaped if sailing was delayed. Normally loading would be stopped in rain. Fred Wheeler, the master, did not normally stop for shelter in any weather. We were over half way towards Aberdeen with an East to North East gale blowing, with a departure point about 10 miles east of Flamborough Head for a direct course to Aberdeen. Roughly twenty miles off Saint Abb's Head, with one very big roll to port, the cargo shifted, probably due to the rolls of paper being wet. This gave the ship a large list and water was halfway across the port side of the hatches. The plugs in the starboard side double bottom tanks' air vents were knocked out and the engineers pumped ballast water into first No. 2 double bottom tank to see if it would correct some of the list – it worked, so No. 1 starboard double bottom tank was also half filled; this reduced the list so that the sea was now just above the hatch coamings on the port side. This took the pressure off the hatch canvas tarpaulins. Captain Wheeler watched the wave pattern and when he was ready several gallons of diesel oil and engine oil was discharged down the officers' toilet on the starboard side. When this had made a large slick, the engine was put full ahead and the helm was put hard over and as the ship passed through into wind and sea, with the ballast tanks being only half full to assist rolling the ship,* Lady Sylvia *gave a big lurch to starboard and the cargo shifted back enough that the bulwark rail capping on the port side was out of the water and with the ballast water adjusted we made it to Aberdeen. Captain Wheeler treated it just as a normal thing – maybe for him being an ex-sailing ship man it was!*

Most small motor ships, when not under way, shut down machinery, except for possibly an auxiliary motor of about 20hp for the generator or ballast pump motors which exhausted up the funnel. In order to reduce the noise in the accommodation, some vessels had their generator in the forecastle. The accommodation was kept free of fumes by following the rule that engine room shoes and overalls were not allowed to leave the engine room except when taking bunkers or lubricating oil aboard. Normally the mate would create hell if there were any oily marks beyond the engine room. The deck department hated the engine room staff when on duty, but off duty in the saloon they were all good mates. Often engineers on duty would ask permission to come on the bridge for a while. This was frowned upon by the deck department, though tolerated, but definitely no engine room shoes!

Many small ships' winches and windlasses were motor driven, each one having their own independent diesel engine. This was common on motor coasters under about 1,200 tons. Those over about 1,200 tons often had electric winches, while ex-Scandinavian vessels had low pressure hydraulic. There were also steam and even compressed air on a few ships. The problem with motor winches was lack of maintenance and poor starting during cold winter weather. They produced thick smoke and fumes when first started – exhaust pipes were turned down towards the deck to keep rain and spray out of the engine but could be turned skywards when in use. Many winches had Lister engines (JP or Freedom types) and the ship's engineer was required to operate them on some ships. There was no training given to crews – they learned by trial and error. Winches on 'Chants' had a friction drive with a huge handle to move from drive to brake, the friction system was designed to the 'Hastie' multigrooved friction drive. Hastie was best known for the friction brake system fitted to ships' steering gear replacing relieving tackles. Most motor winch gear boxes had no reverse so it was heave in and freewheel out. Many small coasters had just hand powered capstans fitted aft.'

Lady Sylvia was sold in 1963 to the Alliance & Consumers Gas Co., who had begun to replace their ageing steamers. She was a near perfect fit for them, literally, as she was the biggest vessel which could comfortably fit in the entrance lock of Ringsend Dock, Dublin where the company was situated. Renamed *Glenbride*, she carried coal to Dublin for the company until 1969, when the company ceased shipowning and she was sold to the Alderney Shipping Co. Ltd, Alderney, who renamed her *Alderney Trader*. Sold in 1973 to the Gemini Shipping Co. Ltd of Cyprus and renamed *Memi*, she was seized in March 1976 on suspicion of smuggling and taken to Cherbourg, where she was eventually sold to be used as a pontoon in 1978; she was finally broken up in 1986.

Often because of the cost and long delivery times for coasters, suitable Thames barges were still being upgraded into motor coasters. Dick Massey recalls joining the motor barge *Gazelle* (166/04), 90.3ft x 23.3ft x9.0ft (registered dimensions), in late February 1958:

'Gazelle had been built in Holland at Krimpen on the River Ijsee in 1904, as an iron-hulled spritsail sailing barge to an English design by Pollocks of Faversham, there being some eight or more sisters built. She was originally named Runic and like many of her sisters, was converted to become an auxiliary sailing barge and had been fitted with a Bolinder engine in 1931. Later, her owners, Goldsmiths of Grays, Essex renamed her Goldrune in 1949, in line with their policy of having 'gold' in their barges' names.

The Vectis Shipping Co. of Newport, Isle of Wight bought the Goldrune in 1949, renaming her Gazelle in 1951. In 1950 they fitted her with two new 3-cylinder, 2-stroke Bolinder marine engines

with twin screws, but these were replaced in 1953 by Kelvins which gave her a speed of 6 to 7 knots, making these craft easier to organise, if weather permitted, and their cargo arrived on time. Three of these barges had sailed loaded with cargo across the Atlantic to the River Plate in 1930, later returning to Pollocks shipyard for conversion to motor barges. Some of these barges had their two cargo hatches made into one long hatch to match the single hold. They could carry 330 tons in river work, but for seagoing, the load line would be 230 tons.

The company had a fleet of barges used around the Solent. The Gazelle, along with their other seagoing vessel Leaspray, traded to any port, from the north east coal ports to the stone and china clay ports of the far south west of England, with some voyages to the Channel Islands, with a crew of five comprising captain, mate, engineer and two deck hands. Who was the cook? Anyone who was free at the time, with many a culinary disaster served up to the crew such as one young bloke who, when told to heat up a tin of spaghetti and a tin of beans did not realise the thing to do was to remove the labels and punch a couple of holes in the top of the cans before standing them in the oven of the Aga. He was then called on deck for some reason which was just as well as with a mild explosion the oven door flew open, first the beans exploded then the spaghetti. For days after, we were finding the latter in some very strange places.

I joined the Gazelle at the Snodland paper mill where she was unloading china clay from Cornwall. The clay was in powder form and the day windy so as I went through the Townsend Hook paper mill – after being on ships with coal, this was opposite – everything was snow white! I wondered what I had got myself into (more experience). Three of us lived in the forecastle; that being the cooking, eating and sleeping area. There were two bunks on the starboard side, the Aga stove across the forward bulkhead and the mates bunk on the port side aft next to the companionway to the deck. In the middle of the fo'c'stle was a large multi-purpose deal table and at the top of the companionway was a large hoodway with a watertight door with a small porthole. Everything seemed to be coated with china clay. Later I was to discover that this clay went into all sorts of consumer goods like toothpaste, stomach powders etc, but here at the paper mill it was to put a high gloss on paper.

Soon enough the hold was empty and our orders were to proceed to Medway shipyard at Rochester to have the steering system replaced. The steering was the original installed in 1904 some fifty-four years previously. I soon found it was a challenge for any helmsman and this was in a calm river. Fortunately for me I only did this one short trip down river. This was enough to show that in calm waters twenty-five degrees either side of the course was the norm. The new steering gear was designed by a modern naval architect and at sea we were later to prove that the new design not only worked, but worked far better than ever expected. The first job after arriving at the shipyard was the removal of the old waterlogged rudder. The yard's crane driver was of the opinion that the rudder weighed over two and a half tons and with the steering gear added came to about three tons. The new twin rudders had already been fabricated and were almost ready for installation and the full steering gear was soon available for fitting.

As soon as the slipway was available the Gazelle was hauled out for the fitting of the new rudders and this was fully completed within a week. During the fitting of the new steering gear the outside of the hull was inspected and painted and soon enough the Gazelle was back in the water and river trials ordered the next day. With the yard bosses, the owner's superintendent and the naval architect on board, the trials showed that the new steering gear was far more efficient and positive than expected. As soon as the trials were over our orders were to proceed to Silvertown on the River Thames to load cattle feed at Silcocks wharf, for Newport, Isle of Wight. The cattle feed being light and bulky, filled the hold completely and when loaded the Gazelle had about seven inches of freeboard amidships. As soon as the ebb tide started we departed Silvertown in fine weather and calm which lasted almost all the way to Cowes at the entrance to the Medina River. The new steering gear kept the barge going in a straight line and from Silcocks to Cowes there was a saving of over six hours and a fuel saving of over fifty gallons.

On arrival at Newport, Mark Croucher, the Vectis Shipping Company's shipping manager, came on board full of enthusiasm for this new rudder system and was now going to consider upgrading any of their poor steering barges. This being my first time in Newport, I had an interesting port and town to explore and all within walking distance of the wharf. On most coasting barges the crew were paid by the share, the share being part of the monies earned from each cargo carried. Vectis paid the crews a weekly wage, plus a cargo bonus. For the crew this was an advantage as if you were held up by the weather you still got paid. Also with Vectis, the crew numbered five instead of the normal two or three of a barge paying by the share. From Newport the next cargo was to be china clay to be loaded at Plymouth.

The young skipper was always at loggerheads with the marine superintendent of the company. The skipper lived in Southampton and wanted to have as much time at home as he could (being on pay) so any excuse would do. If he could find a reason for not sailing he would. This time in league with

our engineer, some small part was required for the engine's water pumps and being Friday afternoon this was thought to be a good time at Cowes for the weekend as nowhere would be open until Monday. The skipper departed with great plans for a long week end at home. Soon after he left, Mr Major, the superintendent, turned up with all necessary spares. He had a full set of spares in Newport. The crew had pulled this excuse before and they were not going to get away with it today. Also the super, predicting where the skipper would be, had already phoned the Red Funnel ferry office to have our skipper phone the office urgently. This worked and with the skipper back on board we were soon on our way towards Plymouth to arrive and load china clay on Monday. All the time I was in the Gazelle as soon as we were in the Solent area some reason for not sailing had to be dreamed up, but the super was also trying to keep one step ahead of the skipper and most times he won. The china clay was known as boulder clay. Most of the Cornish ports never bothered about the dust from clay, but here it was different as the lorries had to pass through the town, so the clay was in lumps about the size of four house bricks with no dust. The problem was that the lumps would stick in the loading chutes and the cargo needed to be trimmed. This involved man-handling the lumps as they were too large and awkward to shovel to get the barge in sea-going trim.

Top: Gazelle at sea loaded in fair weather.

Above: Thames barges like Gazelle had little freeboard and were soon awash as this second picture shows! Both Dick Massey

By early afternoon we had the hatch fully battened down and ready for sea instead of still being in Cowes. With fresh westerly winds we started the run up the English Channel. The Gazelle when loaded was more like a hippopotamus than a gazelle; the only way forward was across the top of the hatch. A single lifeline was rigged from the front of the wheelhouse to the foremast, which meant climbing over the cradle and chocks of the barge's lifeboat. This in daylight was an obstacle course, in the dark with no deck lights and the seas breaking across the hatch making it very slippery as well, was quite something. Many a wet foot was had crossing this hazard and going to the toilet was even more interesting. The toilet door was part of the after deck house and the door was non-watertight and when the sea was on the starboard, the water could be halfway up the door so bowel training was soon learnt. On the run up channel, meals and loo visits were organised for certain spots unless the sea was practically calm. The course would always be via the sheltered waters of the Solent in the lee of the Isle of Wight, as this gave the crew a break for a few good meals, etc. On passing the Nab Tower at the eastern end of the Solent and once more clear of any shelter, if the wind was anywhere between south and south west, this put the seas on the starboard beam or quarter. The door to the engine room was on the opposite side from the toilet, but there was also a very narrow access from the wheelhouse so that in bad weather it could be more easily reached. The next good shelter was after passing Dover, in the Downs behind the Goodwin Sands. From Dover round to the Thames and Medway, much of the route was between the sand banks and shoals of the estuary.

The next voyage was a repeat from Snodland to Silcocks and Newport. On this trip on arrival in the Medina River, being the start of the neap tide, our skipper had a secret plan for getting some time home. Just upstream from Cowes is a riverside pub, the Folly Inn, and with a small error in navigation we grounded on the sandbank handy for the pub and the local bus back to the Cowes/Southampton ferry. Here the skipper and engineer required to be landed in the barge's boat with instructions to me of "If she floats, take her up to Newport", I having only been up the river once. The Medina almost dries out at low tide, so for the couple of days we were stuck waiting for the tides to increase in size, I was able to chart the river and its channels to Newport, using the barge's boat and a pole to gauge

the depth. The Kelvin engines were electric start, but with petrol and spark plugs to start the monsters. Once the engine fired on petrol it was changed over to run on diesel, this was an art I was yet to master, but somehow I managed all this and with our two young deck hands, took the barge up to Newport.

Our next trip was to St. Sampson on Guernsey, this being a 12 hour crossing from the Needles, the departure point on the English coast, to the west side of Alderney. In this area the tides run through the islands at six to eight knots, so careful navigation is required in these waters. Even though the islands are British many goods like cigarettes and spirits were duty free so the crews of visiting craft must be cleared by Customs. The roadstone we were due to load could only be tipped into our hold at low tide when the barge was sitting firmly on the harbour bottom, the tides there being some of the biggest in Europe, over ten metres. Soon we had our cargo on board and with the hatch fully battened down we were ready to depart on the next tide, but Brian, our skipper had a plan – again. Even though the weather forecast was good, he suggested the tides in the Race of Alderney would be wrong for us. The crew were unanimous with his decision as there were lots of friendly young women in St. Peter's Port and soon we were all scrubbed up and a taxi bus ordered to take us all to town. After a night on the town we departed next day and had a calm crossing back to the Isle of Wight.

On arrival at Cowes, having to clear customs back to England, most of the crew had nothing to declare, even the skipper had somehow forgotten he had a carrier bag full of cigarettes – unfortunately for him the customs officer spotted them. This was an expensive bit of forgetfulness for our skipper, but then he had other things on his mind, his plan had worked, the delay in St. Sampsons had us arriving in Newport on Friday afternoon, and with no discharging until Monday he had his weekend at home! After discharging the roadstone we were to proceed to Charlestown to load china clay for the paper mill at Snodland, this being a similar trip to the one from Plymouth. From the Medway we loaded scrap steel for Middlesbrough, then on to Blythe to load house coal for Gweek on the Helford River in Cornwall. By now we were into summer with lots of calm days and at times thick fog. With the barge now steering a straight line, it was very much easier to navigate and know where your plotted position would be. The only aid to navigation apart from the compass was a small radio direction finder. Once out of the complex of sandbanks of the southern North Sea and into the English Channel, the navigation was easier with some long distances between headlands, but with lots more large ships to avoid, so where possible we stayed well inshore, there we only had to dodge fishing boats and fishing gear. The Helford River is just to the south of Falmouth and renowned for its beauty, starting from the hamlet of Helston at its entrance, from there to Gweek at the head of the river, the channel winds and twists across shallow mud flats. As we had made a quicker passage than expected, we now had a wait of several days for the tides to make, as the river would be too shallow for the loaded barge until the spring tides came around. While we waited the skipper decided that we would mark the channel with withys. Withys are no more than small trees trimmed down with a few branches left on. The idea was that at low tide we would row the barge's boat upstream and push the trees into the mud banks to mark the channel. It took us several days before our skipper was satisfied that the channel was well enough marked that we should have no problem finding our way to Gweek. On the morning we got underway, not one of our markers was to be seen – it was then that we began to understand what had happened to all our hard work. Brian, our skipper, on a previous trip had upset the local fisherman who acted as river pilot and wishing to avoid a confrontation had us put in our own navigation marks. Later we were told that as we marked the channel during the day, each night all but the last marker downstream was pulled out. With just one withy there was no way we could find the channel, so we returned to anchor off Helston.

Now we flew the 'G' flag (I require a pilot), but no pilot came. The next day Brian had to go ashore cap in hand and apologise to the pilot who consented to come the following day and take the Gazelle upstream. Our arrival at Gweek caused quite a stir as the coal was not for the village, but for the local RAF base. The system for unloading was by using a very old steam crane that could lift about half a ton. A lorry arrived with about twenty half-ton tubs and these were lowered into the hold and a couple of gangs of men with shovels filled the tubs with coal. The crane then lifted the tubs on to the lorries for delivery to the RAF base. At the end of the first day the crane driver discovered a crack in the crane's jib pivot that put the crane out of service. The next day the RAF sent one of their bomb loading cranes to finish unloading the coal. On enquiring where we could get water as there was no sign of a tap and there must be water for a steam crane, the crane driver showed us where to get drinking water. At the back of the quay was a fresh water spring. With a bucket brigade each evening we eventually filled our tanks.

The small harbour of Charlestown was an important china clay loading port. In this circa May 1959 view, Watson's **Lady Sylvia** of 1952 is ready to sail while beyond, the Thames barge **Gazelle** is loading. She is 'down by the head', suggesting a small parcel of one grade is being loaded forwards to be followed by a larger parcel of another grade which will be distributed to bring the vessel a little 'down by the stern'. Thus, by the time she arrived in the Medway, she would be on an even keel to have the best chance of getting alongside the shallow berths available there. It was the mate's job to load the ship to achieve this and he would have to allow for the amount of fuel and fresh water that would be used on the passage from Cornwall up the Channel. DICK MASSEY

With the coal discharged, our next loading orders were to proceed to Charlestown to load china clay for the River Medway so requiring every trace of coal dust to be removed before loading, but first we required fuel. With a diversion to Falmouth, bunkering was completed in an hour or so, then it was on to St. Austall Bay and Charlestown. By the time we arrived in the loading berth the good weather had finished. The little harbour had a single set of lock gates that might only be opened in good weather with up to a moderate swell, now with a southerly wind blowing directly towards the harbour entrance this in fact closed the harbour. It was almost a week before any vessel could leave and the sea had calmed. After departing the bay, the sea was almost flat calm for nearly all the way to the Thames Estuary. On arrival at Strood we had to wait a few hours for the tide to take us to Snodland and while waiting the captain of the Jim M, came over to ask me if I would like to have my mate's job back as there were now lots of cargoes to be moved and it seemed the ship would have full employment. On arrival at Snodland I signed off the Gazelle and took the short rail journey to Strood to rejoin the Jim M, It was now early July 1958.

The time spent in the Gazelle was interesting, not least for the skipper's lack of loyalty to the owners. However the owners had faith in him. Later when she was sold to Palmers of Gravesend, Vectis Shipping purchased an ex-Dutch coaster which, renamed Vectis Isle, plied the same routes as the barge. The Vectis Isle came very near being wrecked when she dragged anchor while in Portland Bay in a southerly gale with nobody on anchor watch.'

Robertson's next post-war coasters, a pair from the Ailsa Shipbuilding Co. Ltd, Troon, returned to the all-aft raised quarter deck arrangement. Their design was carefully considered and a model of *Olivine* was tank tested at the Denny experimental tank. The engine chosen was a 'Polar' M47M giving 1,310bhp at 300rpm, driving a solid bronze propeller 7ft 2ins in diameter, easily exceeding the contract speed of 11.5 knots. *Olivine* (1,354/52) was completed followed by *Gem* (1,354/52), 227ft 6ins x 38ft x 15ft 5ins. The vessels were well equipped, fitted with radar from new and, interestingly, the central heating system was coal fired. A feature of Robertson ships at this time was the heavy belting on the stern, also the poop deck which was inset from the side of the hull. This was probably to reduce the risk of damage when loading alongside their quarry jetty. MacGregor steel hatch covers were fitted. They were classed as self-trimmers for bulk cargoes and the cubic capacity was 86,600 cubic feet or at least 50 cubic feet per ton, and they were also equipped for timber cargoes. Steering was electro-hydraulic and deck machinery electric supplied by Trige. Electric power came from three 41kw generators driven by Russell, Newbury E4 diesels. The price steadily increased from *Olivine* at £143,292 to £152,850 for the last of the three, *Emerald* (1,382/52). The style of these vessels set the company look for the 1950s, with white painted poop deck and superstructure surmounted by a wide squat black funnel. The short white line on the hull below the bridge was a distinguishing feature of all Robertson ships. The bunker capacity was sufficient for Mediterranean as well as Baltic trading. To suit changing trade requirements, *Olivine* and *Emerald* had their hatch coamings raised by about three feet and this increased their capacity by about 6,300 cubic feet. The raised hatches permitted a slightly deeper draught and so the extra steel weight of the modifications did not significantly affect the deadweight. Stowage increased to a minimum of 53 cubic feet per ton. The changes allowed more pulp to be stowed below deck and made them more suitable for liner work with their partner Thor Thorsen, which was becoming important. Although the vessels are recorded with increased gross tonnage (*Olivine* 1,430 gross, *Emerald* 1,454 gross), Lloyd's Register only shows an increased grain capacity for *Emerald* at 93,160 cubic feet, whereas the original grain capacity of 86,600 remained unchanged for *Olivine*. All the vessels had carefully countersunk manhole covers to protect them from grab damage when discharging.

As the vessels often had to load at out of the way places, there were three 3-ton derricks. The hatches were not altered on *Gem* but her capacity was increased by lengthening her by 29ft 10ins, changing the tonnages to 1,597 gross and 2,182 deadweight. The series was ended by *Brilliant*, a slightly smaller version built in Holland in 1958.

In 1922, William Robertson, took a controlling interest in a North Wales limestone quarry, as the high grade limestone was an important return cargo for the vessels which frequently carried coal from Scottish ports to Ireland. Robertson ships had been regular arrivals at the Llanddulas Quarry jetty of Kneeshaw, Lupton & Co. Ltd to load limestone, often destined for the Glasgow steelworks, from at least the 1880s. The company had also been closely involved in the supply of limestone products from Northern Ireland. At the turn of the century, loading at the jetty was slow and the vessels had to load aground between tides. In subsequent years, improvements were made so that ships could load afloat on the tide. Even at neap tides the rise was 18 feet, so coasters could come alongside about three hours before high water and start to load. This was too risky if there was

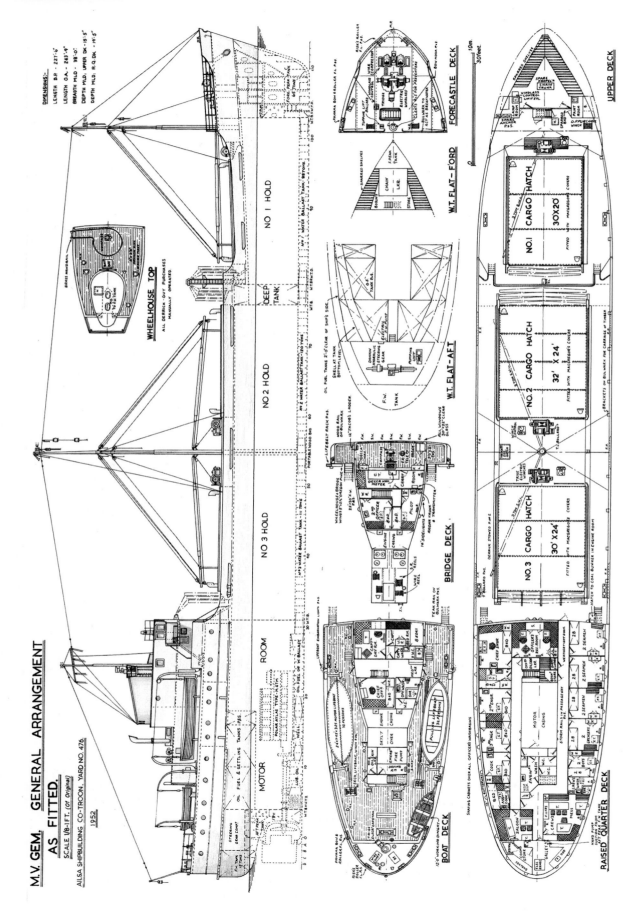

M.V. OLIVINE

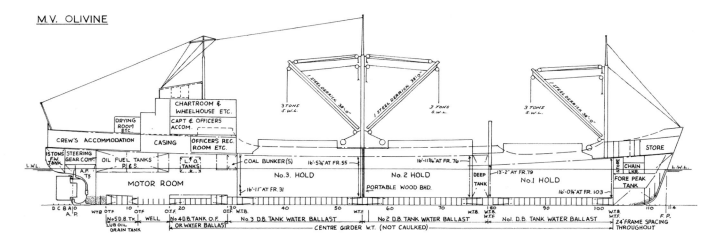

YARD No 475
PLATE LANDINGS
SCALE :- $\frac{1}{2}$" = 1 FOOT
(Of Original)

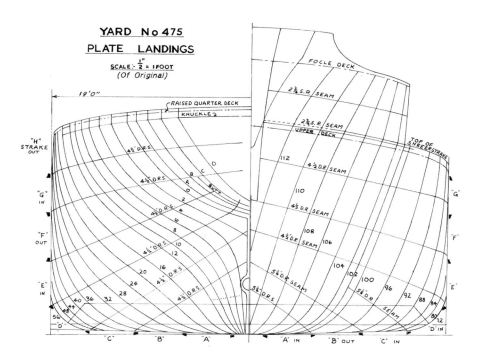

a northerly wind or one was expected, as the vessels could be blown ashore. Fortunately, good seamanship meant serious incidents were rare, the Reverend William Jones recalled. As the size of cargoes customers could accept continued to increase and faster loading equipment became available, the longer Ffordd Newydd (new road) jetty a short distance to the west was used and the old Hen Ffordd (old road) jetty was closed in 1948. The new jetty became even more important in 1962, when the firm's Penmaenrhos Quarry and jetty about a mile to the west was closed, as no more stone could be safely extracted because of the adjacent railway tunnel.

Prior to 1962, vessels sometimes loaded a part cargo in the after hold, then backed off and moved to the Penmaenrhos jetty to complete loading and a young William Jones was sometimes allowed to make the short voyage and walk back to Llanddulas. Beginning in 1969, he made several trips to the Continent in Robertson ships. They were built to a high standard and the accommodation was comfortable, with television from the 1950s for the crews who mostly hailed from Scotland and Northern Ireland. They ate well too; at 8.00am there was a large breakfast of bacon, eggs, toast and marmalade, followed by a mug of tea at 10.00am, dinner at 12.00, more tea at 3.00pm and then high tea at 5.00pm, the three courses having to last until breakfast, although some self catering and tea was possible at later hours. Etiquette was carefully observed and the meal was not started until the Captain arrived, unless he was likely to be late.

The quarries' output had been steadily rising, as the high quality limestone attracted orders from

Olivine and Gem were originally built as sisters in 1952 and the GA of Gem shows their original design. During service they were updated with various modifications and the outline plan above shows the raised hatch coamings which were fitted to Olivine to increase her cargo capacity. In 1960, the capacity of Gem was also increased by lengthening. This was achieved by inserting a section amidships taking care to keep her under 1,600 gross tons. Apart from lengthening the hatches were unaltered. The body plan and plate landings for Yard No. 475 (Olivine), essentially the same for both ships when built, are also shown.

A view of Olivine showing how the poop was inset a few inches, probably to reduce the risk of damage when coming alongside exposed jetties. It was a rare feature but was to be seen as well on some of Stephenson Clarke's small colliers that were also built in the 1950s.
DAVE HOCQUARD

the UK chemical industry and then from overseas. The purity and crystalline nature attracted British Oxygen, who started using it in 1956 for making calcium carbide in Northern Ireland and it was shipped to Odda in Norway for the same purpose, as their local limestone when crushed produced much fine dust waste. This trade is reflected in the voyage notes Reverend William Jones made:

'Olivine 1,430/52. (Captain Thomas Balmer). Llanddulas (North Wales) 7.25am Wednesday 25th June 1969 sailed for West Thurrock (Grays), Thames Estuary with limestone for Thurrock Chalk & Lime. Arrived Friday 27th, Bunkered; 29 tons at 7.40am then went alongside wharf and finished with engines at 11.30pm. Noticeable smell of diesel in accommodation. Saturday 28th: Work had started 6.30am discharging cargo and continued on Sunday until 1.00pm. Monday 30th sailed at 12.35pm for Antwerp and arrived Tuesday 31st at 5.00am, Berth 287. Wednesday 1st sailed at 12.45pm for Antwerp Lock with 1,730 tons of silver sand for Bramley Moore dock, Liverpool, consigned to Pilkingtons glass works at St. Helens. Arrived Saturday 5th at 1.30pm. Speed about 9 knots.

Wednesday June 21st 1972: Llanddulas (limestone) sailed 7.30am for Trolhattan and soon ran into a moderate gale, speed fell back from the usual 9.5 knots to 8 knots, course set to pass west of the Isle of Man by which time the weather had improved. By this time the Olivine had been fitted with an automatic pilot that did the actual steering at sea. The large spoked wheel was locked except for harbour work though a small hand held device marked 'port – midships – starboard' was used approaching pilot vessels, etc. It was sensitive and a Manchester Ship Canal pilot bumped the canal bank while using it. The voyage was via Sound of Islay, Sound of Mull and Sound of Sleat then out into a heavy swell which had moderated by Thursday in the Pentland Firth. Sunday 25th. Arrived Gotenburg. Passed customs and picked up Gota River pilot and departed 3.15pm, passed through the locks and docked at Trolhattan at 11.40pm. Discharged and sailed Tuesday at 1.00pm (light) for Tofte (Oslo Fjord). Wednesday arrived about 8.15am to load 500 tons woodpulp using ship's derricks. By this time the ship's derricks were rarely used for loading. Sailed at 3.30pm for Larvik arriving there at 9.30pm (speed slightly over 9.6 knots). Thursday, loaded balance of wood pulp cargo (1,100 tons) for Barrow-in-Furness and sailed at 5.00pm returning via the Sound of Canna. Arrived Monday 3.20pm and tied up at berth at 6.15pm.

July 6th 1973 (Captain Thomas Balmer) Llanddulas – Zelzate with ⅛ins limestone dust for Sidmar steelworks on the Ghent Canal. Zelzate-Rotterdam (light ship). Rotterdam-Runcorn with borax for Fenton Dock. Average speed outward 8.9 knots and inward (to Liverpool) 9.87 knots.

June 18th 1975 (Captain J. McLaughlin) Llanddulas – Odda with ¹/₈ins limestone dust (Via Treshnish Isles, Passage of Tiree, Sound of Eigg and Sound of Canna). Average speed 9 knots. Odda – Ardal (light ship).

Sapphire 1,286/66 (Captain J. Gillies). 26th June 1971, Amethyst 1,548/58 and Pearl 1,093/53 had already loaded for Odda so Sapphire was loading at Llanddulas (limestone) on a falling tide and with just 400 tons to load was sent out until the next tide at 11.15pm. By this time Brilliant 1,148/58 had arrived and took precedence, but her loading was interrupted by a broken conveyor belt. Sometimes when this happened ships were sent away short of a full cargo especially in deteriorating weather. Sapphire finally completed loading at 4.00am on Sunday and sailed for Odda (via Sound of Islay, Sound of Mull and Sound of Sleat). Passed Cape Wrath at 3.45pm on Monday and arrived Tuesday evening off the Island of Utsira to pick up a pilot, but they were busy, so proceeded to Haugesund and picked up pilot there. Arrived at Odda on Wednesday at 10.30am to find Pearl and Amethyst already there, but we begin discharge first and this continues from 6.00am on Thursday 6th. Sailed for Egersund (light ship) at 12.50am, via Haugesund where 29 tons of bunkers were picked up. Arrived Friday 5.00am at Egersund to load anorthosite for Bromorough, consigned to Lever Bros who use it as an abrasive in cleaners and tooth paste. Sailed at 1.20pm (foggy). Weather fine the next day, but foggy again on Sunday. Anchored off Bromborough at 4.00pm to wait until 8.30pm. Average speed about 10.8 knots.'

While the last of the raised quarter deckers was being built in Holland, the company was well advanced with a larger single deck design, which became *Amber* (1,596/56), 252ft x 38ft 6ins x19ft 9ins, able to carry 2,405 tons on 17ft 0ins. Grain capacity was 112,677 cubic feet or about 49 cubic feet per ton. Two large self-trimming hatches allowed long items to be carried but they could be subdivided by wooden bulkheads, so that four holds could then be worked by four gangs each using one of the four 3-ton derricks with Trige electric cargo winches. The increased draught was acceptable as the quarry jetty had been extended into deeper water. In order to stay under the important 1,600 limit and avoid the cost of a radio officer and radio room, the deep tank used previously was eliminated and the double bottom increased beyond rule requirements to give

This very basic drawing of Robertson's Amber (1,596/56) was published in Shipbuilding and Shipping Record of 4th October 1956 but shows all the essential details, such as what was inside the funnel casing. Apart from the engine exhausts, it also contained the header tanks for the salt water and domestic fresh water, plus the ventilators to the engine room.

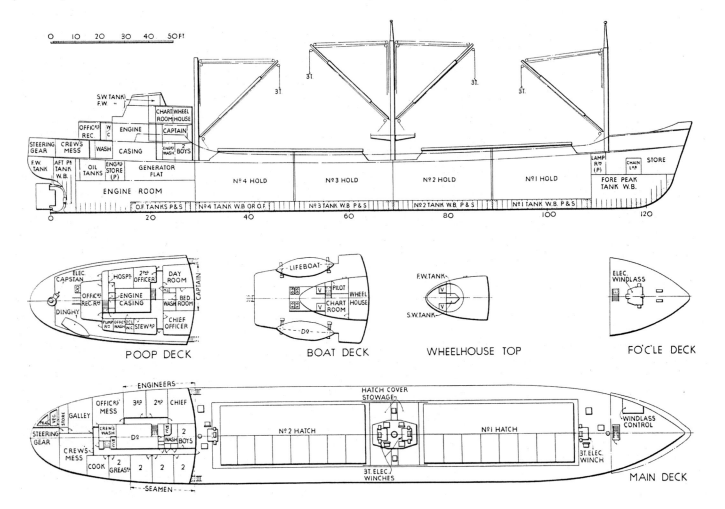

sufficient ballast. The design also took advantage of the new regulations for measuring engine room tonnage, so it was possible to reduce the engine room length to a minimum and increase hold space. This required the three Deutz air cooled generators to be accommodated on a half height platform, where they were totally enclosed in a sound proofed area with the hot cooling air exhausted via the funnel. There was also a return to Deutz for the main engine, which was a direct drive 8-cylinder, 4-stroke RVB8M366 producing 1,650bhp at 250rpm. Interestingly, the domestic heating was still coal fired. Jim Robertson described her as one of their best ships when discussing the fleet in 1974. She was sold to Panama registered owners in 1971 and renamed *Simari*. A slightly shorter version carrying 2,319 tons, *Amethyst* (1,548/58), 243ft x 38ft x 19ft 9ins (moulded), was completed two years later. A return to three hatches was made and a less powerful though supercharged Deutz RVB6M366 of 1,450bhp at 260rpm was fitted. Speed was reduced from the 12.5 knots of *Amber* to 12 knots for *Amethyst*. Experience with *Amber* also led to *Amethyst* being fitted with wing tanks in No. 2 and No. 3 holds to improve sea going qualities in ballast. She had been made slightly shorter to be handy for trade to Goole, though not the maximum that Goole could accept. William Atkinson of Goole did once load his 'Icemaid' type collier *Mayfleet* (2,002/42), 268ft x 39ft 10ins x 19ft 5ins (moulded), at her home port but, as he commented some years later, it was an experience not to be repeated!

As already noted, *Yewmount* (859/39) was used as the basis for some 'Empire' ships. *Yewmount* herself spent the early part of the war as a cased petrol carrier, initially to France, then later made a trip to Norway and was again used as a petrol carrier for the D-day landings. She was sold to Queenship Navigation to become *Saxon Queen* in 1947, probably as good prices were being paid rather than because the design was not satisfactory for post war trade, as the closely similar *Yewdale* (987/49) was followed by *Yewglen* (1,018/52) and *Yewmount* (1,031/56). The building programme was completed by *Yewhill* (1,089/57) and *Yewforest* (1,097/58), built with the coal trade in mind; all had come from James Lamont's yard. The final two made the change to all-aft arrangement and from 6-cylinder, 2-stroke 'Polar' engines to 8-cylinder, 4-stroke Deutz engines. Deadweight had crept up from 1,300 to 1,375, although the moulded dimensions of the hull at 205ft x 34ft x 15ft, was only 6ft 6ins longer, 1ft wider and 5ins deeper than the first of the post war ships.

Queenship Navigation may well have bought *Yewmount* while waiting for the delivery of their vessels of a similar size. The company had its origins in the British Channel Islands Shipping Co. Ltd, which operated a liner service between London and Jersey. They entered the tramp trade with *Jersey Queen* in 1937, by which time Coast Lines had a major interest and the company was completely taken over by them in 1942. The tramping side of the business and its ships were separated and placed under a new company, British Channel Traders Ltd, which was later renamed Queenship Navigation Ltd. Their new ships arrived from different builders, with **Osborne Queen** (1,424/57) 225ft x 35ft 9ins x 15ft 8ins, coming from the Ardrossan Drydock Co. Ltd. She was of a more conservative styling than *Yewhill* but similarly built with the coal trade in mind, with a deep tank separating holds 1 and 2 and a fixed bulkhead between holds 2 and 3, useful for separating different grades of coal. They were often employed carrying coal from Blyth and Goole to Jersey and Portsmouth, and although no cargo gear would be needed for this, it was fitted for use with other cargoes, especially in summer when there was less demand for coal. She was one of several similar vessels built for the Coast Lines Group with different machinery. In her case it was a Sulzer 8-cylinder, 2-stroke giving 1,440bhp at 250rpm, resulting in a speed of 11.5 knots.

She was sold in 1965 along with the company by the Coast Lines Group, who preferred to concentrate on their liner trades. The buyers were Watts, Watts & Co. Ltd, who had decided to diversify from their traditional ocean tramping and had bought two second hand coasters earlier in the year. They were registered in the name of their Britain SS Co. Ltd and were placed under the management of Comben Longstaff. However they ran into financial difficulties in respect of a new bulk carrier and were taken over by Bibby Line, who were not interested in the coasters and laid them up for a short time before they were sold to Howard Lund's Eskgarth and Eskglen companies. From August 1968, *Osbourne Queen* sailed for the Eskglen Shipping Co Ltd, until 1972 when she was sold to the Nefeli Shipping Co. Ltd, Cyprus and renamed *Nefeli* but was wrecked in fog and abandoned five months later near Land's End.

The 'Esk' companies had mostly been involved with ocean tramps but in 1956 took delivery of the coaster *Eskwater* (627/56), 175ft x 30ft x 13ft 5ins, which had a summer deadweight of 800 tons. Although classed with Lloyd's, the west coast of Ireland was excluded from the normal Elbe-Brest limits. The vessel was unusual in several ways. The yard, T. Mitchison Ltd of Gateshead, generally built tugs and trawlers. She was one of the largest vessels they had built and used a hydroconic (hard

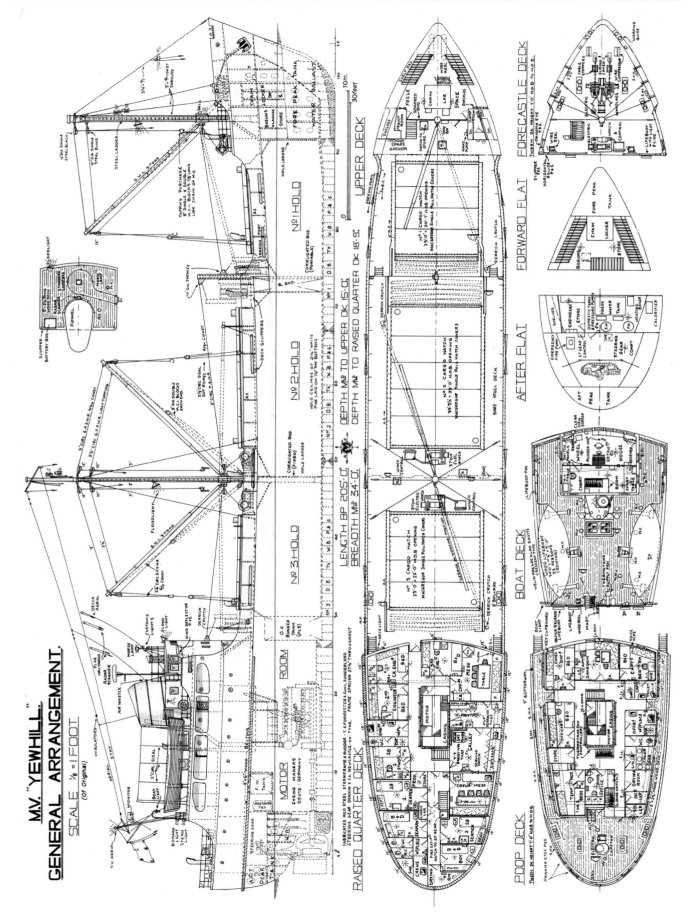

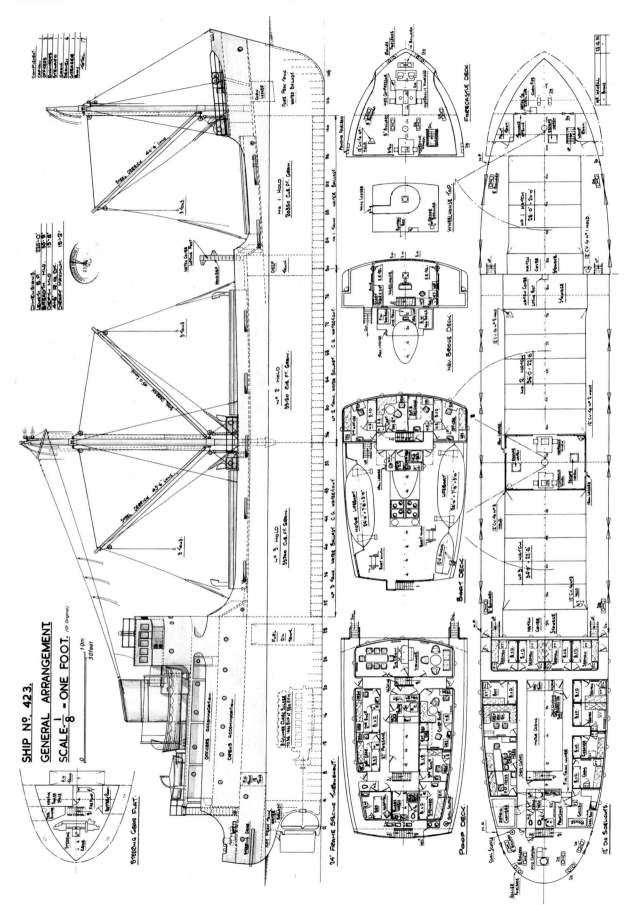

Osborne Queen (1,424/57) was built for Queenship Navigation Ltd (part of the Coast Lines conglomerate) at Ardrossan and designed with the coal trade in mind.

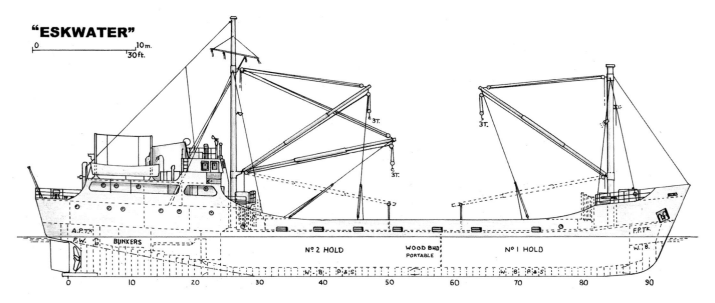

"ESKWATER"

chine) hull design by Burness, Corlett & Partners. In this design system, all surfaces were conical or cylindrical to simplify construction and had become common for small tugs. The most obvious feature of this is the simplified stern shape on the profile. The single long hold, with a portable wood bulkhead, was designed with timber cargoes in mind and for a small coaster was well geared, with two 3-ton derricks serving the after hatch and one 3-ton derrick at the fore hatch. The engine was an 8-cylinder, 2-stroke Crossley of 600bhp at 300rpm, giving about 10 knots. She carried other bulk cargoes but was soon sold to Canadian owners who took all but one of the derricks off and renamed her *Blue Trader*.

Few owners built timber carriers as most Baltic timber cargoes were tied in closely with Scandinavian ships. However, just after the war, with the Government short of foreign currency, British owners were encouraged to enter the timber trade more fully with mixed results, some finding that their ships were too large for the cargoes that merchants could finance as exchange rates fluctuated.

One firm that was to have vessels designed as timber carriers for many years was the Klondyke Shipping Co. Ltd of Hull, which was closely associated with May & Hassell, the timber merchants. The company began operations with a steamer in the early 1950s and ordered a timber carrier from R.S. Hayes (Pembroke Dock) Ltd, a yard not associated with coaster building, resulting in *Kirtondyke* (959/57), 199ft x 35ft x 15ft. The yard had started in the repair business after the Second World War and built a few small craft but *Kirtondyke* was the only large vessel they ever built. The engine was a 'Polar' 6-cylinder, 2-stroke of 960 horsepower at 250rpm, giving a high service speed of 12 knots. She could carry about 1,275 tons on 13ft 4¼ins, at a stowage rate of 55 cubic feet per ton. The accommodation was good and radar was fitted from new, with the scanner as high as possible clear of obstructions, although the main mast and the 'goal post' foremast produced some interference. The bridge was unusual as it was raised above the boat deck to improve the forward visibility over deck cargoes. Deck gear was extensive, with a single mast between the two hatches holding two 3-ton derricks and 'goal post' masts at each end each with two 3-ton derricks. At this time ships often had to load timber using ship's gear and discharge it also.

James Fisher continued to add to their specialist ships for project cargoes with the completion of *Bay Fisher* (1,289/58), 200ft x 36ft 6ins x 18ft 6ins, by the Ardrossan Dockyard Ltd. She could carry 1,550 tons on a draught of 16ft 5½ins. The hatch was 100ft x 24ft, giving access to a hold clear of all obstructions, allowing large machinery or structural items to be transported. *Bay Fisher* was used for example to carry very large items for the construction of Wylfa nuclear power station on Anglesey, such as on 21st July 1966, when two 110 ton condenser beams were discharged at Holyhead which she had brought from Liverpool. The deck machinery was all electric. The engine was one of the popular British 'Polar' 6-cylinder, 2-strokes producing 1,040bhp at 275rpm, giving a trial speed of 11.9 knots. Electrical power came from two 75kw generators driven by McLaren diesels. The hull was strengthened for navigation in ice by fitting intermediate frames beyond frame 77 to the frame spacing, which was 24ins throughout, and scantlings were generally in excess of

Eskwater (627/56) was built as a small timber carrier using simplified hull construction to reduce the amount of bending of plates required. Provisions for timber included good capacity derricks at each end of the hatch, placed high on the masts to clear the deck cargo, and little sheer in way of the hatch for easy stowage of deck cargo. She carried out her trials with timber uprights in place along the rails ready to accept a cargo of timber. Profile from a plan published in Shipbuilding & Shipping Record, *13th December 1956.*

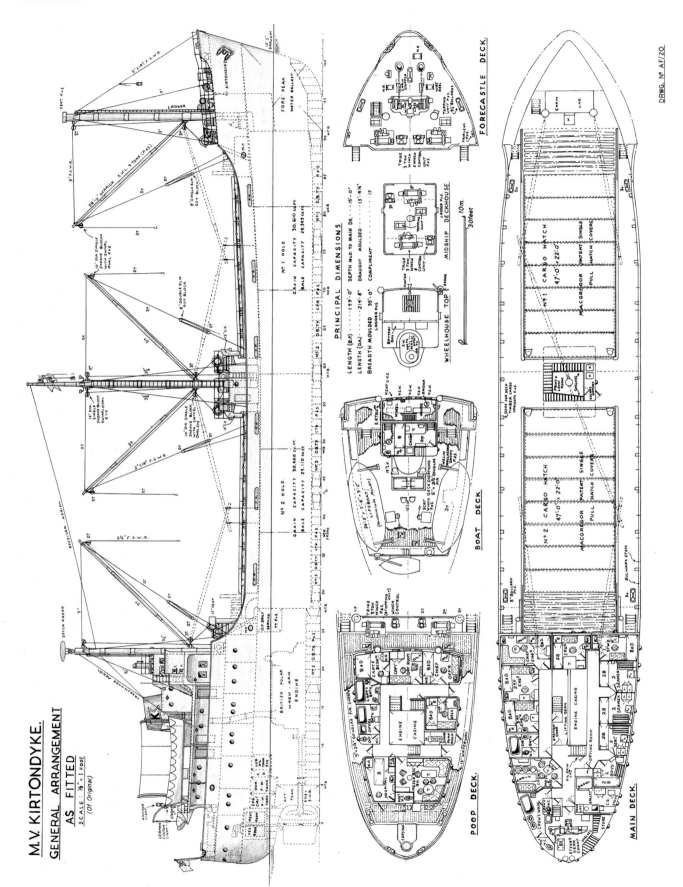

In a useful juxtaposition with the plans above, this side on photograph of the timber carrier Kirtondyke, built in 1957 and seen here off the Hook of Holland, shows the heavy goal-post style masts she had fore and aft. She was in some ways a forerunner of the single deck vessels built in later years as the coal trade became less important to British coasters. DAVE HOCQUARD

(see below)

"BAY FISHER"

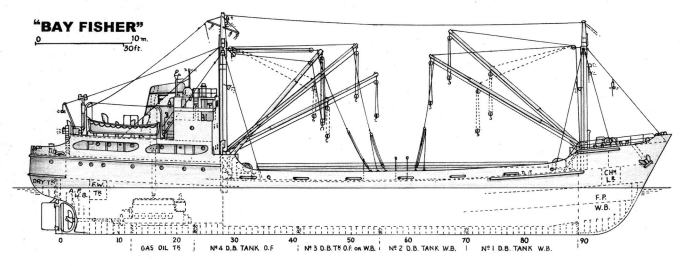

ABOVE: This profile of Bay Fisher (1,289/58) shows her as delivered, with two 5-ton and one 20-ton derrick aft, and two 3-ton and one 10-ton derrick forward. She was typical of the specialist vessels built for Fishers, who regularly carried railway containers and heavy industrial plant such as cargoes for the Central Electricity Generating Board. Profile from a plan published in Shipbuilding & Shipping Record, 31st July 1958.

Lloyd's requirements. Water ballast totalled 361 tons. The shell plating in the forward area was all welded, while the remainder was riveted and end butts were welded with riveted seams, as this was considered the best combination for ease of repair and reduced corrosion. Her first cargo was gun mountings from Rosyth to Barrow-in-Furness for Vickers, their most important local customer, and she was also time chartered to the United SS Co., Copenhagen for their Felixtowe-Copenhagen route. She was sold in 1969 to Pargola (Shipping) Ltd and in 1970 to the Northern SS Co. Ltd of New Zealand, who renamed her Moanui.

Although most new ships were coming from British yards, with a few from Dutch yards, one small owner went as far as Sweden. The Hindlea Shipping Co. Ltd had been formed by Mr Hindmarsh, a marine engineer who had an office in the same building as R. Dickinson Lean, a solicitor, and they went into partnership in 1949. They owned various second hand coasters including the Hindlea, which had been fixed on a ten year time charter carrying cement from London to Jersey, with a return cargo of granite for the Croft Granite, Brick & Concrete Co. A charter for a second vessel was secured, so an order was placed with Kalmar Varv, Sweden, for one of their 499 gross single deckers to suit the company specification for stone and cement cargoes. As built, Marshlea (494/57), 164ft x 31ft 1ins x 13ft 2ins, was equipped with derricks and hydraulic deck gear, with accommodation for eleven crew, though only seven were required for coasting. In 1967 the partners decided to retire from shipowning, so she was sold to Ronez Ltd, Jersey, but continued on the same run, though she was converted to carry cement in bulk. Marshlea loaded at Ronez Quarry for the first time on 30th July 1957 and the last in 1971, and could load 800 tons in about three hours. In 1971 it was decided to convert her to a bulk cement carrier, as the cargoes of granite had ended. The No. 2 hatch was shortened, whilst a deck house was added amidships for the pumping equipment and a suction pipe

BELOW: Marshlea (494/57) was perhaps the only coaster built in the 1950s in Sweden for a British owner.

"MARSHLEA"

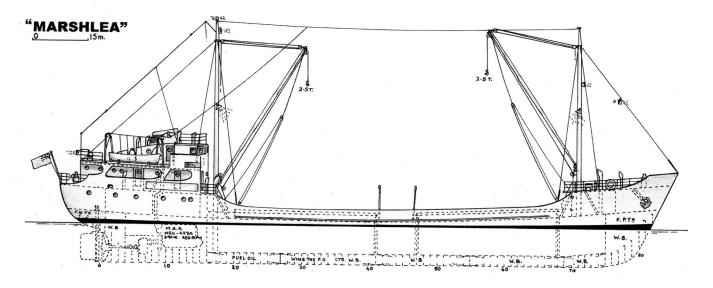

long enough to reach all parts of the hold. The forward derrick was retained to handle the pipe and hoist it to quay level, essential because of the tidal range of the harbour, one of the highest in the world. A final cargo of cement was delivered in March 1982 and she was offered for sale in Rotterdam but was eventually sold for scrap after twenty-five years of hard work, although at times she did carry other cargoes, if they could be fitted in, such as potatoes in season.

There was a slight advantage in buying new overseas, as the appropriate British-approved navigation lights and other equipment could be planned for and fitted. If a second hand vessel was bought, the extra costs of this equipment and its fitting had to be allowed for, so Dutch vessels which were already British flagged often tended to stay with British owners when sold. With coasters generally in short supply until the late 1950s, Watsons bought one of these which became their *Lady Sonia* (199/29). She had been built at J. Meyers yard at Zaltbommel as *Apollinaris III* in 1929 and came under the British flag in 1937 for J. Carter (Poole) Ltd as *Parkstone*, with the registered dimensions 108.4ft x 21.7ft x 7.9ft. Sold in 1948 and re-engined with a 5-cylinder, 4-stroke Blackstone, she passed through several hands before being bought by the Bradleys and renamed in 1954. Dick Massey recalls:

'*Lady Sonia* was purchased to bring china clay to Aylesford paper mill, the main stay for all their small ships. As they had to pass under Rochester bridges all had an air draft of under 25ft. *Lady Sonia* was 21 feet. Her accommodation, all aft under the poop, was fully renewed in 1956 one year after purchase from Ackerley & Co. of Liverpool. The two deck hands shared a cabin at the forward end, on the port side, next, going aft, was the cook's cabin. Opposite on the starboard side was a spare or classed as pilots cabin. Galley and mess room were under the wheelhouse. The forecastle did have accommodation originally when she was *Apollinaris III* and may have been in use when she was first named *Parkstone*. As she was built to carry mineral water, she had a large single hold served by two hatches. The hull shape was a cods head and mackerel tail, and being so fine in the stern there was very little reserve buoyancy. Because of this, all heavy cargoes like cement or fertilizer had to be stowed starting at least four feet forward of the holds after bulkhead. Her tons per inch [tpi] was 5.5 tons. Apart from the china clay our trading ports covered any port between Aberdeen and Bideford. The Continent was North Holland to Channel Isles and Northern France. Later she was on a time charter at about £10,000 a year to part of Eastern Counties Farmers of Ipswich. Due to rising costs she was sold to Intercon Coasters for £5,000, an associate of Eastern Counties Farmers, and now as owners, charterers and agency in house it worked out cheaper for them. She traded anywhere from Hamburg to Brest generally with a return cargo for them. However on one trip loaded with grain the gearbox disintegrated. She had to be towed into Ipswich to discharge her cargo and then to Lowestoft where William Overy the engineers carried out repairs. While there the Board of Trade surveyor spotted some plates he did not like and so the bill was considerable. She continued trading for them until a crew problem and a change of company policy led to her being sold to M.W. Hardy & Co. (Mercantile) Ltd in 1963 and she was to have several more owners until finally scrapped in 1977.'

Tanker Trades in the 1950s.

It was not until the 1950s that coastal tanker owners began to build new tonnage, as petrol rationing finally came to an end, although the Suez Crisis mid decade again affected supplies. Most companies took up war surplus tankers which were suitable for general trade. These tankers had very simple piping arrangements, with the same pipes having to be used for several grades of cargo, so it was customary to discharge the heaviest grade first followed by successively lighter grades, the slight contamination being acceptable. National Benzole with their more specialised requirements ordered purpose built vessels.

One of the specialised trades was the Thames, where low air draft vessels were essential to pass under the low fixed bridges beyond Tower Bridge. There was also the Port of London Authority requirement that their hulls were to be double skinned and inflammable cargoes were limited in size. To meet these requirements, *Ben Harold Smith* (325/52), 132ft x 26ft x 9ft 6ins, was built by the company's usual provider, Rowhedge Ironworks. The displacement was 573 tons of which 300 tons were cargo. A British 'Polar' M441 of 310bhp at 300rpm gave a trial speed of 8.92 knots. In order to give a better forward view, the wheelhouse was placed midships on the trunk deck, while all accommodation was aft. Although primarily intended to distribute company products in the Thames area, she was built to meet the requirements for restricted coastal work between the limits of Hull and Southampton, with the accommodation on a raised quarter deck aft. Hot water was available in the bathrooms but the officers' cabins had to make do with cold water only. The 100 tons per hour cargo pump could be controlled from the engine room or the deck.

The company had already taken delivery of *Ben Hittinger* (446/51), 150ft x 27ft 6ins x 12ft 9ins,

"BEN HITTINGER"

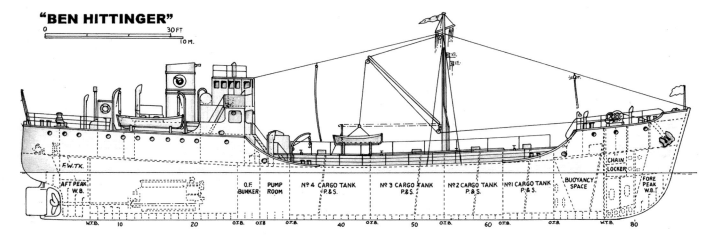

0   30FT
10 M.

Ben Hittinger (446/51) was typical of the many small tankers built to supply coastal depots after the Second World War. Though not immediately visible on this drawing, the trunk did not extend all the way to the poop, ending at the after end of the pump room skylight and just beyond No. 1 tank forwards. The access ladders are shown inside the tanks on this profile. The ship was built in eight months, six months to launching and two months fitting out. Profile from a plan in Shipbuilding & Shipping Record, *18th October 1951.*

and in a break with recent tradition she was built by Charles Hill of Bristol, although they had built the company's first coastal tanker, the steamer *Ben Read* in 1923. However, Rowhedge built a similar sistership, *Ben Bates* (565/56). Contract deadweight was 500 tons on a draught of 11ft 6ins, although the maximum deadweight was 570 tons. The trunk differed from most tankers in not being continuous fore and aft, and was described by Lloyd's as *'a trunk in a well'*. Both tankers were lengthened by 21 feet in 1961, increasing deadweight to 635 tons and both were sold in 1972. *Ben Bates* went to Canada but *Ben Hittinger* went to the Ball & Plumb Shipping Co. Ltd, Gravesend and was renamed *Spirit Carrier II*. The following year Hills built the *Regent Jane* (376/52). The Regent Oil Co. already had a fleet of motor barges for distributing refined products, which operated on the River Severn and went as far as depots at Swansea and Cardiff, supplied from Avonmouth. It was to augment this work that the *Regent Jane* was built and in a break from usual practice, incorporated sufficient ballast capacity so that the cargo tanks could be kept free of seawater on ballast runs. She traded for the company until 1968 and was then sold to Celtic Coasters, Eire and renamed *Breeda J*. *'A thorn in our side'* was how Dick Rowbotham described her, as *Regent Jane*, supplemented by Everard and Bulk Oil tankers, did all the west coast work (Avonmouth to Cardiff, Carrickfergus and Truro) until her sale, when Rowbothams finally got all this trade from what was now Texaco.

Rowbothams frequently chartered tankers to the Regent Oil Co. and their precursors Russian Oil Products, and unlike other owners had no war losses. As their tankers were all clean products carriers, some were taken up as water boats during the war and the others directed as required for the war effort. Rowbotham's operations were essentially confined to the south and east coasts, both before and after the war. For example, *Tillerman* (220/31) and *Guidesman* (233/38) were the maximum size for the Exeter Canal, a trade which lasted until 1964. Tankers were bought and chartered as the company did increasing amounts of clean products distribution for Regent in particular. They also brought fuel in for the 'pirates' (as Dick Rowbotham called the independents!) from the Antwerp-Rotterdam range. Tankers were also enlarged and the most interesting conversion was that of *Helmsman* of 1937, in which the trunk was extended the full width of the ship, increasing deadweight from 586 to 836 tons.

The fleet expansion also led to an interesting order. For many years the Drypool Engineering & Drydock Co. had carried out repairs and conversions for the Rowbothams. Drypool began the excavation of what was to become No. 2 drydock and conceived the idea of building a ship in it while it was under construction. Consequently, *Oarsman* (778/59), 189ft x 30ft 6ins x 14ft 0ins, of 1,000 deadweight, became Yard No. 1. Rowbothams were happy to encourage the project. As Dick Rowbotham explained, they had seen that on the basis of their repair work costs compared with a quotation from Clelands, the price would be much cheaper. *Oarsman* was registered in the name of the Helmsman Shipping Co. Ltd and was floated out on 25th August 1958. She was powered by the first exhaust gas turbocharged Crossley engine, a unit of 875bhp giving a service speed of 10 knots. Although Crossley had run engines at 50% boost, for this first engine a service rating of 28% was set. The Brush-made turbocharger delivered compressed air to the scavenge pump, operating in series, to the after cooler. The exhaust pulse pressure charging, a feature of the earlier Crossley engines, was retained. The weight of the engine complete was 22 tons. Fuel consumption was similar to a non-turbocharged engine of the same power but the turbocharged unit weighed considerably less and took up less space. Although a Spanner boiler was fitted in the engine room in case heating

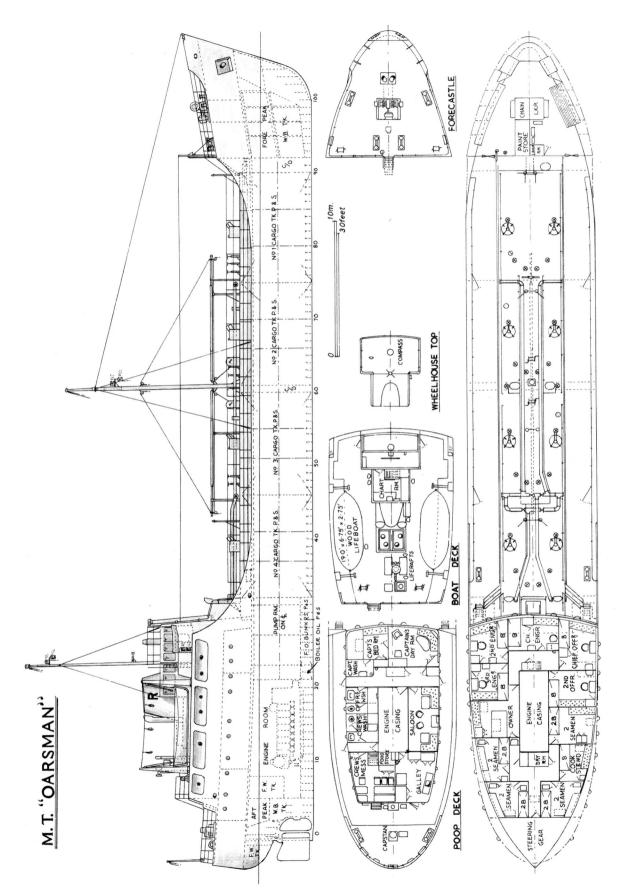

M.T. "OARSMAN"

FORECASTLE

WHEELHOUSE TOP

COMPASS

CHART RM

19.0' × 6.75' × 2.75' WOOD LIFEBOAT

LIFERAFTS

BOAT DECK

CAPT'S WASH
CAPT'S BED RM
CAPTAIN'S DAY RM

OFFR'S WASH
CREW'S WASH
ENGINE CASING
SALOON

CREW'S MESS
FOOD STORE
GALLEY

CAPSTAN

POOP DECK

CHAIN LKR

PAINT STORE

2ND ENGR
CH. ENGR
3RD ENGR
2ND OFFR.
CHIEF OFFR.

OWNER
ENGINE CASING

SEAMEN 2
DRY RM
COOK STEWD
2 SEAMEN

SEAMEN 2B
2 SEAMEN

STEERING GEAR

FORE PEAK W/B TK
No 1 CARGO TK P & S
No 2 CARGO TK P & S
No 3 CARGO TK P & S
No 4 CARGO TK P & S
PUMP RM
F.O. BUNKRS P&S
BOILER OIL P&S
ENGINE ROOM
F.W. TK
AFT PEAK W.B. TK
F.W. TK

10m 30 feet

Oarsman (778/59) was the first of a series of similar tankers built by Drypool for Rowbotham throughout the 1960s. Plan based on that in The Motor Ship, February 1959.

coils would later be required, no heating coils were fitted in the tanks as she was expected to be carrying clean products only (petrols, light oils and solvents). The piping was aluminium-brass for fresh and seawater lines.

Oarsman soon proved very successful and was followed by *Anchorman* (795/62), *Tillerman* (807/63), *Guidesman* (799/64), *Chartsman* (787/67) and finally the enlarged *Leadsman* (843/68), 194ft x 32ft 6ins x 15ft 9ins, the sixth from Drypool for Rowbothan in nine years. Apart from *Oarsman*, all had Drypool-built Brons engines. *Leadsman*, though only two feet longer, was able to carry 300 tons more in total at 1,469 dwt (because of the increase in breadth) and 1,200 tons on a draught of 12ft 6ins, 200 tons more on 3ins less draught. The more powerful 12-cylinder Brons 2-stroke, direct reversing, pressure charged, intercooled uniflow scavanging engine developed 1,130bhp at 350rpm, to give a trials speed of 11 knots. Designed for clean petroleum products, the tanks were coated with Dimetcote D4. Vent-axia fans driven from a separate high pressure fire main were fitted for gas freeing and drying the tanks after washing. These water pressure driven fans replaced the old method of hoisting small canvas sails by the hatches to disperse fumes and dry out the tanks. Built for loading or discharging aground, the main customers were Regent, Phillips, Murco and Conoco, though *Anchorman* was time chartered to Shell-Mex & BP Ltd. Hamworthy pumps gave a discharge of 273 tons per hour at up to 70lbs pressure, with double cross over valves so that multigrade cargoes could be safely carried in the five tanks, each with a centre line bulkhead. Though not initially designed for bridge control, the extensive range of warning and remote controls fitted on the bridge and in the main accommodation alleyway adjacent to the engine room was approved by Lloyd's for the Unmanned Machinery Space (UMS) notation. *Guidesman* was also subsequently brought up to the requirements necessary to have the UMS notation. Like all the later tankers, she was built with a trunk as it improved longitudinal strength and slowed the roll, so making for a more pleasant sea boat.

Rowbothams' business was expanding rapidly with the opening of an office at Milford Haven to handle work for Texaco. There can be some heart stopping moments even for the successful shipowner, however, as was proved when Texaco decided they should put their tanker requirements out to tender! Rowbothams found themselves having to tender for a contract of affreightment requiring over a dozen ships. Loss of the work would have been catastrophic for the company but as it turned out no one else had enough tankers available, so Rowbothams were the only company able to tender.

Esso Poole (754/55) was built of all-welded construction as a bunkering tanker and had the moulded dimensions 186ft x 33ft x 13.5ft, with a cargo capacity of 46,250 cu. ft and a trial speed of 10 knots. The four pairs of heated cargo tanks were connected to two cargo pumps in the engine room. As bunker fuel has a high flash point, a separate pump room was not necessary. From The Motor Ship, August 1955

Apart from Texaco, they also had a 'gentleman's agreement' on charter rates with Esso, so a tanker could be fixed on just a phone call. Unlike other major oil companies, Esso bought few of the war surplus tankers and ordered several vessels during the 1950s. About half were for river or sheltered water work but beginning with the *Esso Poole* (754/55), they ordered a series of bunkering tankers. She was built at Hessle by the Henry Scarr yard, which was about to become Richard Dunston (Hessle) Ltd. *Esso Poole* was to be employed on bunkering duties at Fawley, Southampton. A sister was built by Philip & Son, Dartmouth, at a contract price of £194,314 and though appropriately named *Esso Brixham* (758/57), she was soon employed on the Mersey and also carried bitumen to Goole. The deadweight was about 1,082 tons on just under 12ft. Three slightly larger tankers able to carry 1,300 tons on 12ft 9½ins were also built. All were fitted with turbocharged English Electric 8-cylinder, 4-stroke engines. The varying horse powers quoted for *Esso Hythe*, *Esso Lyndhurst* and

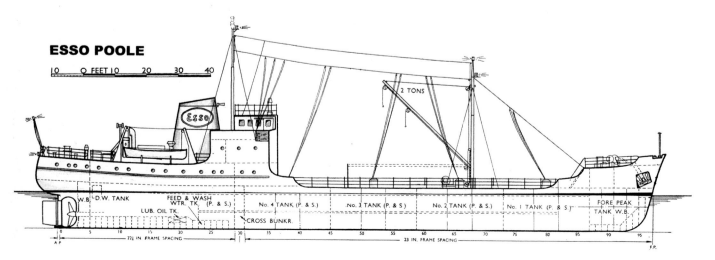

ESSO POOLE

10   0 FEET 10   20   30   40

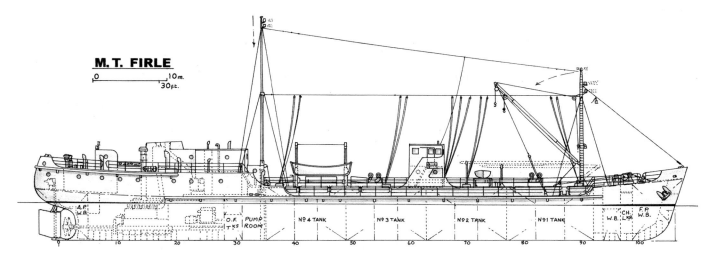

M. T. FIRLE

Esso Woolston were apparently the result of different rating values being recorded. The trials rating was 900bhp at 750rpm, while the service rating was 657bhp at 675rpm, which was delivered to the propeller at 225rpm via an MWD reverse/reduction gear box.

With the general decline in the coal trade and the change over to oil by a number of industries, collier owners Stephenson Clarke began to order coastal tankers for the expanding market and charter them to oil companies. Their main trade was to be in carrying bunker oil and similar products. Apart from these conventional tankers they also ordered two low air draught tankers to suit Port of London Authority rules for Thames work: *Firle* (948/58) and *Friston* (948/58). One of the interesting features resulting from the PLA rules was the narrow dry tanks on either side of the cargo tanks, to protect against spillage in the event of a collision. They were built by Richard Dunston, had the moulded dimensions 200ft x 34ft x14ft 6ins and could carry 1,223 tons on a draught of about 13ft. The main engine was a British 'Polar' M44M 4-cylinder, 2-stroke of 750bhp at 300rpm, which was coupled to a variable pitch propeller. This soon proved its worth in service on charter to Shell carrying clean products. The deck machinery was hydraulic. The foremast, which carried a 2-ton derrick, was hinged while the main mast was telescopic, raised and lowered by a pneumatic winch. Though built with Thames work in mind, they were classed for coasting UK and Eire, excluding the west coast of Ireland but not north of the Clyde or Inverness. Engine speed and propeller setting were controlled from the bridge with a combined telegraph, which also showed the propeller pitch. If necessary, the propeller could be locked and revert to reversing the engine for manoeuvering. Both were sold to Maldives Shipping Ltd, *Friston* in 1975 to become *Maldive Venture*, with *Firle* following in 1976 to become *Covodoro*.

Also diversyifing into other trades was the long established Dundee, Perth & London Shipping Co. who, as their title suggests, were engaged in the liner trade between the ports mentioned. This trade fell away after the Second World War and they then sent coasters to Canada for the summer season but this too declined and they decided to build a tanker to meet a charter on offer from BP Tankers Ltd. *Kingennie* (1,169/58), 215ft x 36ft x 14ft 9ins, was built by George Brown & Co. (Marine) Ltd to carry 1,481 tons on 13ft 9ins. The main engine was a British 'Polar' of 1,120 bhp for a speed of 11 knots. The design was quite old fashioned, with a hatch to a small dry store forward and a steam ballast pump. In contrast, single berth cabins were provided for the entire crew, hence the large accommodation block on the stern. She began an initial five years on time charter to BP at a rate rumored to have been £63,000 per annum. Although sailing for BP, she did so in Dundee, Perth & London colours of red funnel with black top. She was to be the company's last ship and following a voyage from Swansea via Dunkirk and Ghent, she arrived in the Tyne on 3rd March 1967 and was handed over to Cambridge (Tankers) Ltd, London. The company continued to manage her though, until sold to Greek owners in June 1972, who renamed her *Amalia*.

The Lady Grania (1,152/52) built for Arthur Guinness, Son & Co. (Dublin) Ltd, was what might be described as a dry cargo tanker, as she was a conventional coaster in appearance, though with the addition of four pairs of derricks able to lift four tons each. These were for lifting out bulk tanks of Guinness stout, shipped from the Dublin brewery to Liverpool, which were carried in insulated holds. A second vessel, *The Lady Gwendolen* (1,164/53) was built the following year.

The low air draught tanker Firle *(948/58) was built with work on the River Thames in mind. Apart from the main engine, four Lister-Blackstone engines were fitted in the forward part of the engine room, two driving generators which could also be coupled to pumps and two driving Stothart & Pitt cargo pumps through the bulkhead, as well as hydraulic pumps to supply the hydraulic deck machinery. However, tank drying still relied on windsails as the halyards suspended from the line between the masts indicates. From* The Motor Ship, *July 1959*

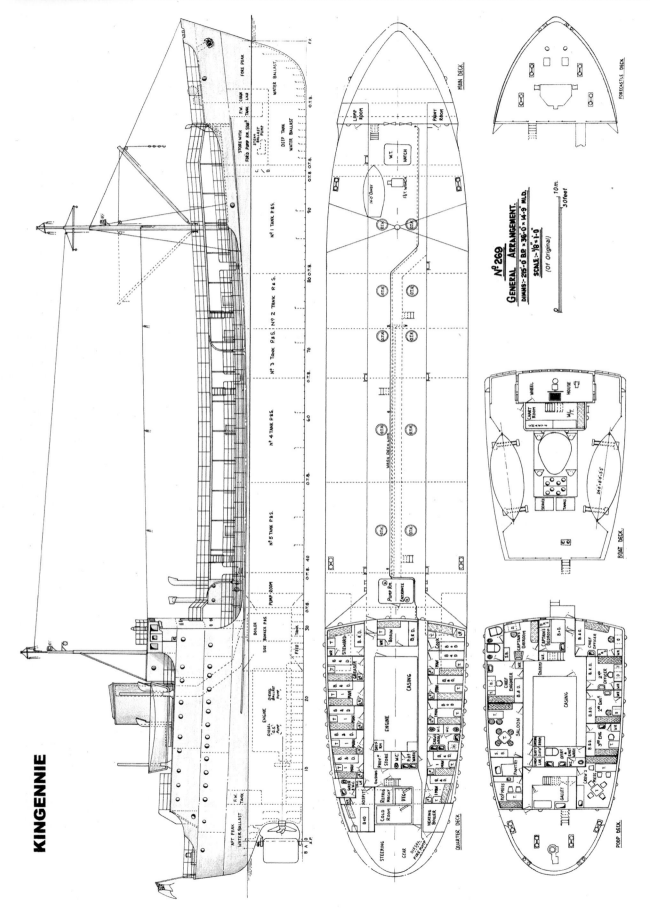

KINGENNIE

CHAPTER 6
THE 1960S

In this chapter moulded dimensions are given unless otherwise stated.

The decline of coastal shipping which began in the latter part of the 1950s continued into the early part of the 1960s, with *The Motor Ship* reporting that on average one coaster was being scrapped every nine days. Of course many of these vessels were old steam coasters but they were often not being replaced and many companies gave up shipowning as the coal trade continued to decline. One of the big steam fleets being rapidly reduced was the collier fleet of John Kelly Ltd, Belfast, although Alexander Hall had just built two motor colliers for them, *Ballyloran* (1,092/58) and *Ballylesson* (1,092/59), originally almost exclusively employed on coal to Northern Ireland. After *Ballylesson* was lengthened in 1964, increasing her deadweight from 1,320 to 1,626 tons, she was employed in more tramping and was not sold until the early 1980s. Meanwhile, the company had taken delivery of *Ballyrush* (1,575/62) and *Ballyrory* (1,575/63) from Hall, Russell of Aberdeen and, like the earlier pair, they followed the traditional long raised quarter deck layout and were rigged with derricks, although these were soon put ashore. Hall, Russell then followed up with *Spray* (890/62) for local Aberdeen coal merchants Ellis & McHardy, to replace their steamer of the same name. Her heavy masts and derricks were fitted with grabs so that she could discharge herself in Aberdeen. However, their coal trade was steadily reducing and she was sold in 1973 to C.H. Rugg & Co. Ltd, who passed her on to Rasheed Enterprises to become *Yasin*, the first Sharjah registered ship, in 1974.

Metcalfs added *Ann M.* (1,203/61), 218ft x 36ft x 15ft, and she followed the usual raised quarter deck style of the time but although her first cargo was coal to Shoreham, her regular employment was intended to be bulk road making materials around the east and south coasts. In later years, under Coe-Metcalf, she was used on the Northern Ireland coal run to ports like Londonderry. She was also the largest for the River Bann and was running coal to Coleraine from Blyth for some time. The machinery

Ballyrush (1,575/62) and sister Ballyrory (1,575/63) were typical motor colliers built for Kelly's coal trade to Belfast. Both had a conventional crusier stern in contrast to Spray (890/62), built next, which has a knuckle at the stern to reduce platework costs. As Spray was intended to be self discharging, particular attention was paid to her masts and derricks, with the derricks placed higher than usual on the masts to aid discharge using the ship's own grabs.

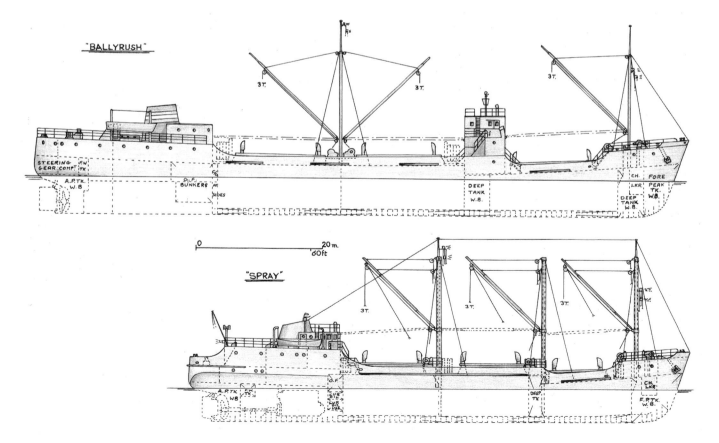

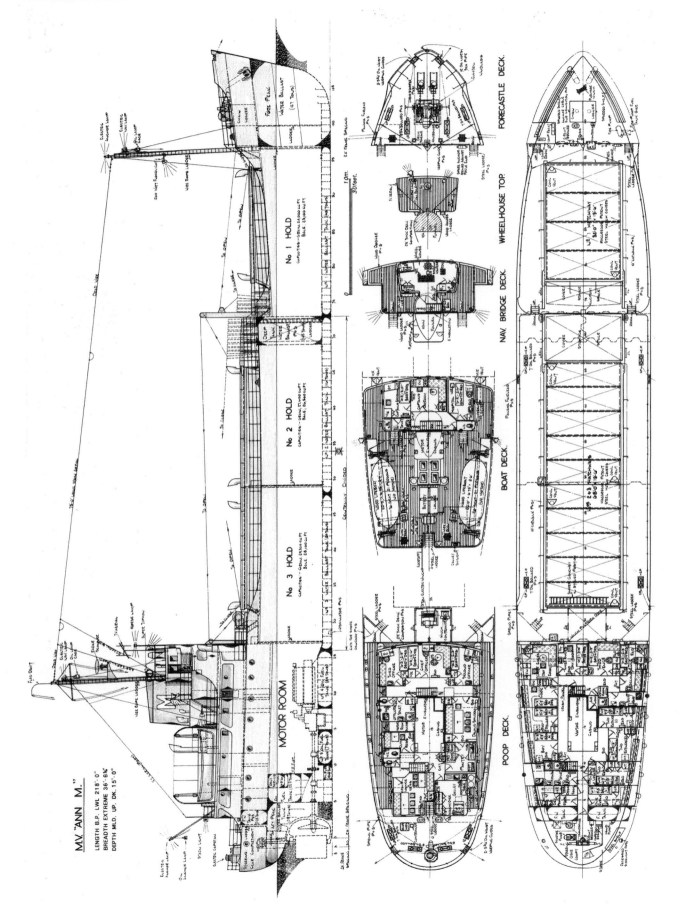

M.V. "ANN M."

LENGTH B.P. LWL 218'-0"
BREADTH EXTREME 36'-6⅞"
DEPTH MLD. UP. DK. 15'-0"

M.V. "ANN M"
LINES PLAN

The hatch coamings for the MacGregor hatches of Ann M (1,203/61) show up prominently as, unlike most coasters of the period, she had open rails rather than bulwarks. Photo DAVE HOCQUARD

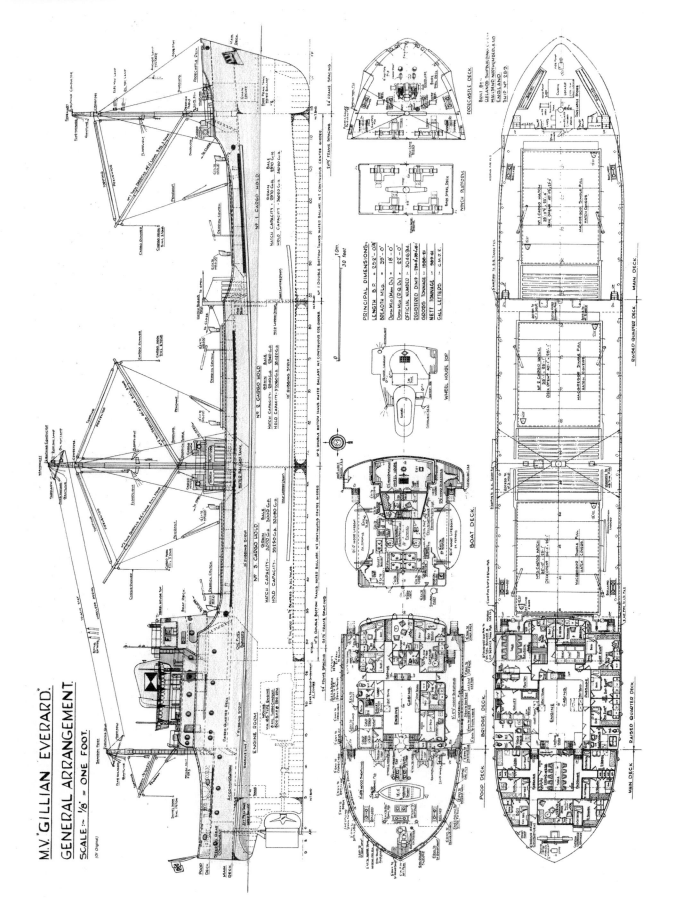

was somewhat unusual in that two 660 bhp Lister Blackstone 8-cylinder, 4-stroke engines were fitted, driving a single propeller at 225rpm via a reverse and reduction gear box. Although delivered gearless, for a deadweight of 1,650 tons on 14ft 8ins, provision was made for fitting gear if necessary, although in practice it was never carried out. Coe-Metcalf was acquired by James Fisher & Sons, plc in 1984 and she was laid up in the Tyne from July 1984. After lay-ups and passing through various hands she was damaged loading at Briton Ferry as *Ann II* in 1989 and was then moved to Menai to await demolition.

In terms of numbers, Everards' fleet had remained about the same at just under a hundred vessels but the 1960s saw various new classes emerge which were not confined to their fleet, illustrating the move to standard designs to cut building costs and take full advantage of maximised deadweight whilst staying just within the rules. Perhaps the most important design developed in the early 1960s was the work of Henry Robson, the naval architect at Clelands Shipbuilding Co. Ltd, who was largely responsible for the yard's design of a vessel just under the 1,600 gross limit which was marketed as the 'Exelship 2600'. Several owners placed orders and the first to be delivered was *Chesterbrook* (1,594/63), 250ft x 39ft x 18ft, for the Williamstown Shipping Co. Ltd (Comben Longstaff & Co. Ltd, managers). The deadweight was 2,607 tons on 17 feet draught and a grain capacity of 119,633 cubic feet. The strange stern (as shown on the plan of **Gillian Everard**) helped to get the most from the rules. The design was described in Lloyd's as having a *'raised deck forward of the poop 142 feet'*. The stern also featured a knuckle just below main deck level which simplified the bending required for the hull plating. Next to take delivery was Everards but the *William J Everard* (1,589/63), 251ft x 39ft x 18ft moulded, was built by Goole under sub-contract (both yards were controlled by the Craggs family) and claimed a higher grain capacity of 121,518 cubic feet. There were other differences too; whereas Clelands had used a frame spacing of 24.5 inches for the main central portion in their design, with the ends reduced to 24 inches, Goole used 24 inches throughout for Everards. Visible differences were the taller funnel of a simplified oval shape and a more rounded stern, so the crew members in the aftermost cabins got about 6 inches more room. Longstaffs ships' retained the concave funnel top style which was introduced on their first motor ship from Lewis of Aberdeen. Delivered the same month was *Penelope Everard* (1,583/63), which had a more complex curved top to the funnel that also featured on **Gillian Everard** (1,598/63) and *Rosemary Everard* (1,599/64).

It seems that Everards noticed that an extra frame space could be inserted in No. 3 hold so the moulded dimensions increased to 252ft 0.5ins x 39ft x 18ft while still staying under the limit and increasing grain capacity to 121,240 cubic feet, with deadweights recorded as 2,635 and 2,593 tons respectively. The lower deadweight for *Rosemary Everard* was probably due, at least in part, to a heavier Newbury engine compared with a Nohab Polar in **Gillian Everard**. All the Everard vessels were fitted with twin 3-ton derricks for each hatch compared with the single derricks fitted to the Longstaff ships and so the latter tended to have higher deadweight as their gear was lighter. Oddly enough the later vessels built for Comben Longstaff, *Corkbrook*, *Caernarvonbrook* and *Clarebrook*, did not incorporate the extra frame space. All their vessels were fitted with British Polar MN16S turbocharged 6-cylinder, 2-stroke engines. Following the success of turbocharging on an earlier ship, all the new vessels were so fitted giving a fuel consumption of 0.35 lbs/bhp/hour. *Glanton* for the Sharp SS Co. was similar. At this point new measurement rules came into force and *Rattray Head* (1,600/65) 255ft x 42ft 6ins x 18ft 3ins, was the first 'Exelship 2800', although the actual deadweight came in at 2,758 due to the owners other requirements. A self-trimmer, she had four hatches and four holds each served by a 3-ton derrick and was intended for the coal and bulk trade of A.F. Henry & MacGregor. A final, rather different vessel was built for Everards, *Ethel Everard* (1,599/66), 262ft x 40ft 9ins x 20ft 4ins, carrying 2,601 tons on 16ft 9ins, she was heavily geared with three 'goal-post' masts and eight derricks. For a number of years in the 1970s she ran regularly in the timber trade from Gothenburg to Grangemouth or Glasgow and Belfast, a trade acquired when Everards took over Glen & Co. of Glasgow. She did have a grain letter of approval but a few cargoes got wet owing to the crew probably not securing the Goterverken hatch covers properly, so did not stay on that trade. Grain letters specified the agreed amount to be bagged for sloping cargo areas and later rules required the cargo to be levelled off with a layer of bagged grain on top. The bags were filled from the loaded cargo and were not closed but left open so that the dockers could tip the grain out ready for discharge. However, the layer or layers of bagged grain stabilised the cargo sufficiently for safe passages to be made.

The 'Exelships' proved good timber carriers but the need for ships' gear was very much reduced after 1967, when Svenska Cellulosa A/B of Sweden began to assemble timber of one size but different lengths into standard packages which were generally loaded and unloaded by crane, followed by a rationalisation programme of loading and discharge ports in order to remain competitive with other suppliers of forest products. From the shipowners point of view this was less attractive, as there was

quite a lot of wasted space. In earlier times, cargoes of deals, battens and boards (DBB) were stowed individually, resulting in a tightly packed cargo. However, if the stevedores were not packing tightly it was not unknown for the crew to go into the holds and push timber into all the odd spaces after the stevedores had knocked off, to improve their cargo bonus!

Longstaffs sold their four 'Exelships' in 1976 to various Greek and Cypriot based companies. Unattractive freight rates and the continuing decline in the coal trade led the Sharp SS Co. to sell *Glanton* to Stephenson Clark who renamed her *Steyning* and two years later they also bought *Rattray Head* from Christian Salvesen, who were the owners of A.F. Henry & MacGregor. G.R. LeClercq recalls:

'My time in the Penelope Everard *and* Rosmary Everard *were good and pleasant. After being in the new* Actuality *(698/66) with Norwinch slewing derricks and Gotaverken folding hatches, things were much heavier on deck. The up side was the accommodation which was huge, plenty of room, large mess room, recreation room, etc and single cabins. As A.B.'s, cargo work was driving winches all day, loading paper pulp in winter in snow and wind left a lot to be desired but the many Swedish kroner were welcome! — Shore rates! We used the twin derricks for union purchase working. The two runners were shackled to a union plate, one derrick over the hold, the other over the quay. The Swedish dockers had a loading method we had to use which was to lower down slings of pulp to shoulder height then all the dockers would start to swing the pulp fore and aft two or three times and on their shout we would drop it, nearly always in the right position. This saved much crow-barring and a better stow, more below and less on deck — less work for us. The space at the ends of the hatches were fairly deep and to stop and reset the derricks took too long as they had no separate topping lift winches or dolly winches. With a full load of pulp up to the winch tables, nothing was better for the North Sea — the 'Old Man' on bonus for every bale on deck. We only carried coal, fertilizer, pulp and timber, all with no problems. One trip I remember in the* Rosemary Everard, *Antwerp to Portishead, cargo potash, not for a bad or uncomfortable trip, but what we did to the poor ship. There was a hard south-westerly gale pilot to pilot. Heavy seas cleared the forecastle head of everything, vents, ropes, wire reels, hawse and spurling covers, partly flooded the forecastle and we had to use insurance wire to tie up in Portishead. The starboard side bulwark on main deck was hanging off for half its length and had to be winched back. Opening No. 1 hatch revealed 6 to 8 feet of water. The hatch rubber seals were bad and with the amount of water going over, let it in. No's 2 and 3 were ok. Lots of suits with brief cases appeared on board! Lots of work all round. I never had a breakdown with the Newbury engines at sea but two in rivers. The year previously in* Superiority *(2,145/47), the timing chain broke shifting from Greenhithe to Tunnel Cement.* Rosemary Everard *also broke a timing chain passing Passage East power station bound for New Ross. Dropped anchor — all ok as ships could just pass at slow speed. A new chain arrived some days later which was fitted and then we proceeded to New Ross. We had never eaten so much salmon — bartered from the Irish poachers during the nights! Apart from that, the Newbury must have been a good strong work horse from a sailors point of view, and being a 2-stroke was simple to run, but heavy on engineers having to de-coke pistons and ports regularly, a hot horrible dirty job.'*

Pulp cargoes carried on deck were finally banned after a few incidences of cargoes becoming waterlogged and near capsizing. One of the last cargoes of pulp on deck was brought into the Thames by *William J. Everard* in the late 1960s.

During 1974, Everards began a re-engining programme for all of their 'Exelships'. *William J. Everard*, *Penelope Everard* and **Gillian Everard** received 8-cylinder, 4-stroke British Polar engines, whereas *Rosemary Everard* and *Ethel Everard* were each fitted with 12-cylinder, 4-stroke Mirrlees Blackstone engines, all with combined reverse reduction gear boxes. The lighter Polar engines and possibly other changes increased deadweight by about 40 tons. *William J. Everard* was sold in 1982 followed by the others in 1984, mostly to Maltese and Greek owners.

A pair of vessels were also built by Clelands for Everards' timber trade to Gunness wharf on the Humber. *Actuality* (698/66) and *Apricity* (692/67), with a deadweight of 1,154 tons, were considered to be the largest vessels suitable for the trade in the 1960s. Fully geared with single Norwinch slewing derricks, they were intended for loading cargoes of DBB's (deals battens and boards) using ships' gear where lifts could be made up to suit the derrick capacity. However, the change to packaged timber made their gear redundant a few years later. They had been built with 6-cylinder, 2-stroke Newbury engines and these were replaced by 8-cylinder, 4-stroke Mirrlees engines after just five years. Inclining experiments with the much lighter Mirrlees engines showed that they were unstable and so all the gear was removed except for the fore and mizzen masts necessary for navigation lights. This was still insufficient so some permanent ballast was fitted in the double bottom. With the new engines they worked as far as the Mediterranean with general cargo, containers and vehicles, returning with bulk cargoes of phosphate, pearlite and pumice. Later they returned to more local work. They were both sold to the Carisbrook Shipping Co. Ltd, Cowes, Isle of Wight, becoming *Greta C.* and *Helen C.*, though

the former spent a few months as *Hughina* with Allsworth Shipping before being sold on to Carisbrook.

Apart from building larger vessels, Everards were now beginning to replace their smaller vessels in order to service customers with draught restrictions or smaller cargo size requirements. For the smallest vessels, they turned to their own shipyard, Fellows & Co. Ltd, Great Yarmouth for three 199 gross boats. The first two were able to carry 287 tons and the last slightly stretched version 324 tons. The latter vessel, *Fixity* (199/66), was built in sections when the yard was not fully occupied with repair work for the fleet. They were all powered by Lister Blackstone engines of 320hp and were the last vessels to be built for the company, as the yard was sold to Richards Shipbuilders (part of United Molasses) in 1970. At 199 tons they were below much of the stricter regulations which covered coasters and their crew of master, mate and two deck hands were largely at the discretion of the owner but they were able to make fairly extensive voyages including to the continent. All were sold to small UK owners between 1974 and 1976.

The advantages of staying below the 199 gross limit but having vessels which met the requirements for coasting had already been exploited by the Hull Gates Shipping Co. (Craggs & Jenkins Ltd) in the late 1950s, following on from experience gained with earlier small vessels. The design was drawn up by Clelands (Successors) Ltd, which was also under the control of the Craggs family. It resulted in some smart little coasters with a mast at each end of the single hatch. The mizzen mast had a derrick arranged to reach over the combined wheelhouse and streamlined funnel casing to handle the single lifeboat, which was placed athwartships behind the funnel. First to be delivered was *Queensgate* (200/59) with the moulded dimensions 110ft 3ins x 25ft x 9ft 2ins. Water ballast was low at 37 tons and the single hold was 72 feet long. *Humbergate* (200/60) followed but her service with the company was short as she sank off Trevose Head on 2nd October 1963, after developing a sudden leak while on passage from Porthoustock to Bristol with a cargo of stone. The last to be delivered was *Paullgate* (200/61), appropriately named as she was built by J.R. Hepworth & Co. Ltd, Paull, Hull. The company had good experience with their small ships in the 1950s, which lead to the orders; however, as Mr S.F. Craggs explained in 1965, 'the intense competition on the east coast from foreigners, particularly Dutch and German, rather forced us to sell. In addition, we had higher running costs.' Both were sold to Ross & Marshall, Glasgow for work around the Clyde and islands. With a deadweight of 290 tons on about 8ft 5ins, they were well suited to that trade. All were powered by Lister 6-cylinder, 4-stroke 264 bhp engines.

Although a fair number of small Clyde 'Puffer' style coastal lighters were built during the Second World War, some of which were diesel powered, they had little effect on the fleets of the Clyde owners of this type of vessel, who continued to rely on steam. It was not until *Glenshira* (153/53) was built for G.&G. Hamilton of Glasgow in 1953 by Scott & Sons, Bowling that the change to motor

Glenshira (153/53) was built for G.&G. Hamilton, Glasgow by Scott & Sons Ltd, Bowling. From a profile in The Motor Ship, *April 1953.*

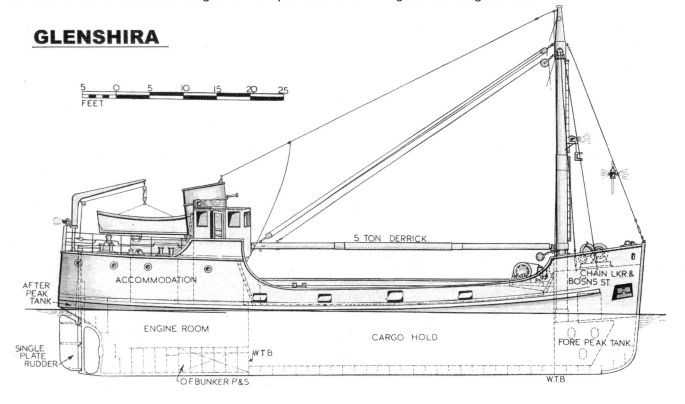

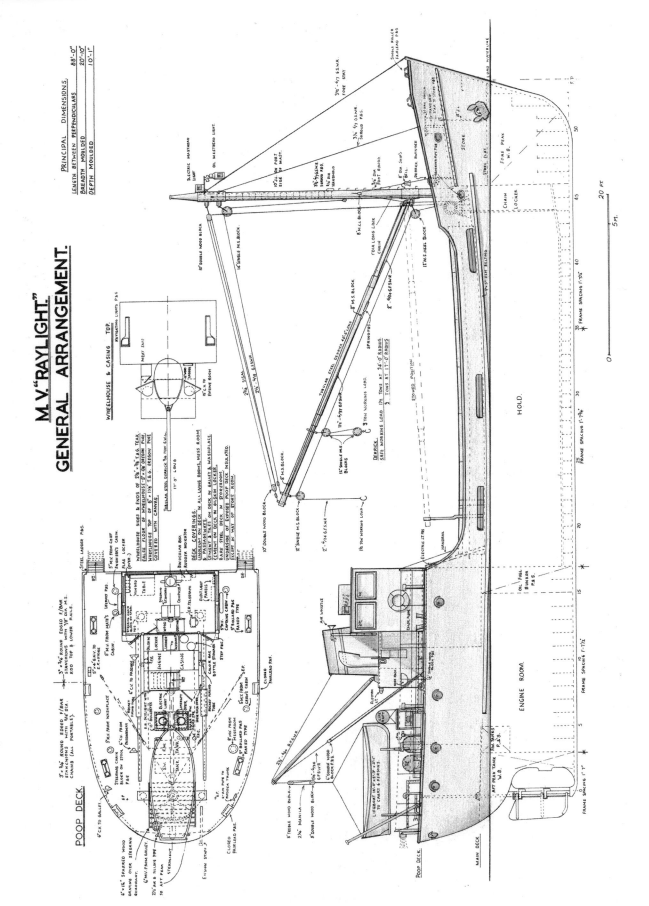

M.V. "RAYLIGHT."
GENERAL ARRANGEMENT.

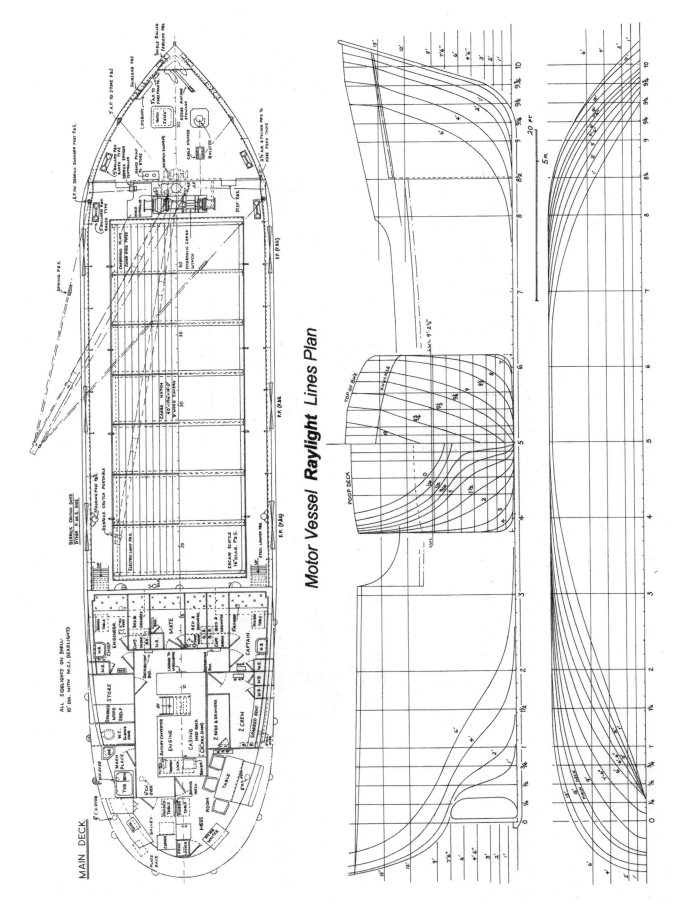

Motor Vessel Raylight Lines Plan

vessels finally began. With an overall length of 86ft 6ins and an extreme breadth of 20ft 3ins, she was the maximum size for the Crinan Canal and resulted in rather bluff lines and a speed of 8 knots from the 270bhp British Polar 5-cylinder, 2-stroke running at 600rpm, which drove the propeller at 200rpm via a reduction gear. By this time there was little trade on the Forth & Clyde Canal, which closed to commercial traffic in 1963, and so the maximum dimensions for the Crinan Canal were used. This canal avoided the need to sail round the exposed Mull of Kintyre. She was able to carry about 190 tons on a draught of 9 feet. As usual for this type of vessel the hull was built to a robust specification considerably exceeding the minimum required by the classification society but essential as she would be frequently in drying harbours or even beaches on occasion. A substantial 5-ton derrick operated by a hydraulic winch allowed her to discharge heavy cargoes like machinery around the Scottish Isles. In 1974, after being laid up for a period, she was sold to Peter Herbert and towed down to Bideford, subsequently being sold to other UK owners. Hamiltons ordered their second motor vessel, *Glen Sheil* (195/59) from Livingstones of Peterhead, which incorporated a controllable pitch propeller combined with an Alpha engine of 310bhp for a speed of about 9 knots; it was one of the first small British coasters to have this combination. In 1963 they merged their management operations with G.&G. Hamilton to form Hay-Hamilton but the companies retained their own identities and funnel colours. Hays had just lost their first motor vessel *Druid* (197/58), which had capsized the previous year on Preston Bar. Righted the next day, she was sold to Preston Corporation to become a radio communications and weather vessel, replacing an old tug which had been anchored at the mouth of the Ribble. Following the link-up, Hamiltons returned to Scotts of Bowling for two more vessels, *Glenfyne* (198/65) and *Glencloy* (200/66), both 100ft 4ins x 23ft x 9ft moulded, with a similar Alpha engine and controllable pitch propeller arrangement to that which had proved successful in *Glen Sheil*. *Glen Sheil* herself was to founder sailing from Ayr in 1973.

Meanwhile Ross & Marshall had their first motor vessel, *Raylight* (184/63), of 220 tons deadweight, built by Scotts Shipbuilding, where she was dwarfed by the ocean ships for which the yard were best known. Machinery selected was the popular Crossley 6-cylinder, 2-stroke engine of 300bhp. She was followed by *Dawnlight I* (199/65), which at 97ft 10ins x 20ft 10ins x 10ft 1ins moulded was 9ft 10ins longer, increasing the deadweight to 259 tons. A novel feature was an Atlas loader (hydraulic arm) in place of a derrick. This proved very successful and was fitted to subsequent vessels. She was regularly employed on various coal runs (latterly from Ayr) until 1988, when she was sold to work on a project and eventually sold on to the West Indies in 1990. Ross & Marshall merged their operations with Hay-Hamilton in 1968 to form Glenlight Shipping but with plenty of small ships available from London owners, no further new ships were built and with larger ships the voyages were not just confined to the Western Isles and Northern Ireland.

Meanwhile, Thomas Watson had ordered *Lady Serena* from Clelands and a much more utilitarian barge-style design emerged, with the moulded dimensions 130ft x 25ft x 8ft 8ins that could carry 361 tons on 7ft 5ins and so was an improvement on the earlier Hull Gates' vessels, which was at least partly due to the fact that *Lady Serena* was gearless. They chose a Bergius-Kelvin 6-cylinder, 4-stroke as they felt that this would be more reliable than a Lister, although it meant a reduction in speed. A new vessel at around £42,000 was considered satisfactory, as Government support was available towards the cost. However, two sisters, *Lady Sarita* (200/65) and *Lady Sheena* (200/65), were both built in Holland. All three were sold in the mid-1970s and were taken up by small local owners, Watsons' china clay work being much reduced as bulk trains had tended to replace coasters.

Following a careful study by Clelands which showed that deadweight could be improved by careful interpretation of the rules, Everards placed an order for what was to become the 'Exelship 400'. The changes included a double bottom and avoiding or reducing unusable space by fitting a ballast tank (exempt from tonnage measurement) below the fore deck, along with an engine room store aft. The previous vessel had wood hatch covers but these vessels had MacGregor hatch covers and this led to rather cramped quarters for the four crew, as space was needed for stowage of the covers when open, as the hatch was as large as practicable for ease of loading and discharge. On the plus side the crew did have the benefit of radar, autopilot and hatches which could be opened in a few minutes. The general arrangement drawing was submitted to Everards in June 1967, of a vessel with the moulded dimensions 129ft 2ins x 25ft x 11ft 1in, giving a deadweight of 425 tons on a draught of 8ft 10.5ins and a double bottom which contributed to a total ballast capacity of 232 tons. This allowed them to make ballast passages in bad weather. The grain capacity was up from 16,530 to 18,435 cubic feet. The initial proposal was to fit a Rolls-Royce V8 medium speed diesel of 340bhp, with a 3.5 reduction/reverse gear box to give a speed of about 9 knots. The engines were manufactured in Shrewsbury as Rolls-Royce had taken over the old Sentinel works, best remembered for their

excellent steam wagons though post-war they built a diesel version.

However, Everards preferred to stay with the less powerful and larger Lister-Blackstone 4-cylinder, 4-stroke for which there was more marine experience. Despite the extra weight, bulwarks were chosen over rails, as the rails on *Lady Serena* had been frequently damaged. First to be delivered was *Futurity* (198/68), although her launch was delayed for a few days when she stuck on the ways. To utilise the space in the yard as efficiently as possible, she was built on the same ways as her sister *Formality* (199/68). By this time the yard had become part of Swan, Hunter Small Ship Division, although no builder was indicated on the plan, only the Yard No. 300. The price was about £75,000 including the Lister-Blackstone ERS4MGR engine of 330 bhp at 750 rpm, with a 2:1 reduction gear to give 9 knots. However, trials on 3rd July achieved a speed of 10 knots light. As usual when Government support was available, owners placed orders rapidly before the support was withdrawn.

A new entrant was Tower Shipping, formed by London brokers who decided it was profitable to become owners under the scheme. *Tower Venture* and *Tower Conquest* were delivered in 1968 and the company returned for a further three in 1969. *Tower Duchess* and *Tower Princess* were built by Clelands but the final vessel, *Tower Marie*, was subcontracted to J.R. Hepworth & Co. Ltd, Hull and was the last to be completed. All these vessels had the Rolls-Royce V8 around which the engine room had been designed, as did the subsequent vessels.

G.R. LeClercq recalls:

'My time in Tower Shipping was good and varied with hard work and good pay. Nearly all the problems in the early years with the Rolls-Royce engines were due to the cooling. When Tower changed over to salt water intercooling and head-hunted the Rolls-Royce service engineer to become marine superintendent, things ran very well. They were good sea ships with just enough horsepower loaded and plenty of double bottom ballast so there was little time lost making ballast passages. The small tank forward of the hatch was not actually used and was just there to reduce the tonnage measurement. They were very easy ships to load nearly always full. With heavy winter wheat it was necessary to be careful with trim and always a slope to bag off for safety. They were also used for general cargo from Glasson Dock to Castletown, Isle of Man. Full down below with flats, generals and full deck containers – a drop of ballast if required – couldn't be better. Never stopped for weather, unless there was no prospect of getting into Castletown harbour with an on-shore gale. We couldn't pull up in time before the swing bridge and then we could be pounding on the rock bottom at low-water! They were very strongly and heavily built, easy to handle and with small alterations to the accommodation, all you needed. Small, yes, but most of the time we ran three handed and if you all got on it worked. Most weekends in the UK everybody got home. I, from Jersey, looked after the ship, opened up for the dockers, pumped the ballast ready for the tide, then crew aboard and away. The share system worked well, the incentive was there and a like-minded crew made good money and it was years before I came near that money in the weekly [wages] boats.'

The next order also came from London brokers entering shipowning, with Eggar, Forrester ordering three which were all subcontracted. *Wiggs* (199/70) was built by Hepworths and the remaining two, *Wib* (199/70) and *Wis* (199/70), were built by the Malta Drydocks Corporation, which was now under Swan, Hunter management. Eggar, Forrester placed management of the vessels with G.T. Gillie & Blair of Newcastle. The final order came from the Aberdeen Coal & Shipping of Aberdeen, as a replacement for the larger *Ferryhill* dating from 1946, the new vessel becoming *Ferryhill II* in 1971. By this time Government support had been withdrawn and no further vessels were ordered.

Eggar Forrester chartered their three to Clyde Shipping for their Glenlight Shipping subsidiary, which had its origins in Clyde puffer owners who operated in the Clyde, Northern Ireland and Western Isles. They exercised a purchase option in the charter. One was lost and the remaining two disposed of, *Sealight* to underwriters following a grounding, and *Glenetive* sold. Tower Shipping kept theirs longer but had sold all but one by 1980. Two went to local owners, the Sully and Palmer families and were managed by Sully Freight, Norwich. In later times, the 'XL400's were passed around various small owners and some went overseas. A transom stern version of the 'XL400' was built by Cooks of Wivenhoe for Watsons. Everards kept theirs longest, being employed where work limited the size of the vessel. They were ideal for cement cargoes from Bevans Wharf at Northfleet to the Isle of Wight and were on the run for many years, although the cement, still warm from the kiln, caused corrosion in the double bottom by producing a warm steamy atmosphere in the empty tanks. Also in connection with the Thames cement works they would go to St. Valery to load cargoes of flints. They were not replaced as new regulations requiring certificated crews were imminent and in addition they were already forced to pay expensive pilotage in the Humber up to Selby, whereas if the same ship and crew arrived coastwise from the Thames for example, the ship was exempt from pilotage.

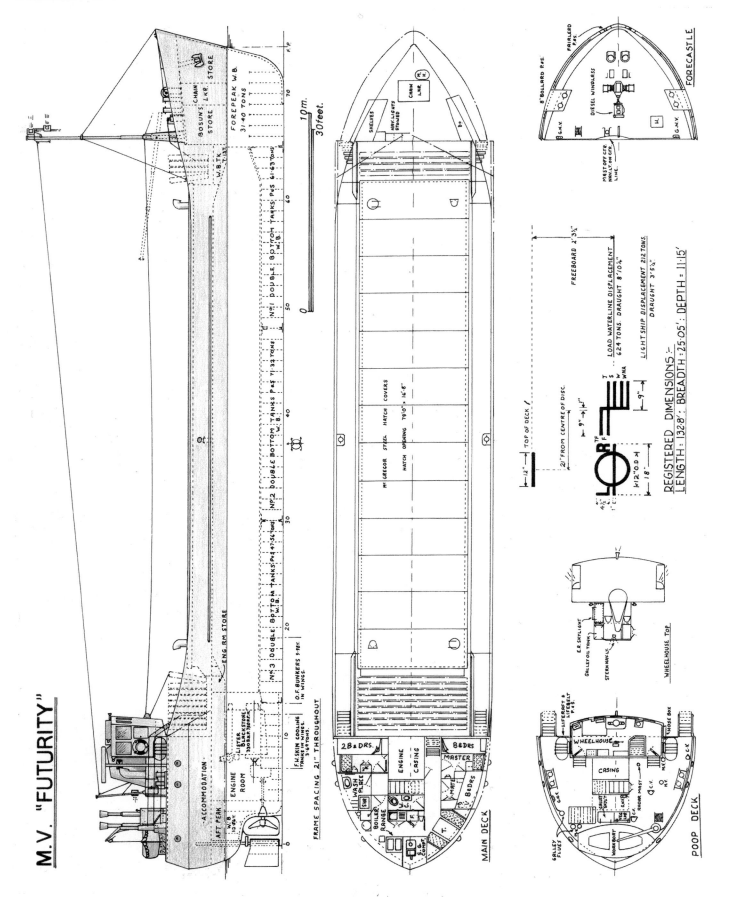

M.V. "FUTURITY"

FORECASTLE

FAIRLEAD P&S.

8" BOLLARD P&S.

DIESEL WINDLASS

MAST OFF CTR.
NAV.LT. ON CTR.
LINE.

G.M.V.   G.N.V.

H.

FREEBOARD 2'3½"

TOP OF DECK

2' FROM CENTRE OF DISC.

LR

LOAD WATERLINE DISPLACEMENT
624 TONS. DRAUGHT 8'10¾"

LIGHT SHIP DISPLACEMENT 212 TONS.
DRAUGHT 3'5¼"

REGISTERED DIMENSIONS:-
LENGTH: 132·8': BREADTH: 25·05': DEPTH: 11·15'

WHEELHOUSE TOP

E.R. SKYLIGHT

GALLEY OIL TANK

STERN NAV. LT.

POOP DECK

WHEELHOUSE

LIFERAFT & LIFEBELT P&S.

HOSE BOX

CASING

RADAR MAST

GALLEY FLUES

WORKBOAT

MAIN DECK

SHELVES

NAV. LIGHTS STOWED

CHAIN LKR.

McGREGOR STEEL HATCH COVERS

HATCH OPENING 79'10" x 16'8"

FORE PEAK W.B.
31·40 TONS

BOSUN'S CHAIN LKR. STORE

W.B.TK.

No.1 DOUBLE BOTTOM TANKS P&S 61·63 TONS
W.B.

No.2 DOUBLE BOTTOM TANKS P&S 71·33 TONS
W.B.

No.3 DOUBLE BOTTOM TANKS P&S 47·54 TONS
W.B.

O.F. BUNKERS 5·18T.
IN WINGS

F.W.SKIN COOLING TANKS IN WINGS.
3·47TONS.

LISTER BLACKSTONE
330 B.H.P. 750 R.P.M.

FRAME SPACING 21" THROUGHOUT

ENG. RM STORE

ENGINE ROOM

ACCOMMODATION

AFT PEAK
W.B.
13·04 T.

2 BERTHS

WASH PLACE

BOILER RANGE

ENGINE CASING

MASTER
BEDRM

MATE BEDRMS

BEDRMS

"SAINT FERGUS."

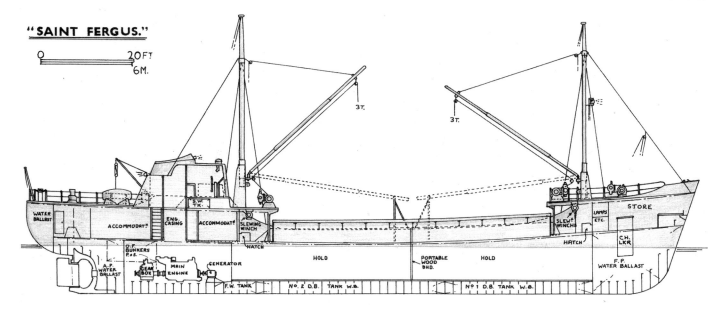

The original quotation for *Ferryhill II* was £80,000 but by the time she was delivered it had increased to £103,000. Her first cargo was coal from Blyth. She could make a hundred voyages a year, the usual sequence being Monday discharge coal at Aberdeen and sail for Blyth in the afternoon; arrive at Blyth twelve hours later in time to load Tuesday, then arrive back on Wednesday and discharge, sail and load Blyth on Thursday, to arrive Aberdeen on Friday. These small vessels were worked hard as this round of voyages shows. The company became part of British Fuels Scottish Division in 1973 and voyages became more varied, covering Inverness, Invergordon and Lossiemouth. Even so, in summer the drop in coal consumption meant that she was free for other voyages such as stone from Berwick and Inverkeithing to the Thames, grain from Rotterdam and Antwerp, and as far as Hamburg to load salt for Peterhead and Aberdeen. She became *Subro Victor* in 1978 for Sully Freight.

Much of the J.&A. Gardner fleet was built in Dutch yards, although in the 1960s orders were placed with British yards and one of those to benefit was Lewis of Aberdeen, who built the coaster *Saint Fergus* (346/64), 128ft x 26ft x 10ft 6ins. She had one hold 76 feet long with a 3-ton derrick at each end and had a grain capacity of 19,950 cubic feet. With a deadweight of 432 tons on a draught of about 9ft 8ins, it is interesting to contrast her trawler-style design with the 'Exelship 400'. Although of the same deadweight, the gross tonnage was much greater and needed a crew of six, or seven if a cook was carried. The engine chosen was a 4-stroke, V-12 Dorman (English Electric) that could be controlled and started from the bridge, developing 495bhp at 1,500rpm. This drove the propeller via a 6:1 reduction MWD gear box which also provided reverse. The engine was turbocharged by two CAV exhaust gas driven units. Only one engineer was carried and a saving of £2,000 per year was expected as a result. The main engine also drove a 7kw, 220 volt generator via a clutch and the total weight of the engine, gear box and spares was 5.9 tons. Two Ruston-engined generator sets completed the engine room, whilst the deck machinery was hydraulic. The main machinery was expected to run for four years between major inspection and overhaul but this proved optimistic and a new engine had to be fitted in 1966. Although good from a weight point of view, these high rpm engines tended not to be as rugged as the slower running types for marine use. The hatches were wood and she was expected to carry granite from the company quarry at Bonawe on Loch Etive to restricted berths, as well as general and bulk cargoes to similar destinations around the Western Isles and the Irish Sea. In 1979, a hydraulic crane was fitted in place of the main mast to speed the discharge of road making materials. She was sold to Singapore owners in 1981 and was renamed *Cape Elizabeth*. Larger new vessels came from Scotts of Bowling and Connell.

While Clelands were developing their 'Exelship 2600' raised quarter deck style design, Goole were working on a single deck vessel capable of lifting 2,650 tons on a summer draught of 15ft 9ins for the Klondyke Shipping Co. Ltd of Hull. The contract had called for vessels of maximum deadweight, cubic capacity and cargo handling, with good crew accommodation, and resulted in *Framptondyke* (1,599/64) and *Revesbydyke* (1,599/64), with the moulded dimensions 260ft x 41ft 6ins x 20ft 4ins. As regards cubic capacity at 124,413, it exceeded that of the 'Exelships' of a similar deadweight and met the tonnage rules then in force in a similar though less obvious way, as the sheer of the monkey poop

Saint Fergus (346/64) was built by Lewis of Aberdeen and, as this profile shows, was essentially a coaster version of the designs Lewis' supplied to the trawler industry. Built for J.&A. Gardner, Glasgow, her main work was intended to be carrying roadstone from their quarry at Bonawe on Loch Etive, delivering it to Glasgow and small harbours and piers around the west of Scotland. Profile from a plan in The Motor Ship, October 1964.

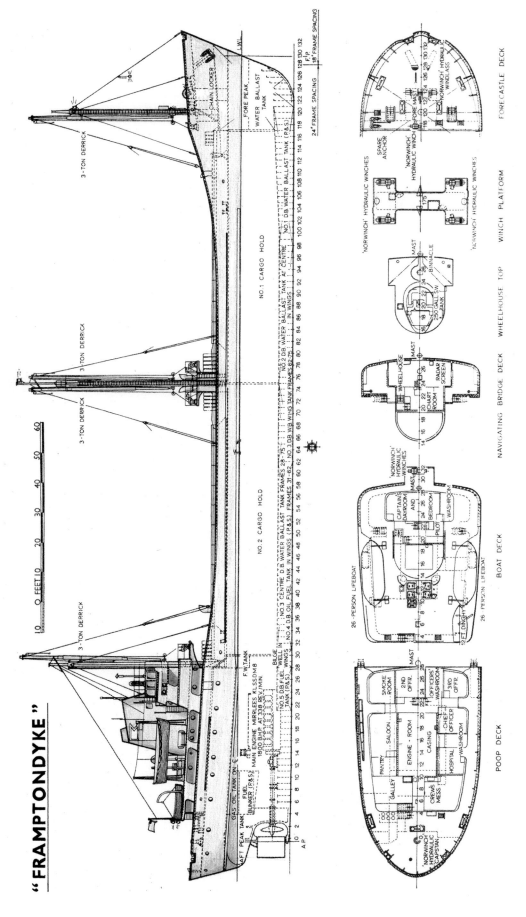

Framptondyke (1,599/64) and her sister were designed and built with the Klondyke Shipping Co's timber import trade in mind and the layout was particularly suited to timber, with sheer eliminated from the main deck and derricks stowed vertically to give ease of stowage of deck cargoes. This Goole design was subsequently developed into a gearless transom sterned version for Everards, built during the 1970s. From, The Motor Ship, April 1965.

deck rose to almost the same height as the tiny section of what would have been the main deck, if extended, at the stern. There was provision for a crew of twenty-one, as the vessels were expected to go beyond the Baltic and Mediterranean and when required, cross the Atlantic, primarily for timber for which they were designed, as well as carry grain cargoes. The first round of cargoes for *Framptondyke* were coal from Hull to Southampton, then grain from Rouen to Poland, followed by timber from Finland to Newcastle. For loading the two long unobstructed holds, there were six 3-ton capacity derricks, four on the main mast between the hatches and one each end on the fore and mizzen masts. Care was taken with the design of the hatches so that they were classed as self-trimmers for the coal trade and had MacGregor single pull hatch covers. A hint of the change to gearless ships reliant on shore discharge and loading was the vertical stowage of the derricks, so that they did not have to be cleared away before the hatches could be opened. The gear was all Norwinch hydraulic, which was both robust and reliable and would be familiar to stevedores loading timber with ships gear in Scandinavian countries. The generators were Rolls-Royce driven and though not turbocharged, should have been in a sound proofed area according to the *The Motor Ship* correspondent, to reduce engine room and accommodation noise. The main engine was a Mirrlees KLSSDM8, which produced 1,800bhp at 338rpm and was directly coupled to a four blade propeller, 7ft 6ins in diameter with a mean pitch of 4ft 8ins. The engine was fitted with a Napier Brush turboblower and air cooler, and was direct reversing. *Framptondyke* was sold to Stephenson Clarke Shipping Ltd in 1975 and renamed *Whittering*. Unfortunately, the following year she collided with *Odin* while on passage from Rotterdam to Cork with wheat. She was abandoned and sank the following day.

Revesbydyke's life was very much shorter as, soon after completion, on a voyage to Brazil she grounded on a sandbank near Itajai in the south of the country and subsequently became a total loss. She was loading timber there for Great Yarmouth but crossing the bar on 2nd September 1965 she developed a heavy list and struck the breakwater. She grounded and heeled over on to the breakwater. The ship was refloated only to ground again on a sandbank because of flooding in the engine room and accommodation, where she remained, her position gradually deteriorating. Divers reported there was a longitudinal fracture about 6 feet long in the port side plating and the bottom plating badly indented overall. On 23rd September, it was reported she had broken between No. 2 hatch and the engine room. Subsequently, *Revesbydyke* slowly sank into the sand with little visible after a few months, although the timber cargo washed off and was recovered in part. The company immediately ordered a replacement, which became *Somersbydyke* (1,598/67). The opportunity was taken to improve the design under the new measurement rules and deadweight increased to 3,120 tons. In 1978 she was sold to Stephenson Clarke Shipping Ltd and renamed *Pearl*, the name suggesting she was intended to augment the ex-Robertson fleet and the limestone trade which they had taken over. Sold later to Bremar Shipping Ltd, Cayman Isles (Lindsay Terminals & Trading Co. Ltd, Leith, managers) she was renamed *Rosemount*. Douglas Lindsay recalls:

'By this time she had become a bit battered from years of bulk cargoes but was otherwise reasonable for her age although she did arrive with the main engine out of tune and not performing properly. We got in a Mirrlees expert and he sorted out the timing, caused mainly by worn parts in the fuel train. She was then operated on long distance trades. Renamed Mull in 1984, she traded for the same owners for a few more years before dire markets forced her into lay-up in 1986 at Avonmouth, then sale.'

After various further owners she was broken up in India in 1998.

Fishers also continued to order coasters with an eye to having them suitable for project cargoes. *Leven Fisher* (1,540/62) was built for them by the Burntisland Shipbuilding Co. Ltd, with the moulded dimensions 241ft x 38ft 10ins x 19ft 5ins and could carry 2,370 tons on a draught of 16ft 9ins. Water ballast was good at 865 tons and useful when carrying bulky light cargoes. Fishers managed three vessels with names beginning 'Marchon' that delivered phosphate rock from North Africa to the Marchon plant at Whitehaven and so she was built to the maximum size for this trade when not wanted for special cargoes. The after hold was particularly long to handle these cargoes and she had three 5-ton derricks if needed. If it was necessary to carry a cargo longer than the hold (and after hatch) the foremast, derricks and winch platform could be unshipped to clear the deck completely. The main engine was a Deutz 8-cylinder, 4-stroke of 1,800 bhp which gave a speed of about 12 knots. Like other Fisher ships, she occasionally helped out on short sea container services, generally for British Railways.

The gear was removed when she was converted in 1969 to carry twelve 50-ton nuclear fuel containers. Following trials in April 1969, she sailed in May via Durban and Singapore for Japan and could make about three round trips per year. She also carried similar containers to and from Italy. This contract came to an end in 1979 and she reverted to more general trading before being sold

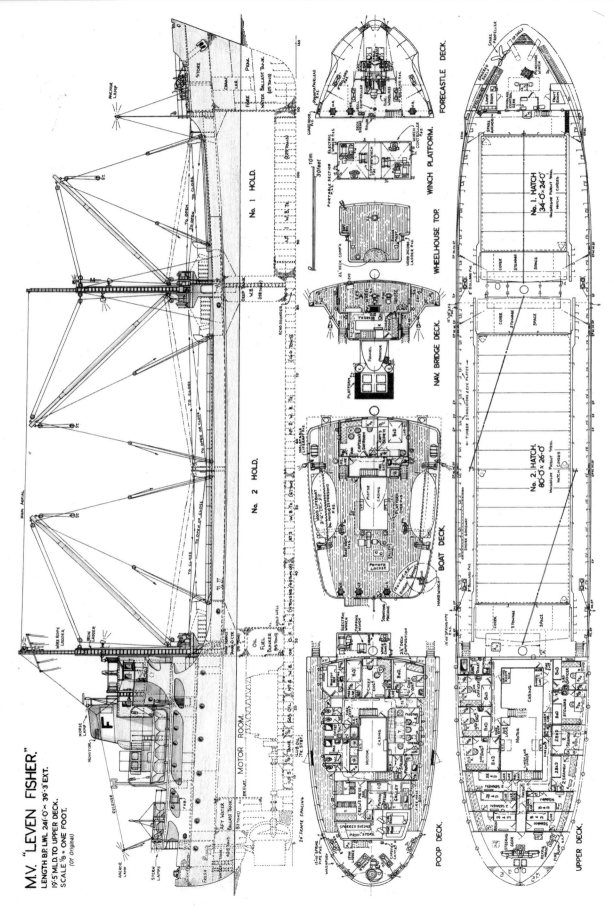

M.V. "LEVEN FISHER."
LENGTH B.P. L.W.L 241'-0" × 39'-3" EXT.
19'-5" MLD. TO UPPER DECK.
SCALE 1/8" = ONE FOOT.
(or original)

FORECASTLE DECK.

WINCH PLATFORM.

WHEELHOUSE TOP.

NAV. BRIDGE DECK.

BOAT DECK.

POOP DECK.

UPPER DECK.

Leven Fisher (1,540/62) was built in 1962 with long and heavy special cargoes in mind and it was possible to unship the foremast and associated gear to permit especially long cargoes to be carried on deck.

to Ali Samin & Co., Syria who renamed her *Haj Hassan*.

The London & Rochester ('Crescent') barge fleet went from being essentially a smooth waters operation around the Thames and Medway to a fleet of mostly new mini-coasters in the 1960s, taking advantage of the favourable situation regarding crews who were not required to have formal qualifications for vessels below 200 tons gross but rather a few years of hands-on experience. The appearance of *Andescol* (191/61) introduced vessels able to carry about 250 tons with sufficient accommodation for more extended voyages. She was registered in the name of Francis & Gilders Ltd, a subsidiary of the London & Rochester Trading Co. Ltd. The Dutch built *Elation* (196/63) was followed by *Caption* (189/63) and *Diction* (189/63) from Richard Dunston's yard. But perhaps the first true small coasters came from J. Samuel White, Cowes with the delivery of *Bencol* (200/64) for Francis & Gilders, followed by near sister *Horation* (205/64). The latter broke her back at Mistley, having arrived from Nijmegen with a cargo of bagged starch in March 1981. The next pair, *Ignition* (199/67) and *Jubilation* (199/67), came from Hepworths of Hull. *Ignition* was sold to C.P.R. Nicholson, Stornoway in 1986 and was wrecked the following year. *Jubilation* went to rough seas too and passed to Mezeron Ltd, Ramsey, Isle of Man as *Laxey River* and then two years later to owners in the USA. London & Rochester's own yard at Strood added *Kiption* (198/68), though she was registered in the name of Francis & Gilders. They were able to carry up to about 300 tons and the last, *Lodella*, was added to the fleet in 1970. All were sold in the 1980s with the last, *Libation* (198/69) sold in 1985; many went to local, often captain owners who had lower operating costs and several became sand carriers on the Thames for Priors.

London & Rochester also ordered four larger types. Eric Hammal recalls:
'*Ambience, Blatence, Cadence and* Eloquence *were a four ship order for 'Crescent' to Drypool Engineering & Drydock [Yard No's 25-28]. The design was Drypool's and the hull form chosen was virtually that of the war-built 'Chants.' Building had already commenced when Drypool bought Cochrane at Selby and to meet the delivery date, the fourth (28) was built at Selby as yard No. 1528. The contract required a total deadweight of 550 tons to be lifted on winter marks. The completed vessels were not achieving this and were facing penalties or rejection. As Naval Architect at the newly acquired yard, I was asked to provide a quick and cheap solution, hence the hatch-side boxes converting the hatchway into a trunk. As the hatch-side boxes were set up as ballast tanks, there was no increase in gross tonnage. Under the rules the trunk allowed a reduction in freeboard and consequent increase in draught and so deadweight which could be carried. Although the conversion added about 7 tons of extra steel, the summer deadweight increased from 568 to 603 tons after fitting, which lifted the winter deadweight over the required 550 tons. The increase in draught was about 5.5 inches. My records noted that the IMCO [International Maritime Consultative Organisation] stability requirements were marginal for the design.*'

All were delivered between May and August 1969. The moulded dimensions were 139ft 0ins x 25ft 6ins x 12ft 4ins and the first delivered was *Blatence* (392/69), which was actually built by R. Hepworth & Co. (Hull) Ltd as their yard No. 104. Next was *Ambience* (392/69), followed by *Cadence* (392/69), both from Drypool, and completed by *Eloquence* (392/69) from Cochrane as Yard No. 1528. First to be sold was *Ambience* which became *Gino* of Guardscreen Shipping Ltd in 1982 and the others followed to various UK owners, with all sold by 1987. Two were operated by Dennison Shipping Ltd, Kirkwall, whilst *Blatence* was lost as *Calf Sound* in 1989, when her cargo of cement and

London & Rochester's Ignition *of 1967 was one of a group of vessels built for the company in the 1960s which made the step from barges to small home trade coasters but remaining under the 200 gross limit to take advantage of the minimal crew qualifications needed. They were soon employed on voyages to destinations where small cargo size or shallow draught was needed, often working around the greater Thames area and the Continent.* Ignition *was eventually sold to Mr Nicholson, renamed* Eilian Roisin Dubhe *and registered in Stornoway. Following an engine failure, she grounded and was wrecked on 30th October 1986 at Loch Carnan; the crew of three were rescued.*

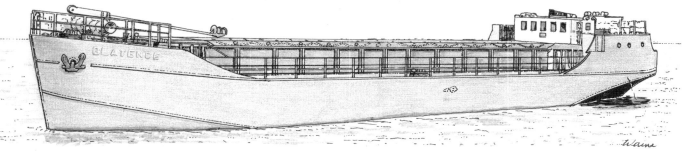

This sketch of **Blatence** (392/69) (ABOVE) shows the original design but it soon became apparent in service that they were unable to meet the owner's specified winter deadweight. At this point, the builders, Drypool, took over Cochranes and their resident naval architect was tasked with solving the problem. The second sketch (BELOW) of **Eloquence** (392/69) shows how the problem was solved by adding ballast tanks along the sides of the hatches (arrowed), so they could now claim to have a trunk deck; the allowance for this additional buoyancy permitted them to carry additional cargo and so meet the contract requirements. In practice, the ballast tanks were not used, their arrangement being purely to avoid an increase in gross tonnage. Also added to the vessels was the white spurketting plate in place of rails at the stem.

prefabricated buildings shifted on a voyage from Berwick-on-Tweed to Kirkwall.

Lapthornes progressed from Thames barges, through elderly Dutch coasters engaged in Thames, Continent and Channel Isles trade, to their first new ship *Hooness* (196/65) of 295 deadweight, which was built for them by J.W. Cook (Wivenhoe) Ltd. A sistership was built and taken on bare boat charter and subsequently bought.

Owners, particularly those just starting out, often preferred to buy second hand Dutch coasters rather than raise the capital necessary for a new ship, as Dutch coasters had generally been well maintained by captain owners. Captain Chris Reynolds recalls:

'They were often stronger than later ships and more tolerant of bumps and scrapes. Compared with the later Yorkshire Dry Dock 'boxes' they were more sea-kindly, were a delight to sail on and much much quieter and without the vibration noise and heat. Of all the ships I sailed on I would have to say Gena F *(500/57)* [170ft 3ins x 28ft 10.5ins x 12ft 8ins] was my favourite ship, we had an excellent crew, made some great voyages and had a good social life. I was in her right up until Geoff French sold her to the Caribbean and she went under the Panamanian flag as Kolanda in the West Indies. The stern of the Dutch coasters was quite pointed, so they parted the following seas allowing them to pass either side; this could mean an occasional pooping in really extreme circumstances, but because of the spacious accommodation and engine room providing lots of reserve buoyancy it was never a problem. The Dutch coasters were much more 'ship shaped' and the bow and stern were designed to cut the waves. They also had bilge keels to cut rolling. They had a reasonable power to deadweight ratio of about 1:1, while in the later 'boxes' like the Hoo Pride of 1984 it was 1:0.52, a much lower ratio hence the lack of speed, especially when it came on to blow a bit. All in all the old style Dutch coaster like Gena F were so much nicer to sail on – designed with consideration for crew comfort and convenience too, something often lacking in the later designs.'

By this time her original masts and derricks had been removed, and even the stub masts required for navigation lights had been arranged to fold to achieve low air draught, as shown on the composite plan combining a capacity plan and a later accommodation plan as *Gena F*.

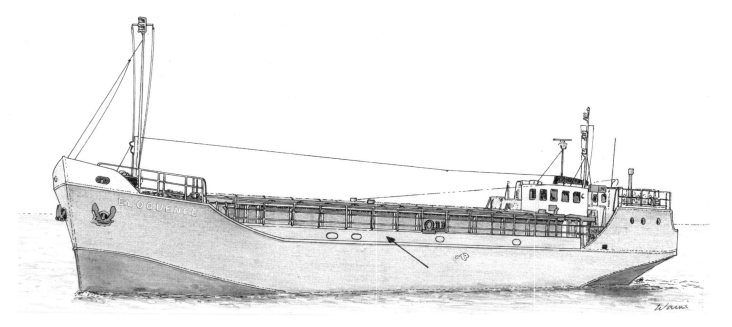

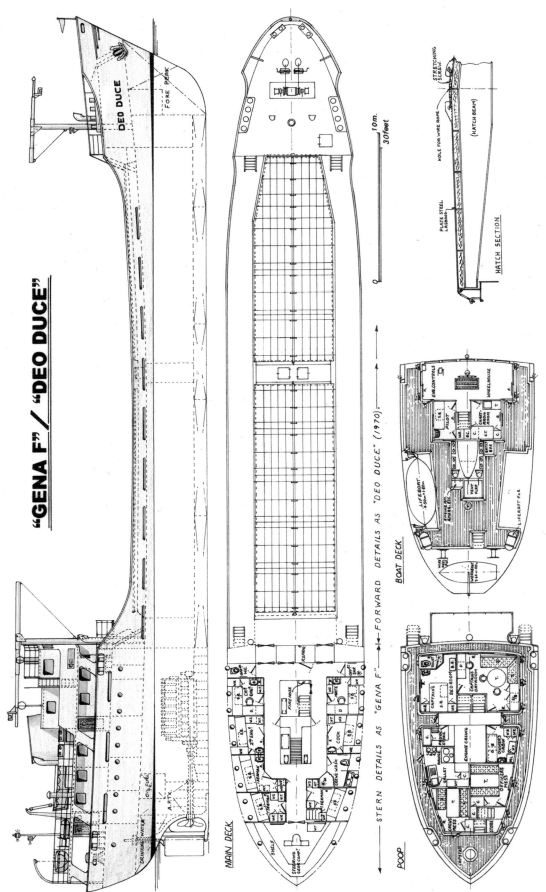

"GENA F" / "DEO DUCE"

DEO DUCE

FORE PEAK

MAIN DECK

← STERN DETAILS AS "GENA F" → ← FORWARD DETAILS AS "DEO DUCE" (1970). →

BOAT DECK

POOP

10m.
30feet

STRETCHING SCREW.

HOLE FOR WIRE ROPE

(HATCH BEAM)

PLATE STEEL LASHING

HATCH SECTION

Gena F was built at Zaandam by Scheepswerf Kraaler in 1957. This illustration was compiled from a drawing prepared for customs requirements showing details of the hatch in particular and how it could be sealed by customs by running a wire fore and aft, through holes in the stretching screws holding the steel bands which secured the hatch boards and covers in place. When the vessel was purchased and came on to the UK register in 1972 as Gena F, the accommodation was refurbished and so detailed drawings of the stern accommodation were made. A feature of many Continental vessels was the advantage gained with tonnage openings. These had originated in the concept of a shelter deck, which sheltered cargo but was not sealed against the sea and so was not counted for gross tonnage. Although she has no shelter deck, the poop accommodation passageways and steering gear were theoretically open to the sea via openings in the front of the poop (marked with closed 'X' symbols) and it is likely that the forecastle was similarly arranged but not shown on the plan. They were closed by boards tightly lashed in place and drains were fitted to clear any water which did get through. Clearly this was undesirable though legal and led to the gross tonnage measurement rules being rewritten to eliminate the practice.

Gena F *was originally built with two masts with derricks and winches but these were later discarded and the masts altered to fold so she could pass under low bridges. She is seen here at Par.* T. NELDER, DAVE HOCQUARD COLLECTION

They were particularly popular with Rix of Hull, who had almost exclusively European-built motor vessels. One of the smaller companies to invest in Dutch coasters was the Enid Shipping Co. of Leith and one of their purchases was *Greta* (382/57,) 141ft 0ins x 26ft 3ins x 11ft 2ins, built by Scheepswerf Kerstholt for J. Schokkenbroek, Groningen, which was renamed *Hillswick*. She traded for them on the local trades until 1968 when sold to G.E. Gray & Sons (Shipping) Ltd, Thomas Whatson (Shipping) Ltd, managers, London. Sales of foreign vessels brought on to the British register tended to be to other UK owners, as all the original navigation lights and other fittings which were not necessarily on the Board of Trade Approved list would have been changed by the first owner, simplifying matters considerably. *Hillswick* was sold to Boston Offshore Maintenance, Boston and lost in collision the following year.

Tanker Trades in the 1960s

The wartime tankers were now being rapidly replaced by new building and, the economy having generally improved, consumption of all types of oil products had risen. Apart from renewing their own fleets, oil companies also offered attractive time charters or contracts of affreightment which encouraged coastal ship owners to build tankers. Whereas in dry cargo vessels transverse framing was almost universal, coastal tankers could also have longitudinal side shell stiffening, particularly in the larger vessels, as the strength of the stiffening could be varied in steps to cater for the hydrostatic head (*i.e.* more pressure at the bottom), which reduced the steel weight, rather than the single size transverse frame (which become unnecessarily thick at the top). Longitudinal stiffening also helps with longitudinal strength, though this is not usually important in small coastal tankers as they were normally built well above the minimum strength required. As time went on, precise calculations of scantlings were usual to produce lighter structures.

Coastal products tankers regularly require tank cleaning to load different products. This was done with Butterworth portable washing machines, which suspended both vertically and horizontally rotating water jets at different heights to wash down every part and drew water from the wash deck line. Small hatches for these are marked as Butterworth openings on some tanker plans. Later tankers had them permanently installed and another supplier was Dasic. Everards preferred these when they became available, because they washed everywhere quickly and as little as one cycle was

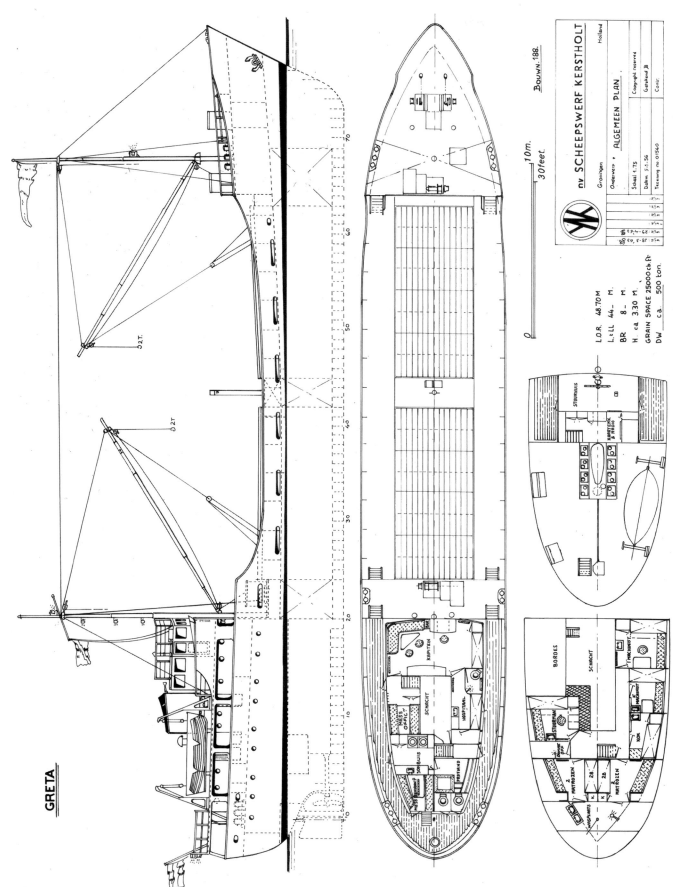

GRETA

nv SCHEEPSWERF KERSTHOLT

Groningen   Holland

Onderwerp ▸ ALGEMEEN PLAN		
Schaal 1.75	Copyright reserved	
Datum 5-1-56	Getekend JB	
Tekening no 01560	Contr:	

Bouwn. 188.

L.O.R.   48.70 M
L.t.LL   44.—   M.
BR   8.—   M.
H. ca   3.30   M.
GRAIN SPACE 25000 cb.ft
DW   ca   500 ton.

Greta (382/57) was built by Sheepswerf Kerstolt, Groningen and was British owned from 1964 until her loss in 1976. The spaceous accommodation for the captain and the much more cramped accommodation below the poop deck for the remainder of the crew suggests it was designed for a Groningen captain-owner.

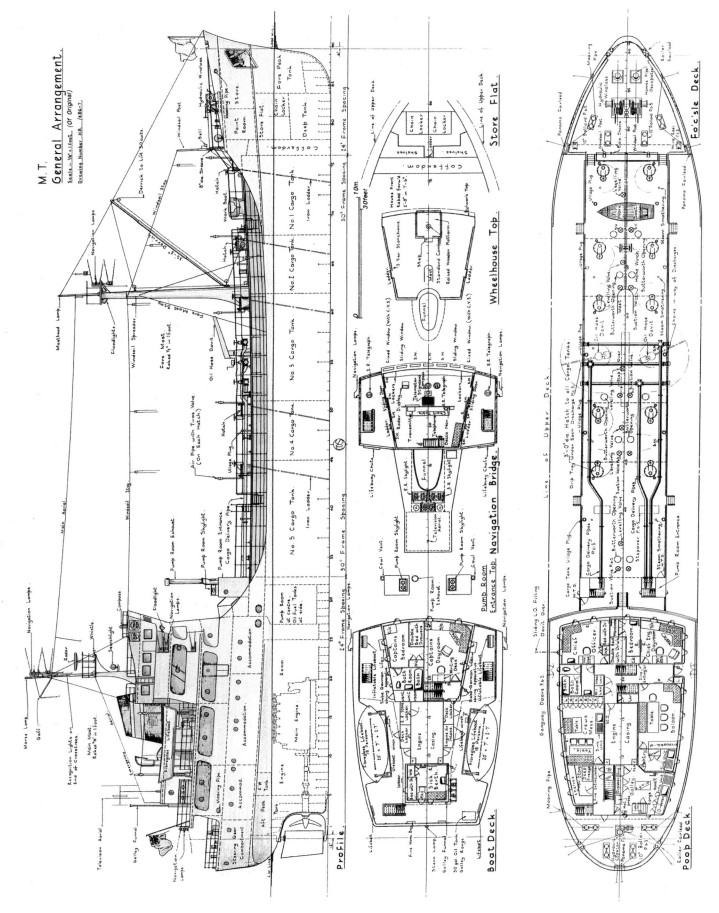

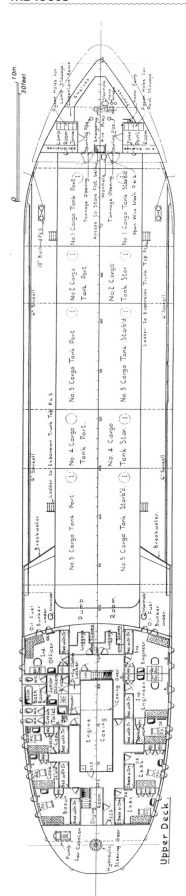

Upper Deck.

*LEFT: Killingholme
(1,182/64) was
the second in
a series of new
tankers built for
the coastal fleet
of Shell-Mex & BP
Ltd in the 1960s.
Later vessels
were fitted with
prominent rubbing
bars as seen in
Ardrossan (title
page).
DAVE HOCQUARD*

sufficient for petrol and similar cargos but more cycles were needed with heavier oils. Butterworth's were slow but thorough. In order to aid tank washing, which became more important to meet oil company requirements, vertical side framing was preferred in coastal tankers. The bottom framing was generally longitudinal to assist drainage when pumping out the cargo. The deck could be either transverse beams in conjunction with the side frames or longitudinal. Transverse support needed for the longitudinals was provided by deep transverse webs, usually spaced four or five (transverse) frame spaces apart, running across the bottom of the ship, continuing up the side shell and across the deck. These webs would usually still be fitted even if the complete tank structure was transverse as they added to the rigidity of the tank structure as a whole, which had to take into account the surge effect of the cargo in the partially filled condition.

In addition, shipbuilders tried to eliminate stiffeners and brackets which could be difficult to wash. In the 1960s, most vessels had troughed (corrugated) plate bulkheads which replaced flat plate and stiffeners, although this was still used for double skin tankers. Tankers by this time were almost completely welded and building was commenced in the centre of the ship, working out to the sides and then the ends.

The biggest building programme was that of Shell-Mex & BP Ltd, the joint coastal tanker operation used primarily to supply their depots around the UK and Ireland with oil products. By 1968, fourteen vessels had been delivered, with a further four on order, made up of six classes. Three of these were primarily for work on the Thames and totalled seven vessels in all. Appropriately they perpetuated names which had been used for a series of motor barges built in 1921 which they replaced. Two of them, *Pronto* (588/67) and *Perfecto*, were classed for limited coastal work as far as Ipswich or to work on the more exposed Mersey. The moulded dimensions had originally been 162ft 6ins x 34ft x 11ft but *Perfecto*, *Poilo*, *Pando* and *Perso* were lengthened in 1969 to 184ft 6ins. There were also three classes of coastal tankers. The first ordered were *Hamble* (1,182/64 – later renamed *Shell Refiner*) and *Killingholme* (1,182/64 – later *BP Scorcher*), which were built by Henry Robb. The moulded dimensions were 202ft x 36ft 11ins x 15ft 6ins, giving a deadweight of about 1,480 tons on a draught of 14 feet and when delivered they were the largest tankers in their coastal fleet. Transverse framing was employed, spaced at 30ins centres abreast the cargo tanks and closed to 24ins elsewhere.

They were of all welded construction and incorporated forward raked bridge windows, which were just becoming a feature of 1960s designs, and unusually a clipper bow. The main engine was a British Polar MN16S turbocharged 6-cylinder, 2-stroke of 1,230bhp at 250rpm, driving a four-bladed bronze propeller. The Stothert & Pitt screw displacement pumps were driven by shafts through the forward bulkhead of the engine room by Ruston Paxman engines and were able to discharge 166 tons per hour of petroleum and 259 tons per hour heavy fuel oil. Discharge connections were amidships. To keep heavy fuel oils sufficiently fluid there were steam heating coils supplied by a donkey boiler. The cargo tanks were of various capacities to permit variations in the quantities that could be delivered. Butterworth openings in the tanks were provided for Butterworth tank washing jets but tank drying by means of fans was not fitted and two parallel windsail stays ran from posts on the forecastle via a crosstree on the mast to the bridge, so canvas windsails could be rigged to aid drying of the tanks. All the deck gear was Donkin hydraulic and the electro-hydraulic steering gear was also of their manufacture. The crew were well provided for, with a cook/steward and assistant steward, and television for officers and crew.

They were followed by two closely similar though slightly smaller (190ft x 34ft 1ins x 14ft 9ins) tankers from Grangemouth Dockyard, *Falmouth* (982/65) and *Partington* (982/65), able to carry 1,094 tons on 13ft 10ins. They later became *Shell Scientist* and *Shell Mariner* when the pooling arrangement between BP and Shell was ended in 1975. The main engines were slightly less powerful British Polar units of 1,120 bhp. *Falmouth* was seriously damaged by fire while fitting out, which required replacement steelwork as well as extensive repairs to the accommodation. This work was carried out by the associated Smith's Dock at North Shields in order not to disrupt the yard's building programme.

Grangemouth then followed up with two 'Hamble'-type tankers, *Dingle Bank* (1,177/66) and *Teesport* (1,176/66), with the same 1,230 bhp British Polar engines. All Grangemouth tankers differed in having a straight stem. A further vessel, *Dublin* (1,077/69), of the same moulded dimensions was built by Hall, Russell, incorporating some modifications to become the one-off 'Dublin' Class and fitted with an 8-cylinder, 4-stroke British Polar engine of 1,200bhp, working through a reduction and reverse gear box. *Dublin* was able to carry 1,537 tons on about 14ft 8ins draught. The engine was replaced by a 6-cylinder Holby of 1,590 bhp in 1974, which increased service speed. She became *BP Springer* in 1976 and was painted red, replacing the earlier black hull with green decks. A further engine change was made when a B&W Alpha of a similar horsepower was fitted in 1988, which reduced fuel consumption.

In the late 1980s, she was mainly running from Grangemouth to the Western Isles with master, two mates, two engineers, bosun, two able seamen and a cook; the whole crew working one month on and one month off. She was finally scrapped in 2004.

Meanwhile Hall, Russell built a group of four tankers, *Point Law* (1,529/67), *Inverness* (1,529/68), *Grangemouth* (1,529/68) and *Ardrossan* (1529/68), all 235ft x 40ft 8ins x 16ft 10ins and able to carry 2,221 tons on a draught of about 15ft 6ins. The first two had 6-cylinder, 2-stroke British Polar engines of 1,280bhp for a speed of 11 knots. The latter two had Vee 12-cylinder, 4-stroke Polars with reduction/ reverse gears and were products tankers. They were similar in style to the earlier vessels but had prominent angled rubbing bars fore and aft, similar to those of offshore supply boats The latter three subsequently became *BP Warrior*, *BP Battler* and *Shell Craftsman* and each achieved over thirty years of service. Soon after building they were fitted with oil discharge and loading booms similar to those fitted from new on the Appledore-built vessels which followed. Subsequently, shore depots were fitted with booms and by the 1980s they had generally been removed. *Shell Craftsman* was lengthened by 8.5 metres to add a new cargo tank section in 1991. New electrics were also fitted and she was re-engined with an Alpha, as were others.

The opening of the all-new covered shipyard for Appledore Shipbuilders in the spring of 1970, following the takeover by Court Line, immediately attracted orders from Shell-Mex & BP, with the prospect of better quality control and cost savings of around 20%. The first order was for two modified 'Dublin' Class tankers, 201ft 9ins x 37ft 7ins x 19ft 1in, which for ease of construction eliminated sheer, had a straight raked stem and a transom stern. A well designed transom stern could improve hull efficiency up to 5%. The result was **Caernarvon** (1,210/72) and *Plymouth* (1,210/72), later *Shell Director* and *Shell Supplier* respectively. The engine chosen was a British Polar turbocharged SF-Type Vee 8-cylinder, 4-stroke, developing 1,200bhp at 750rpm and driving through a MWD 3:1 ratio gear box to a fixed blade propeller. *The Motor Ship* observer noted that there was a marked absence of vibration under almost all conditions. The service speed was 11 knots. The vessel was the seventeenth constructed and indicates the productivity of the new yard. The five cargo tanks were separated by vertically corrugated bulkheads and had a centreline horizontally corrugated dividing bulkhead. The cargo tanks were longitudinally framed with deep deck, side and bottom transverses. Elsewhere, transverse framing was used and flat bar mouldings were extensively used to protect the sides of the vessels. The need for diagonal bar mouldings to protect the stern and forecastle is well illustrated by the numerous scrapes and dents seen in the earlier vessels which lacked them.

All the tanks were fitted with heating coils so that heavy fuel oils could be carried. For gas freeing, fans driven by water turbines taking water from the fire main were used, with air injection nozzles and the appropriate tank openings to give good air circulation – a considerable improvement on the old windsail method used on the first vessels in the series. The cargo pumping arrangements were similar to the earlier vessels but output was increased to 366 tons per hour of heavy oils. The most striking feature was the latticework Sherwin hydraulic loading and discharging derrick amidships, which was able to handle two grades of fuel at once. Appledore then built the larger *Swansea* (1,598/72) and *Dundee* (1,586/72), which were able to carry 2,305 tons on a draught of 15ft 6.5ins but were otherwise very similar except for the main engine, which was a Vee 14-cylinder, 4-stroke Alpha of 1,890bhp, which came as a package complete with matched gear box and controllable pitch

*Caernarvon (1,210/72). Note the longer discharging boom compared with **Ardrossan** and lack of sheer compared with earlier vessels in the building programme. Profile based on a plan in **The Motor Ship**, September 1972.*

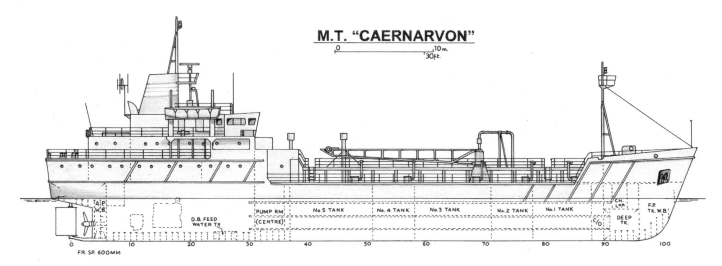

M.T. "CAERNARVON"

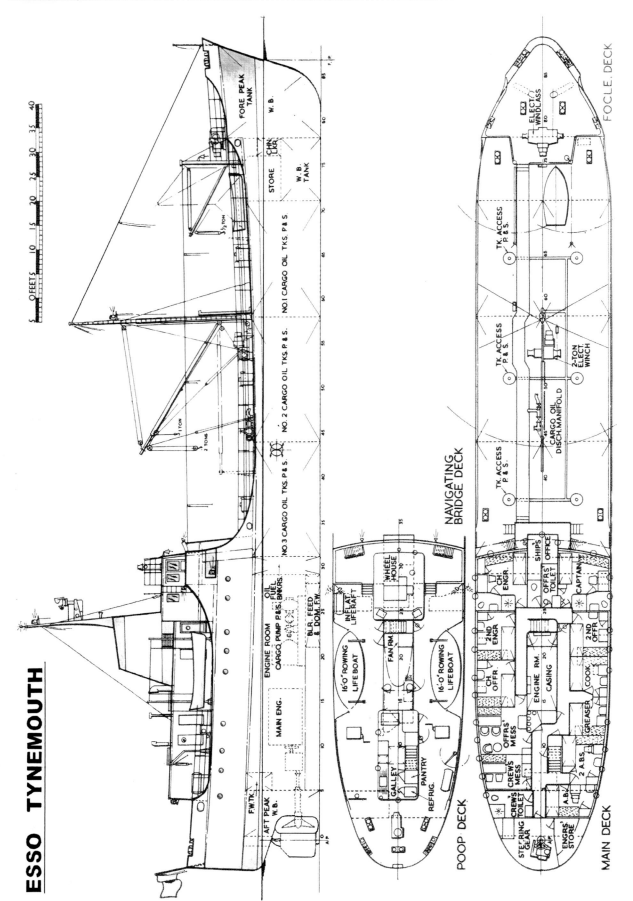

ESSO TYNEMOUTH

FORE PEAK TANK

W. B.

CHN. LKR.

STORE

W. B. TANK

NO.1 CARGO OIL TKS. P & S.

NO. 2 CARGO OIL TKS. P & S.

NO. 3 CARGO OIL TKS. P & S.

OIL FUEL BNKRS.

ENGINE ROOM

CARGO PUMP P&S

BLR. FEED & DOM. FW.

MAIN ENG.

F.W.TK.

AFT PEAK W. B.

FOCLE. DECK

ELECT./ WINDLASS

TK. ACCESS P & S.

TK. ACCESS P & S.

2-TON ELECT. WINCH

CARGO OIL DISCH. MANIFOLD

TK. ACCESS P & S.

NAVIGATING BRIDGE DECK

WHEEL HOUSE

INFLAT LIFERAFT

FAN RM.

16'-O' ROWING LIFEBOAT

16'-O' ROWING LIFEBOAT

GALLEY

PANTRY

REFRIG.

POOP. DECK

SHIPS OFFICE

CH. ENGR.

OFFRS' TOILET

CAPTAIN

2ND ENGR

2ND OFFR

CH. OFFR.

ENGINE RM. CASING

COOK

OFFRS' MESS

GREASER

ENGINE RM. CASING

CREWS' MESS

2 A.B.S

CREWS' MESS

A.B.

STEER'ING GEAR

CREWS' TOILET

ENGRS' STORE

ENGRS' STORE

MAIN DECK

0 FEET 5 10 15 20 25 30 35 40

MAIN ENG.

3½ TON

1 TON

2 TONS

propeller. These Alpha power packs simplified work, costing and fitting for the shipyards.

Esso, who relied more on chartered vessels, added a few mostly small tankers to their fleet, including *Esso Jersey* (313/61), small enough to be able to use the canal up to Exeter. The largest pair, *Esso Ipswich* (1,103/60) and *Esso Caernarvon* (1,103/62), came from J.L. Thompson & Sons Ltd. *Esso Ipswich* was built to carry petrol and similar products, in five tanks with a centre division, from Esso's Fawley refinery to coastal depots and makes an interesting contrast with *Hamble*, with the bridge windows slanted in the opposite direction and the accommodation built out to the sides of the poop. The electrical system was AC 440 volts, which was transformed down to 220 volts for the accommodation. AC was just coming into use and meant that normal domestic appliances could be used aboard ship. The main engine was an English Electric turbocharged diesel giving 969bhp at 750rpm, driving through a MWD 3:1 reverse/reduction gear box. The turbocharger was a Napier TS300 with a maximum speed of 13,000 rpm and illustrates the need for precise engineering and lubrication. J. Bolson & Son Ltd, Poole built two, *Esso Dover* (490/61) and *Esso Tynemouth* (501/60) and although of similar size differed in design, the latter built as a bunkering oil tanker mainly for work on the north east coast. She was of all-welded construction as was normal by this time, using ³/₈th steel generally. Longitudinal framing was used in the bottom of the cargo tanks, with transverse frames at the sides and all the tanks were fitted with heating coils as would be expected. The steering gear featured a Neo-Simplex rudder and a cast iron propeller powered by a Mirrlees 5-cylinder, 4-stroke giving 530bhp at 750rpm, via a reverse/reduction gearbox, for a propeller speed of about 250rpm and 9.5 knots. This could be controlled from the bridge or the engine room. Cargo pumps were in the forward part of the extended engine room, with no separate pump room as permitted for bunkering tankers. Cargo was handled by two Plenty pumps driven via a gearbox and clutch by National/McLaren LES6 engines of 156bhp at 1,200rpm and were fitted with hydraulic starters. Deck gear was also hydraulic and driven by a Vickers VSG hydraulic pump. In 1960, Esso opened their Milford Haven refinery and coastal tankers delivered to the west coast and Ireland from there. All were sold by the early 1980s, *Esso Tynemouth* being renamed *Celtic Lee* by Irish owners in 1978.

Everards were also replacing their tankers in the 1960s, with the older ones scrapped or sold often as their time charters ended. Six new vessels were built by Goole, ranging from *Annuity* (1,599/61), which often carried lubricating oils, to *Acclivity* (299/68), which had been built with cargoes to Paris in mind but spent much of the 1970s carrying lard from Holland to Bow Creek off the Thames. Competition from Dutch yards was now considerable and a group of four stylish tankers came from Niewe Noord Nederlandse Scheepswerven NV, Groningen, the Dutch coasting centre. Dutch yards usually paid particular attention to the profile of their vessels and accentuated this on their general arrangement drawings; the vessels themselves had names in raked lettering similar to the caption on the profile here. Rather built down to a price, repairs could be difficult as some of the pipework was just pushed through bulkheads and welded in place, rather than fitted with a proper union so the pipe could be easily unbolted when it needed replacing. First delivered was *Authority* (500/67), 193ft 8ins x 32ft 2ins x 13ft, which was in effect a standard Dutch design to be under their 500 limit. However, this limit was not significant in the UK so the next vessel, *Asperity* (698/67), was stretched to 214ft 10ins x 32ft 2ins x 13ft 11ins but kept just under the limit for less qualified engineers in the UK. The final two, *Activity* (698/69) and *Allurity* (698/69), were stretched a little further after consideration of the measurement rules (220ft 1in x 33ft 9.5ins x 14ft 7ins) and had their tanks coated so were suitable for carrying liquids up to a specific gravity of 1.5. To save money they went to Poland for coating but the weather was so cold that the coatings took much longer to cure, so there no great benefit was derived

This profile of the tanker Asperity of 1967 is from the original Dutch yard drawing, which was simplified by omitting all external pipework fitted on the deck (or the arrangement was only agreed at a later stage on a more detailed piping plan). Dutch yards generally paid careful attention to profiles of their ships as here, producing an attractive outline. Thought was also given to general seaworthiness, with breakwaters just beyond No. 4 hatch to push seas back overboard and a curved poop front to achieve similar results. They were to prove good sea boats in service.

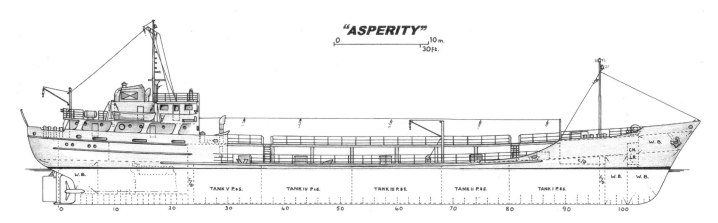

"ASPERITY"

in the end! All were fitted with 6-cylinder, 4-stroke Deutz engines of 1,500 bhp, which gave *Authority* a speed of 12.5 knots and the others 12 knots. The Deutz engines proved reliable but when something did break the parts could be expensive. *Authority* had a 2,000 bhp engine fitted in 1970 and so went even faster if necessary. Although the chartering department would have costed a voyage at the most economical speed, captains were allowed to increase speed if it meant getting to a berth ahead of a competitor, such as one of Rowbothams who then had to anchor off and wait for the berth! All frequently carried clean products for the major oil companies. There were differences in appearance and the last two had a prominent derrick for handling hoses and quite prominent tank vents to comply with chemical tanker rules.

Corys had acquired J.W. Cook's operations in 1958, including the Bulk Oil SS Co. Ltd and the shipyard at Wivenhoe. Corys already had a large fleet of road tankers, as they were distributors for Shell-Mex and BP in the south east, as well as a tank lighterage business on the Thames. They set about replacing the steam tankers with German-built vessels in the 1950s and it was not until the 1960s that any came from British yards, with *Pass of Melfort* (937/61) from the Blyth Dry Dock & Shipbuilding Co. Ltd. She was followed by *Pass of Glenogle* (860/63) and *Pass of Glenclunie* (1,416/63) from Sir James Laing & Sons Ltd, Sunderland. *Pass of Glenclunie* was the last ship built at the Deptford Yard, Sunderland and with her cranked sheer was similar in style to Bulk Oil's pre-war steam tankers. In 1965, Cory Maritime Ltd was formed for the merger of the shipping operations, although Cory Tank Craft remained separate. In 1963, Liquid Gas Tankers Ltd had been formed to consider entering this business but in fact the colliers were placed under this subsidiary in the later 1960s.

Pass of Glenogle suffered vibration problems in service, from her three-bladed, 7 foot screw but following technical considerations this was fixed without drydocking. The vessel went alongside Husbands Shipyard, Southampton and divers from Underwater Maintenance Ltd went down with templates prepared from the original drawings, cutting three inches off the tips to cure the problem. She was sold in 1973 to Ball & Plumb Ltd, Gravesend and renamed *Cy-threesome*. Two chemical tankers, *Cordene* (784/70) and *Cordale* (784/70), were added, lengthened in 1972 and given 'Pass' names – *Pass of Chisholm* and *Pass of Cairnwell* respectively – in 1975. They were mainly employed by Monsanto between their Seal Sands, Teeside plant and Coleraine. Cory were taken over by Ocean Transport & Trading in 1972 and the dry cargo vessels sold, tanker operations transferring to Liverpool in a tie-up with Panocean Shipping & Terminals Ltd, which was eventually wound up in 1983 and the tankers sold.

T.J. Metcalf made a major investment in new tankers in the 1960s, that were designed for distributing a range of refined products, with the central tanks fitted with heating coils allowing heavy oil to be

Pass of Glenclunie (1,416/63) shows how sheer was simplified on some tankers by cranking the deck upwards near the bow and saving on complex bending operations. She is seen here in Cory colours. WAINE COLLECTION

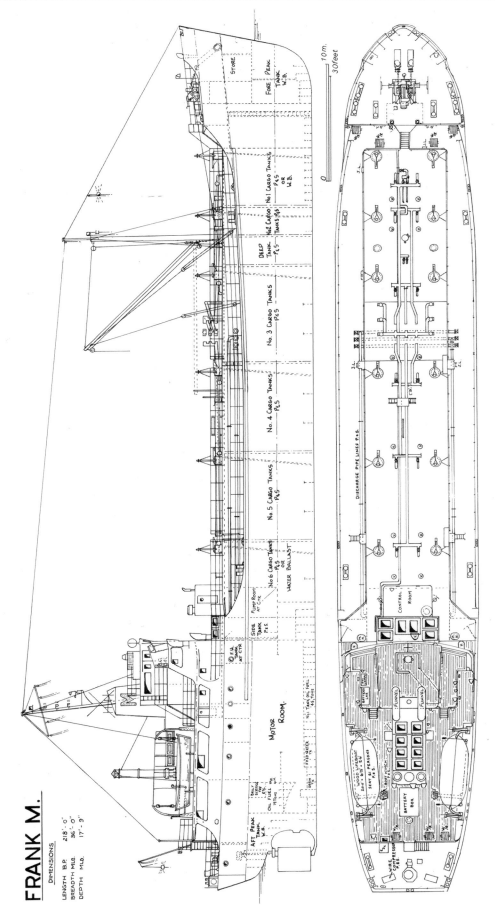

FRANK M.

DIMENSIONS

LENGTH B.P. 218'- 0"
BREADTH MLD. 36'- 0"
DEPTH MLD. 17'- 9"

In the tanker Frank M built in 1965, and two sister ships, considerable efforts were made in the design and construction to prevent cross contamination of the different grades of fuel while being carried to distribution depots round the coast. To achieve total separation, Metcalfs decided to use completely separate filling and suction lines to each of the six pairs of cargo tanks, by connecting the three cargo pumps to the suction lines utilising removable sections of pipe and using three separate discharge lines. Filling was via 6 inch diameter lines to each tank where branches allowed filling either side of the centre line bulkhead. If more than one tank was to be filled, short elbow pipes were used to connect more filling lines on the opposite side from the loading point. Cocks were fitted at the lowest point near the loading station so the lines were completely drained after filling. For discharge, there was a 6 inch main line and a 3 inch stripping line. These pipes ran aft through the tanks to the pump room, where the portable sections of pipe were inserted as required to connect to the discharge line and other connections blanked off. Prior to arrival at a depot, the appropriate lines could be connected up to the three pumps for immediate discharge at up to 600 tons per hour, though many depots could not accept such a high discharge rate. After ten months in service there had been no claims for contaminated cargo. Gas freeing of tanks was by Ventaxia water turbine driven fans, which meant that the tanks could be ready for inspection by the customer on arrival and loaded immediately after inspection.

carried, as well as spirit with a flash point below 150 degrees Fahrenheit. First delivered was *John M* (1,308/63). The main engines were two 8-cylinder, 4-stroke Lister Blackstone units, each of 660bhp at 750rpm, driving a single screw through an oil operated reverse/reduction gear box. The deadweight initially reported as 1,601 or 1,630 tons was later revised to 1,839 tons on about 15ft 11ins. Two more tankers, *Frank M* (1,307/65) and *Nicholas M* (1,308/65), followed with the same moulded dimensions of 218ft x 36ft x 17ft 9ins but with twin funnels in order to give a better view from the bridge. Cargo handling was via hydraulically operated valves from a central control room on deck, from where there was a clear view of operations. The water ballast of 448 tons included a deep tank so that ballast in cargo tanks was avoided and with completely separate pipework, ballast could be loaded while discharging and discharged while loading in an hour, with no delays waiting to discharge oily water to a sludge line. Manoeuvring with the two engines proved most effective and in service speed was about 12.3 knots. Compared with earlier vessels the round trip Fawley to Ipswich had been reduced by up to 40% and slight improvements resulting from experience with *John M* meant the later two were even more efficient. The company was subsequently taken over by James Fisher and merged with Coe in Liverpool to form Coe-Metcalf.

Gas and Specialised Tankers.

The general increase in demand for liquid petroleum gas and other gases in general led to the development of specialised tankers to carry them. Initially, owners moved cautiously, converting existing cargo ships, which was favoured by the fact that tanks separated from the hull were needed. Early vessels carried the gases in pressure vessels at normal temperatures but the weight of these tanks and the need to be cylindrical to stand the pressure made them inefficient. Thus, by the 1960s, there was a move to lower pressure tanks which could be shaped to the hull, coupled with refrigeration. One of the early conversions was *Broughty*, purchased in 1963 by Stephenson Clarke, who had experience of managing the large ocean gas tanker *Methane Princess*, which had been built following trials with the converted cargo ship *Methane Pioneer*. *Broughty* had been built as a 'tween deck dry cargo coaster and these decks were cut away by Hawthorn, Leslie (Shipbuilders) Ltd, who had begun design considerations in 1961 to produce a vessel suitable for world wide trading. The cylindrical insulated tanks were able to carry between 400 and 500 tons depending on the type of gas, in semi-refrigerated conditions to keep the pressure below 100psi, the gas produced being continuously re-liquefied.

George Gibson & Co., who operated in the coastal liner trades to the Continent under the banner Gibson-Rankine Line, began to look at other trades as their traditional business was taken by big container and lorry-carrying ferries, securing a seven year time charter from Imperial Chemical Industries to carry ammonia from Heysham to Belfast and Dublin in April 1964. Their motor coaster *Quentin* (500/40), 163ft x 28ft x 14ft, was selected, as although still in good condition she was commercially obsolete. The requirement was for her to carry about 450 tons of ammonia but the carrying conditions were onerous, requiring the ability to load ammonia and liquefy some of it to overcome heating which would occur in the pipeline to the jetty at Heysham. Carriage then was at -28 degrees Fahrenheit, to keep the pressure below 10lbs per square inch in the tank and deliver it heated up to 23 degrees Fahrenheit. Powerful heating and cooling equipment had to be carried to achieve this and the necessary conversion work was carried out by Henry Robb Ltd. In order to improve the standard of the crew accommodation, the crew was reduced from 11 to 9 by fitting an autopilot and arranging the galley for pre-cooked food so no cook was needed, as hot meals could be quickly had at any time. Even so, one double berth cabin remained and with other modifications the gross tonnage was increased to 574. Gibson engineers were all uncertificated at that time and although the chief engineers had years of experience, all received special training, as did other crew members, to cope with the major hazard of a leak of ammonia. *Quentin* could carry about 458 tons in service and all except about 1 inch depth in the bottom of the tank could be discharged. That which remained aboard was cooled and reliqufied and then sprayed back into the tanks to keep them cool to speed loading on arrival at Heysham. She was scrapped in 1976.

As *Quentin* was a success, the company commissioned two fully refrigerated ethylene carriers for charter to ICI. The ethylene was to be loaded at the North Tees Jetty from ICI's Billingham plant and carried at a temperature of -156 degrees Fahrenheit to their plant at Rosenburg near Rotterdam, for the production of polythene. As in *Quentin*, the small amount of cargo remaining on board was reliquefied and sprayed onto the inside of the tank to keep it as cool as possible on the ballast voyage back to the Tees. The vessels were built by the Burntisland Shipbuilding Co. for the Nile SS Co. Ltd (later the Ship Mortgage & Finance Co. Ltd), the main shipowning company of the Industrial &

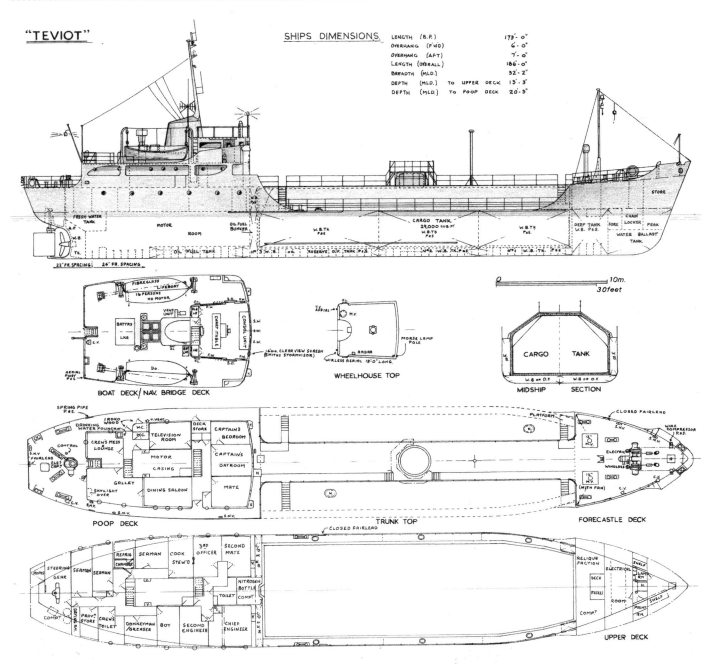

"TEVIOT"

SHIPS DIMENSIONS.

LENGTH (B.P.)		173'-0"
OVERHANG (FWD)		6'-0"
OVERHANG (AFT)		7'-0"
LENGTH (OVERALL)		186'-0"
BREADTH (MLD.)		32'-2"
DEPTH (MLD.) TO UPPER DECK		13'-3"
DEPTH (MLD.) TO POOP DECK		20'-3"

10m.
30feet

BOAT DECK / NAV. BRIDGE DECK

WHEELHOUSE TOP

MIDSHIP SECTION

POOP DECK

TRUNK TOP

FORECASTLE DECK

UPPER DECK

The refrigerated gas tankers **Teviot** and **Traquair** of 1966 were double skinned as the midship section shows and this also provided longitudinal strength. Extensive water ballast was provided for, as the return voyage would always be in ballast. The aluminium/magnesium alloy cargo tank was made by the Gloster Saro factory at Beaumaris and launched into the Menai Straits. It was then towed to Holyhead, where it was loaded as deck cargo for the remainder of the journey to Burntisland. The insulation was of 6 inch polyurethane between the tank and the steel hull structure, and because of the considerable contraction when the tank was cooled down, it had to be free standing within the insulation. A dome in the centre pierced the steel trunk, which had prominent external stiffners. The dome was sealed to the trunk by flexible stainless steel bellows and the void space was filled with nitrogen gas. The gas boiling off from the cargo was reliquefied by machinery in the after end of the forecastle, with a duplicate set on stand-by, driven by shafts through a gas tight bulkhead. Safety valves kept pressure between -1 psi and 4.5 psi. A particular feature of the vessels was the fluorescent fire orange paint scheme to encourage other ships to keep well clear of them!

Commercial Finance Corporation, who then demise chartered them to George Gibson. Though built for ethylene, they were also capable of carrying ammonia, propane and butane, and classed by Bureau Veritas for world wide trading.

Teviot (694/66) was delivered in July 1966, followed a few months later by *Traquair* (694/66), both being 173ft x 32ft 2ins x 13ft 3ins and could carry about 440 tons on 11ft 3ins. The main engine was a Paxman 8-cylinder, 4-stroke of 925bhp at 750rpm. This drove a four-bladed, 7 foot screw at 300rpm via a reverse/reduction gear box. They were crewed by master, two mates, three able seamen, two engineers and a cook/steward. All had separate cabins and the able seamen were on call/day work as steering was by autopilot.

By 1970, Gibsons had converted their remaining dry cargo vessels to gas tankers and in 1972 the company was taken over by Anchor Line, who purchased *Teviot* and *Traquair* from the finance company in 1977. *Teviot* was sold to Kissingland Line, Panama, in 1979 and renamed *Rudi M*. She suffered insulation damage by fire while in London and was written off as an ethylene carrier. She was eventually bought by J.P. Knight (London) Ltd and renamed *Kingsabbey* in 1980, to work as a waste disposal vessel and remeasured at 645 gross tons. On 30th June 1986, she collided with Southend Pier while carrying a cargo of spoiled sugar to the dumping grounds. She was sold to S. McKitterick, Belfast in 1988 and renamed *St. Stephen*.

Tankers were also built to carry corrosive and other hazardous chemicals, as the charter rates on offer were attractive. Because of their specialised nature, they were generally built for time charter to a particular customer's requirements. Building for time charter was one way in which liner and tramp companies could easily diversify away from their diminishing ocean trade. Silver Line sold their liner service and set up Silver Chemical Tankers Ltd in London and ordered the chemical tanker *Silverkestrel* (498/65) from Swedish builders, which was designed to carry caustic soda to Ireland from the Mersey, for delivery to Courtaulds factory there. Apart from the name, the silver theme was perpetuated by the silver grey hull colour used for the ships. *Silverkestrel* proved successful and further European-built chemical tankers were ordered, though *Silvereid* (1,596/69) was built by Hall, Russell to carry tetra-ethyl-lead, a petrol additive, but larger tankers were soon ordered for this trans-Atlantic trade. However, by 1971 the company was overseas-owned by the Vlasof-Dene Group of Monte Carlo. By this time, Buries Markes Ltd, London an offshoot of the French-owned Louis Dreyfus Group had also entered the chemical tanker trades, with the Dutch-built *La Hacienda* (1,452/69) and *La Quinta* (1,452/69), though by 1975 they had become part of Interchem Shipping BV, the Dutch-based managers of the merger of their operations with those of Silver Line. However, the partners retained their distinctive naming styles and the vessels were an important constituent of the UK tanker trades in the 1970s and beyond.

INTERLUDE

BRITISH MOTOR COASTERS IN COLOUR

A busy scene at the Point of Ayr Colliery wharf on the Flintshire coast in north Wales on 28th August 1955. By this time the National Coal Board had invested in a new jetty to handle coal shipments, which usually went to Ireland in their steamers, and Point of Ayr of 1921 can be seen waiting to load. Beyond, Coppacks' Indorita of 1920 has probably just commenced loading whilst beyond, their Fleurita of 1913 is sitting low in the water, ready to sail probably with slack destined for Price's candle factory at Bromborough. Situated at the mouth of the Dee Estuary, almost at the point where it meets the Irish Sea, the colliery had a life of just over 100 years; coal production commenced in 1890 and the mine finally closed on 23rd August 1996, by which date it was one of the last deep mines in Wales.

RIGHT: The colour version of the picture of Coppack Bros' **Fleurita** being overhauled at Port Dinorwic on the Menai Straits in September 1958 is little better than the black and white image on page 18 but pictures of coasters under repair are rare. The hull had been repainted and work on the topsides and deck was continuing afloat. Just to the right of the mizzen mast, a brazier is probably being used to heat up rivets for some topside repairs, perhaps in respect of the boat cradle missing from behind the funnel. The yellow top line, long a feature of Coppack's ships had been partly repainted round the stern. With rising labour costs and falling freight rates in became too expensive to maintain a few years later.

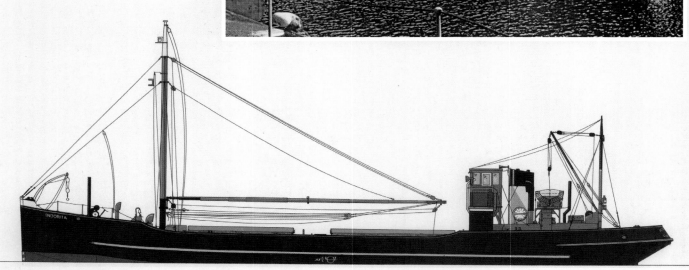

ABOVE: **Indorita** (203/20) is shown here in Coppack Bros colours in the late 1950s and following the fitting of a new Crossley engine, which necessitated the fitting of a larger funnel to accommodate the silencers.

LEFT: **Adaptity** (945/45) alongside in Swansea on 24th June 1964. She was built by the Goole Shipbuilding & Repairing Co. Ltd for F.T. Everard & Sons Ltd, Greenhithe. She was the first coaster for Everards to have single berth cabins for the entire crew. A Newbury diesel gave her a service speed of 10.5 knots and, unusually, her speed in ballast was almost the same.
PETER GLENN, WAINE COLLECTION

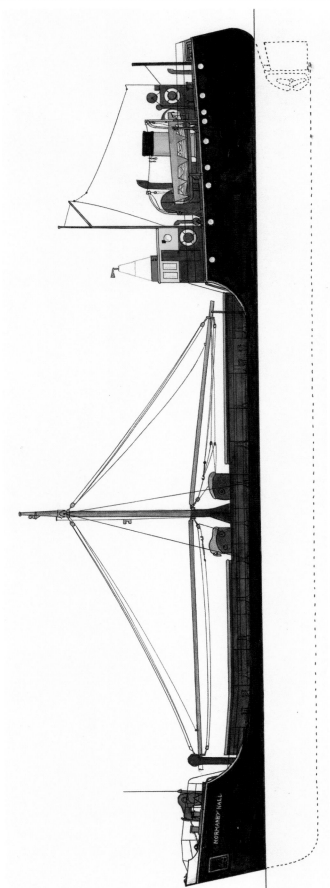

Above: **Normanby Hall** (332/43) in the colours of Coppack Bros & Co. of Connah's Quay in later years. She had been built as the gearless collier Empire Rancher but the mast and derricks were a post-war addition.

Left: The striking hull colour adopted for their ships by the London & Rochester Trading Co. Ltd is well seen here as Eminence (555/45) comes alongside to load. Her all-aft, long raised quarter deck design was to set the style for their coaster building programme in the 1950s. *Waine collection*

W.N. Lindsay's Roseburn (604/47) alongside at Sharpness Docks in February 1970. Beyond to the right is Langfords effluent disposal vessel Fulham, converted from the steam naval tanker Empire Fulham.

ABOVE: **Stability** (1,490/49) was built by the Goole Shipbuilding & Repairing Co. Ltd and the forerunner of a series of similar vessels cosntructed throughout the 1950s for Everards. The vessel is seen here with her original black hull not long after she was built. WAINE COLLECTION

RIGHT: **Similarity** under way in the Thames in April 1974, showing the corn colour which Everards adopted for the larger vessels in the mid 1950s and eventually adopted for the dry cargo fleet. The tankers eventually had grey hulls, with the change over beginning in the 1960s. CAPTAIN C.L. REYNOLDS COLLECTION

Looking aft from the bridge of Everards' Similarity, 1,575 gross, of 1951, when alongside at Greenhithe. She was carrying cement clinker when the photograph was taken on 16th August 1972.

ABOVE: **Olivine** *(1,430/52) heads out from Llandulas with a cargo of limestone for Trolhattan, into a Force 7 north-westerly gale on the Irish Sea on 22nd June 1972.*
REV'D WILLIAM JONES

RIGHT: The officers on the bridge wing of Robertson's **Olivine**, *looking forwards on 27th June 1972. The grey cover in the foreground on the right is that of the lifeboat. Also prominent above the porthole on the left is a 'torpedo' vent, often used at this time for accommodation in the days before air conditioning.*
REV'D WILLIAM JONES

BELOW: **Olivine** *again, passing through the Gota River Locks on 25th June 1972, on her way to Trolhattan with a cargo of limestone. The dimensions of locks such as these were an important consideration for shipowners. REV'D WILLIAM JONES*

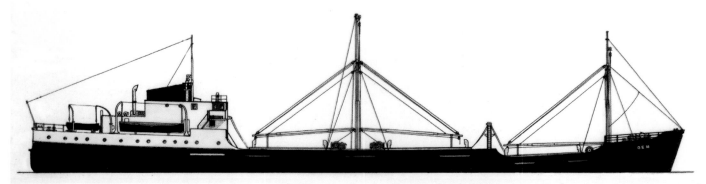

ABOVE: The smart though rather solid appearance of Gem (1,354/52) of Robertson's fleet was typical of the larger British coasters built in the 1950s. The short white line below the bridge was a feature of their vessels.

ABOVE: Glenshira, 153 gross of 1953 and originally built for G.&G. Hamilton Ltd, Glasgow, alongside the small pier at Ardvasar, Skye on 28th September 1970, discharging coal using her derrick. She was later purchased from lay-up by Captain Peter Herbert and towed to Bideford in 1974 but was subsequently sold to Alwil (Coasters) Ltd and eventually scrapped in 1980.

RIGHT: Bay Fisher (1,289/58) discharging a 110-ton condenser beam in the evening of 21st July 1966 at Holyhead. She had brought two from Liverpool that day, destined for the construction of Wylfa nuclear power station. Such cargoes were typical of the heavy project cargoes Fisher's ships were designed to carry. By this time, all except one derrick on the foremast had been dispenced with and put ashore.

Above: **Thameswood**, 1,799 gross, was built in 1957 for the Constantine Shipping Co. Ltd, Middlesbrough and looks very smart here in September 1965, with her white superstructure and white ribbon. She is seen just completing loading coal at Hull and is almost down to her marks, with the last of the cargo going into the foremost hatch. Sold to Greek owners two years later and renamed **Astyanax**, she was subsequently converted into a tanker.

Below: **Malta Faith** (1,334/58) was built by Fleming & Ferguson Ltd as **Sutra** for Christian Salvesen management and was renamed in 1970 following her sale to M.&G. Shipping Ltd, managed by Freight Express Ltd, London. Photographed alongside at Aberdeen in September 1972.

ABOVE: The tanker **Kingennie** (1,169/58) was the last vessel of the Dundee, Perth & London Shipping Co. and is seen here alongside at the Tyne Dock Engineering Co. Ltd, South Shields on 8th June 1972.

BELOW: The tanker **Onward Progress** (345/59) of Fleetwood Tankers Ltd passes under Menai Bridge in November 1967, with a cargo destined for Caernarvon. She takes the deeper water and so is passing the shallower draughted fishing vessel starboard to starboard rather than the normal port to port.

ABOVE: The tanker **Esso Dover**, *490 gross, built in 1961 by J. Bolson & Son Ltd, Poole, heads southwards through the Menai Straits with a full cargo of petroleum products destined for the Esso Depot at Caernarvon on 11th April 1968. The white wires running either side of the mast were to support windsails to de-gas and dry the cargo tanks after they had been washed out. She was sold to Cherry Marine Ltd and renamed* **Cherrybobs** *in 1980 but was soon resold to the St. Helena Shipping Co. for use at St. Helena to supply the island and act as a floating fuel depot between voyages.*

BELOW: The small coaster **Raylight** *(177/63) was built for the Light Shipping Co. Ltd, which was managed by Ross & Marshall Ltd, Greenock and carries their colours.*

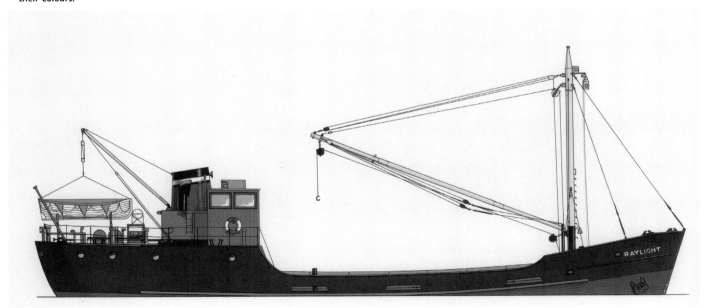

*Above: The almost new **Kinnaird Head**, 1,985 gross, built for A.F. Henry & MacGregor in 1963, alongside at Hull in September 1965 to load coal. However, the MacGregor hatches were yet to be rolled back and the derricks topped up as it was the weekend. Sold to Doreys and renamed **Perelle** in 1972, in 1974 she was towed into Southampton when the crank shaft of her Polar main engine broke and cracked the bed plate. Repairs were carried out by Vosper's yard. She was sold to Italian owners in 1977.*

*Below: **Dawnlight I**, 199 gross of 1965, discharges her coal cargo into a small Ford Transit lorry at Broadford, Skye using her hydraulic Atlas loader and grab on 29th September 1970. She went south in 1988 for a project in connection with Lundy Island but was laid up first at Bideford, then at Appledore and subsequently headed for Barbados in August 1990.*

The tanker Leadsman (843/68) carrying a full cargo on the Thames on 3rd June 1971. She was one of a series of tankers built by Drypool for Rowbothams. Sold for use as an effluent disposal tanker, she later passed on to Greek owners in 1997.

RIGHT: A stern view of Leadsman, arriving at King's Lynn with a full cargo. CAPTAIN C.L. REYNOLDS

BELOW: Jubilence (475/75) alongside at Goole in May 1975. The very squat funnel left hardly any room for the London & Rochester Trading Co's white crescent on a red band between two white bands.

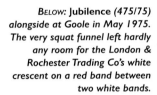

Blakeley (728/71) and her sistership Bude were built by Appledore Shipbuilders Ltd for Bowker & King, London, who had won the contract to move over a million tons of oil products a year around the Bristol Channel, primarily to the east of Swansea. Blakeley is seen here at Sharpness circa 1980, where both were often seen, using the Sharpness Canal to reach the oil depot at Quedgeley. DENNIS PARKHOUSE, NEIL PARKHOUASE COLLECTION

ABOVE: The French owned dredger Cote d'Armor (731/85), seen here at St. Malo on 19th May 2002, started life as the coaster Gwyn, one of the many barge-style coasters built by the Yorkshire Dry Dock Co. Ltd from the 1970s to the 1990s. DAVE HOCQUARD

BELOW: Torrent (999/92) was the last of the dry cargo series and was built for the Franco-British Chartering Agency, who required a low air draught. To achieve this, the bridge was moved forward over the after hatch stowage space by the Yorkshire Dry Dock Co. Ltd, the builders. DAVE HOCQUARD

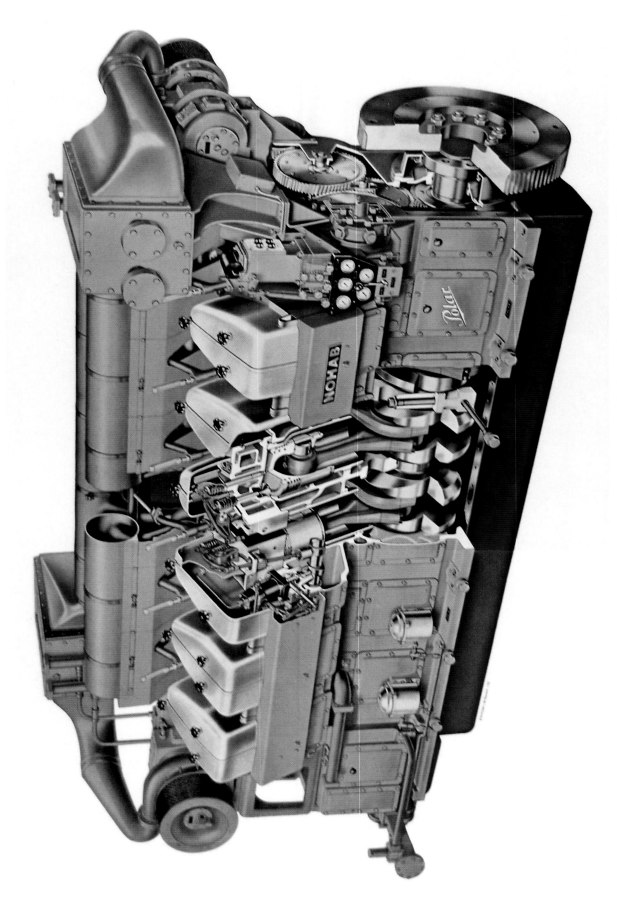

This fine cut-away drawing depicts the V-12 cylinder version of a Nohab Polar F20 type 4-stroke medium speed turbocharged, intercooled engine of the 1970s. As can be seen, there were two separate turbochargers, one at each end on the top of the engine serving the two banks of cylinders. The power developed was 220 b.h.p. per cylinder at 825 r.p.m., and the engine was available as a straight 4 and 6 cylinder unit or as a vee 8, 12 and 16 cylinder unit for higher powers. This V-12 had a maximum rated output of 2640 b.h.p. and weighed 14 tons. However, owners generally asked for a slightly de-rated engine in order to extend the life of the engine and periods between overhauls. The factory, under various names was, based at Trollhattan, Sweden. It eventually came under Nohab control, part of the Bofors Group from 1936. However, despite the ownership changes, they were always marketed under the 'polar' brand name. The licencees for the UK, British Polar Engines Ltd, Glasgow had manufactured a considerable number of the engines destined for British vessels by this time. FROM A NOHAB POLAR FEATURE IN THE MOTOR SHIP JANUARY, 1974

CHAPTER 7

THE 1970S AND
METRICATION

The moulded dimensions etc, are given in metres unless otherwise stated.

The big investors in dry cargo tonnage in the 1970s continued to be the London owners, encouraged by Government support and well placed to move into the Middle Trades (Bergen-Santander range) and further afield but still under 1,600 gross. However, there was a shortage of British qualified officers and a dispensation was instituted; although the ship would need to sign on foreign going articles, the manning and certification was the same as the Middle Trades. These became known as White Sea-Black Sea articles, as the range was Archangel-Black Sea-Casablanca. The latter port was important for return cargoes of phosphate rock, although loading could be slow. Comben Longstaff, part of Amalgamated Roadstone from 1954, often used their ships to carry stone from Newlyn to the ARC Granophast wharf at Deptford. They themselves were taken over by Consolidated Gold Fields in 1968, who wished to diversify away from South Africa and were happy for the shipping operations to continue.

After careful consideration of the market, the company ordered two 1,599 gross ton vessels from Cochranes at a price of £410,000 each in January 1969, with hold ventilation fans so that the vessels could carry return cargoes of fruit and vegetables from the Mediterranean. By May it had been decided to upgrade to full UMS (Unmanned Machinery Space) specification. These changes increased the price by £12,000 but while the first two were under construction, work for a further two was identified and the order increased to four. First to be delivered was *Stirlingbrook* (1,597/70) and *Sussexbrook* (1,596/70), quickly followed by the second pair, *Somersetbrook* (1,596/71) and *Surreybrook* (1,596/71). The moulded dimensions were 80.78 x 12.81 x 6.25 metres, with a deadweight of 2,947 tons on 5.03 metres. They soon proved even better than expected and a final member of the class was ordered, with the shortcomings of the direct current system used in the earlier vessels being replaced by an alternating current system in the last of the 'S-brooks', *Solentbrook* (1,597/72). *Solentbrook* also had a better deadweight at 2,982 tons, as rather than have the floor of the hold covered in heavy composition, thicker steel was used instead. There was a general move to AC, as it was becoming hard to find manufacturers of DC equipment generally and AC equipment was lighter and took up less space. In addition, off the shelf small or domestic AC items could be used.

Each of the four 3-ton capacity derricks was controlled by hydraulic winches of Norwinch manufacture. They were arranged to stow upright to suit timber cargoes and the class all had timber load lines assigned. Apart from the main cargo winch and a luffing winch, there were smaller slewing winches. The four previous vessels had mechanical topping winches rather than hydraulic. The tackles for slewing were attached to stout posts at each corner of the winch house amidships and to similar posts on each side of the fore and mizzen masts on the forecastle and poop. This gear was cheaper than the cranes which appeared on some of the 1970s ships. The fore and mizzen mast had some stays but the mainmast between the holds was unsupported and with both derricks working this mast could flex markedly. The hydraulic pumps for the winches were driven electrically and could at times overload the generators and everything would come to a sudden stop as the overload cut-outs tripped. The AC equipped *Solentbrook* was less prone to problems of this nature.

When the vessels and the company were taken over by Everards, consideration was given to fitting larger generators but there was insufficient space in the engine room. By this time, as the vessels had not been particularly well maintained, hydraulic leaks were also occurring and the gear becoming expensive to maintain, which was not helped by the fact that the hydraulic reservoirs were up the masts. The reservoirs were positioned there as required by Norwinch to maintain the required head (pressure in the system). Also to save money, their Ruston engines had been converted to run on heavier fuel which with filters, heaters, etc, increased the electrical load. However, as they had good lifting capacity they earned a premium rate in the timber trade, as they could discharge themselves and were often fixed with Russian timber cargoes from Archangel in summer. Payment was originally per Petrograd standard, later replaced by cubic metres. They also ventured to Canada for the summer season there. *Sussexbrook* chartered for timber to Shoreham and at the time was the largest so far for the port at 3,199 cubic metres of softwood discharged with two gangs in twenty hours, by Powell Duffryn Wharfage & Transport in 1972. At other times

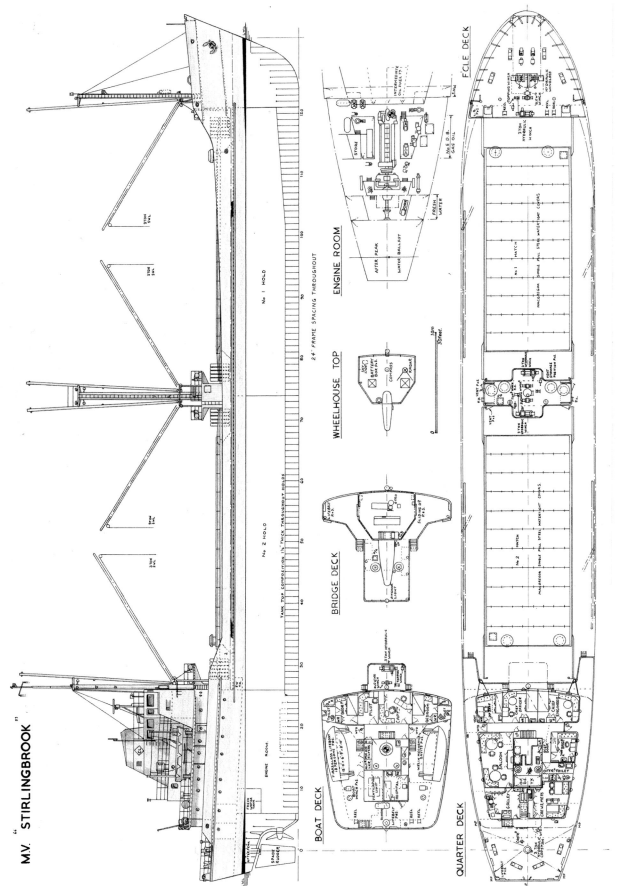

Stirlingbrook, completed in 1970, was the lead ship in a series of five for Comben Longstaff. The layout of the accommodation flat is shown in the plan below.

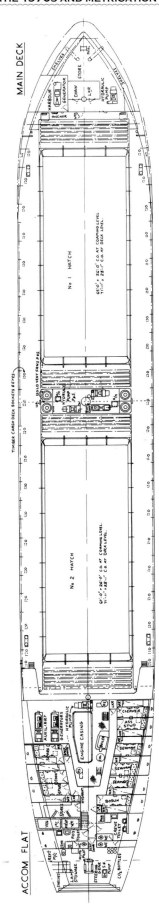

MAIN DECK

ACCOM FLAT

they would load general cargo, including second-hand vehicles outward for the Mediterranean and then look for a return load of phosphate. Further 1,600 gross ships were ordered from Dutch yards in the mid 1970s and some were fitted with cranes. The company came under financial pressure with falling rates at the end of the decade and Consolidated Gold Fields decided to concentrate on core activities, so by 1980, the company and vessels had been refinanced under Everards. The 'S-brooks' were sold off to various overseas owners soon afterwards, with prices up to $830,000 for *Solentbrook*.

Meanwhile Stephenson Clarke, traditionally collier owners (and part of Powell-Duffryn), had opted for diversification into the timber trade. The cranes chosen for *Ferring* (1,596/69) and *Malling* (1,596/70) were from Stothert & Pitt for lifts up to eight tons, plus an 8-ton capacity derrick on a mast adjacent to the bridge. Hall, Russell achieved a similar deadweight of 2,834 tons on 17ft 6ins corresponding to a displacement of 3,954 tons but on the timber load line, 3,114 tons was possible in theory. However, with run of the mill packaged timber, with varying lengths inside each package not being favourable to good stowage, it is probable that they would not have been able to load sufficient to reach this load line, unless the timber was all the same length and was one of the heavier woods. A third vessel was considered but not proceeded with. They were powered by a Mirrlees 6-cylinder, 4-stroke K Major engine which gave them a speed of 12.5 knots. *Ferring* was sold in 1987 to Honduras flag operators and renamed *Ronne*, still retaining her cargo gear. *Malling* had her gear removed to make her more suitable to Stephenson Clarks's traditional bulk trades but was sold to other UK based operators in 1991 and renamed *Torland*.

Everards main investment in the 1970s and utilising favourable government grants, was also in a series of 1,599 gross vessels although theirs were gearless. Two were ordered from Richard Dunston, who went for a rather simple design and were the first to be delivered. *Security* (1,596/71) and *Sincerity* (1,596/71), at 79.25 x 12.65 x 6.20 metres, carried 2,823 tons on 5.075 metres and the air draught was sufficient to pass under the bridges on the Manchester Ship Canal. The main engines were two 6-cylinder, 2-stroke British Polars totalling 1,800 bhp, with reverse/reduction gearing to a single shaft for a speed of 13 knots. The particularly squat funnel caused problems with smoke drifting into the wheelhouse and was eventually corrected by extending the exhausts some distance above the funnel. After arriving in London from the shipyard for the usual reception for marine journalists and customers, her maiden voyage was Tilbury to Glasgow with a cargo of grain. Captain Ken Garratt recalls:

> 'I was given the Security, *a fine ship, when only a few months old and felt very proud. Some months later I visited my buddy on the* Superiority *and realised I had been short changed. The Goole ships were far superior to the pair from Dunston. The Dunston funnel was a free standing affair, quite streamlined whereas the Goole one was connected to the bridge and had space within for some stores and gear. The smaller of the Goole ships were the high point as far as accommodation was concerned, while the larger Goole ships next built were a bit cramped.'*

In *Serenity* (1,597/71) and *Superiority* (1,597/72), 80.75 x 12.81 x 6.20 metres, Goole had managed to increase hold capacity by 11 cubic metres and deadweight by 25 tons on a slightly

LEFT: Malling (1,596/70) with its more traditional hull (80.83x13.11x6.41 metres moulded), makes an interesting comparison with Stirlingbrook, with its transom stern and spade rudder. Although the deadweights were similar, Malling, with its larger machinery space, had less hold space.
From Shipping World & Shipbuilder, April 1970

BELOW: Richard Dunston (Hessle) Ltd built the rather basic bulk carriers Sincerity (1,596/71) and Security (1,596/71) for Everards. The type was further developed by Goole as part of the Swan Hunter Small Ships Division, as illustrated by Summity on the next page.

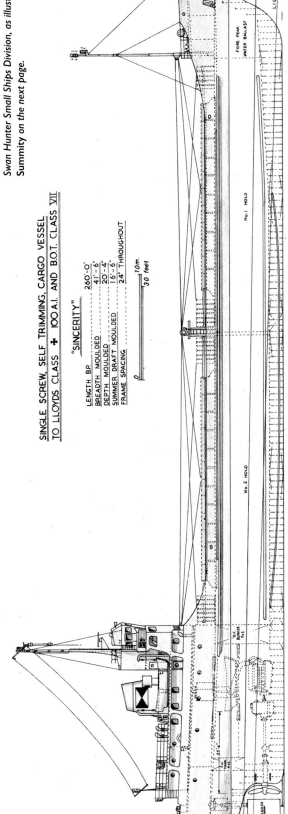

SINGLE SCREW, SELF TRIMMING, CARGO VESSEL
TO LLOYDS CLASS ✠ 100 A.I. AND B.O.T. CLASS VII

"SINCERITY"

LENGTH B.P.	260'-0"
BREADTH MOULDED	41'-6"
DEPTH MOULDED	20'-4"
SUMMER DRAFT MOULDED	16'-6"
FRAME SPACING	24" THROUGHOUT

MALLING

increased draught of 5.144 metres. Thought had been given to the problems of grain cargoes shifting and the ships incorporated a short fore-and-aft bulkhead between the aft end of the hatch coaming and the after hold bulkhead, which was about half the depth of the hold and could be folded away upwards under the deck. A similar one was placed at the forward end of the forward hatch. They were time consuming to rig and secure with wires and so their use was avoided as far as possible. *Superiority* was on a regular run to Italy with china clay for some years. By a more thorough examination of the measurement rules, Goole evolved a revised design for Everards, increasing the depth of the double bottom forward and that under the engine room, using alternate deeper frames and fitting some spar ceiling for the measurement process. They also lowered the accommodation deck but by skilful angling of this, had a small length of main deck forming the steering gear compartment, a feature previously used in the timber carriers built for the Klondyke Shipping Company. The step down for the sunken poop produced a structural weakness, which reduced tonnage but the welds tended to crack and water leak into the hold in later years. Also, the thinner tank tops needed a wood ceiling on deeper battens to raise the ceiling for tonnage measurement. This resulted in the 'Fred Everard' Class, 85.23 x 13.25 x 6.33 metres, able to carry 400 tons more but staying under 1,599 gross and the same draught. But the real attraction was the price. Norman Acaster, chairman of Goole, had secured some extra grants to keep his yard in work and offered the first three ships for £1,000,000 and the fourth ship for a similar amount as the result of reduced grants, so for practical purposes Everards got four ships for £2,000,000. In later years, corrosion in the tank top plates meant that the wood ceiling was discarded and doubling plates fitted over the tank tops.

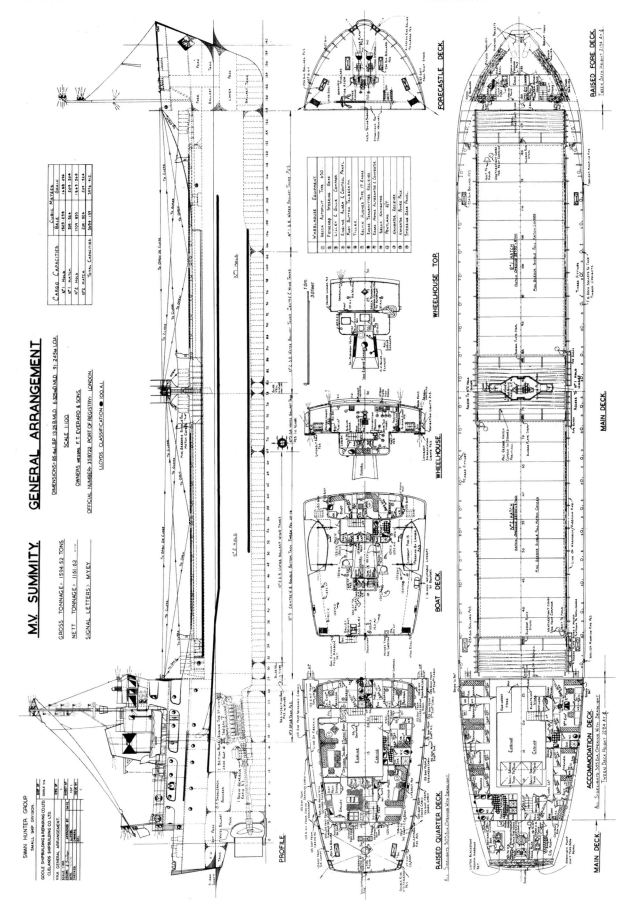

The other big change was to single Vee, 16-cylinder, 4-stroke Polars of 2,400bhp, to give a service speed of 12.75 knots. The earlier four had two engines geared to one shaft, to keep engine room length down and as a result the propeller was right-handed, the reverse of the usual arrangement. *Fred Everard* (1,595/72) was followed by *Suavity* (1,595/72), **Summity** (1,595/72) and *Sagacity* (1,594/73). Originally running in the north European trades with cargoes such as timber to Gunness, they were soon working to the Mediterranean with steel and china clay, often returning with phosphate cargoes. However, they were not fitted with air conditioning so more southern voyages were not practical.

In the case of timber, it was loaded in slings that the owner had to hire, which in Sweden was expensive; in addition, the stevedores would check the testing date tags before using them so the owner needed to keep them within date. Timber cargoes had always had the associated problem of the ship being stable enough to load a full cargo. In earlier times it was normal to keep loading until the ship lolled over and then take a bit off! However, around 1970, an 'M' notice was sent to owners instructing them that not more than a third of the cargo could be carried on deck. Also, starting in 1972, all ships had to carry stability books which came into force as each vessel came up for special survey, that showed what the ship could safely load and had to be adhered to. Timber was still secured between heavy 9ins x 9ins timber uprights (or several planks banded together), placed in sockets in the deck and secured by iron double-ended 'U' shaped hooks which fitted into holes in the top of the bulwarks. If the deck cargo shifted in heavy weather, these uprights could put enough strain on the bulwarks to break them away from the deck weld. The uprights were useful with loose timber cargoes in preventing spillages during loading and unloading but with packaged timber were redundant. The cargo was secured by wires on each side shackled to a length of chain held by a Senhouse slip which, according to Board of Trade theory, a man could release if the cargo shifted and became dangerous. Of course if it did go overboard the man went with it! Another tricky cargo was steel. Apart from the need to secure steel in rolls within the hold, there could be significant claims for salt water damage, so it was essential to check the MacGregor hatch covers were seating properly, usually done by chalking the edge of the hatch, then securing the covers, opening again and looking for continuous chalk lines on the rubber sealing strip. As a back-up, after loading, all the joints between the cover segments were sealed with heavy duty sealing tape. Two vessels of the 'Fred Everard' type, *Kinderence* (1,596/76) and *Luminence* (1,596/77), were also built for the London & Rochester Trading Co. and a further two for Turnbull, Scott management, strengthened for heavy cargoes. Apart from the usual bulk cargoes, *Luminence* was used by Balfour Kilpatrick for cable laying projects with various cable handling equipment. She was used to lay cables across the Pentland Firth and even ventured as far as New Zealand for a cable repair contract, with additional accommodation fitted for the cable handlers and a helideck added to the stern. Other Crescent ships were also used from time to time on cable work.

This busy building period for Everards ended as it had begun with one-offs. The first one-off had been the Dutch-built *Supremity* (698/70), built for the liner trade inherited when Everards took over Glen & Co., Glasgow and the last was *Mairi Everard* (1,599/74), Everards first 'box' hold type, from Clelands with a slightly more powerful Polar engine giving a service speed of 12.75 knots. Although with her smooth sided holds she was ideal for grain, she seemed to get fixed for anything but grain!

By this time it was obvious that European builders were bending the tonnage rules to a considerable extent and Everards were successful in getting the British view of the rules relaxed somewhat, to permit the building of 'tween deck type ships, in which the second deck was of steel in the side tanks surrounding the hold. Also, 'tween deck hatches of no more than plywood resting on steel beams strong enough to support a man within the hold area were acceptable and once the ship had been officially passed, were set aside. Consideration was given to containers and the new ships would be able to carry 122 TEU (twenty foot equivalent units) if required. Their moulded dimensions were 83.19 x 14.20 x 8.56 metres, with a deadweight of 4,156 tons or 4,245 gearless, on a draught of 6.039 metres and they were built to 'Ice Class 3', so they were suitable for trading into the southern Baltic in winter. The engine chosen was a Vee 18-cylinder, 4-stroke Alpha of 2,790bhp at 825rpm, single reduction geared to a controllable pitch propeller. *Singularity* (1,597/77) and *Jack Wharton* (1,597/77) were built with one 20-ton capacity crane amidships and two 5-ton swinging derricks at each end. This proved to be a poor arrangement, as the crane could not load or discharge more than half a cargo of containers but they nonetheless made long voyages across the Atlantic and elsewhere.

They were followed by two gearless vessels, *Speciality* (1,597/77) and *Stability* (1,597/78), which tended to be on shorter runs including carrying coal for the Central Electricity Generating Board, aided by the fact that the notional 'tween deck at the sides of the ship formed the base of topside

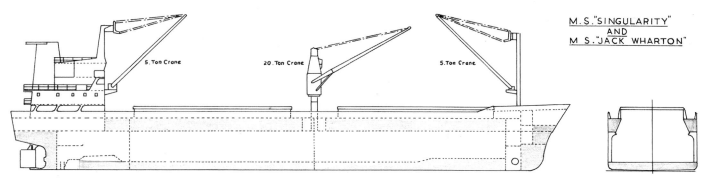

ballast tanks and made them easy to load and discharge. Originally envisaged with a bulbous bow – particularly useful in rivers where it reduced wash allowing greater speed – this feature was dropped at a late stage because of possible damage turning in tight berths. Perhaps this late change was not compensated for sufficiently and with near full homogeneous cargoes they trimmed by the head. Regularly running soya beans from Rotterdam to Erith, they tended to produce a heavy wash and risk of being fined for so doing in the waterways leaving Rotterdam. It also made them unpleasant to steer. It was not unknown for them to fill the aft peak to improve the trim and quietly empty it approaching Erith, as of course this took them over their legal load line. They were easily distinguished from earlier vessels by the load line position, which related to the 'tween deck rather than the main deck and so when fully laden were higher out of the water than a single deck ship, which meant from a distance no one was any the wiser if the ballast tank had been filled. The two geared ships were sold in 1987 and the gearless pair flagged out to the Bahamas in 1989.

Stephenson Clarke also took advantage of the new rules and ordered two vessels from Clelands. *Birling* (1,584/77), 84.28 x 14.51 x 7.75 metres, and *Emerald* (1,583/78), 84.28 x 14.50 x 7.78 metres, but these vessels had full depth side ballast tanks, leaving smooth sides to the hold and incorporating the virtual 'tween deck in the side tanks. Despite the slight variation in dimensions, deadweight was recorded as 3,920 tonnes on a summer draught of 5.449 metres. Depth to lower deck was 5.65 metres. The tween hatches were simple wood covers on steel beams. Transverse portable wood bulkheads were arranged at the ends of the 'tween deck for use with grain cargoes. They were also fitted for timber cargoes and one tier of containers on the hatches. The weather deck hatch covers were Kverner Trans-Roto double skin type and deck gear was Gemmell & Frow electro-hydraulic. The main engine was a Mirrlees-Blackstone KMR Major of 3,300bhp, driving a Liaaen four-bladed variable pitch propeller via a Liaaen gear box, which reduced rpm from 550 to 247 at the propellor. The engine was arranged for operation on heavy fuel, reverting to gas oil when starting and manoeuvring which was assisted with a bow thruster. The crew of sixteen were in single berth cabins with full air conditioning and with an 'Ice Class 3' were designed for a wide range of trading. A speed of 14 knots was reached on ballast trials. *Emerald* then sailed for Copenhagen to pick up spares, continuing to the Baltic for a cargo of Polish coal destined for Northern Ireland. As she was expected to be regularly on voyages to the Baltic, oil bunker heaters from Watson Thermopac were installed. By this time no rigid lifeboats were fitted and apart from life rafts, only a single six-man inflatable boat with an outboard motor was carried.

The main engine driven shaft alternator had a capacity of 250kw, chosen to meet the needs of the bow thruster when entering harbour. It also met the electrical load when on voyage and so no auxiliary generators were run at sea, an arrangement that proved popular with the engineer officers. Mr P.H. Arthur, the chief superintendent engineer of the owners, noted that with marine diesel oil costing £163 and 120 centistroke fuel oil costing £126 per tonne, there was a considerable saving; for example, in the year 1982-83, with each ship averaging 221 days at sea and using 8.6 tons/day, the gross saving was £70,322 annually per ship. From this needed to be deducted diesel oil burned in the boiler heating the fuel oil (about 0.3 tonnes/day), slightly more lubricating oil expense and the extra capital equipment cost for fuel oil but even so, the net saving was about £48,000.

A third vessel, *Harting* (1,589/81) had a deadweight capacity of 4,300 tons and an increase of 380 tons over the earlier two, taking advantage of the latest rules. She carried a variety of bulk cargoes, such as cement clinker from Barry to Magheramorne near Larne from 1983. Also in *Harting*, to further improve economy an exhaust gas heater was fitted, with the idea that the diesel oil fired heating boiler would only be used intermittently. The temperature of the oil fuel was controlled by varying the amount of exhaust passing through the heater. This worked on the acceptance trials but

In Singularity and Jack Wharton, and their gearless sisters Speciality and Stability, the bottom of the wing tanks (shaded) was accepted as 'tween decks and they were allowed to load cargo accordingly. This followed the relaxation of the British rules, which brought them more into line with Continental practice and reduced their gross tonnage on which crewing and port charges were based. The first three were delivered in 1977, followed by Stability in 1978.

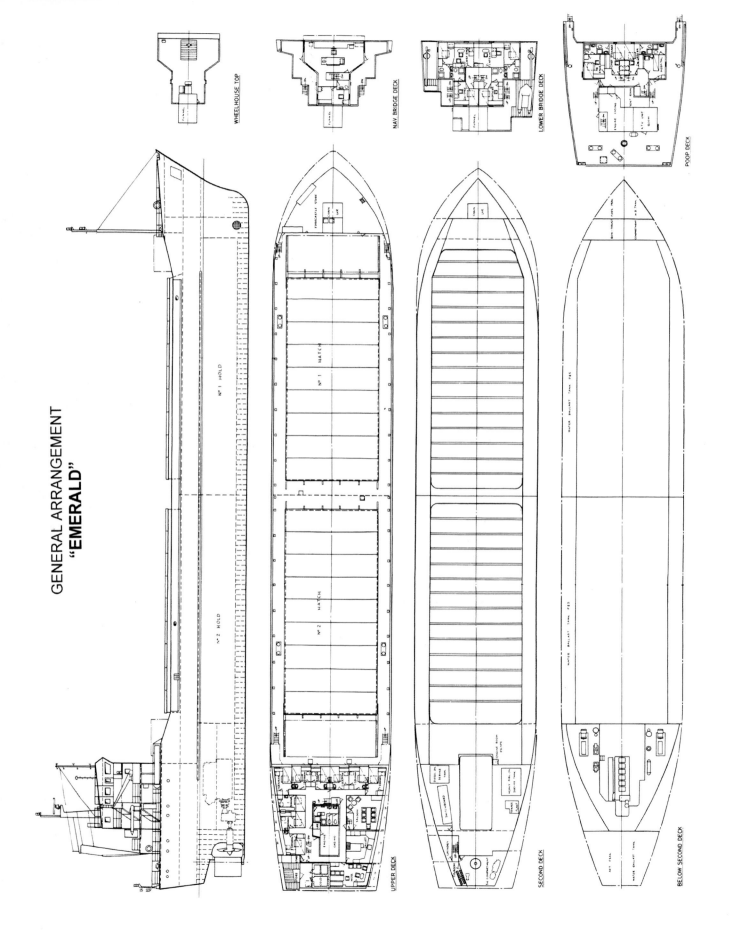

GENERAL ARRANGEMENT "EMERALD"

after some weeks in service the heating system was not working well. After a month of investigations it was found that a baffle plate in the heater was loose and was interefering with the exhaust gas flow. The amount of slow running at sea was underestimated, the temperature drop in the exhaust heater causing the safety system on the main engine to switch over to diesel oil and as the ship operated on an unmanned machinery space rating, it depended on the engineer coming on duty and changing it back when the vessel was running at sufficient speed. How diligently this was carried out depended on the engineer to some extent and *Harting*'s annual fuel cost was actually higher than the first two! However, the principle had been demonstrated and a more efficient arrangement was fitted to the fourth vessel, *Steyning* (1,584/83), which completed the building programme.

Everards still had work for some smaller vessels and six were ordered, four from Dutch builders and two from J.W. Cook (Wivenhoe) Ltd, who had been rejuvenated by Ocean Transport & Trading following their takeover of the previous owners, Corys in 1972. The yard concentrated on producing vessels which optimised the use of flat plates as much as possible and so they were less 'ship shape' than the Dutch vessels and could be stopped by bad weather when the Netherlanders would make a passage. However, they had a better deadweight of 946 tons on a slightly greater draught of 3.252 metres. They were intended for the grain trade from Great Yarmouth to the whisky distillery on the Isle of Islay, carrying malting barley for Scottish Malt Distillers. *Commodity* (582/75) and *Celebrity* (582/75), at 53.65 × 9.91 × 3.92 metres, were built to operate within the Elbe-Brest limits at a cost of about £350,000 each. The main engine was a 6-cylinder, 4-stroke Mirrlees EWSL6MGR, giving 750bhp at 900rpm and driving the propeller at 300rpm via a reduction/reverse gear box. Noise in harbour was reduced by placing the Lister harbour generating set in the forecastle. The system was all AC with 415 and 220 volts. All lights were duplicated and so avoided the need for a separate battery or other system. The crew consisted of captain, mate, engineer and three hands, and they were the last real coasters built for Everards.

The London & Rochester Trading Company steadily added to their fleet, the main beneficiaries being Cooks at Wivenhoe and Clelands. The vessels built by Cooks were similar to *Commodity* built for Everards but with the bridge lowered by half a deck to give a lower air draft, to suit the company's river-sea trading pattern. *Insistance* (475/75) and *Jubilance* (475/75), both 46.49 × 8.84 × 3.81 metres, had an overall length of 49.99 which kept them in the under-50 metres on which pilotage fees were often calculated. Both were fitted with Mirrlees Blackstone 6-cylinder, 4-stroke main engines to give 10 knots and were owned by City Leasing. Leasing deals were an increasing feature of the 1970s, in which banks and finance companies became the listed owners and shipowners increasingly reduced to operators. In earlier times, mortgages were secured against coasters but this would only be apparent from examining the ship's papers. Both were sold to overseas owners in the early 1990s.

Four further Cook-built vessels, originally constructed for Channel Coasters, the shipping arm of Spillers the millers, came under London & Rochester management. The company regularly handled grain movements for Spillers to Gainsborough. Spillers' first two vessels were slightly smaller than *Insistence* and *Jubilance*, carrying 690 tons on 3.252 metres and named *Gainsborough Miller* (427/77) and *Hull Miller* (427/77). Two larger vessels were also built by Cooks for Spillers, *London Miller* (969/79) and *Birkenhead Miller* (954/79), both 68.15 × 11.21 × 4.14 metres but owned by Lombard North Central Leasing. The engines chosen were the Alpha 'package' of an 8-cylinder, 4-stroke with single reduction gear, driving a controllable pitch propeller to give 11 knots. With the subsequent fall in freight rates and the availability of vessels to move grain cargoes as required, Spillers decided to sell, so they were purchased and the leases taken over by London & Rochester. As a result they were renamed *Westerence*, *Xanthence*, *Yulence*, and *Zealence* respectively.

Meanwhile, following the delivery of the two 1,599 gross vessels, Clelands built two low air draught vessels for the company, *Militence* (959/78) and *Nascence* (959/78), although the registered owners were Lloyd's Leasing. They had virtually the same dimensions as the larger vessels built by Cooks for Spillers but had a slightly greater deadweight at 1,431 tons and a few millimetres more draught, whilst also using the Alpha engine 'package'. With freight rates favourable in the mid 1970s, the Cubow Yard, Woolwich added *Ordinence* (470/78).

Cooks were also kept busy replacing Onesimus Dorey's fleet, building three conventional gearless vessels for him, *Rocquaine* (985/77), *Belgrave* (985/78) and *Perelle* (985/79), intended for the Middle Trades but fully fitted for world wide trading. A development of the builder's 'Colne Class' double chine hull, the engine for all three was a Mirrlees-Blackstone 8-cylinder, 4-stroke (999bhp at 815rpm), with a reverse/reduction 3:1 gear box for a service speed of 11.5 knots on 4 tons of marine diesel a day. Deck machinery was electric. The long single hold, though completely free of obstructions for carrying long items, was fitted with retractable bulkheads stowed under the side decks. These operated rather like

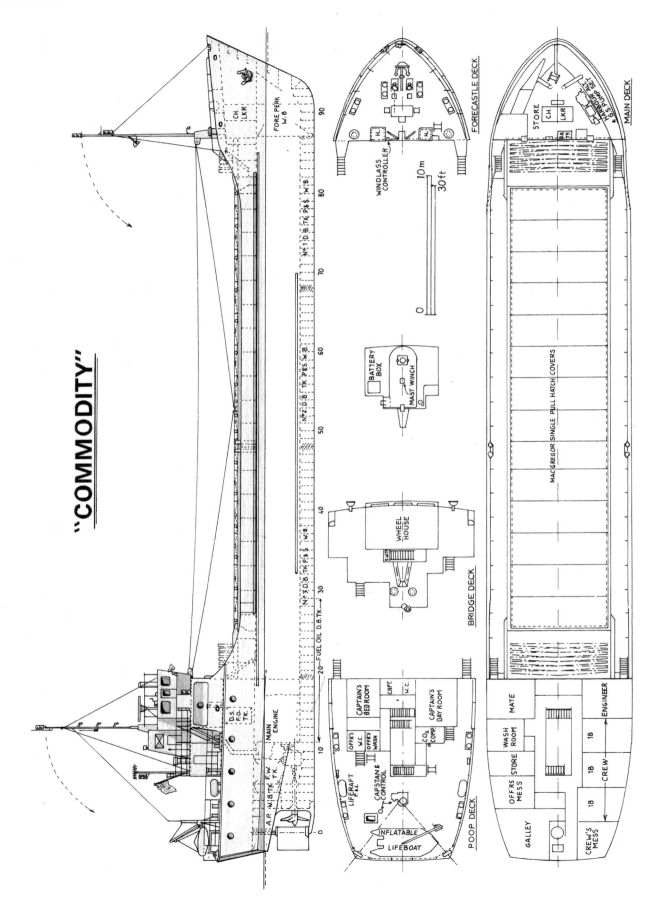

"COMMODITY"

large doors so the vessels complied with the new rules for the carriage of grain in bulk without the need for any to be bagged and placed on top of the cargo to prevent it shifting. Following the drowning of Mr Peter Dorey when sailing in the Fastnet race, and financial difficulties in 1983, the company and its ships were eventually sold to James Fisher PLC, who placed them under the management of Everards until 1986 when they were chartered out and reflagged.

Another important customer of Cooks was J.&A. Gardner of Glasgow. Apart from the *Saint Bedan* (1,251/72,) built by Scotts (Bowling) and frequently employed in the coal trade to Northern Ireland, Cooks built five vessels for the company based on their standard hull type in the 1970s. First delivered was *Saint Kentigern* (469/73), 45.57 × 8.69 × 3.46 metres and able to carry about 550 tons. She was fitted with a bow ramp which, combined with a 'goal post' type foremast, allowed loads up to 6.1 metres wide and weighing up to 120 tons to be driven aboard. There was increasing roll-on roll-off trade for plant required for oil rig construction yards and infrastructure projects in Scotland at the time.

She proved so successful that the larger *Saint Brandan* (931/76), was ordered able to carry 1,394 tons on 4.115 metres and designed for a wheeled load of 175 tons or a distributed load of 360 tons on the hatch, which was specially strengthened. The hold, divided by a watertight bulkhead, was covered with a 63mm hardwood ceiling to accept heavy items inside and she was fully classed for international voyages. The engine selected was a Ruston-Paxman 6-cylinder, 4-stroke of 1,300bhp at 900rpm which drove, via a Brevo 3.5:1 gear box, a four-blade bronze propeller. This gave a speed of about 11.5 knots on about 4.5 tons of marine diesel a day. The generaters and other auxiliaries were all Lister powered. The windlass and capstan were from Gemmell & Frow and to accommodate the bow ramp access, two special windlasses were fitted one each side. Combined with the company's quarrying, the

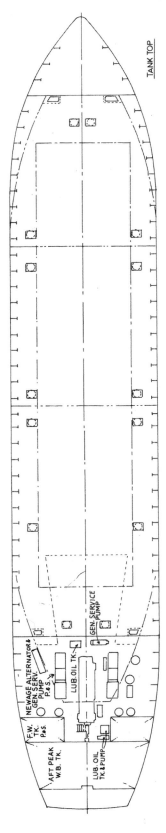

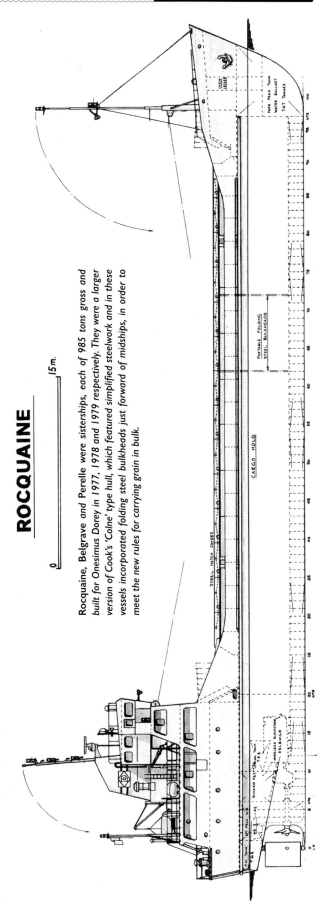

ROCQUAINE

Rocquaine, Belgrave and Perelle were sisterships, each of 985 tons gross and built for Onesimus Dorey in 1977, 1978 and 1979 respectively. They were a larger version of Cook's 'Colne' type hull, which featured simplified steelwork and in these vessels incorporated folding steel bulkheads just forward of midships, in order to meet the new rules for carrying grain in bulk.

GENERAL ARRANGEMENT "SAINT BRANDAN"

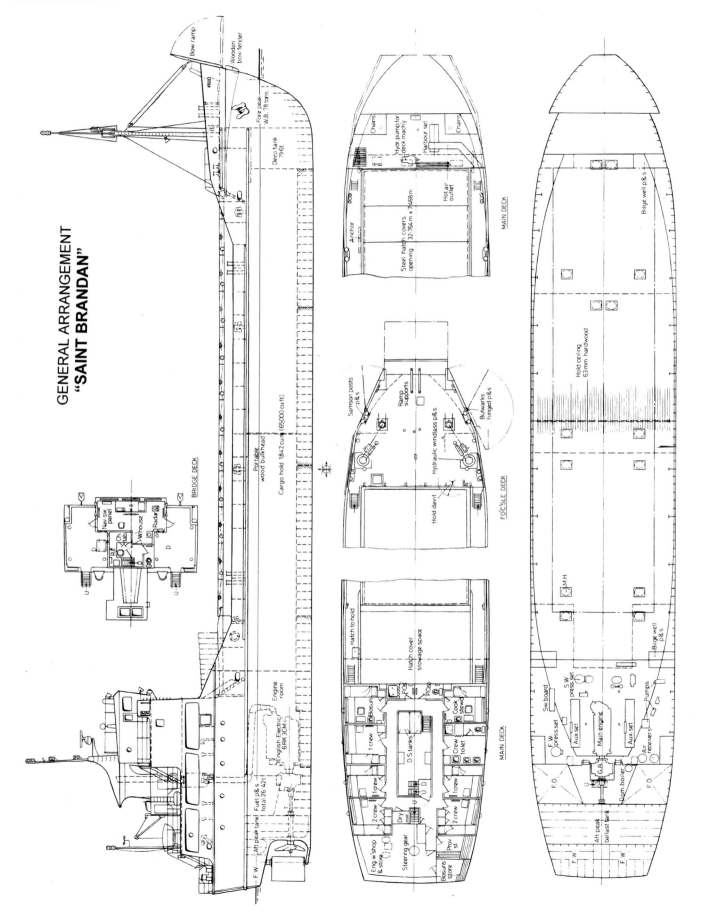

vessels could deliver road laying machinery and material required to the Highlands and Islands. No cargo gear was fitted to this vessel, as it was simple to load a mobile crane as part of the cargo if one would be needed. An improved and slightly larger version was delivered as *Saint Angus* (943/80) at a cost of about £1,200,000, helped by the various development grants available to support Scottish enterprises. Meanwhile, *Saint Kentigern* sank on 3rd November 1979, after grounding at Ketta Ness while on passage from Bonawe to Mid Yell, Shetland with road material. This loss was replaced by *Saint Oran* (573/81), which apart from the now standard bow ramp, had a box hold in which the side tanks were suitable for the carriage of calcium chloride (500 tons) or calcium bromide (640 tons). This meant she could deputize for the company's specialist tanker *Saint Kearan*, as well as handling ro-ro or bulk cargo (720 tons deadweight), which could be assisted by a 2-ton deck crane. She also had a Schilling rudder to aid manoevreability. *Saint Oran* was to be the last ship built for the company, although they managed a later vessel from Cooks, *Peacock Venture* (998/82) for Peacocks Salt.

Cooks also built *River Tamar* (499/81) for General Freight to the maximum width for Selby Bridge (with a 9.2 metres width limitation), as the company, part of Unilever, regularly needed to move animal feed stuffs from the continent, mainly Europort, to BOCM (British Oil & Cake Mills) whose mill was beyond the bridge. Built to the same design as *River Dart* (499/81) from a European yard, both were fully Rhine-fitted so the vessels had a 3.3 metre full cargo draught coupled with a 5.25 metre air draught and a length just under 50 metres overall, so were suitable for a wide range of work. Crew was master, mate and two ratings, with the engine derated to 468 bhp to avoid carrying an engineer.

The Bideford Shipyard also tried to enter the market with a similar design using a simplified hull form but *Peroto*, of 45.50 x 9.01 x 4.50 metres and with a box hold, could carry just 805 tons on 3.614 metres. Built for the Cornish Shipping Co., she required a crew of six including a more highly qualified engineer, as the main engine was 1,100bhp. Although faster at 10.5 knots, she was no match for the Yorkshire economy coaster with just four crew.

In contrast Verolme, the Dutch shipbuilders, had opened a yard at Cork and soon attracted an order for a coaster from James Tyrrell Ltd of Arklow; *Darell* (387/70) was the result but was soon passed on to Marine Transport Services in 1974, becoming *Carrigrennan*. Meanwhile, a larger vessel was completed for the company in Norway, who then placed an order for two identical 1,610 deadweight coasters with the Cork yard, resulting in *Valzell* (1,038/76) and *Serenell* (1,038/77), both 56.50 x 10.25 x 5.65 metres. Built to unrestricted service requirements and 'Ice Class 3', they incorporated box holds free of all obstructions, the full height wing ballast tanks giving a maximum ballast draught of 3 metres, allowing faster ballast passages in bad weather. The hatch covers also followed the latest trend and were Kvaerner Trans-folding jack-knife type, with crocodile hydro-arms which gave the maximum clear hold space, as they required less deck space than earlier covers when open.

A large console in the combined bridge, chart and radio room contained most of the bridge instrumentation, control and communication systems. Also, there were all the necessary alarm panels, fire detection and controls needed for unmanned machinery space operation, so in the home trade the crew was six but there was accommodation for nine on more distant voyages. The accommodation was also to a high standard and both mess rooms had built in refrigerators and TVs, and a well equipped laundry room and air conditioning system. The main engine was a turbocharged and intercooled 6-cylinder, 2-stroke Brons of 1,200bhp at 600rpm, driving via a reverse/reduction gear box a four-bladed propeller at 240rpm. They proved useful ships and were part of the Arklow fleet for a number of years. The Cork yard stopped building in the 1980s and was sold to Damen in 1991.

Valzell was built for James Tyrrell Ltd, Arklow in 1976 and was followed by a sister vessel the next year. As might be expected, the design followed Dutch practiced as it was built by Verome's Cork yard and features side tanks to give a hold free of obstructions. A boat was carried on the port side of the bridge deck. Profile from a plan in The Motor Ship, *August 1976.*

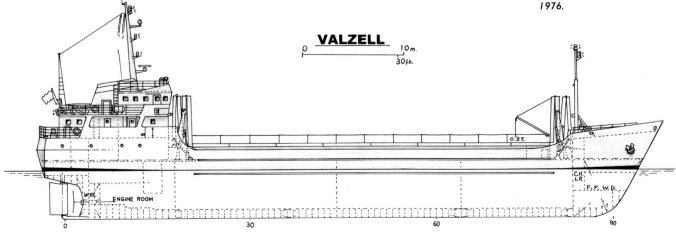

VALZELL

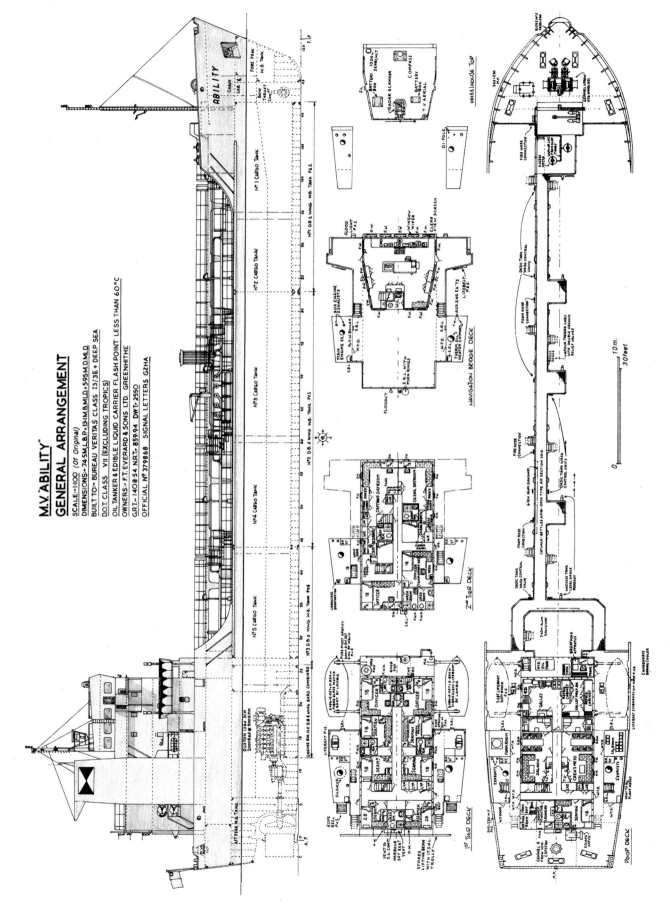

Tanker Fleets in the 1970s

One of the late arrivals on the coasting tanker scene was Bowker & King, though they had been involved with estuarial tank craft on the Thames for many years. The company had its origins in a partnership of 1884 and operated a few tank barges between the wars, expanding rapidly in the 1950s and 1960s as oil replaced coal. The business passed through various hands and became part of the Hays Wharf Group in 1965. The fleet was still mostly confined to the Thames and Medway, with some tankers approved for voyages as far as Ipswich and Dover, having the typical low air draft profile of Thames vessels. Though many came from European yards, several were built by Richard Dunston. The vessels all had names beginning with 'B', a practice which had been introduced by the Stratford family when they owned the company. Union Lighterage and Beagle Shipping had similar fleets of smooth water vessels and these were merged with Bowker & King in 1971. Meanwhile, in 1967, the company had successfully tendered for work in the Bristol Channel. The contract was of considerable importance and involved the delivery of over a million tons of products a year to ports east of Swansea and up the Sharpness Canal to Quedgeley. New vessels were ordered and others modified. Much of the new fleet was supplied by Dutch and German yards but *Bude* (728/71) and *Blakeley* (728/71), both 61.67 × 9.15 × 4.42 metres, were built at Appledore. They were insured to work east of a line from Swansea to Hartland Point, later extended to include Milford Haven so they could load at the refineries there. They could carry about 1,210 tons on a draught of 3.747 metres. Bowker & King's next British built ship was *Bromley* (640/78), 53.52 × 10.61 × 3.61 metres, which was classed for full UK coasting although the actual owners were the Nile SS Co. Ltd (a finance company). She had the typical low profile of most of their ships and was about 844 tons deadweight.

Another late arrival was J.&A. Gardner, who through their long association with ICI, ordered the chemical tanker *Saint Kearan* (441/78) to carry calcium chloride or calcium bromide

This layout for the wheelhouse of the tanker Ability (1,409/79) shows how much the work of the officers had changed, compared with the first tankers which relied on a compass, a wheel and a telegraph to the engine room.

1. Wheelhouse panel had switches for floodlights, overboard lights etc.
2. Stop/Start buttons for main engine.
3. Tank levelling valves and hydraulic alarm.
4. General alarm and overboard light.
5. Newbury alarm panel with Frydenbo steering gear pump unit control.
6. AFA Minerva Marine T870 Mk 2 panel. Fire alarm panel shows location of fire.
7. Chadburn Bloctube whistle control unit.
8. Marconi 10-way talk-back.
9. Telephone type SPT F76 (sound powered telephone). Internal phones round the ship.
10. Frydenbo steering gear hand pump (for use in the event of a power failure).
11. Compass in shelf mounting binnacle.
12. Wynn Mk 3 window wiper control unit.
13. Brunvoll bowthruster control unit.
14. Decca Arkas auto pilot type 450M.
15. Portable tiller.
16. Hand/Auto switch.
17. Engine Telegraph.
18. Whistle control button.
19. Decca Radar display type 914C.
20. Sailor RT 144B VHF.radio telephone for short distance communications (i.e. 'line of sight' to other ships, port control, etc).
21. Battery charger for radio batteries.
22. Decca Navigator Mk 21.
23. Atlas Ecohgraph 460 echo sounder.
24. Pilot's chair.
25. Helmsman's grating.
26. Navigation light panel.
27. Book shelves.
28. Sailor T126/R105 220W radio telephone. Medium frequency radio telephone used for public correspondence via a shore station link, distress calls, etc. A safety of life at sea convention requirement.
29. Battery control unit. This ensured even charging and usage.
30. Radar rectifier.
31. Binocular box.

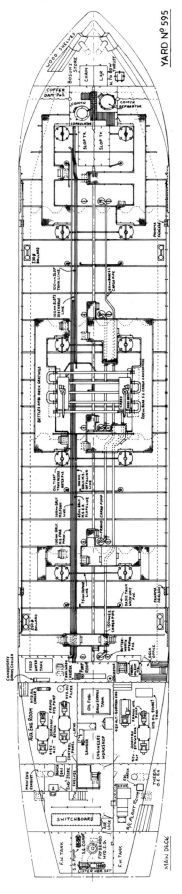

YARD Nº 595

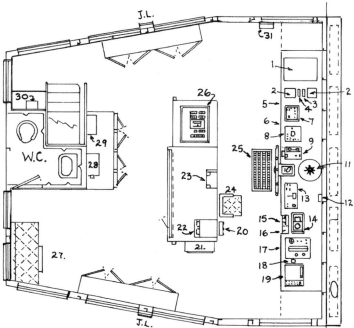

in bulk rather than in tanks, from the ICI plant at Winnington on the Weaver Navigation. The cargoes were taken to Ayr, Peterhead and Aberdeen, and one of the uses was in the processing of seaweed for various products.

In the 1970s, Everards orders were mostly for dry cargo vessels apart from the large tanker *Amity* (2,905/70) and it was not until 1979 that new tankers were ordered. First to be delivered were *Ability* (1,409/79) and *Authenticity* (1,409/79), followed by *Amenity* (1,453/80), which incorporated some changes based on the experience with the first two and extra bunker capacity should she be needed for longer voyages, though as it turned out they were rarely if ever required. They were designed to a higher specification than their previous tankers, incorporating bow thrusters and had separate ballast tanks, so avoiding the problem of contaminated water having to be cleared out of the cargo tanks. The pipework was extensive and allowed for complete separation of products so up to five grades could be carried. Because of the complexity, Everards sent two of their engineers to the yard to oversee matters during construction. The use of higher speed (rpm) more compact main engines and auxiliary sets, also all with turbochargers although compact, increased noise generally in the accommodation. To reduce this, two essentially free standing funnels were used on either side of the accommodation block and meant the ships' lifeboats were placed below the bridge, which also met the requirement that they must be a minimum distance clear of the propeller. As originally designed in 1977, the first tier accommodation had a communal wash room but with a slight reduction in cabin size, by March 1979, shared *en-suite* facilities were incorporated in the final design. All were ordered from Goole and all three carried clean products and lubricating oil around north west Europe, which kept them fully occupied and their ability to carry more varied products was thus not needed. They proved very reliable in service and could run up to eighteen months without time off for repairs. Unscheduled repairs were rarely needed, although there was initially a major problem with the hydraulics on one of the early voyages of *Ability*, when she was discharging, as the all-new set up of hydraulic deep well pumps did not quite work as planned and the manufacturers had to make some adjustments. As they had double bottoms it was possible to have a shallow well in the bottom of the tanks below the pump and so only about a bucket full of product would be left, rather than the gallons left in the older tankers. With all the improvements, the oil companies had to accept that any contamination and loss of product was not the fault of the ship.

The moulded dimensions (74.5 x 13.1 x 5.95 metres) were selected with the maximum for King's Lynn in mind and agreed with the harbour authorities, although the local senior pilot was concerned that the dimensions would leave little clearance. By the time *Ability* was delivered and had been placed on charter, the pilots began to have second thoughts much to the consternation of Shell who were the charterers. After further discussions, one of the pilots agreed to take *Ability*, so she loaded a cargo at Shellhaven and duly arrived at King's Lynn, coming through to the berth with no problems, although she did encounter a badly dredged area which delayed her arrival somewhat. Cargoes were also carried to King's Lynn for Esso, who complained about the slow discharge speed. Since there was no problem with the ship's pumps, a careful check ashore found that the two pipes the ship was discharging into reduced to one ashore inside the depot! When this was pointed out there were no more complaints about discharge speed.

The Rowbotham fleet saw major changes in the 1970s when consideration of future death duties saw the shipping side of the business sold to the Ingram Corporation of New Orleans in 1970. A move to larger tankers had begun with *Wheelsman* (2,897/67) built to carry clean products to the new Regent depot at Southwick and so her size was the maximum for the lock at Shoreham. She was followed by *Pointsman* (2,886/70) and the even larger *Helmsman* (3,705/72), *Bridgeman* (3,701/72) and *Orionman* (3,623/75). Though used in the coastal trades they were fitted for world wide trading. Although oil companies were tending to close depots where there were draught and size restrictions, smaller tankers were required to serve depots in the highlands and islands for example.

Cochranes delivered two vessels under 1,600 tons but still classed for long international voyages should they be necessary. *Rudderman* (1,592/68 – *see page 4*) marked the change to the Cochrane yard and had the moulded dimensions 79.25 x 12.50 x 6.10 metres. The six tanks were divided longitudinally and intended for petroleum products, and she initially went on charter to Phillips-Imperial Petroleum Ltd. The engine chosen was a Drypool Brons Vee 16-cylinder, 2-stroke of 1,530bhp at 350rpm, with direct drive to the propeller of 6.73 feet in diameter. The engines were direct reversing from the bridge controls. The control panel on the bridge had start, ahead, stop and start astern buttons, together with a speed control lever. By the time *Steersman* (1,567/70) was built in 1970, the yard had been taken over from the Ross Group by the Drypool Group. Although the vessels had the same hull dimensions and lines, there were design differences. Experience with

Steersman *was similar to* Rudderman *but incorporated a raised gangway.* KEITH BYASS

Rudderman showed that a centre line railed walkway was not adequate, and the extra cost and weight of a raised fore and aft gangway was necessary. There were also slight changes in the superstructure, as there was a reduction in cabin requirements. The engine was a similar Brons but supplied by the Dutch company's own factory. Speed loaded was given as 12 knots. Both had conventional pump rooms, with the three pumps driven by three Ruston engines, with shafts through the bulkhead from the engine room to the pump room to drive the Stothert & Pitt pumps, for a discharge rate of up to 910 tons per hour. Tanks were washed by Dasic 'Jetstream' fixed washing machines, fed with heated salt water by the port and starboard cargo pumps. It was also possible to connect a fan for ventilating the pump room to the pipe system, for drying the tanks after washing.

Eric Hammal, the naval architect at Cochranes, comments:

'Trunks on coastal tankers, I think, tended to be a fashion or be the simplest means of increasing the cargo tank capacity if the builder was making use of a previously proven hull with set dimensions of length, breadth and depth. The depth moulded to main deck was one of the defining dimensions when it came to calculating scantlings of side shell and frames etc, and this depth probably suited the arrangement forward and aft with regard to poop, engine room arrangement etc, with the trunk being an addition as a lighter structure to obtain the required tank volume for the lighter density petroleum type cargoes. It goes without saying that the construction man hours were greater to have a trunk arrangement rather than a flush deck at a greater depth moulded, but labour costs at that time were cheaper and the benefits of the lighter steel structure were possibly worth having. Later, Class scantlings were amended to use a corrected depth moulded which had a compensation increase to take into account the depth of the trunk. The trunk did of course give a reduction of the cargo free surface effect which to a large extent was nullified by the nominal rise of cargo vertical centre of gravity, with the cargo stowing higher than an equivalent flush deck vessel. The trunk usually did away with the fore and aft gangway although it was not mandatory to fit one on flush deck tankers as long as railed access was available along the main deck at or near the centre line but in practice a gangway was always the better option on a flush decker. Unless an owner specifically asked for a trunk deck ship, my designs were flush decked or a variation i.e. the cranked deck.'

With the backing of Ingram, Rowbothams expanded into the chemical tanker market, which offered good rates at the time. First to be delivered was *Astraman* (1,599/73) and *Polarisman* (1,596/73). They were the first British registered tankers to fully comply with the International Maritime Consultative Organisation (IMCO) dangerous chemicals rules. However, the tanks were not stainless steel but steel with a zinc silicate coating and so the most dangerous acids could not be carried. Eric Hammal recalls:

'The chemical tankers for Rowbotham were an interesting design. The first two were about 1,597grt, 3,200dwt for type 1 [most extreme] cargoes and had to have a speed in excess of 14kts on 3,500bhp. They were the fourth and fifth ships built at the yard for Rowbothams. The previous vessels were conventional oil products carriers designed especially for loading a full cargo of light petroleum spirits with a specific gravity of 0.72. These previous vessels, Rudderman, Steersman and Helmsman, had deadweights of 2,957 tons, 2,932 tons and 6,165 tons respectively. Rudderman and Steersman were built within the 1,600grt limit. They were conventional single skin tankers with cargo tanks suitable for loading mixed parcels of light and heavy oil products for delivery to British and Continental ports. These conventional tankers were capable of carrying certain products which prior to the introduction of the IMCO Code of Practice for the Carriage of Dangerous Liquid Chemicals in Bulk (Resolution No. 212-VII) were not specifically designated as chemical cargoes. The adoption of this code in October 1971 and its introduction by the Department of Trade and Industry in April 1972 meant the phasing out of this previous practice and brought into existence the Chemical Tanker. These specialised vessels were able to carry designated cargoes which the code divided into types 1, 2 and 3, with type 1 being the most hazardous. The code required that any vessel which carried these substances had to meet stringent standards for cargo containment, sub-division, collision damage and survivability, pollution control, crew habitability and safety plus specific cargo type segregation and carriage requirements.

The order for design and construction of the new vessels was placed with Cochranes and they became the first UK built tankers to be designed in compliance with the IMCO code and issued with a 'Certificate of Fitness' by the DOTI (Department of Trade & Industry). The owners would have initially supplied a 'Statement of Requirements' outlining the basic details of the new vessels. The statement would cover such items as limitation on vessel dimensions, usually length and draught dictated by port restrictions, cargo deadweight, gross registered tons limit, classification, type and parcel size of chemical cargoes with any unusual specific gravity requirements, operational trading range, a main engine type, service speed, cargo pump types and discharge rates, cargo tank numbers, etc. For this vessel the following would have been stated: Classification – Lloyds +100A1 Chemical Tanker (selected cargoes). Full International Service. IMCO centre cargo tanks type 1 and 2 chemical cargoes up to SG 1.40 and wing tanks type 3 chemical cargoes. Length overall less than 90 metres, draught less than 5.50 metres, minimum deadweight 3,200 tons, gross tonnage maximum 1,599.99. Cargo capacity (at 100%) approx 3,500 cubic metres, Service speed 14 knots and power 3,500bhp maximum. Manning sixteen officers and crew. Cargo pumps deep well type, stainless steel. Centre tanks individual, wing tanks ring main. Cargo tank coating: zinc silicate.

This was an exacting design for a naval architect, who had to work to a completely new set of regulations as well as meeting the owners requirements. Additionally, a higher than usual service speed for a tanker of this size had to be achieved. It is worth noting here that suppliers of tank coatings specified the number of days or sometimes hours which the coatings were able to resist certain chemicals and so speedy delivery was an important consideration. It was an advantage to have as a basis for the design of the new vessel the recently built Steersman, which although having a similar deadweight within the 1,600 gross tonnage limit, was of single skin construction and had a service speed of about 12 knots.

The design spiral started with a set of provisional main dimensions which were approximated to achieve the cargo tankage and gross tonnage limit, and then using estimated light ship weight (and centres of gravity), to derive a loaded displacement and hull form coefficient (sometimes referred to as block coefficient or Cb). Using these initial parameters, the powering requirements were checked to see if the required ship speed could be attained. It was found that by various iterations, the dimensions of the vessel needed to be approximately 82m LBP x 13.70m beam x 6.10m depth, with a 5.4m load draught giving a Cb in the order of 0.72. Previous tankers for the owner had form coefficients of 0.74/0.75.

With the owner placing a limit on the power of the main engine, it was found that with a form coefficient at 0.72, the position of the Longitudinal Centre of Buoyancy (LCB) became critical and needed to be further aft than for a conventional tanker form having an 0.75 Cb. Moving the LCB of the hull form aft would, however, give rise to an adverse head trim with a fore and aft arrangement of cargo spaces and a flush deck. This was countered by introducing a raised quarter deck over the after section of the cargo tanks, giving a rearward shift of the cargo Longitudinal Centre of Gravity (LCG) and an acceptable buoyancy/weight balance to achieve a level or slight stern trim. This had the additional advantage of giving increased buoyancy and depth aft, which allowed the introduction of a mid level flat in the engine room without an addition to the gross tonnage figure, as this portion of the machinery space and after peak ballast water tank (above the line of the tonnage deck) were treated as exempt spaces for tonnage measurement.

A hull form was derived based on the British Ship Research Association (BSRA) Methodical Hull Form

Series of model tested hull forms, for which powering characteristics were known. On smaller vessels a degree of adjustment was necessary to the BSRA form, particularly around the stern to achieve good water flow into the propeller and an open water aperture with spade rudder was selected for the best all round results.

With the main dimensions of the vessel and hull form confirmed, the layout could be arranged with spaces positioned within the hull for the stern tanks, engine room, fuel oil tankage, cofferdams, cargo tanks, ballast pump room and forward peak tanks. As the cargo tanks were to be discharged by individual deepwell pumps, no cargo pump room was required. The distribution of individual cargo tanks was determined with regard to the Code of Practice, which required a type 1 cargo to be carried in tanks which had to be at least one fifth of the breadth inboard at waterline level from the side shell of the vessel. This gave the two longitudinal bulkhead layout for the full length of the cargo tankage.

The Code of Practice stipulates the types and extent of external damage which needed to be applied throughout the ships length, both for collision and grounding. This affected the positioning of the main transverse bulkheads and also the need to install a double bottom space, which had to be at least one fifteenth of the breadth in depth. With the double bottom in particular, the layout of the ballast piping through the tanks had to be carefully considered, to ensure any applied damage which could penetrate pipes would not result in adverse flooding of adjacent tanks. All spaces surrounding cargo tanks were treated as high risk areas because of a possible cargo leakage and access (from the open deck) within these spaces had to be such as to permit a person wearing self-contained breathing apparatus free movement, not easily achieved on small vessels in double bottom tankage.

Structure: The centre cargo tanks were required to be as free of internal ship structure as practicable, which gave troughed main transverse bulkheads, a flat bottom (tank top plating), longitunal bulkhead stiffening on the outboard side within the wing tanks and deck stiffening external on the main/quarter deck. To a large extent the type of structure stiffeners or troughing was governed by the production capabilities of the plant in the shipyard. The external deck stiffening had to be accepted in way of the quarter deck tanks but it was decided to incorporate the same structure over the forward cargo tanks into deck tanks, in effect a 'double bottom' giving a cleaner working deck space plus additional ballast water tankage. Conventional single-skinned oil product tankers had usually made use of some of their cargo tanks for ballast water to achieve reasonable sea going draughts but the chemical tanker needed to keep its cargo tanks clean, so any additional ballast capacity was welcome and the deck tanks also had the advantage that they were exempt from gross tonnage measurement.

The Code of Practice also had implications regarding the positioning and arrangement of the crew accommodation spaces, which had to be aft of any cargo tank or related cofferdam. Access doors and vent openings had to be at least a defined distance from the deckhouse front, which itself had to be of A60 fire rating, including any windows which had to be non-opening. Access to accommodation and the cargo control room had to be through an airlock system with positive internal pressure. The bridge followed the Code of Practice, which was for it to be fully enclosed and in order to give adequate views fore and aft whilst coming alongside, was extended out to the full beam of the ship. The arrangement of the cabins, etc followed the owner's current practice.

As the layout of the vessel developed, constant checks were made on the gross tonnage to ensure it kept within the 1,600 ton limit. At that time the tonnage measurement regulations required a standardised set of calculated volume measurements, which resulted in a gross tonnage figure. Rules were laid down as to how the vessel would be measured but it was possible to minimise tonnage by accepted 'dodges', such as having deep double bottom spaces, wide alternate transverse side frames, sloped bottom floors, and having ballast tanks and auxiliary machinery spaces above the tonnage deck, etc. There was a slight weight penalty with most of these measures but this was acceptable if it kept the vessel below the tonnage limit. The rounded gunwhale which was the owners' current practice was also beneficial.

Intact and damaged stability were a major requirement in the Code of Practice and a series of loading conditions were investigated, using the detailed estimate of lightship weight and centres of gravity, together with various deadweight components. At this time, the sophisticated software of today was not available to enable every possible variation of damage through a range of cargo loadings and draughts to be computed. Worst condition scenarios were chosen and heel angle and residual stability after damage were calculated, for compliance with the criteria using the added weight or the lost buoyancy methods. Similar calculations would be repeated when the completed vessel had its weight and centres of gravity checked by means of an inclining experiment.

The Propulsion Machinery: Alongside the development of the ship layout and hull form, the required performance had been shown to be achievable within the maximum power listed in the statement of requirements. The configuration of the engine room and related equipment were considered, the main

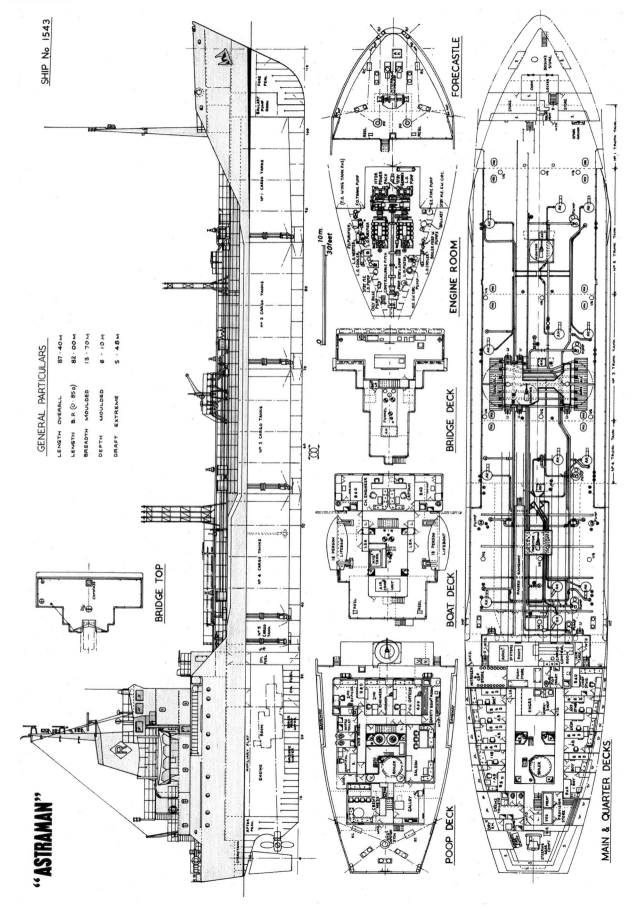

SHIP No 1543

"ASTRAMAN"

GENERAL PARTICULARS

LENGTH OVERALL	87·40 M	
LENGTH B.P. (0·85 D)	82·00 M	
BREADTH MOULDED	13·70 M	
DEPTH MOULDED	6·10 M	
DRAFT EXTREME	5·48 M	

BRIDGE TOP

FORECASTLE

ENGINE ROOM

BRIDGE DECK

BOAT DECK

POOP DECK

MAIN & QUARTER DECKS

10 m.
30 feet

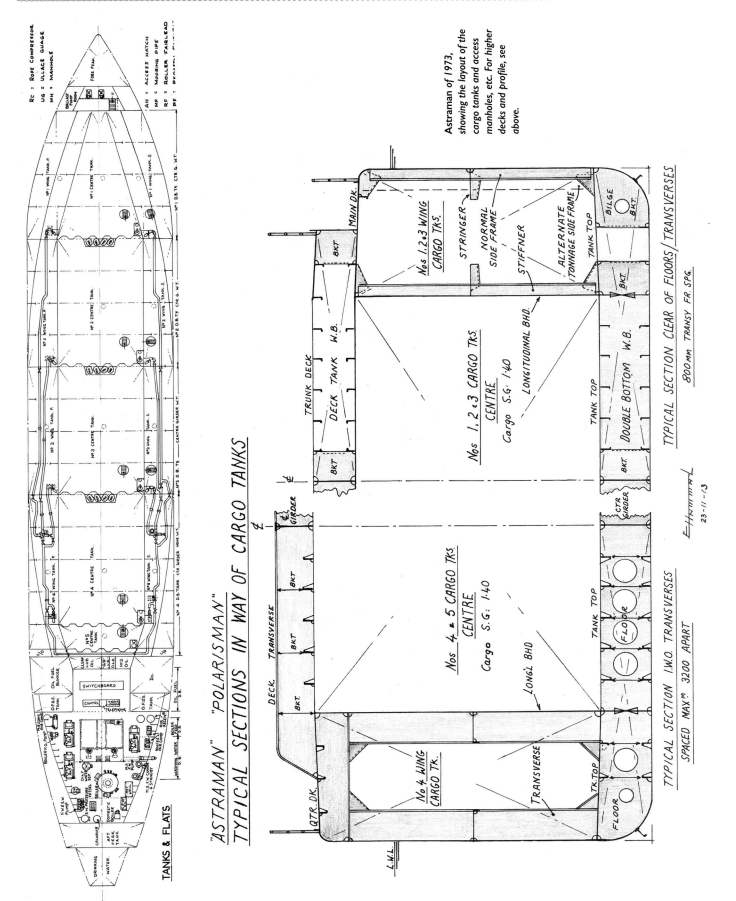

Rc = ROPE COMPRESSOR
Ug = ULLAGE GUAGE
MH = MANHOLE

AH = ACCESS HATCH
MP = MOORING PIPE
RF = ROLLER FAIRLEAD
BF = BREAST FAIRLEAD

Astraman of 1973, showing the layout of the cargo tanks and access manholes, etc. For higher decks and profile, see above.

TANKS & FLATS

"ASTRAMAN" "POLARISMAN"
TYPICAL SECTIONS IN WAY OF CARGO TANKS

Nos 1, 2 & 3 WING CARGO TKS.

STRINGER
NORMAL SIDE FRAME
STIFFNER
ALTERNATE TONNAGE SIDE FRAME
BILGE
BKT
TANK TOP

MAIN DK.

BKT

TRUNK DECK

DECK TANK W.B.

Nos 1, 2 & 3 CARGO TKS.
CENTRE
Cargo S.G: 1·40

LONGITUDINAL BHD.

TANK TOP

DOUBLE BOTTOM W.B.

BKT.

TANK TOP

TYPICAL SECTION CLEAR OF FLOORS/TRANSVERSES
800 mm TRANSV FR. SPG.

DECK. TRANSVERSE
GIRDER
BKT
BKT
BKT

Nos 4 & 5 CARGO TKS.
CENTRE
Cargo S.G: 1·40

LONG'L BHD

No 4 WING CARGO TK.

QTR. DK.

TRANSVERSE

TK. TOP

FLOOR

CTR GIRDER

TANK TOP

FLOOR

L.W.L.

TYPICAL SECTION I.W.O. TRANSVERSES
SPACED MAX'M 3200 APART

23-11-73

engine being the owner's choice of an English Electric RKCM diesel, which in 16 cylinder form would produce 3,600bhp. The single main engine was not ideal, as the owner's choice of hydraulically driven cargo pumps required them to be powered from electric pump units situated in the engine room. After discussion with the owner, it was agreed that a preferred arrangement would be for the single 16 RKCM engine to be replaced by two 8 cylinder units each of 1,760bhp, driving into a twin input, single output gearbox, which would power the controllable pitch propeller but also drive the four-clutched hydraulic pump units. This layout meant that either of the main engines could power the cargo system with reasonable loading. When eventually the detailed drawings of this layout became available, it was obvious that with the conventional layout of gear box aft of the main engines, the extreme width of the main gear box would not fit within the finer hull lines at the aft end of the engine room and the complete assembly would have to move forward, leading to a longer engine room and loss of cargo space. Increased engine room length was deemed unacceptable and the more radical solution of placing the gear box ahead of the engines with the propeller shaft passing aft between them below floor plate level was considered. It was then apparent that with the gear box forward, the complete arrangement of clutched hydraulic cargo pump units was much more accessible and made the hydraulic pipe systems simpler to install, to pass through the top of the engine room and on to the open deck.

Any system that entered a cargo tank and led back to the engine room (such as hydraulics, tank washing water, steam lines, etc) had to be carefully considered and safeguards put in place to ensure that cargo leakage into such systems could not lead to a dangerous situation in the machinery space. In particular, the hydraulically driven ballast pumps normally sited in the engine room were placed in a dedicated ballast pump room at the forward end of the ship. Minor systems were led back to an auxiliary machinery space sited near the deck house front at quarterdeck level. The propeller was a controllable pitch unit operating at 200rpm, of as large a diameter that could be accommodated to give best efficiency and good clearance in the aperture. Auxiliary electrical power was from three diesel driven alternator units each developing 80kw, with usually only one operating at sea and two in port. Steam for the cargo heating was supplied by a Spanner vertical boiler.

Cargo Arrangements: The cargo tankage was designed so that at least five different incompatible cargoes could be carried in the centre tanks, whilst it was also possible to carry further different parcels in the wing tanks provided the ship was not operating as a type 1 or type 2 vessel. It had been decided by the owner that the additional expense of stainless steel cargo tank construction could not be justified in view of the limited number of cargoes that warranted it. The tanks were shot blasted internally after all construction had been completed and immediately coated with a zinc silicate covering suitable for the intended cargoes. Each of the centre tanks were provided with a hydraulically powered stainless steel deepwell pump, with a similar pump fitted in each of the after wing tanks, connected by a ring main suction pipe system to the other wing tanks. An emergency portable cargo pump was carried in the event of a main pump failure. The suction foot of the deepwell pumps sat in a sump in the tank bottom, which together with the cargo piping could be stripped by means of air vacuum and eductors. Each cargo tank was fully segregated from the next to avoid the risk of cross contamination which could be calamitous with some of the intended cargoes. Each tank was fitted with a drop loading pipe, steam heating, closed tank ullaging system, nitrogen inerting (centre tanks only), fixed tank washing using salt and fresh water, air purging, ventilation line taken to a riser stack and fitted with a PV valve, remote monitoring for pump operation and automatic 98% full shut-off.

The complexity of the piping systems running along the main and quarter decks, together with the external deck stiffening, tank hatches, ullage ports, fire fighting foam/water mains and monitors, vent heads from ballast tanks, etc, necessitated careful planning. As an aid to both drawing office and the outfit/installation engineers, a large scale model of the deck, about 10 feet long, was constructed by the shipyard joinery department to enable a three dimensional view to be had of the whole arrangement when designing the layout

The vessels as built had the following principal particulars: length overall 87.40m; length between perpendiculars 82m; breadth moulded 13.70m; depth moulded 6.10m; draught summer load water line 5.47m; total deadweight 3,202 tonnes; gross tonnage 1,597.14; net tonnage 1,330.11; machinery English Electric 8RKCM diesels delivering 2 x 1,760bhp at 900rpm; trial speed (loaded) 14.4kts; cargo capacity at 100% 3,564 cubic metres; ballast water capacity 1,072 cubic metres; fuel oil capacity 265 cubic metres, fresh water capacity 50 cubic metres.

The second pair of ships, Stellaman (1,513/75) and Marsman (1,513/75), both 74 x 13.5 x 6.1 metres, were smaller at 2,320 tonnes dwt and carried type 2 chemicals but still required a speed of 14kts on 2,600bhp. The block coefficient needed to be 0.66 and the longitudinal centre of buoyancy (LCB) 0.2% length forward of amidships, hence the adoption of the raised quarter deck for these, which

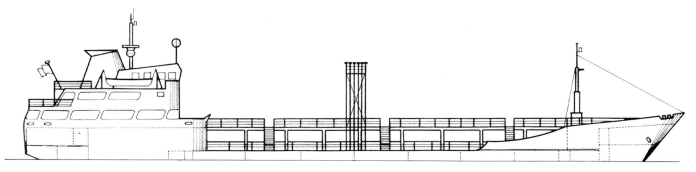

Benvenue (1,550/75) was the first of three chemical tankers built for Ben Line in the Netherlands.

also placed the cargo LCG in the correct position for trimming purposes. As a type 2 vessel requires wing tanks for cargo containment, these naturally became ballast tanks, so there was no need for the deck ballast tanks as on the first pair of ships. All of the deck stiffening was fully external to the cargo tanks, the quarter deck being sloped down to the main deck to maintain strength continuation. As the result of experience with the two earlier tankers which had high noise and vibration levels, despite the usual levels of sound proofing – mainly as a result of the owner's choice of hydraulically powered pumps driven by the main engines, the pipes having to pass adjacent to the accommodation areas (Cochranes had recommended electric pumps). Legislation was due to come into force requiring reduced noise and vibration levels for crew comfort, especially with more powerful engines being fitted. The owners specified that these two ships should meet the new noise levels, which German yards had been achieving by fitting a resiliently mounted deckhouse. The owner was not keen on this and hence the yard prepared a design in which transmission paths and vibration (which creates noise) were eliminated as much as possible from the main noise sources: engines, pumps and hydraulics. This was achieved by removing the accommodation from a poop superstructure, which had high noise transmission paths through the shell and deck, and placing the accommodation in a deckhouse block separated from as much of the ship structure as possible by having physical breaks between it and the main hull. The deckhouse sat directly on the quarter deck but internally it was fitted with a 'floating floor' (about 70mm thick of insulation, reinforcing steel and composition), all internal cabin bulkheads and linings sitting on this floor and these were also isolated by flexible connection to any adjacent steelwork.

The interior of the deckhouse was heavily insulated with high density foam on all external surfaces (also of fire retardant type as required by regulation). Any entry of piping, etc into the block from the engine room was through a single trunk, which itself was highly insulated and the pipe entry fitted with flexible couplings to act as a noise barrier. The block of the deckhouse was separated from the poop structure by a small air gap. As the requirement at that time was to have lifeboats each side of the ship and these were of a size which did not allow their mounting in gravity davits alongside the accommodation block, they were moved forward on to platforms at least 2.4 metres above the cargo deck and which themselves were separated from the deckhouse by an air gap. The main diesel hydraulic pump sets were moved out of the main engine room and sited in the poop 'tween decks at the stern, which removed a major noise source from within the hull and below the accommodation block. This enabled the hydraulic piping to be led forward directly out of the poop front and isolated from the accommodation block. The engine casings were built on the poop separate from the accommodation block. All engine room machinery apart from the main engine and where ever possible was resiliently mounted to break vibration paths as were engine exhausts. The result was a vessel which fully complied with noise level regulations and the experience was applied to subsequent vessels the yard built.'

A change was made to Allen for the main engine, which was a Vee 16-cylinder, 4-stroke of 2,680bhp at 72rpm that gave a speed of 13.75 knots. In addition, two larger chemical tankers, *Centaurman* (2,475/76) and *Vegaman* (2,475/76) were constructed by Hall, Russell. All four were built as dedicated chemical tankers and with a downturn in hire rates due to too many chemical tankers being built, they were sold en block to Hong Kong companies managed by Buries Markes (Ship Management) Ltd, London. Last of the real coasting size products tankers were the Dunston-built *Oilman* (997/82) and the slightly larger *Oarsman* (1,550/80). Dunstons had been bought by Ingram in 1974 and was later sold to the Dutch Damen shipyards in 1988. Compared with the Dunston-built *Quarterman* (1,226/73), this vessel could carry 410 tons more at 2,547 tonnes on 4.86 metres draught, mainly by increasing the length 4 metres. Other changes of note were a return to a conventional pump room (rather than submersible pumps), with pumps driven from the engine room through the bulkhead and the fitting of a slop tank on the main deck in anticipation of the impending new rules; also, No. 3 tank could be used as a dedicated ballast tank for some voyages. It was possible to heat the cargo

from 38 to 54 degrees centigrade or maintain it at 76 degrees if loaded hot using a vertical Spanner Swirlyflow boiler and heating coils. The main engine was a Ruston of 1,880bhp at 750rpm, driving a controllable pitch propeller via a Brevo 3:1 reduction gear. The deck machinery was all hydraulic.

Esso opted to build tankers over the 1,600 gross limit and *Esso Penzance* (2,178/71) and *Esso Inverness* (2,178/71) were built as clean products tankers, while the first of the series, *Esso Tenby* (2,170/70) was mainly used to carry heavy boiler oil to various oil fired power stations, including Portishead and Plymouth. All were built by Appledore.

Ingram added Hull Gates Shipping Co. Ltd's tankers to the Rowbotham fleet in 1982. Hull Gates had been part of the Sir Fred Parkes Group latterly and had been sold en block with other associates to Turnbull Scott, who were the sellers of this fleet of mostly Japanese built vessels. Hull Gates had traditionally been in the dry cargo trades but ventured into tankers with *Humbergate* (1,579/68), followed by *Hullgate* (1,594/70) under the Parkes group. Though similar in appearance, there were some notable differences as *Hullgate* was longer and had a trunk plus heating coils in her tanks. Perhaps the most important change was to a Ruston 6AO 6-cylinder, 2-stroke turbocharged and intercooled engine of 3,000bhp at 450rpm, driving through a 2:1 MWD gearbox and clutch. It was the first AO engine to be direct reversing and together with the fore and aft transverse thrusters giving 1.75 tons of thrust each, were all controlled from the bridge. The service speed was 13.5 knots and her first work was a five year time charter to Esso to carry Bunker C fuel deliveries around the UK.

Turnbull Scott, traditionally in the ocean trades, had moved into the coasting trades at the end of the 1960s and were managers of the Whitehall Shipping Co. Ltd, which ordered two oil/chemical tankers from Richards (Shipbuilders) Ltd, Lowestoft. Fitted with stainless steel cargo tanks, they were appropriately named *Stainless Warrior* (1,561/70) and *Stainless Duke* (1,561/72). They were based on a German design made for a Danish owner and had a double skin and Svanehjoy (Danish) pumps, driven by Brown Boveri electric motors placed on deck. They were also fitted to send cargo vapour ashore to meet regulations for hazardous cargoes but had relief valves venting to the atmosphere if the pressure in the cargo tanks exceeded 3lbs/sq. in. Both were sold in the latter part of the 1970s but *Stainless Patriot* (1,599/74), built in Sweden by Batservice A/S to carry the most hazardous (type 1) cargoes, was not sold until 1983.

Another ocean liner trade company attracted by the favourable rates for handy chemical tankers was Ben Line, who were finding strong competition in their traditional liner services. They ordered three chemical tankers from the Noord Nederlandse yard, designed to carry four fully segregated grades, which could be increased to six grades if the cargo was loaded directly into the selected tank or the ship's deck lines were washed out following the loading of earlier cargo. Each tank had a separate deep well pump for discharge and the tanks and pipework were coated with Dimetcote 4, a zinc silicate coating which allowed them to carry type 2 cargoes. First to be delivered was *Benvenue* (1,550/75), with two sisterships following in 1976. Her first charter was to BP Chemicals Ltd. All were fitted with Smit-Bolnes 2,430bhp engines for a speed of 13 knots but Ben Line too found they were unable to make the vessles pay and dropped out of the trade after a few years.

CHAPTER 8
THE 1980S:
BACK TO BARGES?

The moulded dimensions etc, are given in metres unless otherwise stated.

The beginning of the 1980s saw a revision of trading limits, so the old Home Trade became the UK Near Continental Trading Area. This covered the British Isles and the North Sea coast of Denmark, and south as far as Brest. To this was added the Middle Trade Zone from Orporto in Portugal as far north as Vestfjorden inside the Lofoten Isles of Norway, plus the Baltic Sea. However, some owners were then allowed an extension into the Middle Trade area in certain circumstances, allowing them to reach Poland and south east Sweden and down to north east Spain with no change in manning or certification. To work beyond these limits the vessel and crew needed to be certificated for unlimited trading. Rules were also relaxed on vessels purchased overseas with equipment which was adequate but differed from that approved by the UK Department of Trade. Statutory manning levels and crew qualifications were laid down, including for the first time those vessels under 199 gross. Up until 1977 there had been no precise requirements laid down for the number of crew, which had been governed by customs of trade and agreed with the unions but in this year a voluntary scheme had been set up as a precursor to the statutory scheme.

For some years Kellys, the shipowners and coal merchants of Belfast, which was 50% owned by Powell Duffryn, parent company of Stephenson Clarke, had mainly been equipped with second-hand smaller vessels often from the latters' fleet. However, they finally ordered a pair of new vessels, *Ballygarvey* (1,599/82) and *Ballygrainey* (1,599/83), both 71.81 x13.11 x 6.00 metres, from Goole – the last coasters to be built there. They were single deck vessels with a deadweight of 2,535 tons or 2,020 tons of coal stowing at 1.5 tons per cubic metre and intended for homogeneous cargoes designed with their local Irish Sea coal trade in mind. They had a slightly unusual appearance, as high bulwarks extended a short distance from the poop forwards and the forecastle aft, which extended the poop and forecastle decks as narrow but clear gangways on either side of the hatch stowage area. The main engine was a 6-cylinder, 4-stroke MaK of 2,450bhp, driving a controllable pitch propeller via a single reduction gear and, like most vessels of the period, had bow thrusters. The company was finally taken over completely and merged with Stephenson Clarke in 1990, when the Ocean Group withdrew from shipping. The ships were renamed *Shoreham* and *Cowdray* respectively, to fit the naming pattern used by Stephenson Clarke. *Shoreham* was sold in 1993 and became Barbados flagged but remained in the UK bulk trades in various guises, while *Cowdray* passed to Greek owners.

Perhaps one of the surprises of the 1980s was the success of the 'YDD Boxes' or strictly the Yorkshire Dry Dock 'Economy Coaster'. They began as a grain barge design to meet the needs of the Alexandra Towing Co.'s bulk cargo handling services operations, moving grain from bulk carriers arriving in the Mersey to users along the Manchester Ship Canal, although were capable of making coasting voyages. The order went to Yorkshire Dry Dock who had considerable experience building large barges for use in the Humber area. With a deadweight of about 950 tons, the three barges, designed for a crew of six, were the largest the yard had built: *Seacombe Trader* (480/74), *Seaborne Trader* (499/75) and *Sealand Trader* (499/750, all of 39.60 x 9.50 x 4.75 metres. They were powered by two 6-cylinder, 4-stroke Caterpillar engines rated at about 375bhp, each fitted with Aquamaster drives working very much like large outboard motors, although the engines themselves were fixed but the vertical drive shaft and propellers could be rotated through 360 degrees. The three barges worked for the company until 1987, when they were sold to other UK owners with coasting in mind.

The reports of the vessels in the marine press immediately attracted the attention of John Golding, a manager at Eggar, Forrester, and following a visit to the yard and a trial trip, he discussed with the yard a modified design for a simple coaster version to operate within the Home Trade Elbe-Brest limits. Because of the exposed nature of the Mersey, the original design needed little modification and already had MacGregor single-pull hatch covers on prominent hatch coamings. First delivered was *Wilks* (495/76), able to carry 1,000 tons on 3.901 metres; it had longer bulwarks aft than the next two, *Wis* (491/77) and *Wib* (498/79), which were 1.68 metres longer with the moulded dimensions 42.45 x 9.40 x 4.75 metres and a better deadweight of about 1,040 tons. Also to take note of the design was Giles Prichard-Gordon, on the board of H. Clarkson (Shipbrokers) Ltd and his firm, Giles Prichard-Gordon & Co. Ltd, took delivery of two at the same time, *Alice P.G.* (499/78) and *Emily P.G.*

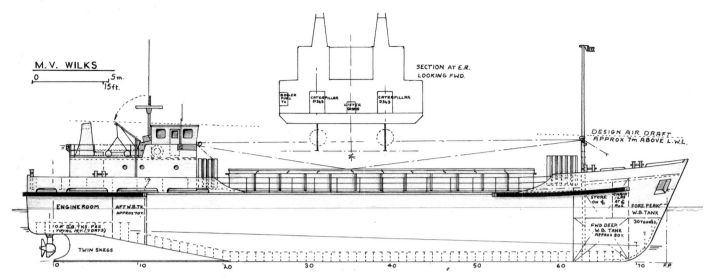

M.V. WILKS

Wilks, built in 1976, was one of the early versions of what was to become the Yorkshire Economy Coaster, as the more refined version was called. The moulded dimensions were 40.76 x 9.50 x 4.75 metres and the block coefficient (Cb) about 80, so rather more barge than coaster. The section shows the positions of the twin engines and their individual casings leading up to the twin funnels, which were side by side.

(499/80), which were managed by G.T. Gillie & Blair Ltd. They traded for Prichard-Gordon until 1988, by which time the company was concentrating on tankers for world wide trading.

Meanwhile, Eggar, Forrester, requiring more ships at short notice, ordered three further vessels from the Danish yard Nordsovaerfret, who could deliver sooner at a lower price but building to a British design by Fairmile. This incorporated a full height poop, giving more accommodation space for a crew of four, although probably not to the captain's liking with his bunk on top of one of the engines! Also incorporated was a higher forecastle and a double bottom, as the earlier vessels lacked water ballast capacity for light voyages. They used two Caterpillar 3408T engines derated to 230bhp, driving Aquamaster units as previously. These units were the product of the Finnish shipyard Hollming Oy. The aquapilot controls for each engine operated from the bridge. Horizontal movement through 360 degrees steered hydraulically, while vertical rotation of the lever first engaged the clutch and then the engine speed through a mechanical cable connection. The complete horizontal rotation, apart from great manoeuvrability, also allowed the propellers to be turned to the reverse position, so that they had some protection afforded by the associated skegs particularly in drying harbours. The ships' main trades were from the east coast between Shoreham and the Firth of Forth, to near Continental ports between Cherburg and Delfzil but particularly working in and out of the Schelde. The main cargoes were steel, fertilizer, scrap and grain; scrap cargoes varied from quite chunky items to fragmented scrap. Incidentally, the rusting process of scrap can remove oxygen sufficiently to suffocate anyone entering the hold and crews needed to be aware of this.

David Lapthorne suggested to various builders a joint venture to construct and finance a coaster to replace his ageing fleet of mostly second-hand, often ex-Dutch, coasters. As the established shipowners had moved into larger vessels, a number of smaller operators had sprung up prepared to work on tighter margins. Masters tended to become owners, particularly of the smaller vessels in the London & Rochester fleet for example. Lapthornes were among the long established owners, though they tended to buy second-hand vessels. However, this was about to change radically, as his suggestion was taken up by the Yorkshire Dry Dock backed by their owners J.H. Whitaker (Holdings) Ltd, who were shipowners themselves. Finance was arranged via the Government Shipbuilding Support scheme for a fixed interest rate loan. Following the earlier success, the design was improved in respect of the accommodation and the harbour generator moved to the forecastle. Advantage was also taken of the measurement rules as far as possible, so that deeper alternate frames were used, as gross tonnage was related to them but allowed grain capacity to be increased and deadweight improved to 1,236 tons. The hull was also tank tested to get the best results while keeping the steelwork simple.

The first of the new series was appropriately called *Hoo Venture* (498/82), 46.42 x 9.40 x 4.75 metres, and at 49.99 metres overall length remained in the 'under 50 metres' for pilotage charges. The Caterpillar engines, though not working at full power, had not proved very robust and so the new vessel was fitted with two 6-cylinder, 4-stroke Cummins KT1150M engines, working at a total of 730bhp at 1,800 rpm and driving two Aquamaster US400 units. Unlike the Caterpillar engines, these had individual cylinder heads with four valves per cylinder, so a single cylinder head could be changed if necessary. It is interesting to note here that, by now, many of the components used

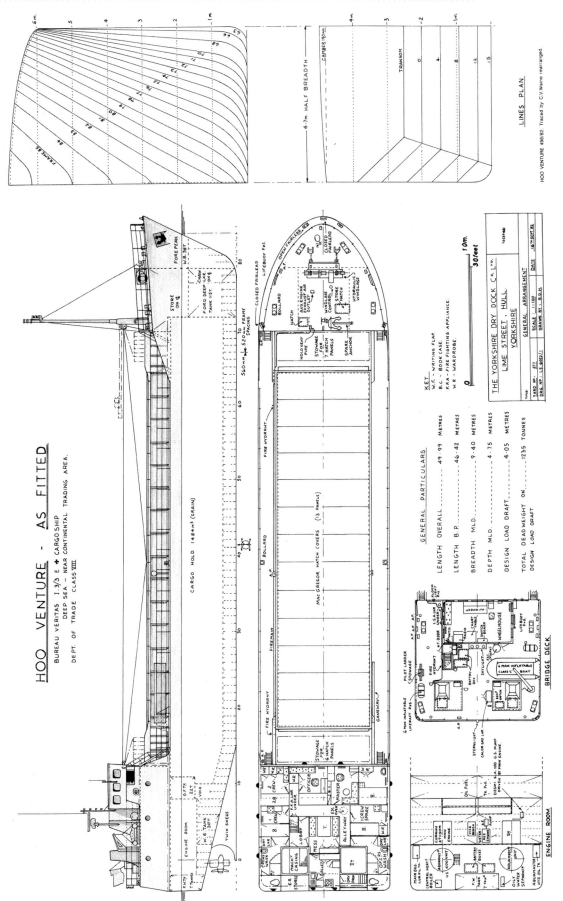

Hoo Venture of 1982 was the first of the Yorkshire Economy Coasters and featured a conventional forebody and a hard chine stern. The accommodation was arranged so that crew cabins were not directly adjacent to the engine casings; even so, they were noisy but low construction costs meant that they could be profitable in the coasting trade, whilst the twin screws, each able to rotate through 360 degrees, meant rudders were eliminated and the vessels were very manoeuvreable.

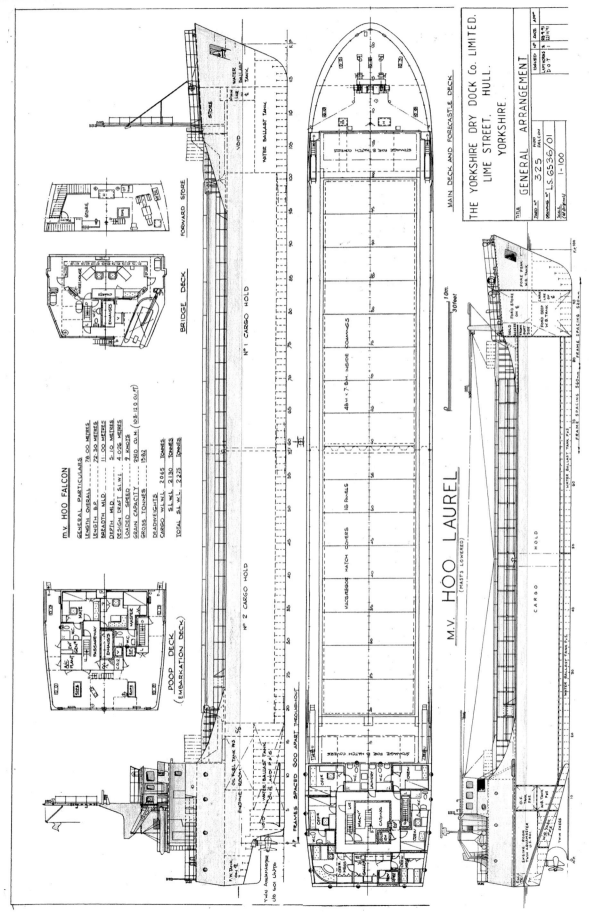

m.v. HOO FALCON

GENERAL PARTICULARS

LENGTH OVERALL -------- 78.00 METRES
LENGTH B.P. ----------- 72.50 METRES
BREADTH MLD. ---------- 11.00 METRES
DEPTH MLD. ------------ 5.10 METRES
DESIGN DRAFT S.L.W.L -- 4.026 METRES
LOADED SPEED ---------- 9 KNOTS
GRAIN CAPACITY -------- 2910 CU.M. (103·120 CU.FT)
GROSS TONNES ---------- 1562

DEADWEIGHTS

CARGO W.L.W.L 2065 TONNES.
       S.L.W.L 2130 TONNES
TOTAL S.L.W.L 2225 TONNES

THE YORKSHIRE DRY DOCK Co. LIMITED.
LIME STREET. HULL.
YORKSHIRE.

TITLE GENERAL ARRANGEMENT

M.V. HOO LAUREL
(MASTS LOWERED)

The main general arrangement drawing for the Yorkshire Economy Coaster shows Hoo Falcon (1,382/92), the largest of the type built, with the profile of Hoo Laurel (794/84) has been inserted to the left of the particulars block to the same scale for comparison.

in British ships were of overseas origin, with American engines powering the Finnish gear box and propeller system. J.I. Jacobs, who had also placed work with the yard, became interested in the vessels as a diversification investment away from ocean tanker operations and so they ordered five ships also for Lapthorne management. These received 'Hoo' names and a sixth vessel, *Ardent*, was built for the Franco-British Chartering Agency.

With the introduction of the new tonnage measurement system, the opportunity was taken to increase the size but stay under the 800 limit, above which a more highly qualified crew would be needed. Despite the poor freight rates on offer, the vessels were attractive because they cost less than £1,000 per deadweight ton to build. Running with a minimum of four men, avoiding an engineer by de-rating the engines, or five men if going round Land's End, they were built to 'Bureau Veritas' classification which would permit wider operation than the Department of Trade Class 'VIII'. The lead vessel was *Hoo Laurel* (794/84), giving a deadweight of just under 1,400 tons on a draught of 3.90 metres. Most were owned by various companies within the Jacobs group for Lapthorne management, though *Dowlais* was built for Harris & Dixon and *Gwyn* (794/85) for the Graig Shipping Co, Cardiff. Last delivered was *Hoocrest* (794/86). The vessels having proved successful and with trade improving, Jacobs and Lapthorne ordered a further five. *Hoo Finch* (794/88) was delivered first and the order was completed by *Hoo Beech* (794/89). Chris Reynolds, who captained several for a number of years comments:

'The Yorkshire Dry Dock Series were a utilitarian design built to save on building costs. They were expected, by the builders, to have an economic lifespan of fifteen years. Although the hull plating was only 9mm thick when built, they have lasted well and have often exceeded expectations by eight years or more. Compared with older Dutch coasters I sailed in, the crew accommodation was both hot and noisy as a result of the proximity to the high revving engines and thin plates. The crew facilities were reduced too. With basically a barge shaped hull and a horsepower/tonnage ratio of about 0.5 the hull was at its limit and this showed itself particularly as the weather worsened. With a force 6 on the nose, speed was down from 8 knots to only 6, by force 7 down to 5, then 3.5 knots at best in gale force 8 in loaded condition. In ballast, force 6 on the nose was the maximum. Although the transom stern of the 'shoeboxes', as they were sometimes called, might appear vulnerable to pooping, it offered a reasonable amount of reserve buoyancy. They tended to lift in a following sea, making the motion more noticeable and thus lively seaboats.'

This liveliness caused problems with the supply of engine cooling water, as the seawater intakes could come out of the water with resultant loss of flow and engine overheating, causing cracked cylinder heads. Everards, who subsequently managed some of the early ones, solved this by recirculating water from the ballast tank below the engine room.

Thought was next given to larger versions and Harris & Dixon placed an order for a more conventional fixed screw type. First to be completed was *Ilona G.* (999/90), 65.20 x 9.98 x 4.85 metres, able to lift 1,700 tons on 3.86 metres draught. The engine selected was a Cummins V-12 driving a single central screw. The Department of Transport still classed it as 'Limited European Area' but the classification society Bureau Veritas gave it 'Deep Sea – European Coasting Service'. The second vessel *Anna Maria* was taken by Cypriot-based associates and traded more widely. The first few trips gave a good indication of the range of cargoes she carried: 3.5.91 Amsterdam sun flower pellets. 7.5.91 depart for Plymouth. Arrive 8.5.91 – hatch had to be opened and closed during discharge because of rain. 8.5.91 Dean Quarry for three grades of stone. No. 20 hatch cover comes off track and falls into aft stowage well. Loading aborted for this tide. Proceeded to Falmouth to get hatch lifted. 9.5.91 returned and loaded stone for Greenwich and arrive there 12.5.91 for morning discharge. Sail for Rotterdam to load bauxite. 17.5.91 depart for Gunness. 20.5.91 depart for Flixborough and arrive 21.5.91 load steel billets. 22.5.91 depart for Antwerp. Arrive 23.5.91 discharge. 25.5.91 load bulk rape seed, depart 26.5.91 for Le Legue. Arrive 28.5.91 discharge and depart 29.5.91. Arrive 31.5.91 Dieppe to load rape seed, depart 1.6.91. 2.6.91 arrive Ipswich. Depart 4.6.91 and arrive Erith to load fragmented scrap. 6.6.91 depart for El Ferrol de Caudillo. Arrive 10.6.91 discharge. Depart 12.6.91 for La Pallice. Arrive 14.6.91 to load milling wheat. Leave 14.6.91 for New Holland. Arrive 18.6.91 discharge and depart for Albert Dock. Hull for shipyard work. 23.6.91 arrive Rotterdam to load soya meal. Depart 26.6.91 for Sutton Bridge discharge and depart 28.6.91. 29.6.91 arrive Rotterdam to load petroleum coke. 1.7.91 depart for Dundalk; arrive 4.7.91 discharge and depart for Llandulas. Arrive 6.7.91 and load stone for Shoreham. Depart 6.7.91 and arrive 9.7.91 discharge and sail 11.7.91... The mate noted for voyage 14 (23.7.91): 'Dean Quarry cargo 600 tons 3mm dust, 500 tons 6mm and 520 tons 14mm. Initial mistake in not loading dust right aft. This then caused 6mm to be loaded forward of centre, hence down by the head. Never did get time to deballast aft peak (which was just as well).

Re-checked all drafts on arrival in calm waters giving 6 tons over marks – loading iffy?' With homogeneous cargo she could usually be trimmed about 50mm or more by the stern.

Lapthornes and Jacobs also placed orders for a larger version but returning to the tried and tested twin Aquamaster format which had been so successful and this resulted in *Hoo Falcon* (1,382/92), 72.30 x 11.0 x 5.10 metres and a deadweight of 2,225 tons on a slightly increased draught of 4.02 metres. Two 6-cylinder Cummins KTA 19M engines rated at 500bhp were used to drive two Aquamaster US601 units, giving a speed of 9 knots. Light ship was 696.53 tons. Last of the Yorkshire dry cargo series was *Torrent* (999/92) for the Franco-British Chartering Agency. She was a smaller version of the *Hoo Falcon* design but differed in having the bridge lower to reduce air draught. To achieve this, it was moved over the hatch stowage space to give a unique profile. With no further orders, the yard closed in the mid 1990s.

As well as the busy Grove Wharf on the Trent, J. Wharton (Shipping) Ltd also owned a small fleet, which in the late 1970s was becoming outdated and so two new vessels were ordered from Cochranes. They were of a fairly traditional single deck design, with the dimensions 56.0 x 11.2 x 4.6 metres, which resulted in *Lizzonia* (798/80) and *Angelonia* (798/80). The single hold was divided by a light steel demountable bulkhead. It was easily damaged and could prove difficult and expensive to fix but did allow different grades of the usual cargoes of coal, grain, fertilizer, roadstone and other bulk commodities to be carried. The well tried Mirrlees-Blackstone engines gave a speed of 11 knots. Everards had been closely associated with the company as shareholders from 1952 and so, in the early 1980s, a new class of 'tween decker was built for both companies, each taking two ships and Everards financing their pair through Investors in Industry. Everards having already had some larger vessels of this type in service, discussed the design of a smaller version with a box hold. One other design feature was to be two movable bulkheads, which would meet the new grain rules; the area of hold used would be full and finally eliminate the danger of grain cargoes shifting, provided of course, the shipper gave the correct stowage rate. If the shipper was in error it was at his expense and not the shipowners! By the time the design and finance had been agreed, it was getting close to the cut-off date for the ships to be built to the old rules, which would remain in force for ten years for ships whose keels at least had been laid before that date. In the event, Cochranes were able to complete laying three of the four keels three days before the 18th June 1982 cut-off point (*Selectivity*, *Willonia* and *Stevonia*), while the fourth (*Pamela Everard*) was subcontracted to Richards (Shipbuilders) Ltd, who also met the deadline.

Although Everards had sent the specification to yards at home and overseas, Cochranes were in a particularly good position to meet the requirements, having recently built *Norbrit Faith* (1,597/82) and *Norbrit Hope* (1,597/83), to a high specification which included two 10-ton capacity Moelven travelling cranes, which ran on tracks incorporated in the hatch coamings The weight of the cranes and the associated strengthening of the hatch coamings to support them probably reduced the deadweight by 60 tons or so. However, the cranes attracted a Government charter for *Norbrit Faith* to make her maiden voyage to the Falkland Isles. Unattractive freight rates soon led the North British Maritime Group to withdraw from UK shipowning and so both ships were sold in 1986 as part of a refinancing plan, to their Dutch subsidiary Erhardt & Dekkers BV and renamed *Norbrit Maas* and *Norbrit Rijn*. They were mainly employed on trades to ports where the ability to self discharge was essential, particularly north and west Africa and later the Carribean. It is interesting to note that the deadweight of these vessels was only 2,350 tons, whereas by adopting the virtual 'tween deck design, the Everard ships could carry 2,415 tons with a gross of only 799. This allowed them to operate with a five man crew in the Near Continent Trade area, although Everards had a dispensation to operate slightly beyond to the southern Baltic and north Spain. The crew of five were non-federated (non-union) and did quite nicely, as they got a small bonus based on cargoes carried, so they were prepared to clean out holds for cargoes like clay, which was greatly simplified by the box hold design. The engine room was also simplified by having a shaft generator running off the main engine and a single Gardner radiator cooled engine to provide electrical power when the main engine was not in use, with considerable automation. Ken Garrett, Everard's marine superintendent, recalls:

'Crews settled down nicely when they got to know each other especially engineer-mate-captain. The two able seamen were moved until all were comfortable. They were built with full air conditioning and were classed for long international voyages with a crew of eight. When their ten year period of working under the old rules ran out, they were remeasured from 18th June 1994 at 1,892 gross, but it was not all bad news as the old rules about draught were done away with and they were allowed to load deeper to 5.1 metres, so they could carry 2,887 tons under the new rules. For a short time also when Everards inquired regarding crew, they were informed that they would be unaffected by tonnage changes, as they

were under 1,600 gross old measurement even when loading deeper.'

Eric Hammal Naval Architect at Cochranes explains:

'Gross and net registered tonnages [grt and nt] were officially assigned to any new vessel but the system of tonnage measurement changed in 1982 when the International Convention on Tonnage Measurement of Ships, 1969, came into force. The tonnage figures then became whole numbers and were referred to as GT and NT (in capitals to distinguish them from the earlier figures). During the change over period, some vessels were measured under both the old and new systems and an intermediate tonnage could be assigned. The new system eliminated the fiddles which brought about the 'paragraph' vessels, which was a false system of measurement affected by depth of double bottom, large side frames, low tonnage decks, etc. The Continentals and Scandinavians were into 'paragraph' vessels much earlier. Their authorities bent over to assist their designers in achieving 499.99 gross, etc. The Department of Trade made no effort to help us and it was always an uphill battle with them to get a good result.

The new GT used a formula which involved the input of total moulded volume of all enclosed spaces, together with a factor from a set table. This tonnage is much more a reflection of the true value of the ship. Owners of many 'paragraph' ships when remeasured found it was possible to apply for a little more draught and hence deadweight. This helped offset the increase in fees, etc from the new GT tonnage. Keels laid before 18th June 1982 could still be built to the British Tonnage Rules of 1967, complete with the various loopholes they contained, hence the rush to lay the keels. Another factor not connected to tonnage was the limit of 1,000 bhp for the main propulsion engine; this affected the qualifications needed by the engineers.

Main engines were often down rated and had stops fitted at 1,000bhp although they were capable of producing more. Although illegal it was not unknown for stops to be removed in service. Anything to do with power and manning fell to the shipowner, who would tell the builder the limits to work to. The 'Selectivity' [class] with the moulded dimensions 73 x 12.6 x 4.325 metres, was designed as a box hold with smooth sides, outer wing tanks and the lower [tonnage] deck positioned to achieve low gross tonnage. This deck affected the load draught [4.55 metres], which was 50mm below the lower deck with this type of vessel, which had a virtual 'tween deck. Virtual because the deck in way of hold space was inside the wing tanks but must have bona fide hatch covers to be treated as a tonnage deck. On the basis that the hatch covers were only there to satisfy the tonnage regulations, it was decided to only fit the lightest weight set of covers comprising of steel hatch beams and plywood sheets. The strength of the covers had to be such as to safely allow a man to walk on them. To give the vessel flexibility when carrying mixed bulks such as grain, two portable steel bulkheads would be carried and these could also form part of the lower deck hatch cover system. When not in use the covers were stowed upright at the after end of the hold. To my knowledge these cover/bulkheads extended the full depth of the hold. They were moved by suspending them from the underside of the main Kvaerner hatch covers which moved hydraulically. These covers were selected in order to keep stowage space to a minimum when open and were also required to open with a 15 degree list and a metre trim by the head or stern.

As far as I know, the tonnage covers were never used subsequently and the vessels only carried a token number of hatch beams and panels in case an Administration check was made at some time in the future. The bow with the vertical stem below the loaded waterline was not new but developed in the yard to suit both ease of construction and a small benefit in hydrodynamics. Ships were not classed as open or closed shelter deckers when Selectivity was designed, so tonnage openings and tonnage wells were no longer required to be fitted.'

Unlike the 'Norbrits', no bow thruster was fitted, manouverability coming from the Schilling rudder which had been developed by Werftunion of Germany and in use there for a number of years. This fairly simple device relies for its exceptional turning ability on its streamlined aerofoil shape, between two horizontal plates at the top and bottom of the rudder. First fitted to the Everard tug *Capable* in the 1970s and subsequently to Charrington's Thames tanker *Charcrest*, it allowed them to turn in their own length and they were soon specified by other owners.

Although, for example, *Willonia* sailed to Spain and Ireland, during the late 1980s most of the voyages were from Amsterdam and Rotterdam to the east coast of England and Scotland, usually returning in ballast. In the winter months the cargoes were coal, usually to one of the private quays along the Humber and Trent. In summer the main cargo was fertiliser to Ipswich, Great Yarmouth or Leith. For ammonium nitrate based fertilizers there is an explosion risk and for this reason one of the portable bulkheads could be effectively used to give the 3 metre separation between engine room bulkhead and cargo the regulations required. For the coal cargoes, loading took from six to twelve hours, with the passage taking about nineteen hours, with about a day for discharge, then a return to the Continent in ballast. Ballast capacity was 1,442 tons and as this was mostly river

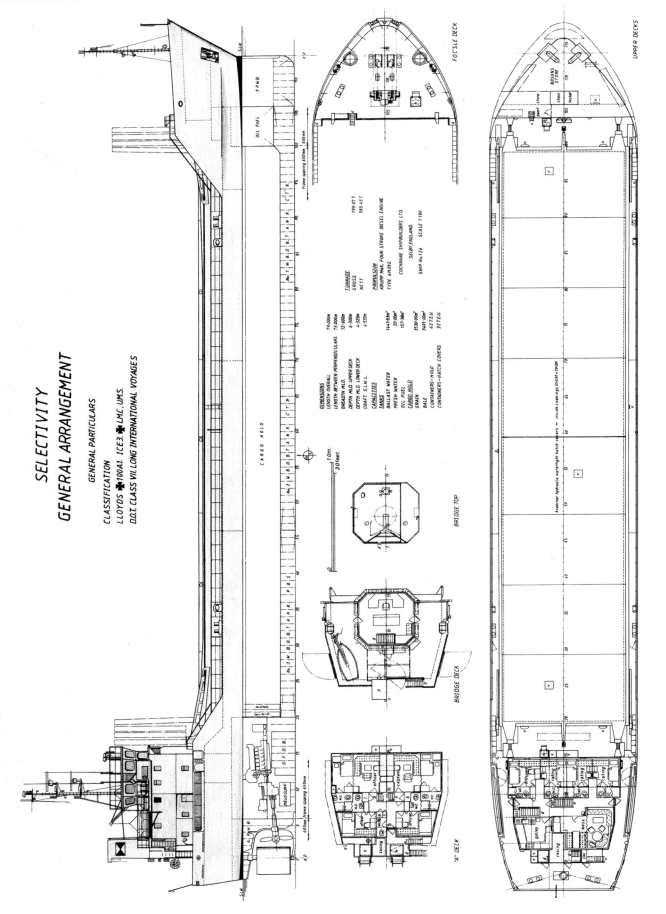

SELECTIVITY
GENERAL ARRANGEMENT

GENERAL PARTICULARS

CLASSIFICATION

LLOYDS ✠ 100A1. ICE3 ✠ LMC, UMS.
D.O.T. CLASS VII. LONG INTERNATIONAL VOYAGES

DIMENSIONS	
LENGTH OVERALL	79·000m
LENGTH BETWEEN PERPENDICULARS	73·000m
BREADTH MLD.	12·600m
DEPTH MLD UPPER DECK	6·300m
DEPTH MLD LOWER DECK	4·325m
DRAFT S.L.W.L.	4·557m

CAPACITIES	
TANKS	
BALLAST WATER	1447·88m³
FRESH WATER	20·000m³
OIL FUEL	157·38m³
CARGO HOLD	
GRAIN	3530·00m³
BALE	3491·00m³
CONTAINERS – HOLD	62 T.E.U.
CONTAINERS – HATCH COVERS	32 T.E.U.

TONNAGE	
GROSS	799·07 T
NETT	585·45 T

PROPULSION

KRUPP MaK. FOUR STROKE DIESEL ENGINE
TYPE 6M282

COCHRANE SHIPBUILDERS LTD.
SELBY. ENGLAND.
SHIP No.126   SCALE 1:100

10m.
30 feet.

FOCSLE DECK

UPPER DECKS

BRIDGE TOP

BRIDGE DECK

"A" DECK

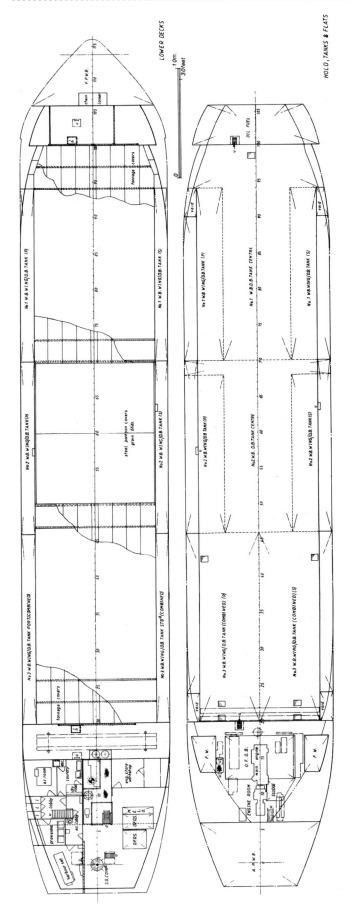

LOWER DECKS

HOLD, TANKS & FLATS

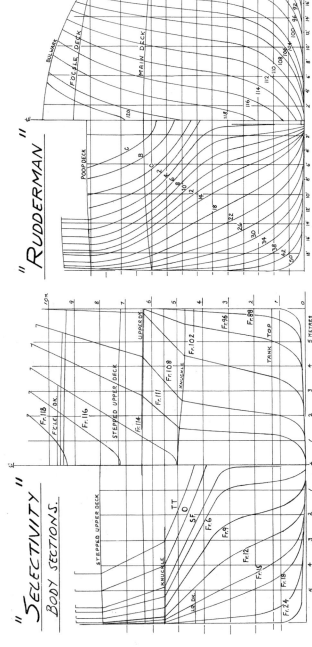

"RUDDERMAN"

"SELECTIVITY"
BODY SECTIONS.

PREVIOUS PAGE & ABOVE: Selectivity (799/84) which had wing tanks the full depth and length of the hold so that it was free of all obstructions. However, in the tanks there was a 'virtual 'tween deck' and corresponding hatches could be fitted in the hold so that the gross tonnage measured to that deck was less than 800 tons, allowing a crew of five to operate the vessel in European trades. Two of the 'tween deck hatch components also doubled as portable grain bulkheads, which was their main purpose but they could also be used to separate different parcels of cargo. Selectivity and Pamela Everard were completed in 1984, followed by Willonia and Stevonia in 1986.

RIGHT: Note the contrast in body plans for the earlier Rudderman, far righ, compared with the later Selectivity, where every effort was made to simplify the plate work to reduce construction costs.

The German-designed Schilling
rudder allowed vessels to
practically turn in their own
length. Two variations were
available. For maximum effect
the trailing edge was widened
(far right) but this added some
drag, so this was eliminated by
fitting a plain edge (right) where
slightly less manoeuvrability was
acceptable.

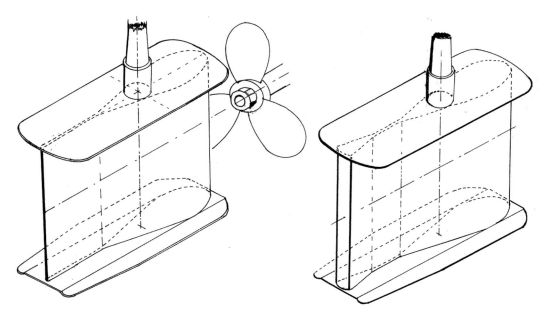

The German-designed Schilling
rudder allowed vessels to
practically turn in their own
length. Two variations were
available. For maximum effect
the trailing edge was widened
(far right) but this added some
drag, so this was eliminated by
fitting a plain edge (right) where
slightly less manoeuvrability was
acceptable.

water, there was a steady build up of sticky mud in the ballast tanks and at a subsequent five year special survey, some 85 tons of mud was removed. Of course carrying this extra weight reduces the cargo that can be carried and various ballast water treatments were used to reduce the problem. The method was to add the treatment to water in partly filled tanks during a voyage, so that the movement of the ship got the mud into suspension and it could be pumped overboard.

The main engine was a Krupp MaK 6-cylinder, 4-stroke of 1,300bhp, de-rated to 999 bhp to allow it to be operated by a Class '4' certificated engineer with a chief engineer endorsement. Even at the reduced horsepower it gave a satisfactory speed of 10 knots. Although the machinery was set up so that heavy fuel oil could be used with simple modifications, the vessels were always run on gas oil by Everards, as the voyages were short and they would frequently be on gas oil when entering or leaving port for manoeuvring. Using gas oil reduced wear on the engine and avoided complex filtering systems. All machinery was selected with reliability and serviceability rather than first cost in mind and a propeller speed of about 168 rpm was achieved with a 5:1 reduction gear box coupled to a controllable pitch propeller, to give a favourable fuel consumption of about 3.75 tonnes/day. There was a control 'black box' in the wheelhouse which calculated appropriate pitch of the controllable pitch propeller and rpm for sea state, and indicated speed and fuel consumption. In order to keep the large diameter screw immersed, the large ballast capacity was used to obtain a ballast draught of 3.8 metres aft.

With a crew of five, the old methods of securing timber on deck, which traced back to the Factory Act of 1920, were completely out of date and impractical, so representations were made by Ken Garratt, Everard's marine superintendent, to use tyrelene straps similar to those in use for lorries but of increased strength like those the German ships were already using. They proved very satisfactory and when officially inspected, the inspector asked what quick release system was to be used in an emergency and was shown an axe! In fact they were so tough under tension it was necessary to cut them with a saw. Packaged timber bundles were loaded with alternating layers athwartships and longitudinally, finishing off with a longitudinal layer on top.

During the 1970s there had been a steady growth in direct cargo movements using river/sea going vessels and with Britain now a member of the common market, interest in these vessels among British owners increased. The small vessels built for the London & Rochester Trading Co. and other Thames-based owners were able to participate in this trade. Some of their large coasting barges, especially the more modern vessels, were essentially small coasters and had the appropriate load line certificates. Many coasters could penetrate as far as Duisburg but to go further on the European canal and river systems, owners had to give careful consideration to both water and air draught to reach Paris on the Seine, Liege on the Meuse, Lille on the Dunkerque-Valenciennes canal or Basle on the Rhine.

As the company's low air draft vessels had been successful, they took the next step and ordered two larger vessels from Cochranes, which were the first to be fitted with a hydraulically raised and lowered bridge, the first such order for a UK yard. This resulted in *Urgence* (699/81) and *Vibrence*

M. V. "AMBIENCE"

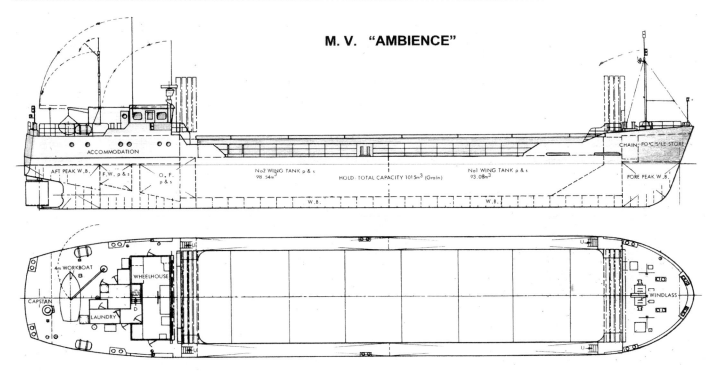

(699/81), with the moulded dimensions 81 x 11.40 x 5.40 metres and the popular Alpha main engine package, with power limited to 999 bhp. The dimensions were selected with Lille in mind, for cargoes of fertilizer in and grain outwards. They were also employed on the Rhone loading grain for ports all around the Mediterranean. The company became active in the commercialisation of the old Chatham naval dockyard as well and used their ships to import and discharge timber there. *Crescence* (492/82) and *Ambience* (492/82) were completed to a Fairmile-style design by Cubow, similar to the Danish built *Tarquence* (499/80). They were built to Lloyds 100A1 Near Continental Trading Area, with the trade up the Rhine as far as Basle in mind and for this purpose also a Schilling rudder was fitted, allowing the vessels to turn in their own length if necessary. The main engines were type 427 4-stroke Callesens, giving 468bhp at 390rpm. Wing ballast tanks provided an unobstructed hold. All were lengthened in 1994 to increase their deadweight from about 840 tons to about 1,020 tons.

Following on the success of *Urgence* and *Vibrence*, a repeat order incorporating some changes from the experience gained from these (mainly the make of the main engine) resulted in *Stridence* (698/83) and *Turbulence* (698/83). They were to be the last British-built vessels for the company, which shortly afterwards changed its name to Crescent Shipping, Rochester and built only one more dry cargo vessel. As older companies faded away, newer ones often expanded. Union Transport for many years concerned themselves as brokers and agents for exports to Switzerland via Basel and, during the 1960s and 1970s, with expanding business, began to time charter. They finally purchased their first ship in 1973, a second-hand German coaster with lowering masts which they registered in Singapore. Following further purchases, the first new ship came from a Dutch yard, suitable for the Rhine and could carry 1,000 ton sugar shipments direct to Basel.

The company continued to develop the Continental trade using inland waterways and ordered vessels from European yards with experience of building low air draught vessels for this trade. Under the business expansion scheme introduced in 1983, which gave tax advantages to investors, Bromley Shipping plc was formed in 1986 and having initially operated second-hand vessels, though now British registered, both companies eventually ordered four low air draught ships with an option for two more from Cochranes in 1988, who were in receipt of an Intervention Subsidy to keep the yard open at a price of just over £3,000,000 each. The specification called for vessels with a ballast air draught of 6.35 metres and a loaded draught of 4.2 metres, suitable for the Rhine and similar Continental navigations. The moulded dimensions were 96 x 12 x 6.35 metres, with an overall length of 99.73 metres. To avoid the impending regulations that vessels over 1,600 gross tons should carry more sophisticated lifeboats, the contract called for the vessels to be built to Germanischer Lloyd classification and so required the yard to buy keel plates allocated for newbuilds from a Dutch yard that were dated prior to the new regulations (a typical Continental practice).

The low air draught Ambience (492/82) was built by Cubow Ltd, who mainly did repairs, to a Fairmile river/sea design for the London & Rochester Trading Co. Ltd, who were part of the same group. The box hold was strengthened to accept 25 ton steel coils.

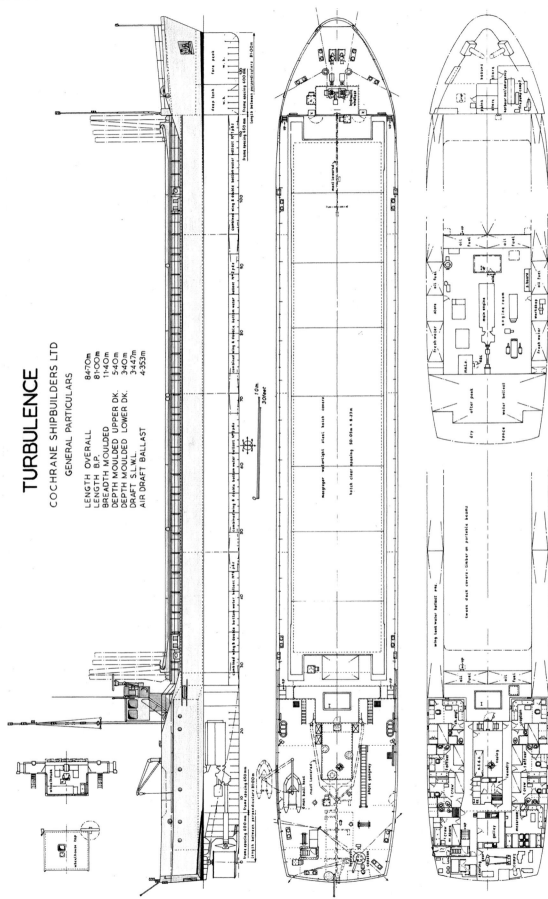

TURBULENCE

COCHRANE SHIPBUILDERS LTD
GENERAL PARTICULARS

LENGTH OVERALL 84·70m
LENGTH B.P. 81·00m
BREADTH MOULDED 11·40m
DEPTH MOULDED UPPER DK. 5·40m
DEPTH MOULDED LOWER DK. 3·40m
DRAFT S.L.W.L. 3·447m
AIR DRAFT BALLAST 4·353m

In the 1980s the trend was very much towards river/sea ships such as Turbulence of 1983, as the Common Market opened up and British vessels could trade in the Rhine and other waterways. Despite the compact nature of this type of vessel, all the crew had en suite facilities, though the officers, particularly the captain and chief engineer, had much smaller cabins than in conventional vessels and no separate saloon.

In order to meet the delivery dates, two vessels were subcontracted to Dunstons who were now part of the Dutch Damen group. Cochranes supplied the drawings and specifications. First to be delivered was *Union Jupiter* (2,230/90), though 1,299 gross under the old measurement. Deadweight was 3,274 tonnes. The two holds each had a movable bulkhead so up to four cargo spaces were possible in the box holds and so were suitable for carrying different grades of china clay for example. The engines were Alpha producing 1,080 kw at 825rpm, with a gear box and a skewed controllable pitch propeller to give 10.5 knots on about 4.6 tons of gas oil per day. This was combined with a bow thruster and an active rudder to give good manoeuvrability. Union Transport cancelled their options, which were subsequently taken up at a favourable price by the Everard group companies, Scottish Navigation and Short Sea Europe plc. The latter also ordered a further ship bringing the class up to seven vessels. The second vessel delivered was *Bromley Pearl* (2,230/90), which came from Dunstons a few months later. By this time the company were claiming against the yard for hatch cover problems. Union Transport had specified MacGregor-designed piggy back covers, with full hydraulic operation including cleating from a remote control panel on the hatch coaming. A cargo of grain suffered some water damage on a voyage to Seville in bad weather. Although the hatch and its equipment was considered to be within tolerance, the resulting dispute led to Union Transport refusing delivery of the next two completed vessels. Consequently, *Union Mercury* (2,230/90) and *Union Saturn* (2,230/90) were laid up and sold to other owners, eventually joining Carisbrook Shipping of the Isle of Wight, which was also a relative newcomer.

The ships for Everards were modified by including additional cross joint panel cleats and external pull-down locking cleats of the old MacGregor type at the sides of the cover panels, so that manual action was needed and ensured the panels were watertight. They were also happy to meet the new requirement for a free fall lifeboat, which was fitted in a special lowering cradle to meet air draught limitations. The three were *Superiority* (2,230/91), *Short Sea Trader* (2,230/91) and *North Sea Trader* (2,230/91). Interestingly, the latter two were purchased by Union Transport ten years later. Cochranes were to build just two more ships, both tankers, before the yard closed in the mid 1990s.

The 1980s Tanker Scene

Whereas dry cargo vessels had tended to become more basic, tankers became even more sophisticated. The three oil majors, Esso, Shell and BP, all placed orders for tankers for delivery in the early 1980s and *BP Harrier* (1,595/80) and *BP Hunter* (1,595/80), with the moulded dimensions 78.0 x 15.0 x 6.7 metres and a draught of 5.75 metres, were built by Appledore. The design specification was produced by the BP Tanker Co. Ltd for BP Oil, the coastal tanker operation, and *BP Harrier* was the first new ship built for the company following the separation of the Shell and BP coastal tanker fleets. They were able to carry up to four white (refined) products such as aviation and jet fuel (and their components) as well as Class '3' chemicals. The tanks were zinc silicate coated and each was fitted with a stainless steel, hydraulically driven Frank Mohn deep well pump, eliminating the need for a pump room. Any two of the three diesel driven power packs was capable of discharging a total of 1,050 cubic metres per hour. For tank washing there was a variable speed Frank Mohn hydraulically driven pump, supplying two tank washing machines and two tank ventilating fans at the same time using sea water. The ballast water was also segregated and a slop tank was arranged for tank washings. The main engines were British Polars of 2,940bhp at 730rpm, driving a controllable pitch propeller via a reduction gear. For manoeuvring there were bow thrusters and this was combined with a Becker rudder. This type of rudder was in two sections, the outer section of which increased the rudder angle so the propeller wash could be directed sideways. Noise in the accommodation was reduced by the free-floating floor method. The lifeboats were high up on the superstructure just behind the bridge. Both were sold to Coe-Metcalf in 1991 and renamed *David M* and *Michael M*, later being given Fisher names when fully integrated into the James Fisher fleet.

Shell's order for three products tankers was split between Clelands and Goole, having both become part of the Small Ships Division of Swan, Hunter in 1967 and so of British Shipbuilders following nationalisation in 1977. The yards were in a good position as regards current experience of this type of tanker, as they had recently built two for Everards. The Cleland yard built *Shell Marketer* (1,599/81) and *Shell Technician* (1,599/82), both 74.50 x 13.10 x 6.50 metres and with a deadweight of 2,575 tons. Meanwhile, the Goole yard built *Shell Seafarer* (1,599/81). These Shell tankers differed from those built for BP, with two prominent funnels side by side right aft behind the rather box like superstructure, which provided air conditioned accommodation for a crew of ten. In these vessels the lifeboats were tucked into a recess directly below the bridge. Designed for a full range of products, ranging from black oils to aviation fuels in five tanks, each was served by a

Framo submerged hydraulically driven pump able to discharge about 750 cubic metres per hour. As usual, there was a centre line bulkhead with a levelling valve between the port and starboard halves of each tank. In all but the most severe weather, the separate ballast tanks were sufficient. The main engines were Mirrlees-Blackstone K6 Majors of 2,700bhp at 525rpm, running on medium grade fuel oil and driving a controllable pitch propeller via a reduction gear. The names were subsequently brought into line with the main shell fleet and given the latin names of sea shells, becoming *Amoria*, *Arianta* and *Asprella* respectively in 1993. All three were subsequently sold en block to Everards in 1999, when Shell decided to leave coastal deliveries to independent tanker owners, becoming *Allurity*, *Activity* and *Arduity* respectively.

Esso placed their order with Cochranes and Eric Hammal recalls *Esso Plymouth* (1,421/80): '*Effects of noise and vibration in crew spaces was being given a lot of consideration in the UK, as with increased main engine and generator powers, noise levels were getting uncomfortably high. The Germans were doing this also and most Sietas-built cargo vessels had resiliently mounted accommodation units and it was thought the only way to meet the impending noise limit regulations was to fit this type of divorced structure, which was not cheap. We at Cochranes could have achieved it by other means, but the Esso technical team went for the Grunsweig & Hartmann system which was well proven. In this system the deckhouse was supported on two fore and aft girders with resilient pads, all service connections being fitted with flexible piping. The engine exhausts were taken out of the aft end of the engine room and up a casing and funnel which was completely separate from the accommodation block. The deck house had restraining bars with resilient bushes to prevent excessive movement in seaways.*'

Following pressure from the German seamen's union in the late 1960s, several German systems had been developed and fitted to coasting vessels but it was not until 1978 that the Department of Trade introduced a voluntary code of practice as regards acceptable noise levels, with a view to mandatory requirements being laid down four years later. On *Esso Plymouth*, the entire four-storey deckhouse, weighing 120 tonnes, was placed on two pairs of longitudinal girders; in each pair a trapezoidal-section rail was welded to the tanker's deck and straddled by a saddle girder attached to the deckhouse. Connecting the girders were a series of composite rubber/steel pads, loaded in a combination of shear and compression. These pads provided the required resilience and load distribution over the whole length of the girders. The lifeboats were also mounted on the deckhouse structure and resiliently attached vertical sidebars below the boats were purely to prevent the lifeboats swinging under the overhang of the side access platforms if the vessel had a list. *Esso Plymouth* was the first British vessel to use the system and provided the thirteen crew with noise levels under the maximum permitted. The main engine chosen was the latest version of Allen's S37 type, the S37G and the first of this model to be manufactured. It was turbocharged and intercooled and the in-line 6-cylinders developed 2,250bhp at 750rpm. This model was specifically designed for reliable operation on residual fuels, although Esso opted to run the engine on intermediate fuel oil. The single reduction gear box and clutch gave the four-bladed controllable pitch propeller a speed of 246rpm and, for increased manoeuvrability, a Schilling rudder was specified. On trials this gave a turning circle 92 metres in diameter on 35 degree helm at full speed of about 12.5 knots and so not much more than the vessel's overall length of 70.80 metres. For harbour manoeuvring, a 75 degree rudder angle could be used as well as a Jastram bow thruster to move almost sideways on to the berth.

Designed to distribute 'white' products such as kerosene, petrol, jet fuel and gas oil mostly from Fawley to the south and east coast, the moulded dimensions of 66.50 x 12.50 x 5.75 metres were

In the tanker Esso Plymouth *of 1980, the accommodation block (shaded grey) was fitted with the Grunsweig & Hartmann supporting system (grey stripes), to separate it from the engine room noise and vibration.*

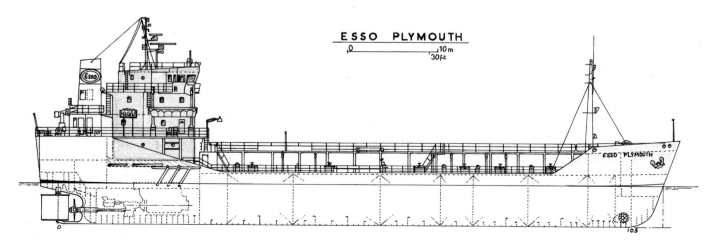

ESSO PLYMOUTH

dictated by the berths available at Ipswich, Dover, Shoreham, Plymouth and the Channel Islands. A deadweight of 2,163 tonnes was achieved on a draught of 4.71 metres. The hull was divided into twelve tanks, all constructed from flat plating with vertical stiffeners. The tanks were all epoxy coated, which gave sufficient protection from corrosion to allow the thickness of the steelwork to be reduced but still be sufficient for the vessel to take the ground at tidal berths. Two pumps, each electrically driven by motors in the adjacent engine room, allowed two grades to be handled simultaneously, while all the deck machinery was hydraulic. Forward there was a double windlass with two drums for mooring wires and a two drum mooring winch aft. At sea all the electrical power was supplied by an alternator driven from the main engine gear box, rather than auxiliary diesel driven sets requiring more expensive gas oil. The whole system had sufficient alarms and monitoring systems for operating with the engine room unmanned. The total cost of building was £2.5 million, with an expected service life of twenty years. In fact she was sold to Rowbothams in 1989 and, as *Guidesman*, sold on to Singapore owners in 1994.

During the 1980s, Rowbotham ordered larger tankers suitable for world wide trading, such as *Echoman* (3,759/82) and *Cableman* (4,916/80), which were often employed running Milford Haven to Eastham. By the end of the 1980s, the company, now owned by Marine Transport Lines, another US company, sold out to P&O who then sold out to James Fisher but no more tankers were built in Britain.

Still ordering what might be described as traditional coasting size tankers were Bowker & King and perhaps their most interesting delivery in the early 1980s was *Banwell* (999/80), built by Cubow on the Thames. The yard was part of the same group and had been formed by a merger of Cunis and Bowker & King's repair facilities in 1971. The naval architects Fairmile also had a share and they supplied the design input, although the yard was sold in 1983. During the rest of the 1980s, a steady stream of vessels were delivered: *Beckenham* (825/80), *Blackheath* (751/80), *Brentwood* (994/80) and *Breaksea* (992/85) all came from Nordsovaerfret in Denmark and were built primarily with the local Bristol Channel and Thames trades in mind, although the radius of operations was increasing as local trades declined. The company moved into full coasting with *Brabourne* (1,646/89) and *Blackrock* (1,646/89) built by Cochranes. The yard ustilised the same proven hull form which had been used for the 'Selectivity' Class dry cargo vessels built for Everards. The engine selected was a Krupp MaK 6-cylinder, 4-stroke. The actual owners of the two ships were Lloyds Plant Leasing Ltd and Lloyds International Leasing Ltd respectively, with Crescent Shipping Ltd as managers, as the London & Rochester Trading Co. were now known. Although Bowker & King had been merged into the latter company, the vessels were still distinguished by the funnel marks, as the ex-Bowker & King tankers had a crescent on a blue band rather than the red band used by dry cargo ships.

Iain Howe recalls *Brabourne*:

'The vessel mainly loaded at oil refineries in Milford Haven and Cork and was employed by the oil majors (Texaco, Conoco, etc) and also customers of these.

We served various ports from Poole in the south to Belfast in the north, also in the Republic of Ireland: New Ross, Limerick always, Foynes, Cork, Arklow, Dublin and a few others. The ship ran normally with a crew of seven: master, first officer, second officer, chief engineer, second engineer, deck hand and trainee. We worked a system of four weeks on and two weeks off and for this we had a total crew of nine; master, relief master/mate, mate, second mate/deckhand, deckhand, chief engineer, chief engineer/second engineer and second engineer. In summer we had two weeks annual leave which was used so that as a crew we did two periods of three on and three off. For this to work some extra hands were employed.

We were paid on a cargo share system, this was a percentage based on rank. This was good on this ship due to being busy and also the cargo capacity of 2,500 tonnes. But this system did produce a problem that on some smaller ships the captain was earning less than officers on our ship. Also because a big percentage of salary was based on cargo share, we vary rarely stopped for weather. An occasion when the master asked the second mate if he had listened to the shipping forecast, he replied, no he hadn't and we would be sailing anyway! – Which we did.

Cargo operations were normally carried out by the first officer who loaded the vessel and the second officer discharged the vessel. This was a new ship and so had lots of improved features: All cargo pipework was on deck. Each of the ten cargo tanks was fitted with an electrical deep well pump as well as the slop tank. The tanks were epoxy coated, so tank cleaning was easier, as well as fixed hot water washing machines. A gas freeing fan was also supplied, these features were required in between certain cargoes and especially used prior to loading aviation fuel. When washing tanks, static was created by the water spray. To eliminate risk the tanks have to be pumped while washing to remove wash water. Also all washing equipment machines, hoses, etc must be bonded. On this ship we had fixed pipework and washing machines so this removed the problem of rubber washing hoses and portable Butterworth

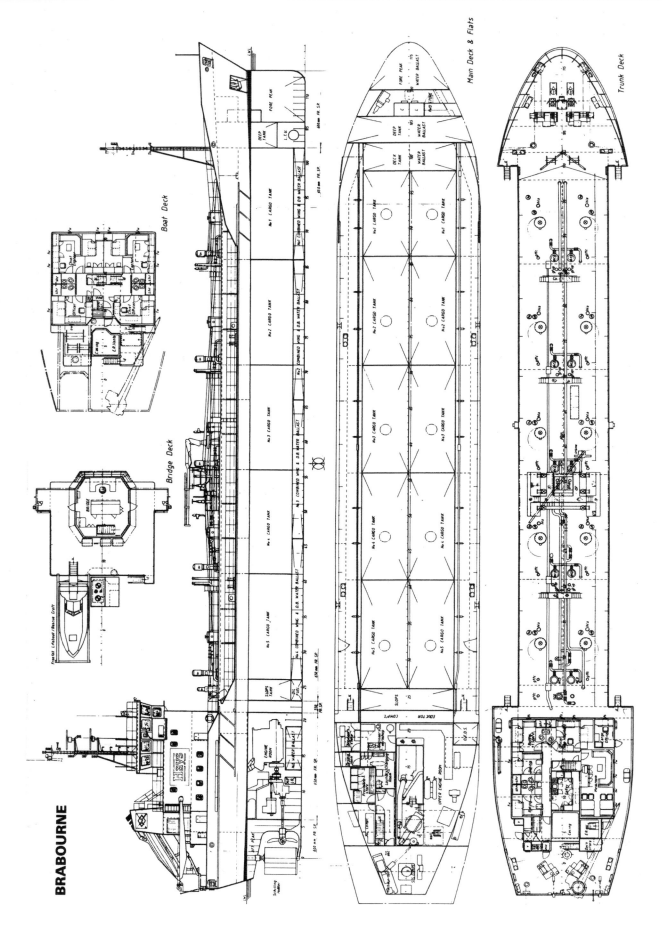

BRABOURNE

Boat Deck

Bridge Deck

Fore/aft Lifeboat/Rescue Craft

Main Deck & Flats

Trunk Deck

machines. When washing tanks you would never introduce anything which may be a conductor to the atmosphere, basically anything metallic. The ten cargo tanks were 1-5 port and starboard, they were paired as follows 1 and 4 starboard, 2 and 5 starboard and 3 on their own. This arrangement allowed five different grades (petrol, diesel, kerosene) to be loaded with the industry standard 'two valve separation' between each different grade. This ship also had a segregated ballast system, so water was carried in separate ballast tanks. This allowed ballasting operations to be carried out during loading or discharging which saved time and the need to pump dirty ballast (ex-cargo tank ballast) ashore. The ship was also nicely fitted out; all crew had single cabins en suite. Galley and mess room were also well equipped, this was a big improvement on most of the other vessels in the Bowker & King fleet. A free fall lifeboat was also fitted, which provided an initial novelty factor. The main safety issues were obviously prevention of fire, explosion and spillage, so sources of ignition were as far as possible eliminated. Smoking was only allowed in designated areas, all equipment on deck was intrinsically safe and procedures to eliminate static electricity were carried out. The latter was a major concern when engaged in tank cleaning operations. She was a nice ship to work on, and with the right cargo and discharge ports arrangement, could be discharged in 2 hours 40 minutes, not bad for 2,500 tons of cargo.'

The tanker Agility *(1,930/90), alongside on 12th January 1992, discharging a cargo in Jersey.* DAVE HOCQUARD

Traditional British coasting and short sea trading, where new vessels were built for British owners by British yards and traded under the British flag with British crews, was now practically a thing of the past and traditional owners and yards continued to go out of business. Everards ordered one last dry cargo vessel, *Seniority* (3,493/91), from Appledore and well beyond the size of previous vessels. She was built to the maximum size that could get up the Trent and limited by length and draught, so the beam was increased a little in order that she could carry cargoes of around 5,000 tons of timber on their regular run from Uddavalla to Gunness, depending on the tides. Tanker rates were better and so an order was placed with Richards for two sophiscated clean products tankers for coastal delivery runs. *Agility* (1,930/90) and *Alacrity* (1,930/90), at a price of over £4 million each, were to be their last tankers built in Britain. Richards also built two gas tankers for Gibson, which were flagged out, and so regular coaster building came to an end in Britain, although coasting vessels were sporadically built subsequently.

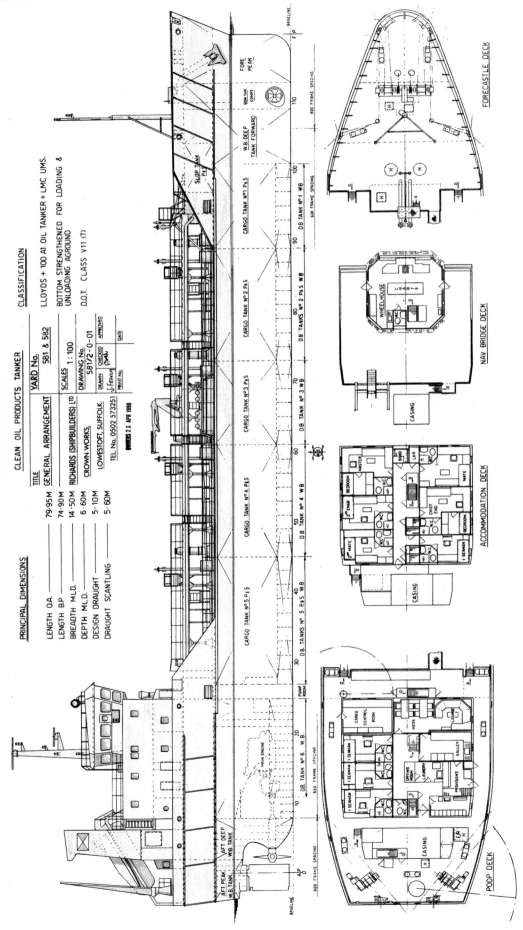

PRINCIPAL DIMENSIONS

LENGTH O.A. — 79·95M
LENGTH B.P. — 74·90M
BREADTH MLD. — 14·50M
DEPTH MLD. — 6·60M
DESIGN DRAUGHT — 5·10M
DRAUGHT SCANTLING — 5·60M

CLEAN OIL PRODUCTS TANKER

TITLE — GENERAL ARRANGEMENT

YARD No. 581 & 582

SCALES 1:100

DRAWING No. 5817/2-0-01

RICHARDS (SHIPBUILDERS) LTD
CROWN WORKS,
LOWESTOFT, SUFFOLK.
TEL. No. 0502 573251

OWNERS 2 3 APR 1990

CLASSIFICATION

LLOYDS + 100 A1 OIL TANKER + LMC UMS.

BOTTOM STRENGTHENED FOR LOADING & UNLOADING AGROUND

D.O.T. CLASS V11 (T)

FORECASTLE DECK

NAV BRIDGE DECK

ACCOMMODATION DECK

POOP DECK

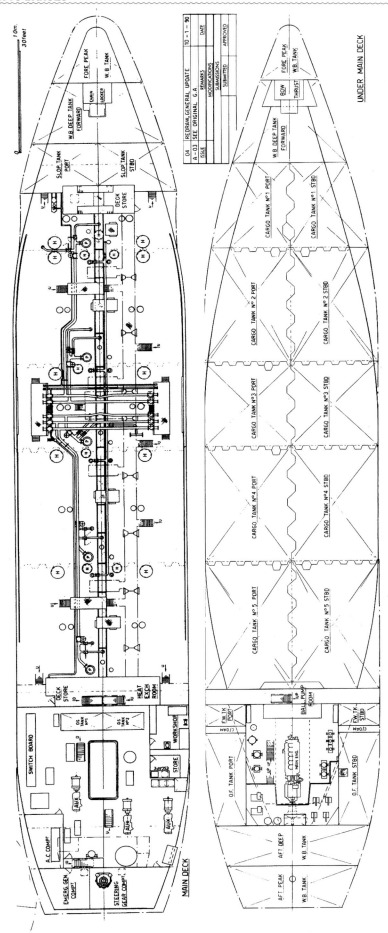

The product tankers *Agility* and *Alacrity* of 1990 were the last tankers built in Britain for Everards and make an interesting contrast with such vessels of fifty years earlier. Perhaps the most striking contrast is the lack of sheer, with straight lines everywhere and flat plate or plate curved in only one direction as far as possible. Other major changes were the elimination of pump rooms and enclosed free fall lifeboats. Below the waterline, changes were just as major, with improved hull forms, bow thrusters, controllable pitch propellers and sophisticated rudders, which combined with the bow thruster allowed the vessels to move sideways on to the berth. In this case the rudder was an Ulstein design. Within the hull the engines were much smaller, and automation and alarm systems allowed crews to be much reduced while radar and related systems meant navigating in fog became much less of a hazard.

INDEX

GENERAL INDEX